AF411558

Communication and Management at Work

Communication and Management at Work

Thomas Klikauer

First published 2007 by
PALGRAVE MACMILLAN
Houndmills, Basingstoke, Hampshire RG21 6XS and
175 Fifth Avenue, New York, N. Y. 10010
Companies and representatives throughout the world

PALGRAVE MACMILLAN is the global academic imprint of the Palgrave Macmillan division of St. Martin's Press, LLC and of Palgrave Macmillan Ltd. Macmillan® is a registered trademark in the United States, United Kingdom and other countries. Palgrave is a registered trademark in the European Union and other countries.

ISBN-13: 978–0–230–51543–7   hardback
ISBN-10: 0–230–51543–6   hardback

This book is printed on paper suitable for recycling and made from fully managed and sustained forest sources. Logging, pulping and manufacturing processes are expected to conform to the environmental regulations of the country of origin.

A catalogue record for this book is available from the British Library.

Library of Congress Cataloging-in-Publication Data
Klikauer, Thomas 1962–
    Community and management at work / Thomas Klikauer.
        p. cm.
    Includes bibliographical references and index.
    ISBN-13: 978–0–230–51543–7 (cloth)
    ISBN-10: 0–230–51543–6 (cloth)
    1. Communication in management. 2. Leadership. I. Title.

    HD30.3.K587 2007
    658.4'5–dc22   2006052192

10   9   8   7   6   5   4   3   2   1
16   15   14   13   12   11   10   09   08   07

Printed and bound in Great Britain by
Antony Rowe Ltd, Chippenham and Eastbourne

This book is dedicated to

Ludwig Numrich

8th August 1891 to 14th August 1988

On the first day of World War I, 60,000 men died. Having been forced
into this war and survived the following four years
of senseless mass-killings, many European workers were bitterly
disappointed with war and capitalism. These returning soldiers founded
revolutionary workers' and soldiers' councils to end all wars and
capitalism. Parliamentary democracy and capitalism were to be
replaced with socialised and deliberative workplace democracy.

My great-grand father, Ludwig Numrich, was a member of the
Darmstadt Revolutionary Workers' and Soldiers' Council, 1918/1919.
This book is dedicated to him and all women and men who fought for
workplace democracy.

*Those who can make you
believe absurdities can make
you commit atrocities.*
Voltaire

Contents

List of Tables

List of Figures

Acknowledgements

Acknowledgements are the usual place reserved for the usual thanks to all those who have contributed to the completion of a book. This book is no exception. I would like to thank Paul Adler, Mats Alvesson, Peter Beilharz, Noam Chomsky, Stewart Clegg, Maeve Cooke, Daniel Cornfield, Braham Dabscheck, Stanley Deetz, John Dryzek, Paul Edwards, John Forester, Boris Frankel, Steve Frenkel, Anthony Giles, Karl Hinrichs, Richard Hyman, Berndt Keller, Douglas Kellner, John Kelly, Stephan Leibfried, Boy Lütje, Dave Lyddon, Thomas McCarthy, Claus Offe, William Outhwaite, Martin Parker, Michael Pusey, Michael Quinlain, Rudi Schmiede, Melissa Tyler, Helmut Wiesenthal, and Robert Young for their highly valuable critique, their comments and their assistance. I have highly valued their support during the initial and conceptual phase of the book. As much as their critique has been helpful, there have been a number of people who have turned my writings and ideas into a book.

My utmost heartfelt thanks go, first of all, to *Khalida Malik* and to my wife *Katja* for turning a highly abstract language – communicating about communication – into accessible language. My gratitude extends to the German Hans-Böckler-Foundation that fully supported my tertiary education in the 1980s and 90s. Finally, I would like to thank the editorial team at Palgrave, *Ursula Gavin, Jacky Kippenberger, Mari Shullaw, Mirabelle Boateng, and Shirley Tan* for their support and assistance in the realisation of this book.

Preface

Books and, above all, academic books are products of someone sitting at a desk somewhere, mostly alone, carrying out the communicative action of writing. In many cases this starts as a two dimensional activity as someone is sitting in front of an empty white page. Today this two-dimensional white page consists mostly of the monopolised *Microsoft Word for Windows* computer screen. When starting to write, the author soon discovers that this page is not only two-dimensional but should – and in many cases actually does – provide for a third dimension, the dimension of depth and critique. To accomplish a serious level of depth a book needs to be able to show what lies behind the ordinary things that are being served up. Books that focus on the third dimension dig deeper into the underlying values of many assertions. They seek to make visible the hidden ideologies that are cloaked behind the so-called *objective* claim. These books are able to show the unmentioned intentions that exist behind the surface structure and make them visible to the reader. They reveal what underlies books that promise to be '*a practical book*'. These books show the truth that is covered up by today's anti-intellectualism often labelled as *a practitioner's handbook that shows facts and figures with problem-solving abilities for the real world*. The anti-intellectualism and anti-thinking biases of these books completely contradict their claim to present management *science*, communication *theory*, or organisational *studies*.

The contradictions are cleverly covered up by reducing theory to a few lines here and there, some easy graphs and figures or a simple *literature review*. These reductions are designed to *sum up*, to deliver a distorted view of *what is out there*. By inventing so-called *key elements* these books carefully avoid the critical power of theoretical concepts: Firstly, they deny the fact that theory and concepts are always in use, especially when the infamous *no-theory but practical* claim appears.[1] Despite this and other claims, theories and concepts are used in every single book ever written *in* and *about* any field of socially constructed *facts* on communication, management and work. The use of theories is unavoidable in any book that contains forms of socially constructed knowledge. Secondly, theories and concepts provide a valuable assistance in the process of uncovering the underlying values and ideologies used in these supposedly *unbiased* books. In short, the theory dimension appears in every book but it appears in two forms. Either it is introduced, used silently and covered up by the *objective* or *practical*, etc. claim or it is used as a conscious reflection on the way knowledge is produced.

One of the core values of these *unbiased* and *objective* books – mostly textbooks – in the field of management is that they fulfil one of *George Orwell's*

(1949:83) most important dictum outlined in his novel *1984: I understand HOW: I do not understand WHY…at one point it had been a sign of madness to believe that the earth goes around the sun.*[2] While today's managers and management students are told that their field is about *HOW* to be a successful manager, *HOW* to communicate effectively, *HOW* to manage the workplace, *HOW* to succeed in the marketplace, and *HOW* to turn *means* into *ends*, the overwhelming force is directed towards the *means* and the *HOW*. Standard management books almost never spend much time on the *ends* and on the *WHY*. Similarly, today we all understand *HOW* the earth moves around the sun. But our understanding of *WHY* the Catholic Church as the prime norm setting keeper of the medieval ideology has taken more than 350 years to acknowledge that Galileo was correct and the Church was wrong is much less known and much less reflected upon. Again, we understand the *means* and the *HOWs* but God forbid not the *WHYs* and the *ends* of the Church's motives. After all it was the most prominent ideological power structure of medieval living for roughly 2000 years. If we dare to ask about the *WHYs* and the *ends*, we might uncover that certain forms of knowledge are dangerous and need to be withheld by those in power, today as much as 2000 years ago. We might also uncover that the *WHYs* and the *ends* lay bare some of the hidden truths about the old institution. And it may tell us why certain truths are kept away from another roughly 200 year old power structure: *capitalism* and its modern administrators: *management*.

In true Orwellian style most of today's management books tend not to ask *WHY* and at which *ends* all this is aimed for as these might be dangerous questions. One might, as Orwell did, suggest this is done for one single reason: *until they become conscious they will never rebel. WHY* and *ends* questions might lead to this, while *HOW* and *means* queries are system integrative and affirmative. They are functional questions that negate and cloak the *WHYs* and *ends* by redirecting attention towards the machine, the mechanism, and the apparatus. They ensure that Orwell's *rebellious* character is denied, hidden, buried, or replaced with the affirmative character that is able operate in *today's business environment*. The headline *today's business environment* is no more than an empty promise found on too many covers of too many management and business books. Deservedly, these books have an average *shelf life* of approximately three to five years as they go with the modern *Zeitgeist*.

While book pages definitely have two dimensions and a third dimension *may(!)* be found in the depth of a book, they sometimes also have a fourth. This fourth dimension has occupied human thinking for thousand of years, from the Greek *kronos* to Albert Einstein and beyond. The fourth dimension is the idea of time. In our days, the idea of time has often been linked to something called *Zeitgeist*. All books encounter this idea. *Zeitgeist* is commonly – and unfortunately untruly – seen as the spirit of the time.

However, *Zeitgeist* or *Zeit* (time) and *Geist* (spirit), according to the inventor of *Zeitgeist,* German philosopher *Georg Wilhelm Friedrich Hegel* (1770–1831) expresses something slightly different. Hegel has been concerned with the *Phenomenology of Spirit* (1807) and how the *spirit* (Geist) or our *consciousness* is connected to *time* (Zeit). Unlike its common understanding today – the spirit of the time – Hegel's thoughts were more directed towards the history of consciousness. He thought that *consciousness,* and in fact any *thinking,* needs to be aware of time. Any thinking or consciousness that is not conscious of time and history is somewhat trapped in its time. Only an awareness of historic processes can result in thinking that is not trapped in time. Therefore, Hegel's idea of *Zeitgeist* means that to be in tune with the *Zeit* is comparable to being a prisoner of time as the reflection on time and history remains unconscious. Only those who are conscious of the time and history in which they exist – and write books – can escape the *Zeitgeist.*

In this sense, all books are a product of their time but two distinctions have to be made. There are books that are written and trapped inside the *Zeitgeist* and those that are aware of time and history and that can escape it. Historically unconscious books that pretend to deliver *a practitioner's handbook that shows facts and figures with problem-solving abilities for the real world in today's business environment* are often exposed to the trappings of the *Zeitgeist.* In other words, awareness of Hegel's idea on *Zeitgeist* can lead an author's awareness of a book's timeliness. Any book that is aware of Hegel's *Zeitgeist* and is furthermore capable of appropriately dealing with the trappings of the *Zeitgeist* might turn into what is commonly labelled a classic. Classics are those books that have withstood *the critique of time.* This '*critique of time*' is not done by time itself but by people. People living at different times, with different perspectives on the world in general and the world of work in particular conduct such critiques. Ever since Hegel's philosophical predecessor *Immanuel Kant* (1724–1084) critique – something largely absent from standard textbooks – has been important to thinking. As Kant once said, *under modernity everything has to submit to critique.*[3] In other words, maybe even in Kant's or Hegel's words, good books are not written unconscious of *time* and *history* nor are they written unconscious of society. Every book also exists in relation to other books in its respective field, in relation to readers, and to society. No book has ever been produced disconnected from society or the readers it has been written for. Books, as an expression of socially constructed knowledge, are always a product of their time and their social environment.[4]

The result of an author's work – a book – is a product that could hardly have been achieved individually and totally disconnected from society. Books are not the result of a *Robinson Crusoe* (1719) like work process. This idea is and has always been a conservative illusion. *Defoe* himself has damaged the conservative *Robinson Crusoe* fantasy of the island man surviving on his own because even Mr Crusoe *used* someone to survive – *a native* appropriately called *Friday*, a working day. This is not to say that all book writers have a *Friday* but people, like the fictive *Robinson Crusoe* or the author *Daniel Defoe himself*, do not exist on fictive islands as lonesome individuals. All books are written in a socially constructed environment. Writers as well as their books have one thing in common – they are part of a society that impacts on them. Like all books, this book is not independent of societal influences and values. It is, however, totally independent from what *Habermas* has called the *power and money code*. It has not received any support from industry, government, funding institutions, universities, etc. It is still possible for a book to be relative independent from the *money and power code*. Despite the fantasy of total *objectivity* and *value-neutrality*, all authors – *without* exception – exist, live, think, and write in a particular society and at a particular time. All authors and all books carry elements of their societal values but while some hide them behind such fictions, others acknowledge them openly.

1
Introduction: Communication and the World of Work

It was a bright cold day in April, and the clocks were striking thirteen is the start of one the foremost books on communication. In George Orwell's *1984*, communication in a future society is reduced to a tool that corrupts our thoughts while BIG BROTHER IS WATCHING YOU and the *thought police* is looking for *thought crimes*.[5] Orwell has provided one of the most powerful images of where society can go when human communication is deliberately distorted, corrupted, abused, and misused. Even though the year *1984* has long since passed, present society, work, and communication have obviously not yet reached an Orwellian stage. However his apocalyptic scenario remains with us. Undoubtedly, Orwell emphasised the importance of communication in shaping our society, our thinking, and how damaging the misuse of communication can be as it reaches into the heart of our society. As much as in 1948 when Orwell wrote *1984*, today, and in a hopefully non-Orwellian future, almost all societies and their accompanying work arrangements exist through communication. Ever since modern mass production ended feudalist peasant life some time between the mid-18th and the early 20th century, demands on communication at work have been on the increase. The way we work is continuously being reshaped and with it the demands on communication. With the continuous rise of modern post-industrial work arrangements, communication has become an ever more important aspect of our present and future working and social lives. Not surprisingly, much has been written on the relationship between the way *work* has been managed and *communication*.

Traditionally, economists, labour relations, and above all communication experts have viewed these developments from somewhat separate standpoints. With the rise of *communication studies* as an independent subject during the last 50 odd years, studies on communication began to be seen as increasingly important for the world of work. Even though the communication field has definitely had an impact on the way the *world of work* is seen today, it is still divided into a managerial and a labour-relations viewpoint. At present, the field of communication at work or *organisational communication*, as it is commonly termed, is still divided into a focus on discussions on *why* people communicate at work while others focus on *how* organisations and *management* communicate and *how* managerial communication takes place.[6] These studies concentrate on *effective* and *efficient* management. Originally effectiveness and efficiency are two management ideas that have been transferred into human communication resulting in effective and efficient communication at work. All too often this widely accepted standpoint tends to result from a rather one-dimensional and ultimately unquestioned management viewpoint. Above all, this effective managerial communication perspective tends not to focus on internal communication as it focuses on customer relations, marketing, etc. Hence *work* is not at the centre either. It is successfully removed as largely irrelevant to management communication. All too often a managerial focus on effectiveness or efficiency takes over and shadows human communication at work.[7] A managerially driven view that uses communication as an instrument inside organisations to support organisational goals supersedes a quest into any *why* of human communication at work. The idea of this book, however, is to remove this rather one-dimensional view on effective communication in organisations which is not driven by organisational goal achieving purposes that see communication consciously or unconsciously as a mere supplement to organisational success.[8] In contrast, it seeks to move communication among people at work into the centre.

It focuses on comprehensive investigations into human aspects that underlie communication at work. Hence the title *Communication and Management at Work* fulfils two essential aspects. It directs attention to *how* and *why* people communicate at work. It shows how communication works as it discusses the inner mechanisms of communication among participants in managerial, industrial, business, and work-related settings. The key aspect is on *why, how* and *in what way* communication at work is conducted in an effort to bring forward concepts leading to a deeper understanding of communication. Of relative importance to an understanding of *Communication and Management at Work* is the construction of meaning among participants in workplaces. Essentially communication is about how information or messages are issued and received. But *Communication and Management at Work* does not stop here. As all participants send and receive messages they also have to understand and interpret these messages in order to understand them.[9] When we receive a message, let's say *a red traffic light*, we not only receive the message, we also understand and interpret it. We interpret this message – *a red light* – by linking it to previous knowledge, i.e. traffic rules that one must obey. In traffic, at work, and in everyday life, every one of us constantly conducts such operations. We do this whether we are at home or at work, whether we are observing signs or reading an introduction to a book on communication at work. As we read these sentences, we seek to understand the author's intentions by reflecting on information that the author issues to us.[10] While reading the introduction we seek to reconstruct the author's argument in order to understand his intentions expressed in *Communication and Management at Work*. As humans we are unable to understand the meaning of any author's introductory sentences without linking them to some form of previous knowledge, to things we already know. This kind of previous knowledge or *a priori* knowledge, as the philosopher Kant (1721–1781) once called it, is a form of knowledge that we all have and share.

Only our ability to link previous – *a priori* – knowledge to newly received messages enables us to enter into a process that creates meanings. It enables us to establish understanding and to construct interpretations. Such a communicative interpretation is also called the creation of meaning. To understand a text called *Communication and Management at Work* is a task relatively easily accomplished as most of us can relate to the two everyday experiences that most of us share: communication and work. For many – whether managing or being managed – communication and work are things we regularly do. Equally, most – if not all of us! – communicate whether at work or not. While we surely communicate outside of work, the focus here is on communication *at work*. Hence the focal point is on the workplace as the place where most of our goods and services are engineered and produced. However, *Communication and Management at Work* does not have engineering, production, or mechanical tools-boxes for business operations or process re-engineering or any other management fads at its core. The task at hand is a substantive inquiry into *Communication and Management at Work* and not into managerial fashions that change, come, and go. In this context, work is not just an engineering fad. It is rather a substantial and socially constructed activity that is at the heart of our present society.

Communication and Management at Work highlights communicative components of work that enable the process of work to become alive. It also focuses on a critical understanding of communication and management at work that goes beyond standard *how-to-do* and *how-to-do-it-better* fashions that all too often are formulated as a handy recipe book.[11] Traditionally, communication has been viewed as a tool or an instrument. Time and again communication and management at work have been constructed inside the framework of instrumental rationality where human thinking is purposively driven towards managerial goals. Inside rational management – often expressed as *strategic* management – such a prescribed way of thinking tends to be preoccupied with finding the right, correct, best, effective, etc. instrument, tool, strategy, etc. for – as it has been claimed – *your* or more accurately – *any* business. Such recipe books are designed to solve *your* as much as *any* managerial problem. This is often done in an approach that could be summarised as: *your business is a very important business – just like everybody else's business!* With a few clever steps any manager can manage communicatively or strategically by moving from being a simple manager to an upmarket position of strategic or communicative manager!

Most unfortunately, this has been transferred into every part of everyday life. All human and societal affairs just need to be managed correctly and the managerial dream of universal success comes true, never mind what success actually means![12] We are told that if we manage our affairs correctly, it improves our family and marriage. It relieves us from pain, emotional stress and misfortune. A raft of *Manage Your…*-books such as *Manage* your Marriage, *Manage* your Finances, *Manage* your First Date, *Manage* your Children, Successful Educational *Management*, Stress and Anger *Management*, *Manage* your Family, *Manage* your Wedding Day, etc. pile up in bookstores and bookshelves at home. Despite the fact that they may not be as helpful or as good as they pretend, most people experience pretty soon that human-, work-, and family life is not as easily fixed as we are being told.[13] That it is not something that can – and in many cases does not even need to be – easily managed. For many, the advice *just follow a simple recipe and your simple life will be okay*, turns out to be a false promise. Despite their doubtful quality in actually providing help, these books are financial success stories as they sell well and *make*(!) money at airport bookstalls around the world. In the words of George Orwell in *1984, books were just a commodity that had to be produced, like jam or bootlaces* (1949:136). These well-selling *Manage Your…* books are the exact opposite of Woody Allen's claim *my movies must be good, they never make any money,* reflecting on his 40-year movie-making career. Maybe good movies and good books hardly *make* money. Maybe they are not designed to make money. Maybe they are designed to enlighten us. Maybe they are not about quick fixes telling us *how* but rather about the secret that resides in *why*.

Maybe most ideas that gave us *Enlightenment* and modernity like Galileo's earth movements,[14] Luther's 95 theses, Copernicus' planetary movements, Newton's gravity, Rousseau's principles, Kant's ethics, Marx' capital, Einstein's relativity, Freud's psychoanalysis, Piaget's development psychology, Kohlberg's ethical development, Habermas' communicative action, or Pinter's 2005 Nobel Prize Lecture were never designed to make money. Maybe they were designed to uncover the often hidden but basic ideas about human communication. While not being positioned in the above listed category, *Communication and Management at Work* is foremost about uncovering the secrets of communication at work. Most likely, it will not turn out to be as funny as Woody Allen's movies but it is designed as a contribution to the enlightenment project. It should – like Woody Allen's movies – be enlightening on aspects of human communication at work. It is not a money-making guide to *Manage Your '…* (insert your subject here)…'.[15]

Most of the *Manage Your…* books tend to focus on narrow subject areas without venturing much beyond their self-set boundaries in which they pretend to have all the answers to your ills. Over and over again they present easy solutions to easy problems that are all to be found and solved in the domain of *how*, never in *why*. While using a language that is easy to understand they all too often exist inside the confines of such language use. As language philosopher Wittgenstein had noted *the boundary of my language is the boundary of my world* (Radford 2005:177). Hence, the simple language of the *Manage Your...* approach already sets strong limits to any deeper understanding of the world, confining this understanding in a self-constructed frame presented in theory-less facts. While facts are presented as given and not as socially constructed complex models, sophisticated concepts and underlying theory are largely absent. If theory is included at all, then it is reduced to a few, if any, simple models and simplistic statements reflecting a KISS approach: *keep it simple, stupid!*[16] While they avoid telling us the theory behind their claims, they still follow a certain chain-logic: the world is simple, your business is simple, your problem is simple, and your solution is simple. Ultimately, there is, however, an unmentioned but equally fatal consequence: you are simple!

These texts tend to confine our thinking *inside* a pre-constructed square which we are supposed to live in without recognising, realising and above all questioning the existence of this pre-constructed square or box.[17] Through these texts, we are more and more led to believe we should be living inside a comfortable box with sharp boundaries and edges. While the almost exact opposite is the case, we are told that venturing outside is complicated, disillusive, dangerous, and non-fulfilling. As George Orwell (1949:163) beautifully remarked in his novel *1984,*

> the world-view of [managerialism] imposed itself most successfully on the people incapable of understanding it. They could be made to accept the most flagrant violations of reality, because they never fully grasped the enormity of what was demanded of them, and were not sufficiently interested in public events to notice what was happening. By lack of understanding they remained sane. They simply swallowed everything, and what they swallowed did them no harm, because it left no residue behind, just as a grain of corn will pass undigested though the body of a bird.

A comfortable domain has been created that allows us to take part without understanding what is happening. We never have to leave our cushioned world of consumerism mediated through corporate mass media that tell us all is fine and that existing in our little boxed-in and closed-off suburban world is a sane thing. Hence even at a somewhat more intellectual level, many follow a quasi-intellectual containerisation of thought that presents the social world of work as being boxed up into a separation of labour relations (Orwell's *Oldspeak*) on the one hand and Human Resource

Management (Orwell's *Newspeak*) on the other. These two boxes are further separated into managerial or organisational communication on the one hand and communication at work on the other, even though management, work and communication occur at the same time at the same place – the place where people work.

Interestingly, an artificial and socially constructed division of academic disciplines – often reflecting no more than an unconscious reproduction of a capitalist division of labour in the minds of academics and management writers – occurs at the same time as the almost universal call for an *interdisciplinary* or *supra-disciplinary* approach is issued.[18] Often, this interdisciplinary approach is presented as a fruitful combination of several disciplines, such as management studies, labour relations, the sociology of work, and communication studies. At the same time it avoids a self-narrowing and self-conforming *containerisation of discourse* (Grant 2004:14). *Communication and Management at Work* is not just another containerised recipe on *how to manage, communicate effectively, manage your communication needs, be an effective business communicator, manage and communicate strategically,* etc. Instead it combines several *disciplinary* areas as a *supra-disciplinary* discourse of *the world of work* underwritten by a critical approach that is linked to critical theory. Such an approach demands that the study is constructed as a critical reflection on communication and management at work from various perspectives rejecting any *one-dimensional*[19] view from any specific viewpoint. Avoiding a specific viewpoint, an interdisciplinary or supra-disciplinary approach, produces challenges to an academically constructed comfort zone of deeply held values inside the well-guarded but ultimately narrowing lines of a sheltered region that is defined by limited academic discourse. A critical multi-viewpoint and supra-disciplinary approach does so by, first of all, contesting the very support mechanisms of containerisation. Such a multi-dimensional viewpoint not only places communication at the centre but also links commonly separated fields as shown in Figure 1.1:

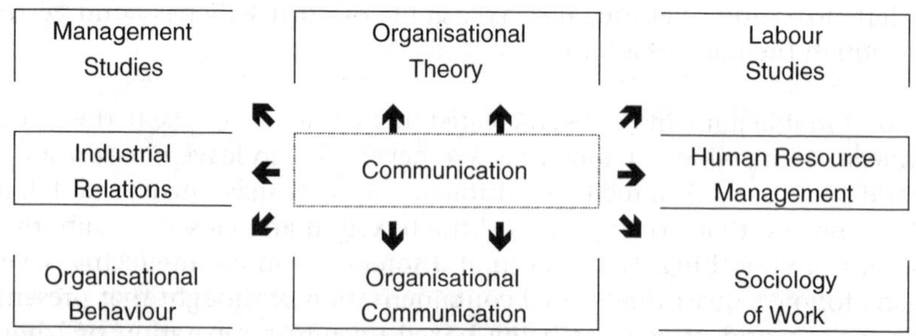

Figure 1.1   From an Inter- to a Supra-Disciplinary Approach

More than just symbolically, Figure 1.1 shows that a previously *inter-disciplinary* approach with borders that can be crossed is moved into a *supra-disciplinary* approach. The previously often closed boxes of academic fields can no longer be seen as closed but have to be opened up as communication at work provides very strong links to surrounding fields. In Figure 1.1 this is shown in two ways. Firstly, all surrounding fields have no borders when linking them to communication positioned in the middle. Secondly, communication is free of any border. The linkage to other fields exists because of communication's communicative ability itself. As shown in the centre, communication itself is not depicted inside a closely guarded box with sharp and thick borders but without any line, indicating *openness* and a *no border* approach towards surrounding fields. While many have traditionally sought to separate not only each field from an adjacent field but also from the linkage field of communication, none of the above fields shown can function or even exist without communication. In short, while there is plenty of communication inside each *box,* there is also a rich collection of communication between each and every of the above boxes.

Communication and Management at Work is neither about communication in each box nor about communication between specific boxes. It is about communication and management at work drawing on all and more than the boxes shown above to highlight the communicative element at work seen from a wide variety of different viewpoints. *Communication and Management at Work* does not live from a once-and-for-all standpoint but seeks to examine the communicative element of work from as many angles as possible. The theme is neither a description of a specific boxed-in framework nor does it seek to assume a middle-of-the-road or mainstream standpoint. It is however not standpoint-less. As American philosopher Isaiah Berlin emphasised in his *Two Concepts of Liberty*: *to realise the relative validity of one's convictions and yet stand for them unflinchingly is what distinguishes a civilised man from a barbarian.*[20] Therefore, *Communication and Management at Work* is a contribution to a civilised discourse that stands firmly on the grounds of a non-mainstream but critical assessment of *Enlightenment,* modernity, and the world of work.

The idea of *Communication and Management at Work* is not to produce yet another standard mainstream middle-of-the-road view displaying an already known mediocrity by conforming to expected conventions.[21] Too often such mediocrity and ordinary views are at the centre of many uncritical but widely accepted ideas on management, labour, communication, and the world of work. Opposing that, reflective and critical scholarship always seeks to honour the German philosopher Kant's dictum *under modernity everything has to submit to critique.* Indeed, scholarship is not about producing more and more themes that swim with one or the other academic trend. Ever since Galileo's *the earth moves,* true scholarship is to be found in those ideas that provide a non-conformist view, even when he was threatened with the instruments of torture, when forced to shut up, when forced to live inside his house, when forced to publish under his daughter's name. Works that follow Galileo and Kant do not drift along like deadwood – only floating Δ downstream in an endless flow of mainstream material. True scholarship that carries connotations of Galileo and Kant swims – and sometimes struggles – *against* the *main*stream as an activity that demands real swimming, not just floating along! Where the floating scholarship can end up has been expressed in George Orwell's (1949:290) novel *1984*, when the hero surrendered, and everything else followed. *Newspeak* made him believe that *he hardly knew why he ever had rebelled*. Today, there seem to be two kinds of scholarship, those who swim with the current and those – like Galileo and many others – who continue to swim against it, who continue to struggle, to rebel and to unearth facts that are inconvenient for mainstream thinking.

Being well inside the Kantian (1781) tradition, Max Weber (1948:147) once noted, *the world of scholarship unearths many facts that are inconvenient for deeply held values.* For philosopher Kant as much as for sociologist Weber the main theme has been to tackle many deeply held mainstream ideas. As a *critical reflection* (Kant) that produces *inconveniences for deeply held values* (Weber), *Communication and Management at Work* is a critical assessment of work and communication as neither can exist without the other. Not only are there no workplaces without communication, we – as human beings – cannot exist without communication either. Communication theorists Watzlawick, Beavin & Jackson (1967) have expressed this as: *You cannot not communicate.* People at work communicate.[22] When they communicate they also establish a second element that is vital to work and communication. They simultaneously establish a communicative relationship with each other.

Therefore people at work are not there to be managed, they establish relationships. These relationships are established through communication in *communicative relationships*. Hence, people at work constantly create forms of communication relationships with each other. The *world of work* (Cheney & Carroll 1997) is a world of relationships among people that has been established communicatively. People at work do not exclusively communicate inside the managerial belief system of hierarchical or vertical top-down arrangements. Communication at work is not reducible into the managerial format of *upward reporting* and *downward commanding*. To a much greater extent, present-day organisational existence of people at work incurs horizontal communicative working relationships by working together as co-workers rather than the old-fashioned *command receivers* or simple task operators.[23] Communicative structures at work are much more elaborate than many writers of business-driven organisational communication who rely on narrow up–Δ–down boxes tell us.[24] Behind these boxes lurks a hidden world of socially and economically constructed relationships between people at work. The world of a socially constructed reality of communication and management at work cannot be pressed into a one-dimensional framework, the framework of managerialism. People at work cannot be neatly containerised and pigeonholed into *human resources management* where *humans* are re-declared to be *resources* that need to be *managed*. If the human world is not only filled with real *humans* but also governed by *humanity* then neither humanity nor humans should be reduced to *resources*. Humans are not to be turned into *objects of power* (Bauman 1989) to be allocated and turned into *organisational* resources forced to behave in accordance with organisational behaviour. Despite many attempts by managerialism and its followers, they have not yet managed to completely turn humans into objects that can be managed instrumentally. Despite libraries filled with volumes of managerialism, endless numbers of journals that glorify the wonders of managerialism, humans still tend to find ways to escape the totality of managerialism at work.

Despite tremendous attempts of the managerial apparatus to antiseptically compartmentalise people at work into pre-determined boxes, people still conduct their work inside social and communicative relationships that relate to the objective world of work. Secondly, proponents of such boxed-in approaches tend to depict the boxes in which work appears as disconnected from history. By doing so, they have often intentionally hidden the historical character of social and economic relationships at work. However, and ultimately unavoidably, there will always be an historic element to the way in which work in present societies is conducted and the way in which people communicate at work. Ever since *The Great Transformation* described the transformation from *feudalism* with master and servants to *capitalism* with owners and workers, the managerial consequences of this process are with us.[25] More or less, these managerial consequences have been commonly termed as *Scientific Management*. However, sometimes this scientific management in its currently existing form is conducted in a more unscientific way (Shenhav 1999) than many academics like to show. Ever since Frederick Taylor engineered his *Scientific Management* (1911), people at work have experienced a division of labour between workers and managers. Even though the current system of production and distribution of commodities has undergone several structural changes between the early days of capitalism starting somewhere in the British Midlands in the early-18th century to present-day's *Post-Industrial Society* (Bell 1973), Taylor's division of labour might have changed numerous times but nonetheless it has not ceased to exist.[26] Again, the two essential categories at work – management and labour – do not exist separately but inside a communicatively established relationship that is at work and that works.

This *relationship* between management and labour at international, national, industry and workplace level has conventionally been seen as a subject and – especially after the event of *The Great Transformation* from feudalism to industrialism – has been allocated to a field of studies called industrial relations (IR) or labour relations. A somewhat outdated view sees this field as the study of collective bargaining or as an equation to trade unionism.[27] Such an antiquated stance appears by far too narrow to cover a widely accepted definition of this field as expressed by former Bill Clinton advisor and MIT professor Thomas Kochan (1980:1) who sees the field as a study of *all aspects of people at work*. The core communicative element of *the world of work* does not lie in the mechanics of technology, the consumer logic of marketing, or the numbers logic of accounting, but in one aspect only: *people*. People at work are seen as communicating people engaged in communicatively constructed relationships with co-workers, managers, supervisors, etc.

Communication and Management at Work is not about management or industrial and labour relations. Nor is it restricted to organisational studies or organisational communication.[28] It reaches far beyond such traditional and one-dimensional frameworks by focusing on the communicative relationship between two agencies: labour and management. Simply focusing on managerial communication would run the risk of being restricted to *how to manage top-down communication*. On the other hand, a traditionalist industrial or labour relations view would rely too much on labour economics, industrial sociology, etc. This perspective relies on a *relationship* perspective that is more akin to communication as all communication necessarily also contains a communicative *relationship*. As much as communication can only be expressed as a communicative relationship, it would nevertheless cut too short for *Communication and Management at Work* to reduce the world of work to communication. Similarly, an organisational studies approach would lean too much towards forms of organisations as discussed inside organisational studies, organisational theory or organisational development, and on how people behave inside such organisations as inside organisational behaviour. In either case, the issue is not about organisations themselves or how people behave organisationally, but how they communicate. While organisational communication is an important aspect and is most closely related to *Communication and Management at Work*, such a perspective would focus somewhat too narrowly on organisations themselves. Nevertheless organisational communication has contributed several significant ideas to an understanding of *Communication and Management at Work*.

The origins of organisational communication can be traced back to the 1930s and 1940s. It fully developed into a field by the 1970s. Redding's (1972) ten postulates of organisational communication transferred earlier studies on top-down management and supervisor-subordinate communication into issues such as meaning, everything is a potential message, message received, feedback, cost factor, redundancy, overload, serial transmission effects, and the organisational climate. Communication moved from *what effects do downward directed communications have on employees?* of the 1940s to issues of supervisor-subordinate, teamwork, and the organisational climate of the 1970s. *Communication and Management at Work* addresses neither the question of the 1940s nor the restricted framework of the 1970s. Passing the 1970s, Wert-Gray et al. (1991), identified four core research interests of organisational communication for the 1980s: a) climate and culture, b) superior-subordinate, c) power, conflict, and politics, and d) public organisation communication. Not surprisingly, *Communication and Management at Work* is more closely related to those than to the issues of the 1940s or 1970s. It addresses issues such as power, conflict and politics. However, it is not restricted to the top-down or superior-subordinate constraints. Between the 1990s and today, organisational and workplace-related communication has been more concerned with an ever wider range of issues that could be categorised into two broad groups:[29] a) non-reflective *how-to-do* issues and b) reflective-critical issues:

Table 1.1   Recent Issues of Organisational Communication

a) Non-Reflective How-To-Do Issues	b) Reflective-Critical Issues
performance and organisational efficiency, groups and teams, leadership, new technologies, intercultural communication, managerial communication skills, communication barriers, persuasive communication, interactive communication, meetings and negotiations, business communication for managers, oral communication, and reporting.	Organisational discourse, communication networks, voice and silence at work, managerial metaphors, groups and teams, leadership, new technologies, intercultural communication, consensus and dissent, fragmented identities, the philosophy of presence, loss of foundation, master narrative, hyper-reality, post-modern forms of communication, communicative action.

As shown in the table above, the field of organisational communication widened during the last decade and a somewhat crude categorisation that also includes some issues in both spheres illustrates that neither a more functional oriented nor a more reflective and critical viewpoint is able to position issues of *Communication and Management at Work* inside either one or the other box. However, several issues in each category touch on *Communication and Management at Work* as they examine aspects covered in this book. Ultimately, none is satisfactory for the issue as category (a) tends to view *Communication and Management at Work* in a top-down, managerial, and functional view while category (b) is predominantly about an organisational viewpoint on *workers* reducing them to a sub-group inside a reflective-critical framework. This reductive view as expressed in Table 1.1 (a, b) also carries connotations representing discussions that can be viewed from the familiar and widely accepted sociological *structure* (i) versus *agency* (ii) matrix (see Table 1.2 below). In both (a, b), workers (*Oldspeak*) or organisational members (*Newspeak*) are viewed as:

Table 1.2   Reflection and Non-Reflection in Structure vs. Agency

	a) Non-Reflective	b) Reflective-Critical
(i) Agency:	part of a *management* framework or portrayed as *'to be managed'*	critical *organisational actor* or critical theory perspective on management
(ii) Structure:	a given functional and supportive system	from imperatives of profit-making to a platform for critical organisational communication

As the table above shows, based on either a (a) non-reflective or (b) reflective standpoint seen as either emphasising (i) agency or (ii) structure, current studies in organisational communication can be located in either one of the four resulting areas. Ultimately, *Communication and Management at Work* cannot be squeezed neatly into one the four sub-areas of organisational communication. The common shortcoming of (a) is its focus on either a functional standpoint or a top-down perspective. Under a more (b) reflective-critical approach, social actors are somewhat neutralised when they appear combined as organisational actors living in an organisational community while the shortcoming of structure lies in the reduction of organisations to mere platforms for human communication.[30] *Communication and Management at Work* avoids both shortcomings. Ultimately, none of the frameworks provided by organisational communication offers a sufficient standpoint from where an examination of *Communication and Management at Work* can depart. However, sociological perspectives based on *agency versus structure* make available an initial starting point for a fruitful journey into *Communication and Management at Work*.

Communication and Management at Work is a discussion on the *communicative* and *instrumental-strategic* expression in the labour-management *relationship* at work. It departs from an organisational perspective in as much as it takes a relationship perspective. Such a relationship approach also departs from a managerial top-down perspective. Traditional industrial or labour relations even though decades old, failed to focus on communication as the issues of communication and managerial strategy are more current and affect every relationship of people at work. Even though there is a span of well over 100 years between British industrial relations writers Sydney and Beatrice Webbs' (1894) original work on the industrial *relation-*

ship of people at work and *Communication and Management at Work,* the issue of communication has been widely neglected by almost all writers during this period. For many years, the labour relations writers' field has been concerned with *problem-solving as the first priority* (Kaufman 1993:66), leading to a deficiency in theoretical development. Already during the 1950s, the late John Dunlop (1958:vi–vii) critically remarked on a seemingly endless growth of empirical data by stating, *mountains of facts have been piled up on the plains of human ignorance.* Consequently, studies of management-labour interaction have been primarily oriented towards practical solutions to stabilise the system resulting in the near exclusion of communication but most devastatingly also resulting in an almost theory-free discipline.

Given the more than 100 years old background of solving problems and delivering facts, there has been only limited engagement with conceptual and theoretical issues such as management's use of instrumental communication.[31] This becomes even more apparent when the issue is examined from a theoretical perspective based on a viewpoint that includes elements of *critical theory.* Hence, traditional conceptual and normative examinations of communication and management at work relied on *theory language* rather than *observation language.*[32] This is no longer sufficient in order to understand the world of work as a world in which people communicate. Unlike all previous inquiries into the world of work, for the first time, *Communication and Management at Work* moves communication into the centre of activity. It does this on a non-empirical but conceptual level by using theory language rather than observation language. *Observation language* expresses empirical cases by using practical examples in support of an enterprise. *Theory language* enables basic explanations of a communicative relationship between labour and management well beyond case studies and empirical limitations.

Here, the emphasis is not so much on *piling up ever more mountains of socially constructed facts* (Berger & Luckmann 1967; Searle 1996) but more on interpreting these *facts* to direct our critical conscience towards *factors* that construct what is presented as *facts.* Already Rabelais,[33] a writer of the year of 1532, demanded such a treatment of knowledgeable *facts* when he called for *knowledge without conscience is but the ruin of the soul.* As much as the world of work – whether expressed in the words of managerialism, organisational studies, labour studies or the like – is a world that is socially constructed, social facts could never have existed without human input. All facts about the world of work that we can possibly know are facts that have been created by humans. Humans have shaped these facts as much as we are able to alter and use them. In the world of work, no *brute facts* (Searle 1969) exist. Today's work does not contain any facts that exist independent from us because we have constructed the way we work. In interpreting these socially created facts, factors, models and *paradigms* are constructed to assist our communicative understanding of contemporary labour and management. *Communication and Management at Work* essentially fulfils Hegel's dictum that the growth of theoretical knowledge is to be seen as an ongoing process of reconstruction of earlier and imperfect theories in order to better attain their goals.[34] Hegel's ideas are not to be understood in Popper's *falsifiable* term. *Communication and Management at Work* does not seek to *proof* older theories as *false* but reconstructs them in the light of communication at work (Popper 1999). In a similar way to Popper's *falsification, Communication and Management at Work* is not a *restoration* and *renaissance* of earlier concepts and theories. A *restoration* would be understood to be a return to an initial situation of *pure* management-labour relations which are seen as being corrupt. This is not intended and restoration is not the task here. *Communication and Management at Work* is not about traditional management-labour relations that had been buried for some time. It does not go back to an earlier stage, does not resurrect earlier theories, and does not falsify them either. It seeks to move on without ever neglecting to look back.

Communication and Management at Work is directed towards the dictum of Danish philosopher Sören Kirkegaard (1813–1855): *life can only be understood backwards but must be lived forward*. While large sections are about theories stemming from the past, the thrust is forward-looking. What has been done is not a *restoration, renaissance, or recycling* of old theories on management-labour relations but a – sometimes indispensably radical – reconstruction of theories and models that explain the communicative relationship between labour and management. This reconstruction seeks to take many of the presently well-established and mainstream models, concepts, paradigms, and theories on labour-management relations apart and put them back together again. This process leads to new forms of theory formation. In this way, a theoretical understanding of communicative relationships at work revises many previously held ideas on management-labour relationships. It makes visible those potentials that have not been exclusively exhausted in earlier attempts.

It goes without saying that *Communication and Management at Work* deals with rather complex theoretical issues. Most contemporary paradigms and models are constructed around some rather basic assumptions when compared with more sophisticated *theories of communication*. In all theory formations there are, however, trade-offs. Those are between necessary simplicities, often expressed in the well-known two-by-two matrixes, models, graphs, tables, figures, etc. On the other hand there is a demand towards an analytical and theoretical grounding of *Communication and Management at Work*. Hence this book is an attempt towards an accomplishment of a goal set by one of the founding fathers of critical theory. German critical theorist Max Horkheimer stood on the shoulders of the Kant-Hegel-Marx tradition of exposing all aspects of our social, individual and collective existence to critical examination. But Horkheimer's vision has also been a reflection on the *practical relevance of critical theory*. Standing on the shoulders of *Enlightenment* thinkers and Horkheimer's Critical Theory, the *Communication and Management at Work* project is able to see a little bit further. As Bernard of Chartres (1159) and Issac Newton (1676) would have put it, *pigmaei gigantum humeris impositi plusquam ipsi gigantes vident*. In other words, *Communication and Management at Work* is no more than a dwarf standing on the shoulders of the giants of *Enlightenment* to see a little bit further into communication and the world of work.[35]

The application of critical theory's *communicative action* to the world of work resulting in *Communication and Management at Work* is as much a critical reflection on the subject at hand as it testifies to the practical relevance of this book. But *Communication and Management at Work* is also about a much earlier critical writer on enlightenment, René Descartes (1596–1650).[36] In the year 1628 Descartes noted *we need a method if we are to investigate the truth of things*. A simple sentence such as *communication at work is about Descartes' truth of things* looks uncomplicated. The crucial element in Descartes' words lies in the equally simple word *truth*. In other words, a discourse on *Communication and Management at Work* is directed towards the truth without interference of instrumental thinking. Hence the guiding light should be *truth* and not corporate efficiency, organisational goals, or managerial demands even when the *truth* produces discomforting facts about long held values. In order to investigate this, Descartes' *need for method* positions an *inter- or supra-disciplinary method* right into the centre. In short, Descartes' *truth of things* and *method* are one of the core patterns of capitalism (Habermas 1997a:336–337), namely the pattern of communication and management at work. In the true sense of the word and as used by Descartes, *method* is applied in its Greek origins providing a *hodos* or *road* and a *meta* or *towards*. Together they build the *road towards* or method towards the *truth* of a *thing* called *Communication and Management at Work*.

Continuing on the road towards Descartes' *truth of things* that is seen as a communicative relationship between labour and management, 100 years after Descartes, we encounter the German philosopher Friedrich Hegel (1770–1831). In a further attempt to understand Descartes' *truth of a thing* of communication between management and labour, Hegel taught us the distinction between: a) understanding, b) dialectical reason, and c) speculative reason. *Understanding* (i) of a communicative relationship leads to a determination and a definition of such a relationship, while *dialectical reasoning* (ii) is a movement of thought that has thesis-antithesis-synthesis at its core. Such a dialectical thesis-antithesis-synthesis concept can be expressed in three ways: firstly, in the thesis of labour and management communication in their respective domains and between each other. Secondly, an antithesis is created as they communicate differently inside their respective domains. Inside the labour-domain, labour can communicate among each other and inside a management-domain management communicates among itself. But both can also meet as members of their respective domains and exchange messages between their domains. A third process is directed towards a synthesis when management and labour enter into a process of communication. Finally, Hegel's speculative reason (iii) seeks to provide a perspective that will explain how two actors with sometimes two contrary agendas fit into a single complex thought of communication at work. This is the speculative or utopian element of Hegel who was, after all, a student of Kant. Kant, as Hegel's predecessor, was interested not only in *what is* but also in *what ought to be*. Surely many had an interest in *what is* of organisational and managerial communication. However, the most intellectually stimulating questions remain today as in the time of Kant and Hegel locked up in the utopian area of *what ought to be*. Today, as in their time, utopian speculations into *what ought to be* remain the most fruitful and challenging enterprise of the human mind. Albert Einstein was correct when he wrote *imagination is more important than knowledge*. Hence, an imaginative investigation into the human condition conducted in the tradition of Kant, Hegel, and Einstein entails three essential value judgements: a) human life is worth living or rather ought to be worth living, b) one can detect societal potentials for a betterment of working conditions, and c) there are ways and means of achieving this goal.

The human mind might have been extended by studies into *what is* but studies into *what ought to be* might enrich the human mind further as thinkers from Galileo to Einstein have shown. Hence any study into the world of work and into *Communication and Management at Work* needs not only to confront *what is* but also, and perhaps more importantly, *what ought to be*. Even after roughly 250 years and many studies into subjects of the human condition at work, discussions on work are still able to produce new thoughts of *what ought to be*. While *work remains the key sociological category* (Offe 1985) and is essential to *Communication and Management at Work's* theme, with work the *workplace* occupies centre stage. Consequently, *Communication and Management at Work* is not written to discuss more of the same. Predominantly, it examines the ways and methods by which information and ideas are communicated, exchanged and shared. Therefore, *Communication and Management at Work* is a dialectic discourse on the *communicative* aspect of the management-labour relationship at work with the workplace as the physical location.

Following from this, *Communication and Management at Work* is written for those who have a professional interest in communication between two actors in the set framework of work, workplace, firm, or company. *Communication and Management at Work* is also written for those who do not stop at Hegel's distinctions (i, ii) but for those with an interest in going beyond understanding and dialectical reason, directing their attention towards speculative reason (iii) and seeking to contemplate *what ought to be*. Hence the core achievement of *Communication and Management at Work* is expressed as a reformulation of Marx' well-known eleventh thesis on *Feuerbach* linked to Hegel's speculative reason and to Kant's *what ought to be* emphasising on Habermas' communicative potentials.[37] Behind the rather complicated theoretical world of Feuerbach, Marx, Hegel, Kant, and Habermas lies a rather simple notion: as empirical studies on what is, gigantic mountains of facts about the world of work have been produced, collected, and interpreted. However, the crucial point is, firstly, to high-light the origins of communication and the role it has played during the rise of modernity, Enlightenment, and capitalism. Secondly, this development has not only impacted on the way society is structured but also on the workplace. Thirdly, to understand modern work-societies, an under-standing of communication at work is necessary.[38] To accomplish these three aspects a certain language has to be applied when discussing the language of language and the communication of communication.[39]

Communication and Management at Work uses *meta*-communication as it communicates *about* communication. This is divided into three distinct areas of communication: a) the construction and production of communication, b) the transmission of communication as a technical process, and finally, c) the reception and appropriation of communication. Communication about communication – *meta*-communication – elaborates these three core problems. This can be transferred into:

Table 1.3   Three Core Perspectives of Meta-Communication

Perspective	Description
semantic and construction	how is a message constructed and conveys a desired meaning;
technical and transmission	how accurately can a message of communication be transmitted;
reception and appropriation	how effectively does a received meaning affect conduct.[40]

The focus of *Communication and Management at Work* – seen through the three elements of the well-known communication theorists (Shannon & Weaver 1949; Thompson 1990; Wood 2004) – is not about the first aspect. Even though most perspectives on communication are located inside the *conduit* model in which communication involves the relatively unproblem-atic transmission of ideas and information between sender and receiver (Mumby 2001:592), *Communication and Management at Work* is not about simple transmissions. It is predominantly about the way communication is used to legitimise managerial decisions, management and managerialism, or expressed differently, how socially constructed actors such as management and labour conduct action in a desired way. Essentially, the central interest of *Communication and Management at Work* is directed towards the problem of a struggle over meaning and how this can affect the conduct of social actors.

To discuss this in an extended framework, *Communication and Management at Work* is set to complete two essential tasks: firstly, it is a contribution to theory development into domination, the mechanism that reproduces conditions for submission, and potentials for emancipation from such domination.[41] It seeks to fill a current lack of a systematic study into communicative aspects of relationships between labour and management at work. Secondly, it also shows that two logics of communication are operative in the domains of labour and management. The different forms of communication become visible as communicative theories are applied to labour-management relations at the workplace.[42]

Having established the three tasks of *Communication and Management at Work*, the final segment of this introduction discusses the *aims*. The first aim is to illustrate communication and its instrumental or strategic use but not as neutral reflections of some objectified reality manifested in the belief that there is a singular truth, the truth of managerialism.[43] However, subjective interpretations in both domains demonstrate that such interpretations succeed the singularity of an objectified truth. The second aim is an *explanation* on how and why communication between labour and management in their respective domains functions or how and why it dysfunctions. The third aim is about *predictions* made on miscommunication between both actors and on the future of communication.[44] A fourth aim can be found in critical theory's inherent aspect of emancipation at work. This part is directed towards action en route for positive social change. The pursuit of social change is not founded on a law-based understanding of theory where a simple causal relationship between x and y is established.[45]

The fifth aim is to show a *correlational* relationship where critical communication (x) and instrumental or strategic communication (y) go together but not to assert that one causes the other. Instead of finding laws that govern communication, the emphasis is directed towards *rule-based* explanations articulating patterns of communication by describing and explaining what happens in work-based communications between labour and management. Such rules or patterns reflect the irregularity of human actors as humanly created rules – unlike physical laws – are subject to social change. The sixth aim includes the assertion of *parsimony* towards appropriate simplicity. This is expressed as: *the best theory is the simplest one that is capable of describing, explaining, understanding, and instigating social change* (Wood 2004:43). This is articulated in the last chapter offering practical usage of the theory of communicative action, even though it might appear complicated from the outset. Wood's statement has also been expressed as *nothing is as practical as a good theory*. The final aim is *heuristic* as it should provoke new ideas, insights, thinking, and research into the communicative relationship of the two actors at work. In this, one has to take some *philosophical elaboration* into account.[46] The world of work is, strictly speaking, not an inherently philosophical subject but relates to it. *Philosophy is in large part the name for all those questions which we do not know how to answer in the systematic way that is characteristic of science* (Searle 2002:20). As questions about communication and management at work cannot be understood by natural-science measurements, sometimes understanding needs to touch philosophy.[47] This can be confronting as *confronting a professional philosopher is to confront one's own ignorance. Nevertheless, the embarrassment must be endured* (Burrell 1994:5). In this respect, one can only hope that *Communication and Management at Work* provides a major embarrassment but one that can be endured by a reader who is willing to adhere to the German *Bauhaus* architect, Walter Gropius' words *the human mind is like an umbrella, it works best when open.*[48]

To the open-minded, *Communication and Management at Work* has not only tasks – pieces of work to be accomplished – and aims – purpose and design – but also several goals. The first *goal* is to provide a new understanding of two sets of familiar materials by treating both in an original and stimulating manner. One set of familiar material is found in the *relationship* between labour and management, while the second set is a link between communication and strategic action. A second goal is directed towards a critique of prevailing assumptions in several academic fields about communication and management at work, while a third goal is set as an educational purpose. *Communication and Management at Work*, then, faces its first theoretical puzzle by applying a theory in a practical way while avoiding to become *hopelessly academic* (Parkin 1996:420). This book is designed to be educational thus reflecting on Orwell and Marx. The educational task set by George Orwell (1949:226) in his novel *1984* is, *there was truth and there was untruth, and if you clung to the truth even against the whole world, you were not mad.* The educational task set by Marx is his eleventh *Thesis on Feuerbach: The issue is not just to interpret the world but to change it!* Hence the final chapter is written as a practical guide that supports these two goals.

To achieve what has been set out above, this book is divided into twelve chapters. After introducing the subject area, the second chapter seeks to lay the groundwork for communication at work by examining the origins and the role that communication plays in today's society. The next chapter relates communication to the development of rationality as a vital contribution to modernity. At the centre is the role of rational communication that is necessary for the work domain to become operative. This has transformed communication into instrumental communication. Chapter 5 discusses how the world of work has been seen and how a critical investigation into the world of work can uncover hidden structures of communicative domination. This is followed by two investigations into the two core domains that are operative at work. Ever since Taylorism, these have been the domains of labour and management. Both take on different forms of logics and communication as chapters 7 and 8 show. Chapter 9 demonstrates how management has been able to use and communicate the ideology of engineering in order to support and legitimise itself. This has been a crucial imperative in establishing communicative control over work. Today's forms of control at work are significantly less reliant on the well-established previous forms of control (Edwards 1979). Unlike these previous forms of control, today's work regimes experience a much higher dependence on communication when establishing and maintaining control. The predominant form of establishing and maintaining control derives from the successfully administered conversion of human beings into human resources. Chapter 11 shows how control is communicated when individuals are converted during the process of primary and secondary socialisation. Chapter 12 examines how modern HR managers communicate control once individuals have been inducted into today's work regimes.

2
The Origins of Communication and Management at Work

This chapter will provide a brief overview of the origins and the role that communication played since our society has moved away from a feudalist past into the present-day system of industrialism, managerialism, and capitalism. While there are many viewpoints from which the role of communication in this process can be discussed, the analytical concept of *critique* provides a particularly fruitful angle as the idea of *critique* has also been at the core of the *Enlightenment* project. Ever since the idea of *Enlightenment* took hold when society left the medieval *Dark Ages,* critique has been a constant companion of modern thinking. It allows not only a reflection on the philosopher Kant's idea of *what is* but also directs our attention to Kant's second idea that might be even more important – the idea of *what ought to be.* Ever since the *Enlightenment* thinker Kant the human condition in society and in *the world of work* has been critically examined using two distinctive viewpoints. The first is a reliance on theories concerned with how things work – *what is* – and the second a reliance on theories that go beyond a simple *what is* entering the domain of *what ought to be.*[49] *Enlightenment's* task has never only been about how things work but has always carried connotations directed towards *what ought to be.* Under feudalism God and religion had told us *what is* and *what ought to be.* Under *Enlightenment,* this was no longer possible. From this time on we had to find out for ourselves *what is* and *what ought to be.* Hence strong scientific demands for our post-feudal society had to be issued.

As much as our civil society changed in the process of *Enlightenment,* working life underwent dramatic changes as well. Feudalist peasants bound to the Lord and to soil became workers,[50] working in factories and engaging in the labour market. These changes also produced significant demands on communication as many new ways of doing things had to be established. No longer were churches, the Lord, and priests able to tell us how society was to function. From now on, people – under the freedom issued in a post-feudalist world – had to communicate their ideas on what society is, how it should conduct itself, and above all how society and people ought to conduct themselves. Overwhelmingly, this was seen to be the task of *Enlightenment* thinkers.

Originating in the 18th century one of the foremost philosophers of *Enlightenment*, Immanuel Kant, sought to identify how things should be done in a modern society as a critical reflection on our feudalist past. Building on Kant's 18th-century idea of critical reflections, 19th-century philosophers such as Hegel and Marx introduced the idea of labour as a core concept for the evolution of human society. But their ideas on work did not remain disconnected from the existing conditions at work. As much as work was seen as part of human evolution, it was also a part of society. Very soon, they discovered that work was done in a relatively harsh world of 19th-century industrialism and capitalism. While connecting philosophical ideas to existing conditions of human society and human work, 20th-century theorists eventually worked core *Enlightenment* ideas such as *society, capitalism, work,* and *communication* into one framework. While doing so, the *Frankfurt School's Theory of Communicative Action* also combined *what is* with *what ought to be*. It saw the need to preserve both as one of the core ideas of the *Enlightenment* project. Once this was done, critical theory had developed the tools necessary to analyse the changing character of capitalist society. In the tradition of *Enlightenment*, the Frankfurt School's critical theory has been able to analyse the following core aspects of modern society and modern work regimes:

Table 2.1   Elements of Work and Society

Core Aspects of Modern Work Regimes and Society

A critical description of configurations of a modern work society,
B social and economic class relations and the social interplay between economy and society,[51]
C the influence and rise of modern mass culture and *mass communication*,[52]
D new forms of production such as Taylorism, Fordism, Neo- and Post-Fordism, the post-industrial service industry, information technology and knowledge economy and modern communication technologies creating new forms of social control at work,
E new modes of primary and secondary socialisation into advanced capitalist and industrial societies,
F the demise of individuality coinciding with the rise of standardised products along with the mediated and often equally standardised mass consumer,
G the successful integration of the working class into consumer capitalism and the withering away of the *proletarian culture* and the proletarian milieu,[53] and finally,
H the unprecedented and previously unseen stability of industrial societies as mediated and communicatively established system integration.

In order to transfer core issues of our society as outlined in Table 2.1. into a workable model, *critical theory* had to go beyond the customary boundaries of traditional theories available in mainstream 20th-century thinking. Some of these mainstream models had developed alongside *Enlightenment*. Two core outcomes of *Enlightenment* mainstream thinking had been *functionalism* and *positivist science*. Both have never been able to leave Kant's *what is*. They remained locked inside Hegel's *Zeitgeist* when explaining new developments of capitalist societies.[54] However and with increasing certainty, *functionalism* and *positivist science* proved to be unable to explain many of the prevailing pathologies of 20th-century social and working life.[55] Therefore, several shortcomings of traditional functionalism and positivist science demanded a *model* based on critical theory that was able to make previously unseen developments visible.[56] Such theoretical model needed to include a link between the *reproductive* domain and the *productive* domain. Labour-management interactions that had been reduced to the *productive* domain without a link to the *reproductive* domain could no longer be used. In short, restrictions that stem from functionalism and traditional positivist theories became too limiting[57] and new developments in the societal and the working domain demanded a new theory that ended all false restrictions of separating the work domain from the social domain. The 20th-century development of critical theory provided sufficient tools that link both domains as outlined above (Table 2.1).

The linkage between society and work can be understood more comprehensively when contemporary working society is linked to communication. Communication in advanced societies always needs to include an understanding of its fundamentals as well as of its organised forms as they appear at work. By doing so, traditional understandings of classical and mainstream management and labour concepts had to be fundamentally adjusted to allow a fully developed comprehension of communication at work. Such reconstructions can only become operative when designed as a *multi-disciplinary* approach capable of coping with the demands issued (Table 2.1). But before the development of traditional labour or management concepts into a comprehensive and above all communicative model to understand modern work relationships can take place, a brief look at some of the core elements of critical theory have to be highlighted.

The origins of the Frankfurt School of *Critical Theory* – a term introduced by Max Horkheimer in 1937 – date back to the year 1923 when Max Grünberg, Max Horkheimer and Theodor Adorno founded an institute for social research in Frankfurt. When Hitler's *Storm Troopers* (SA) occupied the institute in 1933, the Frankfurt School was forced to escape via Paris to Columbia University in New York where it became the *Institute of Social Research*. Like many leading scholars during the Nazi-Regime, they too lived in American exile and the Frankfurt School became known as *Critical*

Theory.[58] Today, critical theory has many representatives inside Germany, Great Britain, the United States of America, Canada, Australia, etc. Apart from the institute's organisational situation, conceptual origins can be found in the ideas of several *Enlightenment* philosophers.[59] Crucial ideas from this period leading to the Frankfurt School came from Kant (1724–1804) and Hegel (1770–1831), but also from Marx (1818–1883), Engels (1820–1895) and Georg Lukács (1885–1971).[60]

Central to Kant's early *Enlightenment* thinking have been his writings on critique as expressed in three major works, *Critique of Pure Reason* (1781), *Critique of Practical Reason* (1788), and *Critique of Judgement* (1790). Unmistakably, Kant (1781:xxiv) stated that *our age is, in every sense of the word, the age of criticism, and everything must submit to it.* Beyond that Kant emphasised that of utmost relevance to present-day thinking is not so much *what can I know?* but *what ought I to do?* Prior to Kant's *Enlightenment* thinking, traditional forms of rationality had often been restricted to simple descriptions of *what is.* Ever since Kant this has changed forever. It gave Kant a secured and somewhat scarily irremovable position in the world of philosophy.[61] Kant's thinking not only introduced the term *a priori* as a fundamental concept of how we can understand the world around us, Kant also sets forward a demand for *what ought to be.*[62] To answer his question of *what ought to be,* Kant formulated a *Categorical Imperative* that focuses on the treatment of people in the same way as one would like to be treated. The *Categorical Imperative* does not see the treatment of people as *a means to an end* or an end *in itself.*[63] Kant's idea on *what ought to be* reaches far beyond that as his ideas always include a possible future state of affairs in a real utopian sense where we would have liberated ourselves from *selbstverschuldete Unmündigkeit* or voluntary servitude.[64]

A philosophical project that ends the state of *voluntary servitude* and includes utopian ideas has been carried forward via critical theory's second intellectual founding father, Hegel.[65] In *Phenomenology of Spirit* (1807), Hegel acknowledged the existence of the *subject.*[66] Hegel also extended the Kantian concept of *a priori* acknowledging a dialectic relationship between Kant's *a priori* and *posteriori* knowledge and between Kant's *subject* and his interest in the *object.*[67] For Kant as much as for Hegel, *subject* and *object* are not artificially, academically or philosophically separated but interdependent. No one can antiseptically separate our being in the world as real existing subjects and our ability to see the objective world.[68] Hence an elementary concept of Hegel's work is *consciousness.* In his *Philosophy of Right*, Hegel discusses animals and human beings and concludes that *labour* is a central category that distinguishes both from each other.[69] Put simply the division between us and the *animal kingdom* is not only our ability to make tools – as tool-making human beings – it is our ability to conduct labour and to work.[70] While animals certainly move, eat, reproduce and so on, they do not conduct structured work in the way humans are able to. Consequently, work and labour are crucial historical elements for the development of human beings and for our present-day human society. Once Hegel and the earlier Kant had located the centrality of human labour and work in the historical development of human society, two other intellectual forefathers of critical theory have taken their ideas even further.

Marx and Engels took the Hegelian analysis one step further by developing a theory on alienated labour and the human potential for emancipation.[71] As humans have the ability to emancipate themselves from the realm of the animal world and subsequent societies – may it be slavery, feudalism and the like – they also carry potentials for emancipation from alien work arrangements, asymmetrical power relations, and forms of domination.[72] Critical theory focuses on these human potentials. In short, critical theory is a product of Kantian and Hegelian *Enlightenment* thinking that culminates in Marx's demand for *a ruthless criticism of everything existing* (1846:8). This is further revealed in the subtitle of Marx's major contribution, *Das Kapital*, that reads, *a critique of the political economy*. As much as Marx's core work is not about communism or socialism as it is *a critique* of the political economy, critical theory's core interest follows very much Kant's and Hegel's request for a critical understanding of present society that cannot be issued without a strong emphasis on emancipation. While critical theory has its intellectual origins in Kant, Hegel and Marx, it is neither classical nor neo-classical Kantian nor classical or neo-classical Hegelian. It is not orthodox Marxian or Marxist as such. For once, a critical theory of the 20th and 21st century has developed far beyond the 18th- and 19th-century philosophy of Kant, Hegel, and Marx.[73]

Furthermore, critical theory also reaches far beyond any version of contemporary labelling in connection to Marx because Marx and all followers of orthodox-, traditional-, unreconstructed-, post-socialist-, neo-, post- etc.-Marxists, had and continue to have *a hard time explaining government intervention, mass democracy, and the welfare state* (Habermas 1997:343). This is especially discomforting for all (*insert your preferred label here*)-Marxists as all three of Habermas' elements are key categories of *advanced* capitalism.[74] Any understanding of modern capitalism is no longer able to avoid these issues. In short, many of the *prefix*-Marxists who rely on Marx tend to fall into what Hegel critically named the trap of the *Zeitgeist* as they remain trapped in the world of the mid-19th century when Marxian analysis represented the most advanced spirit (*Geist*) of that time (*Zeit*) providing a sufficient tool to understand the world. This is no longer possible. However, as advanced capitalism still shows some structures that can be explained by relying on Marx's 19th-century work, they do, nevertheless, show a significant range of signs that demand a substantially extended framework in order to cope with the following trends of present-day work and life regimes (Marcuse 1966:21):

Table 2.2   Structural Trends in Advanced Capitalism

Trends	Explanation
Concentration	National concentration is increasingly replaced by global concentration with state support via international organisations such as GATT, World Bank, International Monetary Fund, OECD, etc.
Military	Corporate Globalisation under advanced capitalism did not lead to an end of armed conflict rather a continuation as military science and technology becomes a function of system integration
Assimilation	There is a gradual assimilation of traditional working-class culture and distinctiveness seen as the proletariat into the middle class with diminished difference between blue- and white collar workers
Welfare state	Although under threat via globalisation and neo-liberalism, welfare state functions as a pacification of disenfranchised and growing sections of the population providing system stability.[75]
Politics	As interest divergence between political parties narrows to a one-dimensional system acceptance, they become undistinguishable as politics is reduced to minor contests as bi-partisanship grows.
Science	Scientific institutions become integrated into advance capitalism as a shift from public-humanist principled education towards a private-market principled system provides functional additives
Private Households	With the shift from work- to *consumer-society*[76] private life is converted into commercial spheres opened up by market access to households as social relations are converted into market relations.
Opening bedrooms	Access of a corporatised and market driven cultural industry is directed toward money, not art or aesthetics. A mediated society opens even bedrooms for commercial advertising.[77]
Standardisation	As mass-mediated reality becomes reality, a standardisation of mass media, mass consumption and communication is established. What follows is a one-dimensional and standardised consumer.
Corporate globalisation	With the rise of global corporations, an international division of labour, product markets and labour markets are reassigned serving globally operative corporations and diluting national boundaries.

Table 2.2   Structural Trends in Advanced Capitalism – *continued*

Trends	Explanation
Political globalisation	Under the demands of corporate globalisation, national welfare and social and labour regulative systems come under threat towards a downward shifting additive to a globalised system.
Trade unions	A merging of working- and middle-class demands unions to shift towards issues previously assigned to middle-class interests as class struggle becomes a routine exercise of minor issues.
One-dimensionality communication	As labour struggles against an overwhelming mass-mediated apparatus directed towards a one-dimensional view of society and work, ideology[78] and communication moves into the centre. Increasingly forms of instrumental communication are established in the reproductive and productive sphere as an ideological support mechanism for system integration.

Table 2.2 above shows, the shift from traditional or early capitalism towards advanced capitalism entails a raft of previously underdeveloped or non-existing issues that Marx could have neither seen nor foreshadowed in the middle of the 19th century. In short, critical theory is neither anti-Marx nor Marxian but a further development of this earlier set of ideas in order to understand the changing character of today's working and social-life regimes. Apart from the failure of much of contemporary Marxist analysis to include the developments of the 20th century, *in other respects a theory of capitalist modernisation developed by means of a theory of communicative action does follow the Marxian model* (Habermas 1997:375). As much as communication in modern society and today's workplace cannot solely be understood in classical or orthodox Marxian explanations, it has to be understood as an extension of it.

One of the early theoreticians of critical theory, Theodor W. Adorno, not only extended Marxian thinking, he also departed from Marxian revolutionary thinking based on two observable and theoretical issues that developed during the 20th century (Morris 2001:119). Firstly and unlike Marxian theory, critical theory's concept of communicative action is a contribution to an explanation why the class structure – already correctly diagnosed by Rousseau (1755:11) in the 18th century as *the extreme idleness of some and the excessive labour of others* – has survived until today.[79] The second problem of Marxian 19th-century thinking that was converted into the 20th and 21st century by Marxists goes to the heart of Marx's theory. Present-day Marxian thinking is still largely unable to provide sufficient answers to a very Marxian question: how can class structures prevail without leading to a revolution as predicted by Marx?[80]

Instead of a foreshadowed revolution, what has been dominant in the 20th and 21st century is *The Affluent Society, The Affluent Worker in the Class Structure, The New Middle Class,* and *The One-Dimensional Man.*[81] This is enshrined in a rather mythical but equally wide accepted formula: *growth means affluence and affluence means democracy.*[82] This formula carries strong connotations of Fordist mass production, mass consumption, and mass democracy. 19th-century thinking had been unable to predict the rise of Fordism that resulted in a massive transformation of capitalism through a dramatic increase in the accessibility of consumption and concurrent wage rises culminating in Ford's famous $5-Day. For relatively large sections of the working class in most major industrialised countries the entire social setting of wage and class relations altered fundamentally under Fordism.[83] It transformed large sections of a previously impoverished working class of the mid-19th century into reasonably affluent classes by the mid-20th century.[84] The Fordist transition, however, also came at a cost, as *those whose life is the hell of the Affluent Society are kept in line by a brutality which revives medieval and early modern practices.*[85] Most crucially however, Fordism did neither end the economic and social division of those who are forced to sell their labour and those who buy it. Our mass-consuming society is still divided into sellers and buyers of labour. Nor has it ended the division into those *who manage* and those *who are managed.*[86] In spite of that, Fordism has significantly contributed to the exact opposite of what Marx had predicted would happen.[87] Marcuse (1969:17) diagnosed the end of Marx's 19th-century prediction of an increased impoverishment of workers as:

> In the affluent society, capitalism comes into its own. The mainsprings of its dynamic – the escalation of commodity production and productive exploitation – join and permeate all dimensions of private and public existence.

In contrast to the predicted revolutionising consciousness and subsequent revolution, the majority of organised labour shares the endless and often somewhat meaningless consumption of commodities and the concurrent stabilising *ideologies* of the middle class.[88] A working-class identity is no longer a viable option as the mass media and the mass-mediated society continuously present a displacement of representation of workers and their culture (Zengotita 2005). The image of the consumer society is powerfully mediated through mass media displacing the image of a working-class society. *The might of industrial society is lodged in men's minds* (Adorno & Horkheimer 1944:7). In a mass-mediated society, the separation of workers from the means of production has not vanished but is successfully glossed over by a mediated reality as systematic integration of working-class consumption into advanced capitalism is established. Despite all efforts by corporate mass media, perceptions of class have not totally vanished in a *mediated mass consumer and classless society.*[89] This is shown in Table 2.3:

Table 2.3   Class Distinctions and Patterns of Consumption

No	Patterns of Consumption
i)	At the bottom, people tend to believe class is defined by the amount of money you have.
ii)	In the middle, people grant that money has something to do with it, but think that education and the kind of work you do are almost equally important.
iii)	Nearer to the top, people perceive that taste, values, ideas, style and behaviour are indispensable criteria of class, regardless of money or occupation or education.[90]

Table 2.3 shows how patterns of consumption relate to class distinctions. It appears as if working- and middle-classes' perceptions (i–ii) of what constitutes class has more to do with *how much* you can consume while the upper class (iii) believes *how* you consume is relevant.[91] Consumption, even though it might appear at its surface to be an individualised process, is in fact a socially organised activity under the system logic of advanced capitalism. In sum, mass-mediated and mass-guided consumption redirects social energies into a system integrative process preserving social relations in the reproduction sphere via an unconscious process necessary for system stability.

The consumption process diverts the focus on wage labour relations away from the world of work towards consumer relations. It essentially moves from the production domain to the reproduction domain as an elementary modality of present relationships.[92] Relevant to both domains – production and re-production – however is a relationship character as a necessary condition of system maintenance for production and mass-mediated re-production. More than ever before, working- and middle-class consumption relies on the individual ownership of commodities as consumer goods, not as investment goods. Increasingly consumer relations have replaced solidaristic working-class relations.[93] The old human-to-human relationships have been altered to human-commodity-human relationships as *The Privatisation of Everything* takes hold.[94] Commodity relations demand new techniques that squeeze the commodity between human-to-human interactions. The technique of selling and advertising infiltrates every corner of life as children are singing advertising songs that have long replaced the nursing rhyme. *Today the private space has been invaded and whittled down by technological reality. Mass production and mass distribution claim the entire individual, and industrial psychology has long since ceased to be confined to the factory* (Marcuse 1966:12). The affluent mass-consumption society created the totally mediated and incorporated individual and elevated Marx's *commodity fetishism* to new heights as the repressive form of commodity consumption moved to centre stage.[95] Fordist *consumption* removed creative energies of the working population from the domain of production into the domain of reproduction. In the reproductive domain, Fordist standardisation of mass products resulted in a standardisation of consumption. Ultimately, the standardised consumer standardises their living and social relationships while at the same time the mediated society keeps up the pretence of individuality.[96] More than anything this is symbolised by the shopping mall. Upon entering any standardised shopping centre, a human is miraculously transformed into a standardised consumer. This consumer lives the illusion of being able to purchase anything on the pre-constructed and mass-mediated consumer want-radar. The fact that one can only purchase what is presented to the consumer – and these are exclusively standardised products – is hidden behind the illusion of individualism. In the affluent society the mass-mediated reality has conquered consumer's behaviour successfully and elevates it above everything else.

The *mediated society* presents a largely televised picture of society that attests to the media's yearning to be the dominant source of a class-suppressing reality via the transformation of workers into consumers and their integration into the consumer society. This is most evident in the consumerist behaviour visible in the act of hunting material goods, cultural merchandise, standardised fun, commercialised beauty, prestige objects, and pure luxuries all of which have long passed the necessities of life. The affluent society is most prevalent in the concept of *discretionary income* exemplifying the extent of a commodified consumer society. *Discretionary income* is indicative of income earned and spent on other than basic needs. Former luxuries have become accessible to the average consumer when sumptuous goods were converted into everyday commodities constantly creating and satisfying new needs and demands. As *Your All New Silver Credit Card!* replaced the ordinary credit card, soon the gold card had to replace the silver card and soon after that, the platinum card replaced the gold card only to be replaced by the black card. This process is made never ending as is the process of consumption itself. In such a process it is *your*(!) newly issued credit card representing yet another status symbol that constantly carries in it notions of replacement to reflect the stratification of present-day society. Without options for reflection in today's mass-mediated society the standardised consumer appears to be dripping along unconsciously, seemingly accepting his fate. In present society, the endless shift between consumer and labourer at the level of humans is linked to an infinite alienation constructed out of an equally endless shift between the world of work and the world of consumption at the structural level.

The 20th century endlessly shifting world of consumption and production is worlds apart from the 19th-century world of impoverished workers struggling to keep alive, struggling against a harsh working regime, and struggling against capitalism. Rather than becoming the revolutionary proletariat or the gravedigger of capitalism, the workers of advanced capitalism are turned into a petty middle class. And those who do not comply with the system are gathered at the bottom of an apparently classless society. *It is of course nonsense to say that middle-class opposition is replacing the proletariat as the revolutionary class, and that the Lumpenproletariat is becoming a radical political force.*[97] The welfare state has successfully eliminated the *Lumpenproletariat* by integrating them into the welfare system or marginalising them as working poor into political insignificance. System integration occurred when a raft of welfare mechanisms forced the *Lumpenproletariat* into integration. Such integration is a highly valued option that pacifies the *Lumpenproletariat. Criminalisation* and imprisonment of the *Lumpenproletariat* serve the same purpose.[98] This section of society has been pacified, marginalised, and covered up by corporate mass media locating it on the fringes of – not only the televised – society. The *Lumpenproletariat* only appears in the living rooms of the middle class as televised victims or perpetrators of crimes which, as it is simultaneously portrayed by the same mass media, demand ever harsher sanctions.[99] Meanwhile at the middle level, the salaried petty bourgeoisie or middle class has been equally pacified and largely incorporated into the affluent consumer society in a process of *embourgeoisiement.*[100] In sum, the rise of 20th-century advanced capitalism saw the rise of the social-democratic welfare state as functional complements to deficiencies of free-markets and the affluent consumer society, adjusting those who the consumer society failed to adequately integrate.[101]

Despite these rather significant developments, many Hegelian and Marxian ideas on the centrality of work and labour for our present society have remained unchallenged. In simple terms, having just watched the latest TV show does not negate – in reality it more likely supports – the fact that you just spent eight – or more – hours working. Maybe late night TV shows serve above all those who work longer and longer hours and who work in highly fragmented working-time arrangements. Despite this, the economic foundation of present society still lies to a large part in work. Consumption has neither managed to eliminate work nor has it replaced work as the creator of wealth. Socio-economic relations and the wealth of present society are primarily based on the productive domain and not on exclusivity of the re-productive domain. However, the consumer society concept makes visible the pathologies of present-day affluent society just as much as contemporary work arrangements are central to the pathologies of our present work regimes. Despite consumerism, the world of work remains a key category of present-day life.

Viewing *Work as the Key Sociological Category* and having a strong interest in uncovering the hidden mechanisms of the pathologies that come with it, Herbert Marcuse – a member of the Frankfurt School – developed strong interests in labour.[102] Studying workers' democracy and non-*authoritarian* forms of work organisation during the 1920s, his interest was directed towards the transformation of work itself. Essentially, Marcuse argued there *ought* and *can* be creative and productive work by an individual that is not an atomistic entity. However, present forms of work could only be understood alongside *domination* and *alienation* (Agger 1979:194). Marcuse saw domination as a key to unlocking the world of work. In our society, according to Marcuse, any positive social transformation of work is prevented by domination. Ever since the event of capitalism, domination – Max Weber's term was *Herrschaft* – has remained one of the dominant features of work regimes.[103] The suppression of the individual occurs via the acceptance of hierarchical structures as a universal concept. Inside this universal acceptance, domination has an external and an internal component. One refers to the external exploitation or the extraction of surplus value,[104] the other explores self-disciplining mechanisms that prevail at work allowing external domination. Domination cannot be understood through the principles of *coercion* only but must be explained rather as a process whereby subordinated groups actively participate in the construction of their own subordination. It occurs when a *structure-agency* relationship is fixated or frozen as an asymmetrical association establishing the singularity of managerialism over the plurality of social relations at work.[105] Domination freezes an asymmetrical power relationship allowing advantageous interest supremacy over all other but equally important interests.[106]

Some of the strongest accompanying elements of domination inside current work regimes are socially constructed hierarchies, a feature of a social relationship that is absolutely necessary for the present system of economy. According to the *emancipatory* goal of critical theory, this needs to be replaced by an organisational rationality based on non-domination and non-hierarchical forms.[107] These ideas can be found in the early research programme of the Frankfurt School as this programme was oriented towards issues in the domain of work. However their programme was not to be understood in a narrow sense of present-day's relations at work that derived from a 19th- and early-20th-century understanding of *relations at industry* that had been termed: *industrial relations*. Their programme always dealt with fundamental problems such as those of domination and emancipation inside the dialectics of work and society.

Within the dialectic relationship between *work* and *society* on the one hand, and the failure of traditional Marxian theory to predict the non-occurrence of a revolution on the other, the early Frankfurt School had to deal with a much more dangerous problem facing human society and humanism (Moore 1966). Much to the astonishment of many Marxists during the mid-1930s, capitalist development took a somewhat unforeseen turn to the worst expression of economic and social existence in modern times. *Fascism* was on the rise almost everywhere. Bourgeois democracy had not only failed to forestall *fascism* in Europe but democracy had – sometimes actively and sometimes passively – led to its own opposite: tyranny.[108] With the rise of Nazism in Germany during the late 1920s, one of the early research projects of the Frankfurt School was designed to gain insights into the psychic structure of manual and white-collar workers in pre-Nazi Germany in the year 1929.[109] In contrast to many Marxists, workers – as it appeared during the 1920s and early 1930s – had not been immune to the rise of *fascism*. Based on their study the Frankfurt School concluded that if one's economic working life and one's social life is administered by an instrumental-technical apparatus that conforms to domineering social and work norms, one loses potentials for self-determination and individuality. Once an individual became part of a capitalist and industrial machine of total domination and administration, the step to become part of a totally dominated and administered Nazi-machine wasn't impossible.[110] The new mass-mediated fascist state based on modern and capitalist techno-rationality seemed to have fulfilled one of Voltaire's direst warnings: *those who can make you believe absurdities can make you commit atrocities.*[111]

The two decades of the 1920s and 1930s showed that Marxist assumptions and existing political reality were worlds apart. The Frankfurt School's analysis of workers on the eve of German fascism had shown that there was no revolutionary working class left that could have militated against the fascist onslaught. The Frankfurt School had designed a research program to investigate precisely this failure of German workers and develop emancipatory strategies directed against the rise of *fascism*. A new set of theoretical tools had to be developed for such an emancipatory program that enabled workers to provide tools against the fascist nightmare.

The experience of fascism and the theory-reality cleavage expressed in revolutionary expectations and fascist takeovers led the Frankfurt School to a new set of dialectic relationships between society and work where social life had to be increasingly characterised by a division between the formation of consciousness and the actual division of social labour. Following that, the Frankfurt School developed two leading answers to the problem of fascism. Firstly, Wilhelm Reich's seminal work on *The Mass Psychology of Fascism* (1946) and secondly Franz Neumann's work on *Behemoth: The Structure and Practice of National Socialism, 1933–1944* (1944). Overall, the fascism-capitalism link had to be explored. In the wake of this Horkheimer wrote *one cannot be discussed without the other* (Held 1997). Having survived the Holocaust of fascism and its German version of *Nazism* in exile in the United States of America, post-WW II interests of the Frankfurt School moved towards three issues: firstly, the prevailing structures of capitalism, secondly, post-fascist societies, and finally state bureaucratic systems that prevailed in the Soviet Union.

Work and communication in present consumer society

In the aftermath of fascism and war advanced western societies had to find new ways of integrating society as the forced integration of humans into the Nazi-machinery had ended in Auschwitz. The post-1945 world demanded new forms that allowed the integration of society into the apparatus of capitalism without running the danger of repeating the horrors of fascism. Hence, several different domains of post-war developed society had to be integrated in new ways. Habermas wrote (1997a:115) *whereas primitive societies are integrated via a basic normative conscious, the integration of developed societies comes about via the systematic interconnection of functionally specified domains of action.* One of the most important domains is located in the functional domain of labour. The labour domain is largely governed by market mechanisms that decentralise and de-politicise all guiding forces that lie behind it. Regulative elements developed by market forces are expressed in the un-equal distribution of *money and power*.[112] This structure establishes principles that infiltrate all domains of social life. New conflict lines between market enforcing competition on the one hand and society depending on solidarity on the other were opened. Traditions of mechanic, organic, or even imagined solidarity have been destroyed by the penetration of highly complex *market systems* without reproducing structures that secure society.[113] Increasingly, market forces are the driving force of industrial capitalism resulting in social anomie.[114] To counter this move, forces towards system integration are established, seeking to integrate [*Nutzbarmachung*] elements of *solidaristic* societies into advanced capitalism. As *system integration* via money and power has proven to be incomplete and failed to establish total control over work and society, a new space was opened up. This new space is present when contradictions in present society cannot totally be administered even when relying on the most powerful sources of system integration. This structural incompletion unwraps space among social actors to direct their attention towards *social integration* of resistance using social norms and social values that are communicatively established. Inside these spaces social actors can establish competencies for emancipation by using concepts such as communicative action where social action is guided through communicatively established understanding. To accomplish communicatively established understanding the complexities of modern societies must be understood. This needs to occur inside a critical framework that starts with a full comprehension of the role of communication in present work and social life. To achieve this, traditional theory cuts too short. What is needed is a theory that goes beyond *what is,* criticises *what is* and reaches far into *what ought to be.*

What is distinctively different between traditional and critical theory is the relationship between social analysis and critique that is built into the framework of theory. As much as traditional sociological theories might have been able to capture the essence of early capitalism, these theories are no longer adequate. They are insufficient to explain the complexities of domain links in advanced capitalism. Even though many earlier theories had critique as an item in their construction, they never located critique at the centre. Similarly, any analysis of the complexities of present capitalism demands a more substantial inclusion of critique. In short, Kant's earlier and rather simple notion of *critique* is no longer sufficient to reflect the changing character of present society. Today, all forms of knowledge, communication, models, theories, etc. need to be seen as expression of a more complex world. The modern world of work and society needs to be exposed not just to simple critique as demanded by Kant but to a multitude of different types of critiques. When allowing *critique* – as understood in the thinking of modern critical theory – to be of more substantial character, it can be understood in four ways (Giddens 1992):

Table 2.4   Four Types of Critique

4 Critiques	Description
(i) Intellectual	That is inherent into any discipline as a rejection of any *reformulation of contradictory statements for the sake of consistency in the scientific realm* (Adorno 1976:115). This criticism amounts not to a rejection, e.g. on grounds to falsify, but to a demonstration of inadequacy with regard to a proper analysis of social phenomena (Flöistad 1970:176). Overall, Horkheimer(1937:128–129) saw *a philosophy that thinks to find peace within itself...has nothing to do with critical theory.*
(ii) Practical	This version of critique is geared towards a *technical* application of knowledge as an engineered usefulness of practical knowledge.
(iii) Ideological	It asks questions such as 'who will use this knowledge and for what ends?' and is concerned with 'how a particular research study is incorporated into asymmetrical power relations. A good example of such a critique within IR can be found it Giles and Murray's recent work (1997:103).
(iv) Emancipatory	It is *the unreserved discussion of propositions. It employs all available techniques of refutation and goes beyond 'socially critical' by being rigorous in the sense of an appropriately rigorous form of social theory that is comprehended in terms of a quasi-Kantian model. It is a return to human emancipation of Enlightenment including power and reason attained in communicative action. Criticism is not a method of testing, it is this test itself as discussion* (Habermas 1976a:210).

Table 2.4 shows how critical thinking is directed towards a politics of self-actualisation reflecting on four uses of critique. At the first level (i) is an avoidance of two positivist traps. The first trap mistakenly sees *facts-as-facts* without seeing the factors that created the facts. The second trap lies in *speak-for-themselves* without seeing the need that facts always need to be interpreted and understood by human beings. In short, any modern understanding of the world of work needs to reflect, first of all, on *intellectual critique* (i).[115] This has been incorporated into any social thinking that ever since Kant's simple critiques has not only been part of *Enlightenment* but has also been part of our understanding of the world. At the second level, *practical critique* (ii) needs to critically reflect on the way communication, language, speech, etc. is formulated as a technical instrument. It needs to assess how it is being used in the world of work. At the third level, *ideological critique* (iii) takes the ideological character of managerialism into account reflecting on how it shapes communication at work. Finally, at the fourth level, *emancipatory critique* (iv) supersedes all three earlier versions of critique as it directs attention towards the goal of emancipation. This goal is to preserve the emancipatory element in Kant, Hegel, Marx, Horkheimer, and many others. It seeks to radically reconstitute the project of transformation of present society directed towards human emancipation. Ultimately, it calls for emancipatory social criticism. In short, while the traditional understanding included some form of critique that had never proceeded beyond the first three levels (i–iii) critical theory has at its core a fourth dimension. The fourth level of critique is designed to act towards the development of *emancipatory critiques*. Consequently, no longer can a critical understanding of communication at work stop at the third level (Table 2.4). The fourth level (2.4–iv) is significantly different from a traditional understanding of communication at work. This level includes intellectual, practical, and ideological critique. Most crucially however, the final level goes one step further. It includes the level of emancipatory critique. In essence, this is more than just an *add-on*. Kant's original idea of *under modernity everything is exposed to critique* applies to all three previous levels. Above that a further level of emancipatory critique is created. Consequently, all four forms of critique – from Kant's *Enlightenment* to today's critical theory – are not simply added but play a crucial role in understanding today's world of work. Therefore, a comprehensive and critical understanding of the communicative demands in the world of work must reflect on all four forms of critique.

At level four (Table 2.4), one of the core tools that eclipses rather than enlightens the world of work is the search for more and more facts constructed inside the traditional positivist paradigm. The mere collection of endless facts about the world of work has hardly enabled a deeper or critical understanding of present-day work regimes. Instead it remains on the

surface while extending this surface more and more. In short, while producing ever more details about the world of work, none of these details has
led to an emancipatory understanding of it. Knowledge collection activities
have prevented rather than enhanced emancipation of the world of work.
Inside the traditional approach to understand the world of work, known as
industrial or labour relations, critical advances in emancipation have come
to a standstill. This dead-end of present industrial relations has been
summed up by Horkheimer's (1937:191) critique on traditional theory. He
argues

> the assiduous collecting of facts in all the disciplines dealing with social
> life, the gathering of great masses of detail in connection with problems,
> the empirical inquiries, through careful questionnaires and other means,
> which are a major part of scholarly activity, especially in the Anglo-
> Saxon universities since Spencer's time – all this adds up to a pattern
> which is, outwardly, much like the rest of life in a society dominated by
> industrial production techniques.

In other words, traditional theory tends to uncritically reproduce bourgeois
society by constructing a false consciousness of a tradition that had never
existed. Ever since the beginning of *Enlightenment* the element of critique
and *what ought to be* has been at the centre. Separating *what is* from *what
ought to be* inside the scientific endeavour, as positivism tends to do, does
not produce a truthful reflection of the origins of science. It hinders rather
then enhances scientific understanding, reasoning, communicative rationality and above all *Enlightenment* and modernity. Instead, traditional
approaches have manipulated our view of *Enlightenment* as domineering
elites have managed to control public and academic discourse. This has
been done through repetitive symbolic activities that refer to re-constructed
past practices. It masks their manipulations by reinventing a scientific
tradition that never existed. The scientific tradition of *Enlightenment* has
never seen a separation between *what is* and what *ought to be*. It has never
added critique to the scientific process. It has never added value to science.
It has never separated an observer from real existing social relations. All of
these separations are artificially created after the event of *Enlightenment* to
justify and legitimate a version of science that is dominated by domination. None of this has ever been part of science or *Enlightenment*. Neglecting
or denying *Enlightenment*'s inherent demand towards critique means to
create a nihilistic view. This view has produced an endless array of intellectuals inside the positivist club of mainstream science. They tend to
accommodate structures of economic and political domination by narrowing their research tasks to simplistic *what is*, *problem-solving*, or *toolkit*
approaches.[116] This is visible in almost any discipline represented in our
socially constructed understanding of work and society. But most crucially,

it is operative in the domain that directly deals with the economic domain of the present order, the domain of the world of work.[117]

Once mainstream theory and its subsequent historically re-constructed view of the world of work dissected into two separated domains with society here and work there has been overcome, the historical and dialectical evolution inside the upper or reproductive and the lower or productive domain starts to become visible. Similarly, a critical understanding of the world of work needs to go beyond traditional views. These views are still locked inside a self-serving and all too often self-created but ultimately self-limiting box of *what is*. In overcoming these limitations a critical understanding of communication at work unlocks system integrative demands inside each domain.

The communicative relationship between the social and the work domains can be carried through from feudalist belief systems into early capitalism, eventually reaching advanced capitalism. In advanced capitalism, a middle class has developed together with a movement towards urbanisation and a rapid development of the mass-production domain. These three developments demand significant adjustments in the re-productive domain. Once these shifts had been accomplished during the transition from feudal life to early and to advanced capitalism, societal coordination had to be transferred from religious belief systems to a public domain that was able to pacify revolutionary as well as democratic demands that would challenge the ruling elite. Steering demands on society could no longer be met through religion or through the public domain. Increasingly, society replaced the steering media of the public domain with the two most prominent media: money and power. Alongside these changes different elites developed. While under feudalism the elite consisted of kings, queens, and priests, the early capitalist elites consisted of merchants and manufacturing-capital owners. In the advanced stage, these elites consist of financial and IT companies as well as owners of corporate media.

As these elites settled most of the challenging conflicts between classes and system integration, a relative minor transition from early liberal capitalism to advanced capitalism enabled the most significant reorganisation of the public domain. No longer was the previously open public sphere needed as a forum for conflict resolution. Powers from the productive domain began to infiltrate the public domain. As corporate mass media began to colonise the public domain, critical enlightening science and modern knowledge creation became increasingly instrumental in the creation of the present system. Unlike *Enlightenment*'s quest for truth present corporate media started to convert all information into a commodity as they largely occupied and defined the public domain today. Unlike craftshops that manufactured a limited number of commercial goods during early capitalism, advanced capitalism operates a system of *mass*-manufactured mass-consumer goods. However, it also turns every necessity of life into a mass commodity. The character of mass commodities enters deep into knowledge and information. Hence terms such as information society or knowledge society seek to capture these developments. New, however is that information and knowledge are converted into tradable commodities. Their prime role is no longer to enlighten us but to be a commercial good that can be bought and sold. Sometimes they are only produced so that they can be sold with no other intention in mind. As much as such entertainment, information, and knowledge merge, new *infotainments* enter the market.[118] News is not there to inform us but to be presented in the most entertaining way. News and even the truth are subsistent to this. They are no more than a commodity. As the information commodity gained importance in the advanced version of capitalism, advanced capitalism has commonly been labelled *information or knowledge society* to divert attention away from its underlying capitalist structures. Even though the very base of this society is for sale as information is sold and bought in the media market often rendering knowledge to the instrumental demands of commodities rather than truth, the true character of the economic foundations of the system is hidden behind the term information society.[119] As we are told *we all live in an information age*, information and even truth enters into an instrumental relationship constructing information and truth as commodities. This fact is harder and harder to hide as not only all necessities of life but also the public domain become commodified.

As much as the present order remains based on mass production and mass consumption, it also operates the public domain as a transmission medium that structures today's mass consumer. In this mass-communicated society the increased complexity of simultaneously operative domains also increases demands towards communication. These coordination demands have significantly increased as steering requirements inside and between domains have amplified. No longer can the world of work be neatly separated from the world of consumption. In advanced capitalism, societies have truly entered the age of:

mass production = mass consumption

Figure 2.1   The Production–Consumption Equation

Under this equation, humans are no longer defined simply as people. They are constructed as producers or workers. In managerial *Newspeak* (Orwell 1949) terms such as *human resource* or *associates* are applied. In the reproductive sphere, they are constructed as mass consumers. In both domains we are exposed to a highly functional, structural, and instrumental environment that has a *Janus*-face like appearance of producer/worker on one side of the face and a mass-consumer face on the other.[120] Even though people have been transformed into either worker or consumer they are still the same person when walking into an office, a factory, or a workshop or when walking into the shopping mall. The more both are fundamentally necessary for the present system, the less can the productive *world of work* be artificially separated from the reproduction domain as the *Janus*-face of worker/consumer becomes reality. Equally, these domains can no longer be seen as functional without communication. Increasingly, communication is an absolute necessity inside each domain as much as between the domains. Without it, both domains can no longer exist and exchanges between both domains can no longer be organised. Communication inside and between domains operates under system imperatives. It needs to integrate workers into a work regime and a consumer into a consumption regime. This occurs as a double structure of mutual influencing and stabilising elements. On the one hand, system stabilising elements from the ex-work domain can increasingly be utilised to keep the work domain functional. On the other hand, system stabilising elements from the work domain, such as managerialism, can increasingly be utilised to keep the reproductive ex-work domain functional. This double character establishes the strongest communicative link between the world of work and the ex-work domain.

As complexities inside the world of work grew, system integrative imperatives from the ex-work domain became increasingly central to the steering needs of the work domain. When system integrative rationality and instrumental communication infiltrate the work domain, the world of work is ever more closely linked to the ex-work domain. These links only exist through communication. Subsequently, today's understanding of communicative structures is indispensable for an understanding of the world of work. Similarly, no longer can the world of work be understood by using tools that have been created as part of a positivist paradigm. No longer can the world of work be understood with restrictive and narrow tools that viewed the domain of work as an enclosed, measurable, and functional system. Increasingly, an understanding of our socially constructed reality of work and society cannot be limited to an image of *the natural equals the social* world. Such traditionalist instruments are no longer sufficient to understand the socially constructed communication demands of the work domain. Understanding of these issues cannot be achieved by simply collecting more facts or by reducing our understanding of the world of work to the simple paradigm of *problem-solving*. Present complexities of work and society can only be understood via a model that accurately reflects the communicative conditions inside the world of work. This has to be dialectically linked to communicative conditions inside the ex-work domain. The time that saw the world of work as a domain to be understood inside *problem-solving* and *fact-finding* paradigms has come to an end.

In enhancing such a view, Horkheimer and Adorno's original critique on positivist traditions showed several deficiencies of the conventional *problem-solving* and *fact-collecting* paradigms when applied to the world of work.[121] Their critical rationality approach combines *rationality* with *critique*. In a second step, critical rationality needs to be extended towards *communicative rationality*. Only with an understanding that is constructed via *communicative rationality* an understanding of the world of work can provide the crucial knowledge that is required. Any comprehensive understanding of the world of work cannot be gained through the application of natural tools or through the confinements of system stabilising elements applied to the world of work. A comprehensive understanding must always include elements from the ex-work domain that have increasingly been utilised to keep the work domain functional. This ex-work–work linkage can only be understood through *communicative rationality*. Constructed as a discourse under conditions of *communicative rationality* participants in such discourse can draw upon the critical knowledge needed to comprehend the domain complexities of work and society. This will assist in the process of reaching communicative understanding about a common situation. Tools that are able to overcome the shortcomings of traditional theory's *problem-solving* and *fact-collecting* paradigm have to be based on a new way of creating knowledge, a new way of epistemology. Such an *epistemology* needs to examine traditional theories critically.[122] Inside the reality of work and society, *communicative rationality* is designed not only to understand the '*what is*' but also the '*what ought to be*'. Therefore, it enters into the idea of *communicative action*. It is designed to assist the process of critical reflection among participants leading to *communicative action* and ultimately to social action directed towards emancipation. However, *communicative action* is never to be seen as a purely theoretical tool. If it is seen simply as a theory, it has failed its most important test. This theory is a theory of society conceived with an emancipatory as well as a practical intention.[123]

In conclusion, a brief look at the theoretical, philosophical, and historical role of a critical understanding of the issue of communication, management, and work as established in our present society has found that the origins of such critical understanding date back to *Enlightenment*. This is enshrined in Kant's early demand to produce a *critical* understanding which needs to transcend *what is* by entering into *what ought to be* as any critical understanding of the role of communication inside the world of work is historically bound to the origins of critical thinking. *Enlightenment* is not only enshrined in philosophical ideas but also in the most dramatic change of work ever seen. It fundamentally altered thousands of years of peasant life when converting peasants into workers as factory life became established. Ever since these changes, an understanding of the world of work can only come from a theory that links both work and society.

Enlightenment also produces – as a rejection of religion – not only an assessment of *what is* but *what ought to be* as it had to find new ways of societal existence. As much as a critical understanding had led to a rejection of religious manipulation in the pre-*Enlightenment* period, a critical analysis of present work and society leads to a rejection of today's mass manipulation as experienced in advanced capitalism. Critical social science is a reflection on *Enlightenment* philosophers such as Kant, Hegel and Marx who have contributed significantly to a critical understanding of reality during the 18th and 19th century. In a second step, contemporary theory development is much more a reflection of historical events that took place between the 18th and the 20th century. Both, theory development and the link to the historical development of work and society have shaped pre- and post-*Enlightenment* theory construction for more than 200 years. With the event of modernity feudalist thinking has ended. This allowed the creation of *Enlightenment* and early capitalism. It significantly shaped theory development during the past centuries.

As society, work, and capitalism developed, so had the tools to understand them. 20th-century events such as the rising mass consumption that occurred concurrently with rising mass communication impacted strongly on our understanding of work and society. Both also impacted on the development of theory. As complexities between society and work grew, theory development had to grow with these complexities. Once both domains had developed communication as their main linkage, work and society had to be understood in this context. No longer was an understanding of society and work possible without communication. Similarly, theory development was no longer possible inside the narrow margins of *problem-solving* and *fact-collecting*. Understanding needed to go beyond a simple understanding of *what is*. It had to enter into *what ought to be*. Present understanding had to include Kant's demand for critique as a substantial element of theory. The fundamental issue of critique can no longer be negated. Critique has assisted our society in overcoming a feudalist past. Critique has been able to show some of the pathologies that developed alongside advanced forms of capitalism. In sum, a sufficient understanding of the complexities of work and society can no longer be established inside a traditional framework that limits the examination of *problem-solving* and *fact-collecting*. A future understanding of work and society needs to be based on a model that highlights elements of critical rationality inside our present working society.

3
Critical Rationality and Present Working Society

Rationality is one of the most distinguished concepts lifting society out of the dark days of feudalism and moving it towards *Enlightenment*.[124] Rationality is with us today, defining many of the most basic rules of human conduct.[125] This reaches deep into our present society and our working arrangements. At work as well as in society, we are supposed to act rationally. While a simple communicative statement like *please act rational* appears to be nothing special, the ideas behind it are somewhat more complex. First of all, to act *rational* and *rationality* are both parts of the *Enlightenment* project. Rationality has two forms. One is the idea that rationality ended pre-rational belief systems when foundations of our society moved on to a rational base. The rational base or rational justification is the second form. Unlike in feudal times, human action could no longer be justified by a reference to some higher authority, usually God. From now on, humans had to justify what they do. As rational science advanced around the 17th and 18th century, the world was increasingly understood by scientific rationality. This affected society in two fundamental ways. Advances in *natural science*, such as physics, biology, mathematics, chemistry, and medicine altered our understanding of the natural world.[126] Advances in the *social science* of economics, politics, and philosophy altered our understanding of the social world.

As rationality took hold in the *natural* and the *social* world, *Enlightenment*'s rationality served two important functions. On the one hand, rationality as part of natural science gave us rational instruments, on the other, rationality as part of social science presented us with critical rationality. An example from the biological and the social world illustrates this. The human voice could no longer be perceived as God-given but as a biological function. In the same way a ruler could no longer assume his social position as God-given. Social rule had to be rationally justified via democratic legitimisation. The feudalist assumption – held for thousands of years – that the human voice as well as social rule are God-given, had ended. They were replaced by the two defining concepts of *Enlightenment*, instrumental rationality and critical rationality. Both assisted us in the ending of irrational foundations of a feudalist past. Instrumental rationality and critical rationality are inextricably linked to *Enlightenment,* both carried human society into modernity and have been a part of modernity ever since.

A critical understanding of work and society stemmed from a time when rationality was established as a form of thinking. This challenged many assumptions of the pre-*Enlightenment* period. It established critical examination not only of *what is* but also of *what ought to be*.[127] Since the Enlightenment period the relationship between critical and rational thinking has proven to be more challenging than originally thought. While any rational thinking during the 18th and 19th century provided enough critique on feudalist and traditional thinking, during the 20th century demands on critical thinking increased as forms of production and societies changed from feudalism to early capitalism and towards advanced capitalism. In order to keep up with these societal and economic developments, theory had to progress as well.[128] One of the most significant theories that developed during the early 20th century and was able to address these changes is Horkheimer's work on *Traditional and Critical Theory* (1937). He constructed the basic parameters of critical thinking that reflected on new societal developments. He clarified the fundamental difference between traditional and critical thinking. *Traditional and Critical Theory* (1937) is widely regarded as the founding document that coined the term *critical theory*. The most basic assumption is that all theory, whether traditional or critical, can be seen as *stored-up knowledge, put in a form that makes it useful for the closest possible description of facts* (Horkheimer 1937:188). Theory in this sense always constructs a number of possible worlds and possible series of new entities that are invisible in everyday language. While everyday language often prevents a deeper understanding of work and society, theory enables exactly that. However, traditional theory and critical theory are fundamentally different in the way they seek to achieve such understanding.

Historically, traditional theory assumed its role as a critique on religion challenging the hegemony of a feudalist regime when God as the supreme supervisor was replaced with human supervision based on rationality.[129] It assisted in the cessation of feudalism by establishing reason and rationality as new forms of knowledge.[130] Such conceptually formulated knowledge presented as theory, has been seen as the sum of propositions about a subject. These propositions are linked to each other to formulate a theory. In very general terms, theory gained validity from being consistent with facts. In a second step theory is tested on actual facts. As a general rule, facts have to be subsumed under theory. However if theory and factual experience contradict each other, they must be re-examined. Therefore, the relationship between *facts* and our understanding of them via *theory* always remains hypothetical. Both can and often have to change or be altered. In other words, our understanding of facts changed over time much in the same way as our theoretical models changed. These changes had to occur in two domains. As the *social* world differs from the *natural* world, so do theories. One set of theories explains the natural world while another set explains the social world.

However, traditional theory disregards the distinction between *social* and *natural* science and transfers methods developed in the domain of *natural* science into *social* science. It assumes, often unconsciously, that our society operates like the laws of mathematics or physics even though humans hardly ever behave accordingly. Given its natural-science background, traditional theory tends to operate as an enclosed system of propositions. It sees science as a whole attempting to discover law-like foundations of society. These are supposed to operate naturally and are seen as being neutral to historical developments. Traditional theory seeks to maintain the illusion of the separation between social existence and theory. Critical theory is the opposite. Here, theory arises *within* a social fabric that constitutes the involvement of human beings capable of intervening and articulating themselves.[131] The difference, in short, is that critical theory admits that theory can only develop inside our society and is inherently connected to our society. Traditional theory does the same but pretends an assumed independence or disconnection between society, economy, and history on the one hand and theory on the other. To maintain this illusion is an important part of traditional theory. Usually it is achieved through the claim to be objective. In any case, the artificial separation between historical and economical development of society and theory development has been expressed as:

> The traditional idea of theory is abstracted from scientific activity as it is carried on within the division of labour at a particular stage in the latter's development. It corresponds to the activity on the scholar that takes place alongside all of the other activities of a society, but in no immediately clear connection with them. In this view of theory, therefore, the real social function of science is not made manifest; it conveys not what theory means in human life, but only what it means in the isolated sphere in which, for historical reasons, it comes into existence. As opposed to his, critical social theory is to become conscious of the self-referentiality of its calling; it knows that in and through the very act of knowing it belongs to the objective context of life that it strives to grasp.[132]

Traditional science is founded on a perceived certainty of the existence of a totality of propositions that emerge from theoretical work in a systematic manner. Often this occurs under classificatory thinking assuming that simple classification or *The Order of Things* (Foucault 1994) produces understanding or even theory. It assumes that there are given certainties – usually called invariables as opposed to variables – and that these have to be put in order in accordance with an invented system of classifications. It establishes an *Order of Things* by linking assumed variables to equally assumed invariables in the form of hypothetical *if-then* constructions. In a second step, the hypothetical *if-then* construction is presented as a scientific fact. Often such law-like hypotheses are developed in anticipation of law-like regulators in society without any empirical justification for them. Classifications and an assumed *Order of Things* disregard the existence of a number of important elements: firstly, contradictions are eliminated, secondly, there is an absence of superfluous and purely dogmatic elements, and finally, society and subjectivity has no influence on the observable phenomenon. Traditional theory has a tendency to be expressed in logical and purely mathematical correlations. Until today, these models have had and still have a strong influence on social science.[133]

In contrast, critical theory is a product of *Enlightenment* thinking. It is linked to rationality much in the same way as the rationality of society coincided with the development of productive forces under capitalism. Some of these productive forces developed an ever more refined method and technique running capitalist firms.[134] In order to understand this development, *the Marx-influenced and Marx-supplementing thinker* Max Weber analysed the institutional framework surrounding and supporting the capitalist economy.[135] Unknown to 19th-century Marx who saw science and technology as unambiguous forces for emancipation within the civilisation project that started modernity, 20th-century Weber correctly assessed that they themselves had become a medium of social repression.[136]

Max Weber is viewed as one of the *Godfathers* on how to understand capitalism, capitalist companies, modern management, organisational studies, and above all bureaucracy.[137] However, *Weber is known in management texts only as a management consultant who recommended the value of bureaucracies and got it wrong, an error the textbooks forgive on the grounds that he was writing so long ago, before management knowledge had really developed* (Harding 2003:55). While standard management texts tend to misrepresent Weber heavily, today's dominance of managerial ideology – known as *managerialism* – also tends to hide Weber's crucial concept for an understanding of modern business affairs.[138] To a relatively large extent the concept of *Herrschaft*, crucial in order to understand our present system, is elementary. While discussing bureaucracy Weber perceived *Herrschaft* first and foremost as the clearest expression of domination. This fact is all too often and conveniently swept aside.[139] Unfortunately, Weber's concept of domination does not fit into standard management ideology and therefore it is conveniently pushed aside.

Standard management writers tend to portray management as something like *there is no more important area of human activity than management, since its task is that of getting things done through people* (Harding 2003:28). The image presented is one of a total absence of domination. Weber's domination is altered into *getting things done through people!*[140] The critique of management in Weber's writings on bureaucracy and domination is miraculously converted into a one-dimensional management ideology of organisational discipline necessary for the modern organisation. *For Max Weber, it is the guarantor of technically and economically necessary organisational discipline, which then becomes the model of the entire discipline required by modern industrial society* (Marcuse 1968:213). Hidden behind management's ideological niceties of *getting things done through people* remains the brute fact that science and technology have assisted the establishment of a highly domineering system.[141] Weber was correct in saying that it is *Herrschaft* or domination, not bureaucracy that is the defining element of management. While hiding this, present managerial systems have almost completed Weber's ultimate form of managerial *Herrschaft*. Weber's metaphor of an *iron cage* represents management's totally administered and totally reified world in which means-ends, purposive, and instrumental rationality supports domination. In the work domain and in the societal domain it fulfils the same goal. This version of rationality is disconnected from *ethics* unleashing potentials directed towards a dehumanised society where people struggle to find meaning in life.[142] While Weber's rather pessimistic appraisal of scientific civilisation mistrusts a rationalisation process that is reduced to means-ends, managerialism has successfully detached Weber's writings from ethical value orientation.[143]

But Weber was not the only theoretician with a rather pessimistic view when looking at managerialism, the bureaucratisation of society, and working life. An almost equally pessimistic outlook was put forward in Horkheimer's *Eclipse of Reason* (1947) and in Marcuse's *One-Dimensional Man*[144] (1966). While Horkheimer and Marcuse viewed *Enlightenment's* rationality in a somewhat negative and at least partly even depressing light, they nevertheless did not fail to highlight modernity's potentials for emancipation. They also rejected the Orwellian or Kafkaesque nightmare of Weber's *iron cage*. This has been summed up in the final words of Marcuse's (1966:261) groundbreaking thesis on modernity's tendency to operate one-dimensionally. Unlike Kafkaesque, Orwellian, or iron-cage visions of society, Horkheimer's and Marcuse's vision is more hopeful reflecting *it is only for the sake of those without hope that hope is given to us.*

Horkheimer and Marcuse rejected society's end destination inside an *iron cage* watched by Orwell's *Big Brother*. Both represent the sharpest contrast to Weber's *iron cage*, Kafka's inescapable nightmare of bureaucracy, and Orwell's (1949:311) visions of *but it was all right, everything was all right, the struggle was finished. He had won the victory over himself. He loved Big Brother. The End. The End* as Orwell wrote does not lie in the love of *Big Brother* but in hope and human emancipation. Critical theory, nonetheless, shares substantial parts of Weberian and Orwellian critique of Western modernity and Eastern Soviet state socialism.[145] Weber's, Orwell's, Kafka's, Horkheimer's and Marcuse's critiques have been directed against three developments. These were Soviet-style Stalinism, German fascism, and American consumerism. They considered all three of carrying tendencies directed towards totalitarianism, domination, and hierarchy in society and at work. Furthermore these forms of domination, authoritarianism, and totalitarianism have been an outcome of the *Great Transformation* between feudalism and capitalism and its subsequent development of modernity.[146] On the positive side, Horkheimer and Marcuse also saw that modernity was the foremost affirmation of autonomy against every traditional and social order that stabilised pre-modern societies.

Rationality, work, and society

Max Weber's *Iron-Cage*, Marcuse's *One-Dimensional Society*, and Orwell's futuristic *1984* are images that were only possible after the *Great Transformation* that converted society from feudalism into capitalism at the superstructure or reproductive domain and at base or productive level.[147] The reproductive superstructure domain includes ideology, the state, laws, and status systems. The base or productive domain includes work, workers, management, and industry. Both domains are in a dialectical relationship. In the reproductive domain, the belief in God and religion has been replaced by science and rationality.[148] These changes and subsequent developments are the underlying factors of modern society. On the one hand, today's managerial rationality of everyday life already shows signs that indicate a future development into what Weber, Marcuse, and Orwell predicted. On the other hand, in today's society human action is no longer based on irrationality, superstition and a mythical past but has to be justifiable based on rational behavioural patterns. More than ever before human action in today's society has to be justified on rational grounds. Under modernity human behaviour has been based on Weber's (1922, 1924) four principles of rationality:

Table 3.1   Four Types of Rationally Grounded Behaviour

	Rational Behaviour	Explanation of Patterns of Social Behaviour
i)	Purposive-rational	involves that expectation of social behaviour of external objects or individuals serve as a condition or means of a rational and success orientation geared towards ends.
ii)	Value-rational	concerns a conscious belief in an ethical or aesthetic mode of behaviour that occurs independent of any prospect of strategic success.
iii)	Emotional-rational	is largely determined by an actor's current affections and emotional stages.
iv)	Traditional-rational	is determined by deeply embedded and long held patterns of behaviour as a consequence of long-term rituals, routines, and habits.

As Table 3.1 shows, traditional forms of rational behaviour can be closely linked to pre-modern patterns of pre-rational forms of behaviour. Apart from emotional (iii) and traditional (iv) rationality, it is purpose-rational (i) and value-rational (ii) behaviour that forms the clearest modes of behaviour. Both (i and ii) signify modernity as the end of faith-based behaviour that supported pre-modern belief in God. These two (i-ii) are the most modern forms of behaviour expressed as market rationality. Rational behaviour expressed in market rationality could only be established alongside the societal transformation from feudal to modern forms of social and economic organisation of society. As faith in God was replaced by faith in market and rationalism, science and rationality grew. At the base or productive level, feudalism based on land-ownership, serfdom, and local lords was replaced by capitalism. Two essential features grew out of this development: the creation of consumer goods or commodities and the division of labour. Links between the reproductive and productive domain are communicatively established through a dialectical process that guarantees each sphere semi-autonomous operation.

As *early* capitalism became *advanced* capitalism steering requests for social welfare and economic regulation had to be met. In contrast to the initial *Great Transformation* from feudalism to capitalism, a somewhat minor transition shifted capitalism towards a refined and more advanced form of regulated market capitalism. The shift from early liberal capitalism to a markedly more coordinated version of capitalism that entailed the social welfare state did not replace the centrality of the consumer commodity nor did it replace the centrality of the division of labour.[149] Both remained core values. But they added some new forms to the existing economy. No longer was capitalism able to neglect the problems and pathologies of its production method. Rising problems in the social domain forced the creation of a welfare state onto it.[150] With the conversion of early capitalism that located most modern products outside the reach of the proletariat, the development of the consumer society altered the worker-consumer relationship fundamentally.[151]

With standardised mass production, a standardised mass consumer had to be created. Somehow mass consumption had to be communicated to the masses. Technical developments in the sphere of communication assisted this via radio, mass newspapers, magazines, TV and Internet. Access to these spheres of communication as well as to consumer goods became *democratised(!)* as everyone could participate. The mass-consumer society not only structures mass consumption it also structures mass democracy. Mass consumption and mass democracy are safely removed from the productive domain.[152] Neither do we have access to goods nor do we vote at work. Consumption and voting are located in the reproductive domain, i.e. the shopping mall and the voting booth. In a mass-consumer society democracy became a *massively* organised ritual of the state.[153] It is an organisation that incorporates everyone into a system. It is system integrative. It is also a massive communicative effort affecting millions of people.[154] It strongly communicates that we are to *give* our vote on a regular and ritualistic basis whenever it is communicated to us. In democracy, we can *give* something that is given to us – and sometimes taken away – usually by the state. This ritual has been summed up by Poole's *Unspeak* (2006:198) as: *in modern democracies, the electorate exerts its democratic right to choose its leader every four or five years; in the interim, it appears, the people may safely be ignored.*[155] Today, this communicated ritual follows the methods of mass advertisements where political parties are reduced to a product to be voted for. Just like *voting for* one product or the other, just like picking up a can of soup in a supermarket, we accept our given fate to choose one soup over the other or one candidate over another. The voter is reduced to a standardised political mass consumer-mediated through equally standardised corporate mass media. Economic and state regulation further enhance the ritualistic exchange – one vote for a leader another one for a can of soup – elementary to the present order of assumed democracy that applies only to the reproductive superstructure as the productive base is a democratic-free zone. In both domains, society and work, most have accepted that they are governed not so much by democracy but by two other elements that are needed for the steering of society and work:[156] *money and power.*

Money and power as two steering media have been elevated well above democracy. Their capacity in directing society and work remain largely unaffected by changes that occur from time to time in the reproductive domain. Being unaffected by the democratic process, money and power are of increasing importance in society. The *system-integrative* force of power and money streamlined an ever more conformist society into a highly standardised or one-dimensional existence. Marcuse (1966) has diagnosed the pathologies of such a streamlined and conformist society. His *One-Dimensionality Thesis* has been summed up as a process that alienates humans in the work and society domain. As early capitalism and technological advances shaped industrial societies, an increased accommodation of economic-social and work affairs has appeared. Both have constructed the work and society domination via administrative powers. Therefore, *Manufacturing Consent* (Burawoy 1979) affects work and society in much the same way.

Engineering ideas such as efficiency and mechanical ideas of administration overwhelmed the individual at work and society.[157] Gradually, with the loss of core elements of critical rationality such as autonomy, dissent, and the power of resistance, society became *one-dimensional.* Humans were degraded to one-dimensional human beings when exposed to the structural forces of money, power, and the instrumental use of language.[158] Such one-dimensional use of power and language has been expressed in Watson's *Death Sentence* (2003:3) as: *they will tell you it is in the interest of leadership, management, efficiency, stakeholders, the bottom line or some democratic imperative, but the public language remains the language of power.* The use of public or managerial language is subsumed under the power that severs one-dimensional goals whether at work or in society. The one-dimensional language of power supports an equally one-dimensional link between society and work. This language of power subscribes to instrumental rationality much in the same way as it subscribes to a totally administered economic, welfare, or social order. Conditions of such a one-dimensional working society are achieved when the following five elements are successfully established:

Table 3.2   Five Characteristics of Advanced Capitalism

	Form	Content
i	Productivity and mass consumption	A high level of industrial productivity achieved through advancements in technology, automation, and mechanisation capable of satisfying mass needs governed by mediated mass consumerism is successfully established.
ii	Integration of opposition	A largely absent or domesticated political or economical opposition achieved through repressive state machinery and through system integration via consumerism and political rituals.
iii	Mass needs	Corporatised mass-media power converts humanist demands for emancipation into needs that can be met via mass mediation and mass consumption.
iv	No working-class revolution	A rebellious working classis converted into a petty bourgeois middle class under the auspices of an affluent society where work-related conflict is ritualised and largely replaced by conflicts in the do main of reproduction.
v	System integration	Private and working life has been successfully integrated into a system of commodity production that appears to benefit a one-dimensional society.[159]

As Table 3.2 above depicts, advanced capitalism has truly left its earlier forms when the following five elements are completed. Unlike its earlier version, advanced capitalism shows a much greater capacity towards system integration. This is largely achieved through *Fordism* (i). Productivity levels unseen by Marx have resulted in a system of mass consumerism along with the rise of material and social welfare conditions. These have successfully pacified workers as they have been converted from a propertyless but revolutionary proletariat into middle-class mass consumers with houses, cars, suburban living, and mortgages (ii–iv).[160] This system has successfully converted early manufacturing workers into standardised mass-production workers and consumers with standard pre-fabricated houses, standard cars, standard mortgages – and standard coffins. These workers are well-integrated into a system of production and reproduction, and rather than opposing it (ii), protect the system (v).

Today's standardised mass consumerism is communicated via mass advertising. This move also positioned communication from a relatively minor side-issue during early capitalism to the centre. More than ever before the present system depends on communication. Communication's ability as steering media increases as demands on mediation between the working and consumption domains grow. The present order could no longer function without the reliance on communication. In a standardised world of mass-communicated culture that is mediated through corporate mass media, people are increasingly reshaped. The reshaping of society takes place via a conversion of humans into consumers. Today, people at work are no longer workers but a *Human Resource* or, to use US supermarket chain Wal-Mart's label, an *Associate*. The existence as an associate or as a human resource is one of the clearest expressions of modern managerial *Doublespeak* (Orwell 1949:53). In the future we might end up as *Shopping Resources* or *Consumption Associates* when walking though the gates of the shopping mall.[161] Our present world redefines and reduces us to mass consumers. Consumption occupies consumers without engaging them. Participation and democracy are excluded from the working and the shopping domain as people are kept busy working and consuming in a never-ending *rat race.*[162] *It is possible to consider capitalism as the ideal form of democracy, consisting of a grand procession of innumerable little electoral moments, when consumer choice is exercised in the supermarket or the cinema or the car showroom* (Poole 2006:203). Consumer's choice, voting-shopping, and rat races convert us into little consumer rats constantly choosing, voting, consuming, and running the treadmill towards *Affluenza* where affluence has become a disease.[163]

Being trapped in the system-treadmill of consumerism and mass-mediated democracy moves preferences to the centre of the system.[164] Democracy is either centre-left or centre-right. It is inside the system, not progressive or backward conservative. It does not break the system. It does not move forward or backward. It only moves a tiny bit to the left or to the right. Society remains stagnant inside the margins of the system. Choice has been converted into simple left-right alternatives just like the choice between *Pepsi* or *Coke!*[165] Only the famous *'Would you like fries with it?'* seems to be absent.[166] Such a mass-structured society does not leave much room outside the confines of these system integrative pre-set choices. Even somewhat independent forms of grassroots democracy are converted into a communicative ritual of advertising-guided and mass-mediated events concealing the true supremacy of money and power. As Marcuse (1966:20) emphasised, *when this point is reached, domination – in the guise of affluence and liberty – extends to all spheres of private and public existence, integrates all authentic opposition, absorbs all alternatives.*[167] This represents the height of system integration.

System integration under advanced capitalism is further enhanced by the creation and subsequent satisfaction of mass needs that divert attention from social protest and emancipation. The working class as analysed by Marx and Engels and depicted in movies such as *Metropolis* or Charlie Chaplin's *Modern Times* becomes a consumerist middle class. Class conflict is pacified via mass consumption and mass democracy. Today, the transferral of conflict from the work domain into the non-work domain has been accomplished. Industrial conflict is less and less regulated at the point of origin but removed and dealt with in committees, commissions, social or labour courts, councils, labour law and the like. Finally, advanced capitalism has achieved a one-dimensionality that has been unimaginable by its earlier forms. The earlier struggle that exposed conflict of interest between labour and capital has been mediated. A *mediated society* is not only able to obscure divergent class interests but also to convert workers' interest into one-dimensionality.[168] Unlike its predecessor, advanced capitalism relies ever more on the reproductive, upper level, or superstructure domain to achieve system integration. At the reproductive domain advanced capitalism has successfully developed its ideological foundations. These foundations are made up of scientism and rationality directed towards a one-dimensional modernity that places instrumental domination via science and rationality in the centre.[169] During the transition from early to advanced capitalism adjustments in the reproductive domain showed a move from Enlightenment's rationality towards *One-Dimensionality* which established previously liberating science and rationality as instruments of domination. This is communicated across classes and across domains.

The rationality of the communicative domain

Unlike the traditional base-superstructure model, the inclusion of communication into the base domain and the superstructure domain enables an understanding of these transitional processes seen as communicational processes (Figure 4.1, Chapter 4). The *Great Transformation* from feudalism to capitalism as well as the minor transition from early to advanced capitalism has been supported by changes in the communicative domain.[170] No longer can the superstructure-base dichotomy be seen without its communicative element as shifts in demands on communication occurred alongside both transitions. During *Enlightenment* an old feudalistic regime of mystic communication via God, religion, and church lost ground to a democratic and open *market place* of ideas that constructed the *public sphere* of modernism.[171] As the steering instruments of feudalism ended, the public domain had to fulfil these steering elements. God and his earthly representatives such as lords, barons, counts, and aristocrats no longer dictated the conduct of society. From now on, society had to do it on its own and find ways in which to conduct its affairs. Such conduct could only be established communicatively, hence the public domain. In order to establish a truly *public domain* where a new form of public communication occurred four elements had to be satisfied:[172]

Table 3.3   Four Elements of the Public Domain

Elements that need to be in existence
i   an open and democratic society,
ii   access to the public sphere is open to all members of a society,
iii it is a forum for discourses that concerns all members of the domain, and
iv   there are commonly shared interests among those members.

The four elements in Table 3.3 could only come into existence when feudalism moved into the background of human society thus creating an open and democratic society (i). As formally independent workers and rising city-based middle-class citizens demanded access to forms of communication that allowed critical discourse, the feudal order started to decline. Once proletarian workers and enlightened citizens began to free themselves from the communicative bondage of feudalism, both demanded voice and political participation based on rational forms of communication (ii). Open discourse among all members of society (iii) enabled the establishment of common agreement on the ways human society should conduct itself (iv). This, sometimes violent, breaking up of feudalist forms of communication between church and peasant enabled a communicatively established rationality to push more and more towards modernity.[173] Once modern and rational communication was sufficiently established, forces in the productive domain began to take over communication in the reproductive domain. Increasingly, privately owned mass media began to infiltrate the public domain. Elements from the productive domain began to colonise the public domain when commercially institutionalised media increasingly challenged communication in the reproductive domain. Free speech in the freed-up reproductive domain became increasingly a question of power and money as commercial imperative stemming from the productive domain infiltrated communication in the reproductive domain.

   Public discourse became ever more guided by and through these privately owned mass-media organisations. This occurred increasingly via highly concentrated corporate media outlets rather than through participation of democratic citizens.[174] Communication was not directed towards truth. Information became a commodity bought and sold to the highest bidder. The idea of reaching common understanding has been replaced and shifted towards commodified exchange.[175] *Exchange* rather than *use* value converted information and discourse into an instrument of capitalist exchanges. Increasingly, the open forum for communication took on forms of domination establishing a one-dimensional regime. These regimes are commercially driven market forms of communication smothering access to open and public debate.[176] More than in previous periods, communication during advanced capitalism is identified by distortions and instrumentality as the commodification and centralisation of mass media takes hold. More than via state control (i and ii), the public domain has been restructured via economic factors (iii–viii). This restructuring of the public domain can be shown as:

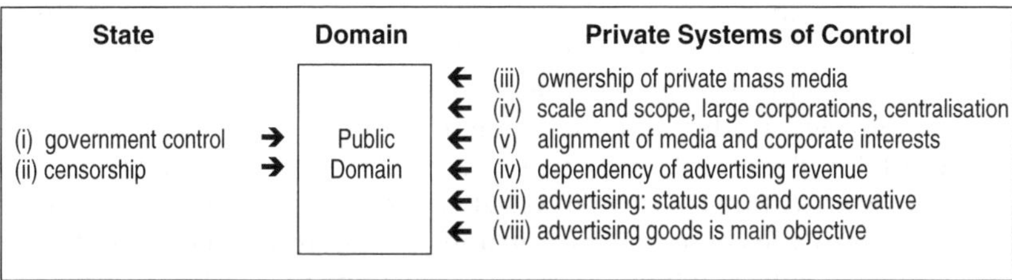

Figure 3.1 The Restructuring of the Public Domain

Unlike George Orwell's predictions in his work *1984*, Figure 3.1 shows that the public domain has not been restructured by an omnipotent police-controlled state but by the private sector. Corporate rather than state interest have not only infiltrated but also colonised the public domain. Not the power centralised by the state but the concentration of power in the hands of a few large global corporations has restructured the public domain. Present society is not the end of history but rather the beginning of a history of unparalleled media concentration and media infiltration of everyday life.[177] In present life, it is hardly possible to meet 99% of all societal members. Therefore, our ideas of societies, country, nation, etc. are shaped by mass media that mediate between individuals and society. Mass media establish, create, and shape our ideas of anything beyond the primary groups to which individuals have personal contacts. We comprehend our society or country via the picture portrayed in the media, not by meeting the members of our society or nation. Mass communication – structured as one-way communication – links us to society. We only receive a mediated reality of what society is.[178] This mediated reality is not so much shaped by state-controlled media but by privately owned media where private interests rather than the state control the public domain, a domain that is of vital importance for democracy.[179] Therefore, democracy is much more challenged by private than by state media. As the public domain works best when a significantly large variety of uncontrolled media have access, the restructuring comes from a significant narrowing of participants on the public domain. The concentration of private-media ownership might have led to proliferation of trivialities broadcasted in increasingly indifferent programmes and channels while at the same time the range of interests has narrowed due to the concentration of media in the hands of a few global-media corporations.

As shown in Figure 3.1, state-sponsored censorships (i) and the direct control of journalists and media (ii) have largely been overtaken by one-dimensional interests of corporate mass media.[180] The *corporatisation* of media has led to the representation of one interest, the interest of corporations (iii). As mass media become larger and larger, they tend to focus on economics of scale (iv). Programmes are increasingly trivial, petty, crude, and unsophisticated as they are intentionally narrowed down to a common denominator.[181] In that way, they can be used in different markets, different societies, and different countries. With that an alignment of media interest and corporate interests takes place (v). As corporations depend on advertising revenue, programmes are structured to serve this goal rather than the public need.[182] They tend to portray the commercialisation and commodification of everyday life as a normal, happy, and fulfilling event.[183] All alternative views are excluded, thus leading to a one-dimensionality of interest, the interest of the commodity. On the whole, advertising and the adjacent programs tend to be conservative, hostile to criticism and other viewpoints (vii). The advertising of goods takes over democratic needs of society as communication is redirected from communicating the truth towards instrumental communication.[184] The main objective is not Enlightenment and critical rationality but the avoidance of controversies, challenging ideas, serious political debate, etc. This is reduced to entertainment as news are reduced to *infotainment*. It contains or containerises our thoughts not unlike locking them in a container. The idea of the public domain is no longer to be seen as a means for democratic debate and open discourse but as an end. This end is the commercially driven instrumental communication. Today, the public domain has been completely restructured from a democratic domain into a vital link between mass consumer and mass production (Figure 4.1).

4
Understanding Communication in Today's Working Society

As much as all societies need communication to establish themselves as societies, needs for communication shift when societies change from pre-historic to slavery societies and to agrarian-feudalist societies. These shifts are required as the forms for production and reproduction change. Communicative needs have changed when pre-historic communities moved into more organised forms of hierarchical social structures. When these societies grew larger as more and more food became available due to ever more sophisticated production arrangements, changes in the communicative needs in the non-productive structure were required. In order to exist and reach agreement in relatively large human formations, these social structures needed new forms of communication. Sophisticated forms of enlarged production and the resulting social structures demanded that communication moved at a somewhat higher and more sophisticated level. With the end of societies that had been built around the exploitation of slaves and the rise of feudalist forms of food production, communicative needs changed again dramatically. No longer was the slave at the centre of production; the peasant and the lord who rented soil to the peasant became the cornerstones of the new societal arrangements. For thousands of years prior to the most dramatic transformation these arrangements had been able to sustain human existence.

The Great Transformation ended all forms of feudalist living and moved humans into modernity. It radically altered all previous forms of peasant life. From now on, modernity and Enlightenment took hold. For the first time in human existence, the soil and agricultural forms of production became secondary. The system of production was no longer based on peasants, soil, and the lord, but on workers, machinery, commodities, and above all, capitalists. This process radically restructured the way humans reproduced and organised their societies. In this process, not only all previous forms of societal living (A) and economic production (C) changed fundamentally, also the communicative needs altered again. Once peasants left their thousands of years old traditions and became *double-free* workers – free from feudal chains and free from the ability to produce because the means of production had been taken away from them and transferred into the domain of capital that now owned machinery, factories and the like – these free workers needed to sell their labour on the labour market. But they also demanded their voice to be heard. No longer could the lord dictate the affairs of society, nor were the capitalists, the newly established form of economic power, able to govern the public domain (B) on their own. Those who had been made workers demanded access to the communicative domain.

The communicative element (B) of modern relations between the re-productive (A) and the productive domain (C) can be shown during the most significant change from feudalism (i) to early capitalism (ii) and to advanced capitalism (iii). While under the traditional view of production and social relations outside of production the superstructure-base link was seen as dialectical, a critical-communicative perspective demands that this link is understood as communicative. The link between A and C is not only theoretically dialectic but also communicatively established. Only communication is able to link A to C. This is shown in B. With B, a new *linking* domain is established as this domain is not only a go-between or connection domain (⇕) but has also developed as a dynamic domain. The communicative domain B takes on an own task as it is ruled, governed, and structured by a separated dynamic that is not the same that governs domains A and C. At a somewhat simplified level the development of modernity, rationality, and communication can be constructed as follows:[185]

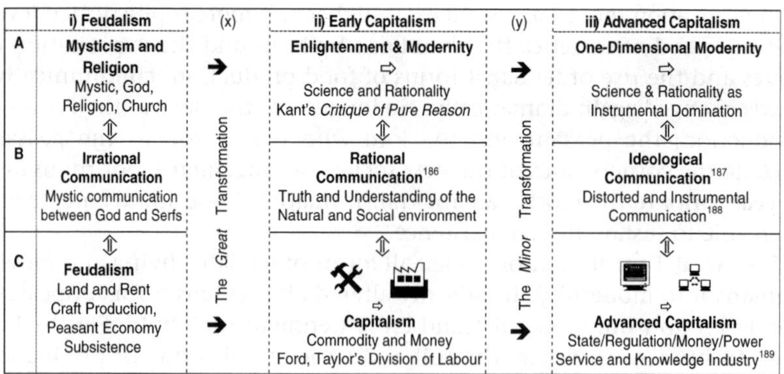

Figure 4.1   A Historic Process Model of the Development of Rationality and Communication

Figure 4.1 shows foremost the historic development of rationality and communication. Rationality and the need for communication have changed throughout the last centuries. Above all, it is communication that links specific domains to each other. Between the production domain (C) and the non-productive or reproductive domain (A), the communicative domain (B) is established as a linkage domain. As rational ways of producing commodities replaced early craft-based workshops (C^i) unable to deliver the goods needed in modern societies (C^{ii}), communication ($B^{i=ii}$) changed as well. This can also be seen when society moved from mass manufacturing (C^{ii}) to advanced capitalism based on the service and knowledge industry (C^{iii}). At the upper level (A), rationality is linked to society and the institutions that support the productive domain via domain (B). Finally, changes in the communicative domain (B) altered the way rationality was used to support developments in domain A and C.[190] These changes occurred as work (C), society (A), and communication (B) underwent two transformations (x, y). These transformations also changed the way we work (C), the way we live (A), and the way we communicate (B) when we moved from feudalism (i) to early capitalism (ii), and eventually to advanced capitalism signified by the service industry and the knowledge economy (iii). This occurred alongside three developments in all three domains: (A) the superstructure or reproductive domain (B) the communicative domain, and (C) the basic or productive domain. The first transformation (x) has commonly been termed *The Great Transformation* as it involved the most significant change in human society during the last three centuries. The next change occurred when early capitalism moved into its present advanced stage (y). This did not include a fundamental shift as dramatic as witnessed during *The Great Transformation* (x).

Figure 4.1 also shows the impact of the first transition (x) that *took shape in the 17th century in the northwest corner of the European system of societies, in Great Britain, Holland and France [creating] the industrial revolution, the democratic revolution and the educational revolution.*[191] With these changes modernity had been established. One of the strongest expressions of modernity has been the rejection of feudalist regimes creating modern human principles such as *liberté, egalité, fraternité* applicable to all humans as codified in *The Universal Declaration of Human Rights* (UN 1948). It took roughly 150 years from 1798 to 1948 to codify universal human rights.

Similarly, in domain A and C modernity also meant a significant increase in our ability to control nature. Secondly, modernity indicates the development of moral social norms that make possible a post-feudalist form of society based on humane forms of conflict resolutions and advancement. Only with a global move towards the completion of these humanist principles can modernity be fully established.[192] Until today, this has not been achieved, hence Habermas' (1985) *modernity the unfinished project.*[193] Only when all provisions in *The Declaration of Human Rights* are fully achieved, the project of modernity can be completed. As long as there still is inequality among men and women, slavery, starvation, violation of human rights, exploitation, and sexual exploitation, we cannot truthfully speak of modernity. The idea of *post-modernism* cannot flourish while the project of modernity remains unfinished. In order to achieve the human goals of modernity, elements directing our attention towards the educational and democratic improvements (A-B-C) still have to be accomplished. Focusing on the material results of the *industrial revolution* of the 19th and 20th century alone cannot achieve modernity. However, the changes in domains A and C have been unimaginable without changes in the communicative domain C.

In addition to the changes in the communicative (B) and the reproductive (A) domains, the most fundamental change occurred in the basic or productive domain (C). The shift in (C) meant that the way in which a society produces and distributes goods and services altered most fundamentally when the system that replaced feudalism was created. This new way has been termed *industrialism* (C) or *capitalism* and when the welfare state was added, it developed into *advanced capitalism.* As the capitalist economy replaced feudalism, two mechanisms of exchange developed. These two mechanisms are a *firm-to-firm* internal exchange and a *wage-labour* exchange on the one hand and a *tax-state* exchange on the other. Crucial to both exchanges is the single most exchangeable medium of any modern society: money.[194] When monetary exchanges became the basic foundation of our lives, modern societies created economic and social pathologies that have started to appear alongside capitalist modernisation.[195] When feudalism's serfdom was replaced by early capitalism's brutal collectivisation and domestication of labour further pathologies developed. These occurred as equally brutal colonialism was carried into many corners of the world. As capitalism advanced to the present version of capitalism, the system failed to solve many of these pathologies. While early capitalism has proven to be incapable of solving these problems, advanced capitalism has produced its own. It has added new and equally horrific pathologies. One of these visible in the reproductive domain (A) has been the unfulfilled promise of early liberal philosophers that institutionalisation of bourgeois freedoms would lead to freedom and equality.[196] While the power of aristocrats over peasants under feudalism has been replaced by the power of the capitalist class over labour, the promise of equality under modernity has remained unfulfilled. Instead, what has occurred is the institutionalisation of equal citizenship in domain (A) neutralising economic inequality in domain (C).[197] Men and women are no longer feudal subjects as they have become legally equal but economically unequal citizens. In the words of Orwell's *Animal Farm, all animals are equal but some animals are more equal than others.*[198]

Portrayed as animals in Orwell's farm story, humans, now living in modern times, are experiencing that some humans are more equal than others. But they are experiencing equality at the same time as inequality. With modernity conflicts are no longer between two contradictory norms –

feudal political order versus modernity – but between two new norms, the civil norm of equal citizen rights on the one hand and the reality of socio-economic inequality on the other. Under modernity, inequality remains as a system imperative while at the same time political and citizenship equality have been institutionalised. This process of a parallel existence of equality and inequality has been accomplished via three means. Firstly, a false *hierarchisation* (C) of equals has developed. In the productive domain *people do not come together freely and spontaneously to set up work organisations, as propertyless many are forced by their need for a livelihood to seek access to resources, owned or controlled by the few* (Fox 1974:284). Secondly, an *ideological equalisation* (A) occurred of those who in fact remain unequal.[199] And thirdly, a *communicative inequality* (A) of citizens has been established where many are excluded from access to the communicative domain. These three elements of modernity are manifest in the productive domain (C), in the reproductive domain (A), and in the communicative domain (B).

In many instances these domains have been artificially separated. Most standard views of history are limited to discussions of shifts in the upper domain – Kings, Queens, Prime Ministers, Generals, etc. – pretending they are in charge. Equally, there are purely economic views that disconnect society (A) from its economic foundations (C). Furthermore, there are purely communicative studies seeking to hide how domination is established communicatively (B). A modern and truly critical view always locates the world of work (C) *as the key sociological category* (Offe 1985) into the centre of activity. But it never does so without positioning work as a connected issue that is inextricably linked to the domains of re-production (A) and communication (B). Between the productive and reproductive domain, system integrative forces can only be mediated communicatively. Hence any critical view of the world of work can no longer be separated and portrayed to be operative inside one domain only. Consequently, forms of domination and the rising pathologies of advanced capitalism such as the decline and ritualisation of democracy and authoritarian forms of work organisation can no longer be understood in a singular mode (Adorno et al. 1964). Only an approach that links these three domains is able to produce a comprehensive understanding of the world of work and to deal with one of the most fundamental questions of the 20th century.

As the world of work (C) is linked to A and B, an analysis of why the workers' revolution as predicted by Marx did not take place can only be answered via a three-domain model. The three-domain model also provides fruitful insights into why the revolution did not occur during the 1920s and 1930s culminating in one of the worst disasters in the history of mankind. Why did some sections of the German – and other European – working class turn to *fascism?*[200] The early research programme of the Frankfurt School, oriented towards issues of people at work, tried to answer this question. This research also assisted an understanding of the seemingly uncontroversial adaptation of post-war mass production and mass consumption.

Instrumental and communicative rationality

During the post-WWII period of the late 20th century, while fascism had been defeated, domination remained a feature of societal and working regimes. In order to understand the rise of post-war prosperity and Fordist mass production, critical theory proponents were aware that social relations at work could no longer be discussed inside a separated domain that is commonly labelled as *industrial relations* (IR) or *labour relations*.[201] For too many years traditional IR studies had restricted our understanding of issues such as institutions, job regulation, *rules, conflict, and negotiations* without linking them to the reproductive and communicative domain (Edwards 2003:338). These traditional restrictions are no longer viable. A critical and comprehensive understanding of the world of work can only be constructed as an interdisciplinary research program when dealing with fundamental problems such as those of domination and emancipation. Such a research programme needs to include the three domains as outlined in Figure 4.1. It can only be constructed inside a dialectic relationship between the work domain, the society domain, and the communicative domain.

The communication domain discusses how actors communicate in this domain. Communication is also seen as a medium linking all domains. Hence, the double aspect of communication as domain and linking medium has been included. In sum, a critical view of the world of work does the exact opposite of many traditional viewpoints. It strongly rejects the compartmentalisation found in traditional positivist social science largely governing IR studies. It equally criticises a *positivist* view that restricts and limits knowledge which was gained by separating these domains. Thirdly, it also rejects a positivist expression that structures knowledge according to technical usefulness.[202] Any knowledge that is gained from a comprehensive look at all three domains can no longer be restricted to *what is* technically useful but must be directed towards uncovering underlying forms of domination with an intent directed towards emancipation.

Consequently, any critical viewpoint is markedly different from traditional sociological theories that sought to explain the world of work *as such* or as a *thing in itself*. Work *as such* or as a *thing in itself* can hardly exist in a socially constructed reality. In a critical approach the relationship between social analysis and critique has been built into any framework that seeks to understand the world of work. Essentially, this is nothing new. *Enlightenment* philosophy such as Kant's *Critique of Pure Reason* (1781) has already directed our attention towards a politics of critical self-actualisation. What prevents such self-actualisation is the socially constructed fact of domination. In short, one of the core fundamental assumptions of critical theory is that today's social order entails forms of domination. *The critical-emancipatory interest underlies the struggle to change those relations of domination-subordination* (Morrow 1994:149). The central goal is not only to preserve the emancipatory element of *Enlightenment* but also to radically reconstitute the project of the transformation of society directed towards positive social change. This sort of theory demands the end of domination, human emancipation, and the liberation of social criticism.

The goal of human emancipation and social criticism can no longer be restricted to a simple form of rationality. Today's understanding cannot be limited to validity gained from being consistent with facts. The assumed, but rather weak, fact-meaning link becomes exposed to critique. Any rationality that gains validity from natural science through a transformation of concept from the natural to the social world has expired. Put simply, the social world does not operate along the lines of natural science but along social and critical rationality. An approach as expressed in statements such as *the median income level of a hundred selected families in an urban industrial universe correlates .76 with population density – not .78 or .61 but .76, and that's a fact...just like physics* is no longer able to reflect the complexities of social reality.[203]

In a second step, positivist understanding (such as *median income levels)* was tested on actual facts (such as .76 or .68). Examples like this are one of the clearest expressions of an uncritical acceptance of self- or socially created facts. They are presented as *given facts, just like physics!* This was done without any critical reflection on what created a *fact*. It neglects or hides the fact that the term *fact* derives from the Latin word *factum* which is the neuter past particle of the verb *'facere'*, meaning *to do* or *to make* (Searle 1996:210). The assumption of facts without any consideration of the *factors* that *make* a fact is one of the most common and dangerous fallacies of our present understanding of the world of work. Unconsciously, most traditional studies on the world of work operated *as if they were in a deductive theory testing mode even when their theoretical commitments are less than clear [and] references, data, variables, diagrams, and hypothesises often used to cover up a lack of theory and actual theory testing* (Deetz 2001:20). In sum, our traditional understanding of the world of work has disregarded distinctions between social and natural science by transferring methods developed in the realm of natural science into social science. This is no longer appropriate. By doing so they eclipsed the:

social world = natural world

Figure 4.2   The Social–Natural Equation

dilemma through an emphasis on technical methods developed in the realm of natural science.[204] Forms of *fact=as=fact* rationalities are no longer sufficient to understand the world of work. Nevertheless this has been a decisive factor in our understanding of the world of work. Such an understanding, as it is presented to us as a *fact!*, has been part of our socially constructed understanding for centuries. While it might have had a long history, the presentation of the idea of *social facts just like in physics* does no longer appear to be plausible.

The French writer Auguste Comte (1853) has developed one of the most crucial themes of *Enlightenment*. Comte's inquiries into the social world had been constructed as: *if man would only apply the discipline of the natural science to the study of man, then only a sufficient expenditure of time, money, and thought would separate him from the good society.*[205] With Comte elements of natural law began to be transferred to the social world. Karl Marx partly continued the *social-world equals natural-world* idea. The idea of *the natural men = the science of men* has plagued the world of knowledge ever since. Originally, it had occurred as an instrument developed against feudalist thinking. It has been transferred into today's modern social science. Essentially, a social science that still operates in the tradition of Comte has fallen into the Hegelian *Zeitgeist* trap unable to reassess and critically reflect on the development of *Enlightenment* thinking during the last 200 years.[206] While sociological methods and technicalities have become ever more refined, a positivistic understanding of the social=natural world lineage appears to be trapped in a *time* (Zeit) when such a way of *thinking* (Geist) was appropriate. Hegel's idea of Zeitgeist refers to thinking (Geist) that is trapped in time (Zeit) without any historical understanding. It describes the inability to think and understand – for example issues such as the world of work – as a historical development, one of Hegel's core interests.

One of the greatest problems of our understanding seems to be that modern social thinking has spent 200 years of refining technical methods but simultaneously the natural-social link has been insufficiently questioned. The positivist social-science idea that the social world equals the natural world had tragic consequences. It appears that *the* defining issue that lent purpose to *Enlightenment* had been eliminated. That is the issue of *critique*. The critical understanding of the *natural* world and the critical understanding of the *social* world had been sacrificed on the altar of an obsession with *what is*, with *how* things work and not with *why* they work. Modern tools appear to deliver ever more on the *how*-scale while the *why*-scale is cut shorter and shorter. Positivists' interests in *what is* and *how* appear to be most eager to fulfil George Orwell's (1949:83) *I understand HOW: I do not understand WHY*. While being locked in ever more refined techniques that tell us the *how*, ever less attention seems to be spent on the *why*.[207] As in Orwell's *1984*, an understanding of *why* appears to be much more dangerous than an understanding that is restricted to *how*. But before entering into the seemingly dangerous world of *why*, there are some elementary criticisms on positivist restrictions that limit our understanding of *how*.

For many positivist scientists and their unconscious entourage, the positivist *natural-world=human-world* assumption neglects three core dilemmas. The first dilemma is that experiences made '*of*' as well as '*in*' nature are disqualified. They are wilfully excluded under the pretence that they just do not exist or can be neglected. The dialectical relationship between both remains hidden or put aside even though it cannot be denied.[208] We – and even Popper's (1965) positivism – cannot disconnect the *socially constructed* world from the *natural* word (Searle 1996). Secondly, the social=natural idea excludes the dilemma that uncertainty does not simply belong to *values* but also to *facts*.[209] Finally, it excludes the dilemma of man's impossibility to be an *extra-natural observer* outside of nature. Any human, scientific or casual observer can only ever be part of nature from which *s/he* arose (Shalin 1992:257). In order to make Popper's (1965) positivist dream work, these three dilemmas have to be neglected, denied, or simply hidden. In sum, positivism appears to be a somewhat nihilistic idea. It negates or denies substance and challenges.

Finally, unlike investigations into natural science such as physics or chemistry, investigations into the world of work concern management, labour, work relations, and *Human Resource Management* (HRM). They do not deal with a naturally constructed world but exclusively with a *socially constructed one*.[210] Too many positivist investigations into the socially constructed reality of the world of work are often no more than uncritical re-interpretations, re-creations, or reproductions set up inside the specific meaning-framework of instrumental rationality. Such a framework, unconsciously or consciously, prevents emancipation from domineering structures of social conduct at work rather than highlighting domination.[211] In other words, while work and the tools to understand it are socially constructed, the idea of a social = natural world negates two things: a) that work is not naturally constructed and b) understanding can never come from instruments developed for natural science. One of the core instruments of natural science that has been used in social science is the idea of system.

This instrument constructs our understanding inside a closed system in which numerous variables not only depend on each other but also seek to establish *equilibrium*. The physics model of *equilibrium* has invaded social thinking as it concurs with the natural = social model. The attempt to discover system conforming and law-like foundations of society is part of this view. System demands towards equilibrium are likely to be constructed as physical-mathematical systems. They eclipse social constructions and historic origins. By transferring the equilibrium notion from physics into socially constructed realities, many social scientists unconsciously reproduce instrumental goals. These goals remain hidden in the system and are unquestioned, hidden behind the drive towards equilibrium.[212] This is generally accompanied by an uncritical assumption and acceptance of a social equilibrium expressed in social harmony. It operates either as keeping a status quo or is directed towards a future status quo. Social phenomena such as disharmony, revolt, protest, conflict, maladjustment, pathologies, contradictions, disorganisation, resistance, or emancipation are viewed as system disturbances that need to be fixed to establish equilibrium. Equilibrium is an implicit element of system stabilising thought. System stability is implied as a desirable goal for society.[213] System and equilibrium are, almost by definition, conservative notions as they seek to preserve the status quo of an assumed social order. The danger of system and equilibrium does not lie so much in the goal of a stable social order. It resides in the fact that social science affixed in system and equilibrium either consciously hides or unconsciously reproduces the implicit goals of system thinking. The danger stems from a prevention of understanding the true state of affairs in society and work by restricting understanding to system, equilibrium and above all the goal of status quo in society.

In summary, the spin-offs of equilibrium establishing elements are viewed as good things and those disturbing the equilibrium are viewed as bad. The idea of system equilibrium tends to carry connotations of totalitarianism as it reduces or excludes reality rather than dialectically incorporating it. It is a clear expression of a rationality that leads to irrationality by restricting a comprehensive understanding of society and work. Above all, it operates seductively because it suggests harmony rather than contradictions, critique, or conflict. Conflict, contradictions, critique, and *critical thinking*, and above all critical theory are system alien as traditional theory emphasises natural equilibrium.[214] It delivers a textbook-like harmony between inharmonious relations in society and at work. It seductively plays on the human mind portraying society and work as harmonious. Disturbing elements are portrayed as negative, which can be fixed by using some easy tools out of the toolbox of instrumental rationality.

Inside the system thinking of traditional positivism technical reasoning and *instrumental rationality* build an integral part. This can amount to some forms of irrationality as capitalist rationality produces more problems than solutions to present societies. While technical reasoning might demand the system of a corporation to act in a certain way, such actions can have a devastating effect on larger issues.[215] System theory helps to reduce our focus to company level. It is a particularly useful tool in neglecting or negating the devastating impacts of capitalism as it operates as a closed system.[216] Pathologies created by the present order are located outside the system and remain cut off from system imperatives that operate inside the closed system of a corporation.

However, despite all attempts system pathologies are still visible in worldwide poverty, global warming, environmental destruction and the like. Increasingly, such system approaches are no longer able to explain the complexities of present society. The system approach is too narrow to explain the realities of the world of work connected to the ideological and the communicative domain. In some extreme cases, this has led to *hyper-*

rationality expressed in the belief in the omnipotence of technical system-rationality. An emphasis on rationality grounded in techniques, tools, or instruments has been made part of the non-communicatively established rationality. Unlike communicatively established consent among people, technical rationality seeks consent that is enforced via technical forces and enshrined in technical or mechanical systems. Rather than being communicatively agreed upon, these systems establish a domineering power over and above their participants. Such a technical and non-communicatively established system in our social and working lives operates through eight key elements:

Table 4.1 Constituting Elements of Instrumental Rationality

No.	Rationality	Descriptive Characteristics
i	Instrumental or tool rationality	Rationality is grounded in the use of *tools, instruments, or implements* or *apparatuses*. Traditionally, they are applied as a means-ends-rationality.
ii	Means-end	A *means-end-rationality* is expressed in actions as *means* in relation to a given *end*. Usually some specific group establishes such goals in the world of work. This goal-setting group tends to be upper management. It divides strategic management (ends) from operative management (means).
iii	Law and system	Rationality-emphasising instruments that perform such actions are often directed towards either law-like functionalist elements, or system-theory constituents that signal such functions.
iv	Rational choice	The overarching concept of rationality is grounded in an individual's free choice expressed as *rational choice* or *normative rationality* limited to operations inside the confines of a system.
v	Value as an attachment	Normative rationality is reflected in value rationality based on ethical standards that are attached to it. They are not viewed as inherent as they are portrayed as being an add-on to rationality.
vi	Objective and value-free	Research conducted under auspices of instrumental, tool or system rationality accepts the present form of capitalist enterprises as a natural existing object open to description, prediction, and control. Such commercial *organisations* are usually discussed in economic or managerial terms relating to *objective* economic or managerial goals. Research is portrayed as apolitical and value neutral.
vii	Managerial rationality	The world of work is constructed as an orderly and integrated world supported by so-called organisational members. Commonly, it is subsumed under the managerial rationality.
viii	Instrumental communicative	Under *means-end-rationality*, instrumental communication is not seen as open discourse but is reduced primarily to the administration of information and messages.

Among the elements shown in Table 4.1 modernity's concept of rationality has resulted in a technical or instrumental tool-like approach (i) to rationality providing a structuring principle in the world of work. According to Morrow (1994:100) *instrumental rationality refers to the efficiency of the means realising given ends (values), where efficiency was based on calculations and expertise was based on scientific techniques*. It seeks to apply *means-ends* themes (ii) to human action in an attempt to structure human action through goal-achieving instruments. Instrumental or managerial rationality operates via three conditions: (a) a goal must be determined independent of the means of intervention (b) this state must be brought about instrumentally and (c) the objective world is to be altered towards a goal. In short, managerial-instrumental rationality separates the goals from the means while in reality they are inextricably linked. Under the exclusion of any ethical or external consideration, instrumental thinking is narrowed to the use of instruments or managerial tools to achieve their goals. Lastly, and this is the major reason of the whole exercise, the world – that means the world of work – has to be altered.

Law- (iii) and choice-rational (iv) systems assist the operation of means-ends rationality as they confine a supposedly free or rational choice to the means-ends doctrine. The means-ends doctrine deals with values in two ways (v, vi). This process excludes ethical or moral values. The first option is to portray values as a non-intrinsic entity that can be attached (v). The second option is the pretence of being value free (vi). More than (v) this is able to hide the intrinsic values of managerialism (vii). This managerial rationality constructs workers as organisational members fulfilling a set task inside a system that is equally rational or at least presented as such. Finally, managerial, system-conforming, or instrumental communication (viii) eliminates unwanted and unwarranted discourse and tailors it towards the needs of means-ends rationality. All this occurs as means-ends rationality and is set to support a system in which social action derives from imperatives inherent in rationality (i–viii). Management does not need to seek common understanding that demands communication. Rationality will deliver it. Management is free to pretend to be just a means, to *get things done through people* (Harding 2003:28).

On the basis of the historical development of rationality, management pretends to be the clearest expression of rationality as it links three rational aspects that stand equal to each other:

Enlightenment's rationality = rational capitalism = management's instrumental rationality

---

Figure 4.3   The Enlightenment–Capitalism–Management Equation

Through the equalisation (Figure 4.3) of these three elements, the objective world of capitalist modernisation uses instrumental rationality as a functional necessity. As this process continued from early to late capitalism, instrumental rationality surged beyond the boundaries of the economic domain deep into previously communicatively structured domains. Up to that time, these domains represented spheres of life that sought to establish moral-political regulation via communicative means. This was no longer the case when instrumental rationality took over both domains.

Once instrumental rationality had been established in all three domains, it became a guiding principle for all actors in all domains. The move beyond different domains can be detected relatively easy. Instrumental rationality seeks to structure the contact of all humans in all domains. Everything and sometimes even everyone becomes a mere function of means-ends rationality. Seeking to infiltrate every corner of our social and individual life, instrumental rationality crosses borders between our objective, social, and subjective existence. In several of the domains shown below (Table 4.2), instrumental rationality has not been able to totally overcome other forms of social regulation. Some forms of social and political regulations are still achieved through communicatively established common agreement and understanding:

Table 4.2   Three Domains of Rationality Shaping Human Existence

Domain	Description
(i) Objective	Actors in an *objective domain* relate to the world in an objective manner based on existing state of affairs grounded in facts that can be shaped via manipulative intervention. This is the domain of instrumental-rational models of action and interventions.
(ii) Social	The *social domain* relates to normative contexts established communicatively through forms of human interaction. This domain is based on shared values of social groups setting ethical norms for participating members of a domain. Such norms create forms of behaviour that is universally accepted.[217]
(iii) Subjective	Lastly, a *subjective domain* is seen as an inner sphere of personal experience with connotations of thought, attitudes, wishes, feelings, etc. The key to a *subjective world* is that accessibility penetrates deep into one's personality and is only provided to the self.

Ever since *Enlightenment* thinking replaced feudalist thinking, work and society have been seen as objective (i), social (ii), and subjective (ii) domains. They have become core spheres of human existence. The domains (i) to (iii) also define our relationships at work as they shape them via (i) objective work demands, social relationship with others at work (ii), and our subjective attitudes to work (iii). In the world of work, the *subjective domain* (iii) shapes thoughts and attitudes on, of, and while being at work. To a large extent, the subjective domain has escaped instrumental rationality. However, these subjective – and often non-rational but subjective attitudes – influence our social relationships at work. Despite all attempts to create purely instrumental rational foundations for work in which rational means-ends concepts replace social relationships social activity still remains. Although work occurs under objective means-ends conditions enshrined in modern production concepts, it is still an employment relationship. The present world of work is not totally governable via instrumental rationality as the objective domain has not been able to totally infiltrate and structure the social and subjective domains.

Inside the world of work three versions of rationality meet. These three rational forces come from (i) managerial rationality, from (ii) social reality, and from (iii) subjective reality. They not only meet at work but are able to result in conflict and contradictions. Viewed from either a managerial or from a labour perspective, different elements of the three domains might be encouraged or reduced. Most commonly, the managerial viewpoint tends to adopt instrumental rationality's means-ends ideas. It seeks to reduce all dangerous elements of the social domain (ii). It also seeks to reduce subjective rationality (iii) especially those attitudes that are not in management's interests or encourage people to pursue non-managerial courses. On the other hand, labour seeks to enhance the opposite. It seeks to reduce instrumental rationality (i) but it encourages social rationality because work is essentially a social activity (ii). It also encourages those subjective elements that are beneficial to work (iii).

In the objective-social-subjective model of Table 4.2 the clearest expression of divergent interests between labour and management can be found in the objective (i) and the social domain (ii). While the subjective domain (iii) is a sphere where labour and management might seek to encourage or reduce different feelings, domain (i) and (ii) testify much more visible conflicts and contradictions. Conflicts of interest and contradictions between management and labour are more visible in the objective domain of means-ends and the social domain of the relationship at work. These two domains (i, ii) tend to be crucial to the constitution of work. In domains (i) and (ii) two types of rationality meet: a) instrumental rationality that seeks understanding as an outcome of rational imperatives and b) social rationality that seeks awareness as an outcome of common agreement established communicatively. The rationality of (i) and (ii) also sets the two parties at work – labour and management – clearly apart as they have divergent interests. These two actors have different rationale. One is instrumental and the other is social and communicative rationality. In the world of work, objective rationality and social-communicative rationality show significant differences when related to a) the *context* of work, b) the *relations* at work, c) actor-*attitude* to work, d) work *values*, and e) *social action:*[218]

Table 4.3   Objective and Social Domains at Work

Domains	Work Context	Work Relations	Work Attitude	Work Values	Social Action
(i) Objective Work-Domain	Existing state of work	Objective relationships	Cognitive and means-ends	Instrumentality and effectiveness	Strategy and success
(ii) Social Work-Domain	Socially created work norms	Social relations based on norms	Normatively regulated	Truth and rightness	Communicative action

Table 4.3 shows how the *objective* (i) and the *social* (ii) domain which together build a structure are governing work. As Table 4.3 shows, any simplistic idea about *labour meets management* at work is shown to be a much more complex affair. It shows that two conceptually different domains struggle over the work domain. In a work context, objective affairs are expressed as existing managerial relations. This is expressed in management that structures work in accordance with instrumental rationality. In the social domain work norms and community codes of social behaviour structure affairs at workplaces. Overall, relations at work link two groups, management and labour. They relate to each other under objective as well as social conditions. On the one hand, the work relationship is shaped by a struggle between socially established conditions that create social norms at work. On the other side of the struggle are objective and cognitive forms of rationality directed towards means-ends ideas that underpin management's instrumental rationality.

In the social domain (ii), attitudes towards work are regulated via norms that are communicatively established, while in the objective domain (i) they are structured via means-ends rationality. Similarly, work values are instrumental and directed towards effectiveness in the objective domain. They are directed towards truth and rightness in the social domain. Finally in the social domain communicatively established agreement and mutual understanding govern social action. In the objective domain strategic success is accomplished via goal-achieving management directions. These are managerial actions that support the present system of production via utilisation of reasoning that has been instrumental ever since the event of industrialism.

Inside the objective domain the equation *Enlightenment's rationality = rational capitalism = management's instrumental rationality* (Figure 4.3) appears to be linear, causal, and of logical appearance. As much as there are attempts to link *Enlightenment* with managerial capitalism and instrumental reason in a linear way to shield it from critique, it does not escape critical examination directed towards exposing contradictions. Of utmost importance is the development of two versions of rationality that operate in two different ways. It ends the illusion of a simple linear development of rationality that portrays managerial rationality as a logical consequence of *Enlightenment*. This can no longer be accepted. In order to reflect on the conceptual demands of the world of work, the *Enlightenment's rationality = rational capitalism = management's instrumental rationality* equation needs to be seen as:

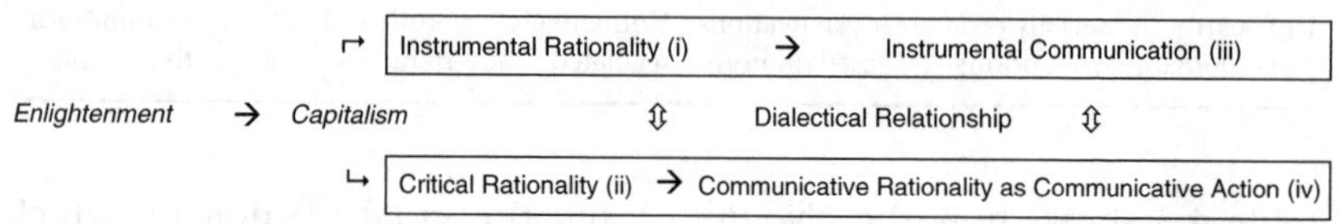

Figure 4.4   The Development of Instrumental and Critical Rationality

Figure 4.4 shows the *Enlightenment's rationality = rational capitalism = management's instrumental rationality* equation in the present stage. No longer can the *Enlightenment = capitalism* equation be seen in such a simplistic way as it negates a vital part of *Enlightenment*, the part of critical rationality. It is crucial to see the divergence in the development of *instrumental rationality* and *critical rationality*. Both have not only produced two different ways of thinking but have also developed into two different ways of communication. Figure 4.4 shows that instrumental rationality has developed into *instrumental communication* (iii) and *critical rationality* (ii) developed into communicative *rationality* or communicative *action* (iv).

First of all, there is no '=' equation linking *Enlightenment* and capitalism as it is not a logical consequence of it but exists as a dialectical relationship which cannot be shown as an equation. Therefore, what is portrayed to be '=' can only be shown as '⇔'. These are not equations but dialectical relationships. To this day capitalism has used and misused elements from Enlightenment in support of this system. On the other hand, however, Enlightenment and capitalism are mutually dependent and historically unthinkable without a strong link between each other. Similarly, *instrumental* rationality and *critical* rationality are not in an '=' equation relationship but in a dialectical relationship. However, as both belong together as part of *one* development, they cannot be shown in an equation either. Their relationship can only be presented as '⇕'. It is a mutually influencing and forward-moving relationship. This relationship continues when instrumental *rationality* becomes instrumental *communication* and critical *rationality* becomes communicative rationality or communicative *action* as both relate dialectically to each other.

Enlightenment and capitalism could not have developed without creating (i) *instrumental* rationality and (ii) *critical* rationality. While (i) contains a necessary functional element for the development of natural science and capitalism, the other (ii) has been a crucial necessity for the separation between religion and rationality. Only with both developments capitalism was able to flourish. Later these two versions of rationality developed into two separate but connected entities. As capitalism advanced, system-integrative elements that belonged to the domain of communication began to gain importance. Once viewed from conditions of communication, *instrumental* rationality has led to *instrumental* communication (iii), while *critical* rationality led to *communicative* rationality or *communicative action* (iv). The meaning of rationality seen as *communicative rationality* becomes the constitution of consensus among people implying that rationality is intrinsically connected with communication. The core issue is that rationality has to be established communicatively while instrumental rationality views communication in instrumental terms. It sees instrumental communication as a form of rationality. Communication is guided via means-ends rational obligations (Figure 4.1:B[iii]).

The concept of *communicative rationality* carries universal as well as pragmatic connotations as the search for truth and mutual understanding is issued universally. As much as instrumental rationality and instrumental communication are universal forms of rationality, critical rationality and communicative rationality are universal in character. However, there are some core differences between instrumental and communicative rationality. Unlike communicative rationality, instrumental rationality carries much stronger connotations of *bounded rationality*. Under conditions of instrumental communication the people participating in a communicative process are somewhat limited to the system demands of instrumentality. In other words, means-ends connotations function as boundary-setting imperatives. Therefore it is more likely than in the case of communicative rationality that discourses under conditions of instrumental communication do not always strive for the maximum result. Discourse outcomes can be limited as instrumentality sets boundaries on communication. Participants in instrumental communication are more likely to be satisfied with a sub-optimal situation. The costs of meeting their aspirations and abilities can be too high when operating outside of instrumental communication. In short, the limits of instrumental rationality tend to inflict limitations on a discourse that is structured in accordance with instrumental imperatives. This applies to instrumental conditions operating in management and corporations.

Selznick (1943) explains why people in corporations do not always behave rationally. They do not behave according to instrumental rationality as demonstrated in quasi-economic theories such as the *rational choice-actor* model. He has highlighted irrational choices of managers during rational problem-solving. It shows why the display of technical foolishness by managers often concurs with a version of instrumental communication that is bound to fail as it establishes meaning under strict conditions of goal-setting rationalities. The fatality of instrumental goal-setting and rationalities that structure communication are expressed in the *3Es-equation:*

Economy = Efficiency = Effectiveness

Figure 4.5   The Economy–Efficiency–Effectiveness Equation

Even though their communicative limitations and structural shortcomings are known, they are rehearsed over and over again as the keys to understand modern and rational managerial thinking. The *3Es-equation* (Figure 4.5) serves an additional and perhaps even more important purpose for management. One of the key outcomes of rationality that assists our understanding of Figure 4.5 is the function of instrumental rationality directed towards *system integration.* The idea of system integration is one of the most powerful ideas of instrumental rationality as instruments can be utilised to serve in an integrative way. Integration into rational systems such as capitalism, managerialism or even management of a corporation is a decisive function. According to Lockwood (1964) *system* integration is directed towards the analysis primarily of contradictions in advanced capitalism. On the one hand, this involves the relatively abstract structural principles of private appropriation of capital. On the other hand, it involves social characters of production.

Marx's core interest was the problem of *system* integration while Weber's focused on the *social* integrative aspect. Both cannot be viewed as independent but as important functions that support our current society and way of working. Giddens (1984:139–144) emphasised that *system integration directs questions to the reproduction of institutions – social orders – across time and space. It takes place behind the backs of actors.* In short, *system integration* seeks to integrate labour into instrumental rationality without their knowledge or conscious contribution. Often this is established through instrumental communication. Habermas has applied the *system* versus *social* integration concept to communication. In other words, communication can be used for *system* integrative or *social* purposes. Habermas (1997a:150) proposed that *social* integration occurs through communicatively achieved consensus. *System* integration is established *through the non-normative steering of individuals' decisions not subjectively coordinated.* Hence, *social* integration refers to an internal agency-oriented view of the social world as face-to-face interaction. It is directed towards achieving communicative agreement among social actors, hence social integration. *System* integration points to an external perspective that reaches through and beyond action. Such actions are systematically mediated interactions. They do not have to be communicatively established but are externally forced upon social actors or achieved *behind their backs* (Giddens 1984).

As system integration remains one of the main forces behind many forms of action in the world of work as well as society in general, it has drawn strong criticism. One of the core critiques on *system* integration is that it infiltrates areas such as the economic system, the administrative-political system, and the world of work. Relatively large decision-making areas in the world of work are achieved non-communicatively.[219] They are achieved upon imperatives that come from instrumental rationality. For example, a managerial decision is taken on the basis of means-ends rationality or the *3Es*-equation. Such decisions are instrumental to management. They do not need to be communicated as they are presented as coming from an internal rationality enshrined in instrumental rationality. They are presented as rational while excluding all forms of communication, shielding managerial decisions from any exposure to communicative rationality.

As relatively large sections of system integration are not established through communication, it developed two steering media to co-ordinate human action. These are money and power.[220] Money and power can best be understood via the notion of *system integration* as both operate silently behind the backs of people as well as in the open. At work they are linked to performance management or performance-related pay while in the reproductive domain they are linked to commodity, consumerism, status symbols, and *Affluenza* (Hamilton & Denniss 2005). In the productive and the reproductive domain, both – money and power – have developed into powerful instruments of non-communicative instrumental rationality. Their ability to steer extremely huge sections of society and the world of work remains largely unchallenged.

In conclusion a brief look at critical rationality versus instrumental rationality has shown that both are an outcome of *Enlightenment*. Both have influenced not only our society but also our way of working. Both are inextricably linked to each other. Increasingly, however, forces behind instrumental rationality have managed to disconnect the most important part of the *Enlightenment* project – critical rationality – from instrumental rationality. By the separation of rationality into instrumentalism and critique, proponents of instrumentalism have paid a disservice to *Enlightenment*. This way of thinking has also spread into many parts of human society and the world of work. It has profound impacts on the way we live, work, and above all, communicate. Only on the basis of the development of rationality – divided into critical rationality and instrumental rationality and its subsequent consequences – can the world of work be understood comprehensively.

5
Understanding Modern Relations at Work

While there are many *concepts* and *models* that seek to explain the world of work, there has also been a lack of comprehensive *theory* that allows a deeper understanding of work. Such an understanding must be linked to Enlightenment's idea of critical rationality. Although it is not specifically geared towards the world of work, a theory that is able to support the project of a critical understanding of the world of work can be found in critical theory. Central to such an idea for a *critical theory for work* are two major works:[221] *Knowledge and Human Interests* (1987) and *The Theory of Communicative Action* (1997). Both have constructed a relatively new normative foundation for critical theory. The theoretical understanding must be formulated comprehensively as an incomprehensible theory is basically a useless theory. While Habermas' first major work on *Knowledge and Human Interests* represents three knowledge creating interests that can be found in all scientific enterprises, *The Theory of Communicative Action* establishes theoretical foundations for communication. In *The Theory of Communicative Action* Habermas' ideas can be traced back to the development of earlier foundations. Original sources that supported the project of a critical understanding of communicative aspects of work have also come from the following sources:

Table 5.1   Intellectual Ideas Supportive of Communicative Action

Supportive Ideas
i)   Wittgenstein's, Austin's and Searle's philosophies of language.[222] These three see language, speech, and communication as essential to human existence.
ii) A second idea relates to the communicative aspects of work. It can be found in a hermeneutical tradition of Husserl and Gadamer.[223] Their philosophy of meaning created an understanding directed towards the question of *how* we understand things.
iii) A third influence has been Pierce's and Mead's philosophy of universal pragmatism and symbolic interactions that are directed towards how we understand the world around us using the language structures given to us since birth.[224]

The three supportive ideas outlined in Table 5.1 share one aspect of communication. There is a common human interest in understanding and even changing the world around us. This has created an interest in knowledge ever since the evolution of human society. Every human society has created knowledge and since Enlightenment human knowledge is seen as rational and scientific knowledge. It has adopted a much more scientific form that is one of the driving forces of modernity. The creation of new knowledge has always been linked to interest. Natural and social scientists have been driven by a certain interest that guided them into discovering new things, thus creating new knowledge. Overall, this interest can be divided into three core interests that drove scientific endeavour. Firstly, there is an interest in an empirical understanding directed towards *how* the world works. The second interest comes from an interpretation of what reality actually means. The third interest relates to the fundamental concern that is not only directed towards an understanding of the world but also seeks to change the world. Before discussing the issues of meaning and changing, the first issue to consider is our interest in an empirical understanding of our world.

An empirical-analytical understanding of the world of work

Essential to *Knowledge and Human Interests* (1987) are three knowledge-guiding or knowledge-constructive interests that humans have.[225] Humans have a desire to make forecasts and predictions and to control nature. This is expressed in the controlling and *technical* interest. The creation of *technical* knowledge occurred in communities of humans that needed to understand the world and create meaning of it. At a later stage, humans were interested in self-reflection leading to autonomy, empowerment and emancipation from the domination of nature and the dominating structures of society. Before humans reached this stage, an empirical understanding assisted human society to move forward.[226] The relatively high importance of the technical or empirical-analytical interest is very much expressed in its potential applications one of which is control. Human societies always needed control. From the hand mill, to the water mill, the steam mill, the electric mill, and to computerised production milling, it has been and still is important to have control over production, time, workers, input and output, and other issues related to the world of work.

Overwhelmingly, our understanding of the world of work – especially when seen as labour-management relationship – takes place within the empirical-analytical approach. Understanding and controlling this process is often guided by the existence of *pure scientific values and a passion for truth*.[227] The *pure scientific* idea tends to exclude the unsolvable dilemma that experiences are made *of* as well as *in* nature. We observe the world as we live in it. Constructed as situational non-determination or standpoint *un-bounded-ness* of an individual researcher, this view portrays knowledge as nature independent and objective. This view *emanates from the power-lessness to hold fast the insights gained into the objective distortion of truth.*[228] This view has produced some devastating consequences.

One of these consequences has been an almost classical misunderstanding by many labour-management researchers of *bias versus subjectivity.* Unfortunately, this has been formulated in a demand for *unbiased research* (Adams 1993:11). This seems to suggest that the field of labour-management has remained somewhat naive about its own prejudices. Extreme care is taken in individual case studies and large surveys to avoid *bias.* But microscopically little work has been done in labour-management studies to examine the bias of heavily over-used methods and concepts that appear to be unquestionably accepted as a whole. Critique is often only directed towards a *correct* application of methods and the relationship between the application of methods and the results gained. Once methods are deemed unbiased, results are admitted as proper, sound science, value free, objective and objectivism.[229]

Critical theory views positivism as hiding behind the veil of *objectivism.* It limits research to statements such as *a statement is held to be literary meaningful if and only if it is either analytical or empirical verifiable or if it can't be seen or measured, it is not meaningful to talk about* (Miller 2000:50). In such a *not-seen, not-measured and not-talked about* version, objectivism and empiricism

> violate the empirical, for in it speaks the mutilated, 'abstract' individual who experiences (and expresses) only that which is given to him (given in a literal sense), who has only the facts and not the factors, whose behaviour is one-dimensional and manipulated. By virtue of the factual repression, the experienced world is the result of a restricted experience, and the positivist cleaning of the mind brings the mind in line with the restricted existence.[230]

A *positivist cleaning of the mind* as outlined by Marcuse does not only come from a false idea of *not seen, not measured,* and above all *not talked about.* Sometimes it is not so much the issue *not talked about* but the way in which it is talked about as all scientific knowledge has to be communicated in one way or the other. Therefore, and this is to the disdain of some positivists, science and language are inextricably linked. In its communicative expression, *linguistic positivism* is all too often unable to see – or unwilling to talk about – anything beyond the linguistic form.[231] In other words, research is presented unaware of the power of language and the ability of communication to frame facts in a particular way. In the words of Adorno and Horkheimer (1944:23), *the blindness and dumbness of the data to which positivism reduces the world pass over into language itself, which restricts itself to recording those data.* Hence, recording data and establishing links between such data – often consciously and unconsciously transforming *correlations* into *causality* – becomes a prime activity of linguistic positivism. It pretends to represent facts as they are, without realising or recognising that this frames facts in a particular way by not reflecting on the science-language link. This unconscious or conscious positivist framing infiltrates not only language but also supports a reduction of communication to neat modelling under system theory imperatives.

This has extended to communication itself. Positivist communication studies operate inside the demands of system theory. The closed-up world of system theory allows the framing of science in a particular way that is conducive to many of the claims put forward by positivism. Consequently, scientific facts are constructed inside a socially constructed linguistic system of phonetics, grammatical, and lexical forms of language.[232] At the same time, important issues have been undervalued. These are outlined in Table 5.2:

Table 5.2 A Frame for Constructing Scientific Facts

No.	Framework
i)	the ideological factor in language,
ii)	the social history of language,[233]
iii)	the critical reflection of communication,
iv)	the socially constructed reality of communication,
v)	the political economy of communication, etc.

As outlined in Table 5.2, the standpoint-less idea of positivism is not supported by any of the above (i–v). Critical theory constitutes the opposite of positivism by not only reflecting on the points outlined above but also taking them into account when presenting scientific knowledge. Critical theory argues *all knowledge is 'perspectival' and flows from certain metaphysical, epistemological, and political commitments* (Agger 1998:179). It argues that truth cannot exist independent from the subject. Humans or subjects produce scientific truth as much as philosophical truth. These subjects or humans live in human societies and are part of it as much as their truth is part of it. As Brown (1998) has successfully shown researchers are not positioned *over and above the social totality* but a unit of it from which life cannot be detached. Inside this context, researchers need to be self-reflective (Habermas 1976a:131, 1997:122).

One attempt to be *over and above society* is seen in empirical-analytical research that seeks to establish *hypothetical-deductive* connections of law-like hypotheses. Here empirical content is used to control observations, experiments and models. Such knowledge attempts to justify the validity of exact knowledge by recourse to the source of knowledge. It is grounded in the objectivist illusion that observations can be expressed in basic statements relating facts in a purely and objective descriptive fashion.[234] In reality, however – and this applies above all to labour and management science – all non-natural sciences operate from a self-created interpretive framework. Therefore, they must give up the claim to produce objective or factual knowledge. As they present their knowledge constructed inside a self-created interpretive framework they can no longer assume to be objective. Rather than being dependent on objectivity, they are dependent on their own interpretive framework, a framework that is socially constructed.[235] Searle (1996:211) emphasises that *facts are not complex objects, nor are they linguistic entities; rather they are conditions, specifically, they are conditions in the world that satisfy the truth conditions expressed in statements.* Therefore, no research can be done in conditions where a researcher is disconnected from the conditions of society. Any researcher is always part of a scientific or research community. There is virtually no field of scientific endeavour that is excluded as almost all researchers and scientists belong to some sort of scientific community.[236] In the end, the acceptance or rejection of so-called scientific findings in the world of managerial studies and the like are made in accordance with a respective research community and not in respect to law-like rules disconnected from society and researchers. An established research community lays down the rules for findings to be accepted into their respected body of knowledge. Often this is decided purely on how newly discovered knowledge fits into the existing body of knowledge without challenging it too much. The idea is to advance but not to contradict the existing body of knowledge. More often than not, the production and admittance of new knowledge is dependent on the research community and nothing else.

For Habermas (1968:290), this version of knowledge is the *cognitive interest in technical control over objectified processes.* It is *organisational knowledge* insofar as it sets the labour power of researchers in motion to largely support an already existent body of knowledge. Therefore, new scientific knowledge is used to establish and expand the power of technical and *bureaucratic* control (Edwards 1979). The task of an established and well-regarded body of researchers in this process is to create knowledge in support of technical and bureaucratic control. To a large extent the creation of knowledge serves not only the scientific community inside which it is created, interpreted, discussed, and allowed access to publishing outlets, it also serves the societal system in which it is created. Consequently, all too often research reflects what Habermas (1976a:141) has called *auxiliary science.* It supports and stabilises the rational administration of science and society. It neglects any critical examination of the conjunction between the three key elements shown in Table 5.3:

Table 5.3   Three Constitutive Elements for a Critical Examination

No.	Key elements
i)	system stabilising conditioning that has conditioned a body of researchers to serve without realising it is serving;
ii)	servants of steering systems reduce science to technical control systems; and
iii)	controlled action that serves the prevailing conditions of society inside a scientific system that controls social action as demanded from external sources.

These three conjunctions (Table 5.3) have issued strong pressures on positivist science ever since positivism came to light in the wake of Enlightenment. Those who are unconscious of the real task of positivism are those who live in danger of being no more than an *auxiliary science* to industrial capitalism. Inside the vision of a *positivist auxiliary science,* science has proven over and over again that it is incapable of delivering the liberal promises set forward by Enlightenment. Developments since the industrial revolution have proven that natural science, technology, technical rationality, and technical knowledge do not guarantee the *material* liberation they are supposed to bring about.[237] All too often such research is subsumed to a support function for purely technical recommendations that support such a process.

Any research that restricts itself to empirical-analytical research would only be in a position to *examine the self-preservation and self-destruction of social systems in the sphere of pragmatically successful adjustment processes* (Habermas 1976b:222). Barbash (1997:19) has located work relations precisely here when he writes *problem-solving necessarily puts a high premium on pragmatism* which he finds *more serviceable than high-theory*. The same can be found when pragmatic policy-oriented and empirical research is emphasised. In order to avoid any critical and reflective approach to science, they are advocates of an applied-scientific enterprise directed towards technical usefulness. The world of work is constructed inside a framework of applied technical rationality.

A brief examination of empirical-analytical positivism has shown several shortcomings. Its critique has resulted in an understanding that this version of positivist science tends to frame the world of work inside a closed system of technical rationality. A critique of this view has shown that it is unaware or wilfully or skilfully rejects or avoids any reflection of the role of science in society and how science depends on a socially constructed reality that is communicated inside a research community. This has narrowed the scientific endeavour to an empirical-analytical problem-solving case. Narrowing scientific knowledge to problem-solving has been only one of several troubles of the empirical-analytical interest. A second problem of empirical analysis has been the creation of an almost unlimited number of facts. The endless accumulation and collection of an overwhelming number of facts has a rather limiting effect. It restricts any meaningful understanding of these facts. In contrast to an empirical-analytical interest, the historical-hermeneutical interest seeks to solve this.

A historical-hermeneutical understanding of the world of work

In sharp contrast to empirical-analytical research, *historical-hermeneutical science* is the science of interpretation with an interest in an understanding of human expressions.[238] It is an important philosophical outgrowth of literary theory beginning with bible studies (Gadamer 1974, 1976). Historical-hermeneutics seeks access to *facts* by understanding their meaning. Scientific understanding comes from the interpretation of facts and not from observations. Accordingly, the term *hermeneutics* has a relationship to *Hermes*, the messenger God of the Greeks.[239] In order to deliver the messages of the Gods, Hermes had to be conversant in their language as well as the language of the mortals for whom the messages were intended. These two parts of Hermes' tasks are shown in Table 5.4:

Table 5.4   The Two Communicative Tasks of Hermes

No.	The Two Essential Tasks for Hermes in Constructing Meaning
i)	He had to understand and translate for himself what the Gods wanted to convey to the world; and
ii)	He had to translate and articulate his message to mortals

Table 5.4 shows the original model of constructing meaning as developed in ancient Greece. This is clearly a model of communication that looks familiar to us in the transmission of information from one domain to another. In communicative terms, Hermes was simply carrying a message from the Gods (senders) to the mortals (receivers).

But the problem was not so much a simple sender-receiver problem. His problem as well as that of hermeneutics in general is not concerned with what happens in the *minds* of the Gods or the *minds* of the mortals. Instead it seeks to address *the role of Hermes* and his ability to understand a discourse from one domain (the Gods) and articulate the understanding to a very different domain (that of the mortals). Hermes represents the *labour* and the *effort* required to read and understand text produced in one place and time and to articulate its meaning in a different place and time. Such creation of meaning is always constructed somewhat differently depending on the context in which it is created. This is not purely a hermeneutic problem. The translation of scientific facts that were gained from research into the domain of everyday language or even into the domain of a scientific community also exists in the minds of the purely empirical and positivist researchers.

Even positivist thinking has to attach contexts to *facts* as meaning could otherwise not be established. One of the most crucial dilemmas for positivists lies in this fact-context-meaning predicament. Challenging for positivist claims such as *facts-speak-for-themselves* is not only Einstein's (1949:11) dictum that *thinking is necessary in order to understand the empirically given* but also that any contextual thinking, interpretation, sense-making or hermeneutical study must also take ideology critique very seriously because its own enterprise is at stake in its claim.[240] Consequently, facts are neither able to speak *for* themselves nor are they objective or independent of us. Despite all the claims by positivists, they are a social construction belonging into the sphere of '*We*' and not of '*I*' as they are established communicatively. Most simply, the positivist idea of *facts-speak-for-themselves* is only possible when humans speak *about* or *of* them. Only human forms of communication turn a thing into a fact. They hardly do it themselves. Facts are not able to speak. They cannot communicate or perform speech acts. Only humans can do this. But an understanding of facts is not simply a flow from one mind to another. To understand facts we must add our mental process to what is given to us communicatively. It is always a dialogue between us and facts as only human intervention can create, construct, and interpret facts. In short, our factual reality is socially created.

In *The Construction of Social Reality* (Searle 1996) we can find two kinds of *facts* that are relevant to an understanding of the world of work. Searle (1996:2) sees them as shown in Table 5.5:

Table 5.5   Searle's Two Versions of Facts

No.	Two Kinds of Facts
i)	'institutional' facts [that] are so called because they require human institutions for their existence [and]
ii)	'brute' facts [that] require no human institutions for their existence.

The distinction between these two kinds of facts is that there are things that exist independently of humans and things that only exist because of humans. One might also think of this distinction as shown in Table 5.6 (Searle 1996:61):

Table 5.6   Facts, Language and Thought

No.	Versions of Facts and Thoughts
i)	language-dependent facts and
ii)	language-independent facts that require no linguistic element for its existence or as
iii)	language-dependent thoughts or as
iv)	language-independent thoughts.

Language-dependent facts or thoughts construct social reality as social facts. This is not an *I*-activity but a *we*-activity. Individuals do not create social facts as these are created by what Searle (1996:27) calls *collective intentionality* using a system of constitutive rules. One of Searle's favourite examples of a social fact is money. He writes (1996:32), *if everybody stops believing it is money, it ceases to function as money, and eventually ceases to be money.*

Unlike money, mountains are an example for brute facts. Even if everybody stops believing them to be mountains, they are still mountains.[241] Unlike mountains, social facts such as *institutional facts* – i.e. management, work, teamwork, etc. – need us to create them. But institutional facts have another distinctiveness attached to them. They are often created when a specific function is attached to them. The institutional version of social facts is often created via a specific process of declaration. For example, a chairperson is appointed, or established through an agreement between management and labour, or officially declared to be in operation. By doing so a social fact becomes an institutional fact. The position of a chairperson or an agreement has become an institution. After such institution-creating acts, these newly established social-institutional *facts* demand interpretations in order to understand them.

The interpretation of labour-management arrangements or other texts such as collective agreements, unions' rulebooks, HR policies, industrial or labour relations issues, committee minutes, etc. enables us to understand them. However, it also does something else. By establishing *facts* through interpretation we use certain standards that, in themselves, constitute yet another set of socially created facts.[242] In short, original texts of agreements, etc. are socially constructed facts while the standards we use to understand and interpret them are a second set of social facts, and finally, the results of our interpretation are a third set. In sum, hermeneutical interpretations and understandings are always directed towards the *production* of a text and the *reception* of a text.[243] In both, knowledge is mediated through language as a necessary pre-understanding that derives from the researcher's initial situation. Every expression and action occurs necessarily as part of a context or situation as a whole. Consequently such knowledge is formed inside a communicative consensus on an established scientific framework established by a research community.[244] In sum, hermeneutics is not satisfied with the production of *facts*, but with the understanding of their meaning. In other words, the hypothetical-deductive system of the empirical-analytical model is replaced by the hermeneutic explication of meaning. This is linked to the core interest of hermeneutics. This interest is guided by the possibility that interpretations and understanding can support *the orientation of action within common traditions* (Habermas 1968:292). One of the clearest expressions of an application of hermeneutics that supports action inside common traditions is the subject of history and historical understanding.[245] In Habermas' view history is not *story-telling* but *the ongoing struggle of humanity to free itself from the dehumanising consequences of its relentless drive to perfect the production forces* (Shalin 1992:243). Such an interpretive viewpoint often comes from reflections of a past state of affairs transported into modernity and used as a critique on modernity, the modern production process, and the world of work.[246] The idea behind this is to save or record forms of working lives in all their complexities and creativities before they are lost to modernity and instrumental rationality, new forms of domination, asymmetric work relations, and distorted forms of communication.[247] Such hermeneutical approach directed towards the understanding of past work regimes is not designed to purely uncover new historical facts and present them inside an historical story. It is, as Habermas (1968) emphasised, directed towards an emancipatory interest.

A critical-emancipatory understanding of the world of work

In contrast to empirical-analytical and historical-hermeneutical science, critical-emancipatory science goes beyond both. The critical-emancipatory interest includes a critique on the ideological content of all research. It strongly rejects the idea that research can be narrowed to questions of methods. It does not see methodology as *the application of statistical techniques* or pure technical devices.[248] Critical-emancipatory science criticises such *techniques* as pure rituals in order to legitimise a certain form of knowledge. A critical interest seeks to reveal illegitimate power relations and their obscured and suppressed conditions.[249] Critical-emancipatory research not only includes the use of empirical tools, it also uses non-empirical methods such as self-reflections. The need for self-reflection is determined by an emancipatory interest founded in autonomy and responsibility (*Mündigkeit*). It originates in the core demand of Enlightenment, to be free from all forms of domination. Habermas (1976b:222) has summed this up as:

> under the conditions of reproduction of an industrial society, individuals who only possessed technically utilisable knowledge, and who were no longer in a position to expect a rational enlightenment of themselves nor of the aims behind their action would loose their identity.

In other words, the interest of critical-emancipatory science is directed towards any analysis that frees consciousness from its dependence on hypostatised powers and from its neutral-scientific associations (Adorno 1976:113). Therefore, a neutral understanding of work is impossible because any researcher must always choose either to present a condition that is empirically given as self-evident (*what is*), or to contrast it with a potential state of affairs (*what ought to be*), in Kantian terms, those conditions that could also have been realised. Finally, the link between knowledge and interest challenges empirical-analytical and historical-hermeneutic science because it eliminates the power of objectivism, *the illusion of pure theory*, value-neutrality, value-nihilism, and pure *facts* by exposing their ideological content through critical reflections on the connection of knowledge and interest.[250] While looking at research, theory, methods, etc. from the viewpoint of interests, the link between interest and knowledge itself is of interest. *The unity of knowledge and interest proves itself in a dialectic that takes the historical traces of suppressed dialogue and reconstructs what has been suppressed* (Habermas 1968:283). In short, it directs scientific knowledge towards an expansion of the domain of freedom, liberation, and emancipation (Marcuse 1969). Sociological knowledge of the world of work is always self-critical and self-reflective. Criticism can only be seen as dialectic of knowledge and interest as a reflective method of research and theory (Adorno 1976:111). Following Adorno, Habermas sees the task of Critical Theory as (1997a:375):

> The theory is also critical of social-scientific approaches that are incapable of deciphering the paradoxes of societal rationalisation because they make complex social systems their object only from one or another abstract point of view, without accounting for the historical constitution of their object domain (in the sense of reflexive sociology). Critical social theory does not relate to establishing lines of research as a competitor, starting from its concept of the rise of modern societies, it attempts to explain the specific limitations and relative rights of those approaches.

Critical theory's task is concerned with power as it operates in the context of social relations among individuals and groups to explain the social and communicative process through which conditions of hegemony arise. Hegemony always involves a struggle over communicatively established meanings and the process by which social reality is formed. Hegemony is a condition describing a *process of a struggle* rather than an existing state. Critical Theory looks at values and interests that underlie knowledge claims as there cannot be a claim of knowledge as being *value-free* (Kant 1781) but rests upon a set of assumptions that are frequently hidden, sometimes even to the researcher. Critical theory research directed towards communication seeks to highlight these hidden assumptions via an analysis that includes deep-seated and underlying value systems that drive and guide certain research while neglecting other interests. Research results are not to be found in the application of specific tools and methods but in open and domination-free – rather than value-free – discourses about research and research results. The aim of critical theory is to move beyond walls constructed of empiricism by moving from technical rationality towards communicative rationality where critical reflections on research lead to consensus formation about research results. For research on the world of work, the task of critical theory is to support the creation of a working environment that is free from all forms of domination. This is to be established in a way that allows all participants to contribute equally to production which is directed towards human needs.[251] Unlike traditional, orthodox, or unreconstructed Marxist theory, critical theory is not anti-management per se. It critically analyses management in its present forms of established domination. It carries strong connotations of resistance but also of emancipation.

A critical investigation into the world of work

The most fundamental difference between research conducted under traditional and research conducted under critical theory lies in their theoretical approaches. All too often, research into management, labour, and the world of work has firmly remained inside *traditional theory* with a strong emphasis on empirical findings.[252] Such research has not advanced much beyond the two domineering paradigms covering today's understanding of the world of work. These paradigms are constructed inside the traditional framework of *agency versus structure*.[253] Ever since the creation of the 2-by-2 *paradigms* for agency and structure, studies on the world of work have tended to reside in them. They guard their borders and narrow theory development well inside these socially constructed walls. Paradigm consensus is conducted in all fields of knowledge. It is especially prevalent in management studies, organisational studies, organisational communication, and labour relations all of which rely heavily on borders secured through communicatively established paradigm consensus. The insecurity of theses fields – sometimes expressed in: *are we a field or discipline* debate – has led to an overemphasis on domineering paradigms. This has restricted theory or concept development. As a result, knowledge is carved up, dissected, dismembered, and disconnected from human subjectivity and societal conditions. Knowledge is neatly categorised, ordered, shelved and boxed-in, and mummified by disciplinary gatekeepers called journal editors, keynote speakers and the like.[254] In contrast, critical theory always seeks to include the wider society as a subject. Neither research, knowledge creation, theory, concepts, models, etc. nor society happen at different levels. Research, knowledge, society, and the world of work cannot be *levelled out*. Paradigm consensus is in reality no more than an artificial and socially constructed separation of things that belong together as they exist in a dialectical relationship. This separation is no longer acceptable even though it remains a constant feature of present research into the world of work. This is most prevalent in management research. Managerially guided research often occurs at different levels or inside compartmentalised boxes such as HRM, HRD, PRP, OB, OT, OS, IR, ER, OP, IT, OHS, MS, CMS, OC.[255] All of these – and more – are nothing more than socially created – and accepted – levels that differentiate the world of work into orderly boxes.[256]

Critical theory views society as a whole. Hence a critical research object views the world of work as part of a wider society. Critical theory always demands the avoidance of the creation of artificial divisional boxes as well as any disconnection between theory and society. It issues a strong demand for dialectics. Whatever research might be conducted, it always needs to be linked to a theory of society (Habermas 1997:5). Being part of a society as well as being created inside this society, critical theory sees research on the world of work as being focused on the relations of production and those institutions and social mechanisms that *specify in what way labour can be combined with the available means of production* (Habermas 1975:290). In short, critical theory rejects any notion of research niches either as a special field that discusses work or within work-related studies.[257] It advocates the opposite. Critical theory criticises that research is often grant-driven and opportunistically directed towards *usefulness* to help ironing out problems without conceptualising major structural flaws, such as capitalism, racism, domination, patriarchy, and sexism.[258] An extreme version of *useful* research can be found in parts of labour economics where research often *fulfils the original positivist vision of knowledge as mathematics, which is as old as the Enlightenment* (Agger 1998:157). In this form, research linked to labour economics is measured in numbers and strongly tends to support a positivist view. Inside the positivist framework of problem-solving and ironing-out, scientific knowledge on the world of work has also been created at universities. It has often been reduced to a productive agency for the creation and dissemination of technical and administrative systems. Today, almost any scientific knowledge of the world of work is well-integrated into an occupational system supportive of advanced capitalism. Hence, many forms of critical argumentation have been separated-off and compartmentalised into critical theoretical discourse. It is reduced to a side arm of mainstream teachings. Meanwhile positivist and useful scientific knowledge on the world of work is assigned to the *value-neutral* scientific enterprise.[259]

Under the guise of value-neutrality that is in reality no more than value-rejection or value-*nihilism*, practical issues are debated inside the limitations of a business, managerial, political, or legal sphere. At the same time aesthetic criticism is assigned to the artistic and literary enterprise. By rejecting it, social relations at work are seen as an extension of production procedures governed by technical and instrumental means. Academic fields studying such social relations at work become restricted to a means-ends analysis of work systems. Theoretical models on the world of work become models of production designed to solve problems in a practical way. The whole thrust is directed towards the design of *methods of better management, safer planning, greater efficiency, closer calculation. The analysis, via correction and improvement, terminates in affirmation; empiricism proves itself as positive thinking* (Marcuse 1966:175). Hence, understanding the world of work very rarely escapes its assigned sphere and when it does it does so in the form of problem-solving policy advice directed towards *the problem of order*. In sum, the functional role of any analysis of work is to support an institutionalisation that negates class conflict in favour of technocratic solutions.[260] This is most obvious in the area where classes meet, the area of collective bargaining. The institutionalisation of collective bargaining can no longer be analysed as a sphere for class conflict. The technocratic orientation of collective bargaining has brought about the pacification of the class conflict inside the social welfare state. Here, wage labourers' compensation is solved inside a framework that sees them simply as an element with a structurally weaker position in the market. Consequently, collective bargaining under conditions of the welfare state has been successfully reduced to adjustment problems of distributive patterns governed by institutions and technical rationality.

Many traditional studies on collective bargaining have failed to take into account that class conflict expressed via bargaining occurs under conditions of an accumulative process driven by capitalists that are protected by state interventions.[261] If not eliminated as individual bargaining altogether, collective bargaining has been reduced to one of many functions in a well-functioning system of advanced capitalism. Since the event of advanced capitalism this has been synchronised with the growth of the interventionist welfare state. The unequal distribution of material rewards can no longer be traced back to class position in any unqualified way. Hence, studies on collective bargaining are reduced to a functional additive to the four core domains that govern the existing system of relations: economy, state, private, and public. The collective or individual worker is constructed inside economic means-ends. A worker is either a state-supportive taxpayer, or a private consumer, or a participant in a democratic and public process. Such a worker is also constructed as part of a managerially organised workplace, an office, or a corporation. Unlike many present ideas of constructing workers as associates – in modern *Newspeak* terms – inside the *economy-state-private-public* framework workers also appear as a non-historical entity. Even the very idea of workers and collective bargaining started with the historical rise of the factory. In other words, to understand today's role of labour, one needs to understand the history of the factory. In short, the domination of labour in the modern production process has a history. Without a thorough understanding of this history, a comprehensive understanding of work is not possible.

The historical process of domination of labour can be divided into three periods. Originally, the rise of the *factory system* was accompanied by a *proletarianisation* of labour.[262] The history of the factory system is linked to the *formal subordination of labour*. This continued with a period of *labour homogenisation* that saw mass labour opposed by large corporations. Between the 1930s and the 1950s the structure of labour moved into *labour segmentation* when labour lost many of its homogeneous features very much in the same way it had lost its proletarian features earlier (Shenhav 1999:23). While employees have lost their *proletarian* features with the continuous rise in living standards, conflicts over distribution have also lost explosive power.[263] Aided through traditional studies into the world of work, class conflict as expressed via collective bargaining has become an increasingly minor aspect of the technical problem-solving apparatus.

Traditional work-studies have tended to support the problem-solving paradigm in which the role of labour is reduced to a problem to be solved. These studies delivered the technical expertise necessary for a normative regulation in a very specific area of knowledge. This specific area has been labelled industrial relations, employment relations, or industrial sociology.[264] The application of system-conforming knowledge can be further observed in the increasing number of IR, HRM, and ER departments and degrees leading to qualifications functionally related to managerial demands. This occurred concurrently with the rise of the managerial class. Whyte (1961:8) once noted that *managers are the dominant members of our society…they talk to each other [innocently] over the front lawns of their suburban* homes. Ever since the firm establishment of managers, not only on the suburban lawns as noted by Whyte (1961) but also and foremost at work, the concept of the manager has come a long way. Today, the idea of managers is well-established, almost as self-evident as the idea of *managerialism.* Both dominate not only Whyte's front lawns but also today's educational systems. Achievements in the educational system of function-science is expressed in the *master* degree of the Master of Business Administration (MBA) or equivalent Master of Operations Management, Master of Human Resource Management, Master of Accounting, Master of Marketing, and so on and on and on. Today's master, however, no longer reflects philosophical, personal or intellectual interests but is an indication for a technical competency.[265] Today, having obtained a master's degree means no more than being a certified *master* of a highly structured pre-set subject matter. All too often they can master no more than that as the volume of knowledge to be mastered is presented not in books but in the modern idea of the *textbook.*[266] To become a *master* these textbooks have to be memorised rather than understood.

Harding (2003:210) concludes in his examination of management textbooks, the textbook offers its readers a pattern. More than understanding the world of work, future managers can construct themselves. To do so, a pattern is created based on a so-called *original* manager who most mysteriously has no origin because the history of management is avoided as it holds too many unwanted truths. In such cleansed history, managers are presented as functional. Textbook readers are drawn in through the seductive creation, layout, and presentation of the text. This enables them to construct a managerial self that involves portraying themselves as managers. It maintains the visual façade of management. Readers are able to control themselves strictly to prevent the construction slipping, thus becoming the pastiche of the modern manager. Once *educated*, or better, *conditioned* in such a way, the modern manager is a functionally educated master who can master the demands of the system without the need for critical reflection. The invention of the *textbook* is most crucial as it separates critical and reflective knowledge from functional knowledge by masking controversial issues.[267] Driven by academic markets such textbooks appeal to the broadest, often lowest but always non-conflicting and neutral readership presenting the so-called dominant view of a subject. More than the market for original books with original ideas, the textbook market is the clearest expression of a truly *unfree* press because its function is to sell functional texts for business. A truly free and real book presents ideas while textbooks present marketable patterns solely directed towards a market. What goes into such texts is what sells – no more, no less. Academic freedom is rendered ineffective in the face of bestsellers on the textbook market.

The standardised textbook-consumer is guided through standardised and above all sellable textbooks through easy-to-read descriptions, handy hints, convenient models, little boxes, useable case studies, and stories creating a theory-free pre-modelled reading environment. They display a disowning and denigration of science and particularly social science academically detached from human and social science faculties, securely positioned in business schools. The precedence of non-science over science is manifested in a particular flavouring that favours anecdotes, homilies, personalised encounters, user-friendly hypothetical examples, and un-referenced and partly invented quotes from so-called real managers with real experiences from the real world.[268] All of them tend to be presented as simple facts.

Rather than presenting science or scientific theory such textbooks often claim to be scientific by heavy use of scientific rhetoric.[269] Ideas and stories are cloaked in scientific facts while at the same time hiding the construction of these facts. Which *factors* construct these *facts* remains in the hidden world behind easy graphs, tables and a *quasi-scientific language* that is derived from natural science rather than social science.[270] The complexity of social affairs is reduced to manageable facts that are presented as *objective* masking managerial ideology that underlies these *objective* facts.[271] Many mainstream text-*books* (!) are simply mediocre publications as they tend to exclude almost any hint of a critical or alternative view. If presented at all critical views are reduced and clearly marked as alternative, controversial, or radical views. They are placed in distant corners of textbooks, telling the reader or better the consumer of textbooks: *one better stick to the mainstream!* The mainstream is constructed and presented so that is can easily be accessed, memorised, and reproduced. Learning objects are clearly identified in bold characters using boxes, internal summaries, leading questions, etc. and providing an efficient conditioning for functional students. Increasingly, functionally conditioned students are produced at university levels as the development of capitalism had an increasing demand for *scientific knowledge* when it moved from *routine production services* to *in-person services* and eventually to *symbolic-analytical services* (Reich 1992; cf. Kerr et al. 1960). Science, technology and universities are intimately bound up with industrial capitalism. Their role as a productive force of the system is ever increasing. Today's universities maintain support functions via science and scientists. Those who tend to perform functionally and show system conformity are recruited. In return, they tend to re-recruit system conformists useful in maintaining the state-supported capital-university system.[272]

Like a motorcar, a piece of toast, or a house, universities and university education were assigned a function. Like a commodity university education provides the functional support mechanism for capitalism. This was not its original function as historically, universities used to be places for thinking, reflection, critique, humanity and unhindered science. This is no longer the case. Today's universities are incorporated into the productive system. They are part of a functioning system. They have a specific function attached to them. As Searle (1996:14) emphasised, *functions are never intrinsic to the physics of any phenomenon but are assigned from outside by conscious observers and users. Functions, in short, are never intrinsic but are always observer relative.* Originally, the idea of universities and university education had been the advancement of knowledge directed towards the improvement of society. Today other functions are assigned by outside observers such as business associations or lobby groups, in short the *business community*.[273] When someone says *the function of a university is…*, such function is assigned or increasingly re-assigned to serve a specific purpose. The function assignment often results in a determination of what a university is which is in fact quite remote from the original humanist idea of a university or university education. Increasingly our understanding of university education is determined from the outside.

As the influx of external research funding increases, universities and research programmes become more open to manipulation. Such an externally driven re-assignment of university research is often directed towards pleasing the grant-givers.[274] But the influx of external research grants has far more implications than just redefining universities. With it managerialism enters research and universities. The way research is conducted is organised and driven by managerial concepts culminating in managerial ideas such as cost-benefit analysis, transaction costs, and means-ends. In short, while reducing research to instrumentalism via a significant increase in so-called *applied research*, it also takes away the humanist aspect of research.[275] Research is less and less geared towards the greater good but towards pleasing grant-givers inside a means-ends framework.[276]

This has not only implications for research itself but also for the internal structure of universities. Research into the world of work becomes complicit in system-maintenance as it establishes hierarchical and bureaucratic research organisations which structure research in the image of managerialism. Power is closely held at the top acting against participation in policy formulation and decision-making at all lower levels. Research becomes hierarchical while scientific colleagues become competitors. The greater the mastery of bureaucratic system-maintenance over research funding and conduct, the less room is left for questions of meaning and value. The more organisational and instrumental reasoning structures the internal affairs of universities, the narrower the scope becomes for critical choices. The further business interest extends its bureaucratic procedures into research, the heavier its domination over the critical individual.

Any alternative ways in organising academic discourse including the institutionalisation of science is put aside in favour of managerialism. Today, academic discourse and science are almost exclusively organised in a dependency on bureaucratic structures. Research is arrested in hierarchy. In sum, all of this systematically decreases the likelihood of discovering communication practices that might produce critical-emancipatory alternatives. Rather than being directed towards human betterment, emancipation, and Enlightenment, research takes on the face of being standpoint-less – and perhaps pointless. It is value-neutral and objective.[277] Any provider of external research funding wholeheartedly supports value-neutral and objective science. This assures a masquerading of political non-neutrality. What follows is beyond any doubt the reduction of research to the managerial ideology of technological rationality. The chief interest of functionalist contributions to research positions, programmes and decisions of research is to solve system problems. Relatively unnoticed and eclipsed by managerial ideology, meaningful engagement shifts from critical rationality to system supportive rationality.[278] True autonomy in research is relentlessly weakened. Domains of research activities emerge that are no longer integrated through mechanisms of mutual, communicative, and non-distorted understanding among researchers. Consequently, the charade of value-neutral techniques is a step towards a *dehumanised society* (Bauman 1989). It weakens any traditional resistance of universities against the two most commanding steering media in our society, money and power. As much as capitalist domination establishes itself in every corner of society it does so in science, research, and universities. Universities and research have lost not only their autonomy against these steering media but also their ability to develop critical theories (Disco 1979:177–178).

Once research is transferred from critical rationality into instrumental rationality, functionally related system demands take over. Theory and even more so critical theory are seen as obsolete. Notwithstanding the development of several models and concepts, instrumental research into the world of work has not attained the level of a theory. In spite of a few notable attempts to write a *theory* for the world of work, most attempts have ended up in – what Giddens (1979:246) has termed – *forms of cookery book knowledge*. Here, one can simply choose or tick ☑: a) ☐ a theory, or b) ☐ two or more theories, or c) ☐ all of the above, or finally ☐ no theory at all (Adams 1993:12). Trapped inside an instrumental problem-solving paradigm, none of these attempts has ever developed any comprehensive – nor critical – theory for the world of work. Even if one sees theory development as a never ending and never final but always moving process, past and present scholars engaged in research into the world of work have on the whole stayed clear of such development. Consequently, our understanding of the world of work remains significantly below the level of theory. It is trapped in the instrumentalism of concepts, ideas, models, or simple arguments.

Despite the lack of any theoretical understanding of the world of work, one can still identify three core theories that allow a deeper understanding. These are, in short, meta-theory, empirical theory, and normative theory (Morrow 1994:41). The first is linked to epistemology, the philosophy that is concerned with theories of knowledge, theories of argumentation or the criteria for determining whether a theory is scientific. Most present *theories* of or for the world of work are far removed from such meta-theories. Most of our present understanding of the world of work is generated from within a field of knowledge that can be viewed as firmly locked inside so-called *empirical theories*. These carefully exclude almost all critical and philosophical reflections. A critical understanding of the world of work is directed towards the exact opposite. It locates critique and communicative action within a framework that builds cooperative bridges rather than segregations. However, disciplinary segregation has been almost self-evident as our understanding of the world of work has been neatly separated into, at least, two faculties. One is the domain of labour studies and the other the domain of management studies. This is the prevailing mode of our divided understanding of the world of work throughout most of the existing empirical research into the field. Knowledge creation for either labour or management via positivism can be seen as being part of empirical theories, because it involves a rather descriptive and analytical language through which social phenomena of *what is* are interpreted and explained. Typically, many labour-management studies endeavour a functional-systems analysis where variables are isolated and hypothetical relationships posited. This establishes the hidden values of managerialism that are taken as a given end. Inside the hidden-value framework of managerialism norms, roles, processes, and institutions are viewed either as functional or as dysfunctional.[279]

However, and somewhat contradictory to the concealed and narrow but value-adding view of functionality, theories for the world of work – in order to end all segregations into partitioned faculties – need to establish an intensive *relationship* to faculties that have the non-work-related world as their core interest. So far our understanding of the world of work tends to focus only on relationships inside a self-constructed faculty. No longer should our understanding of the world of work be restricted to relatively closed-off domains of either labour studies or management studies. The present dichotomist structure comes close to structuralism because it relates to a philosophical view of the reality that sees social relations as functional and structural rather than substantial. Consequently, structuralism has tended to colonise those faculties engaged in an understanding of the world of work. To a large extent, our understanding of work is shaped in terms of functional model building used to construct our understanding. These functional models explain relationships by isolating the experience of actors from their historical and social content. However, both are unconsciously used as constitutive elements that build such models.[280]

Functional model building allows research to portray an understanding of the world of work expressed inside a linguistic frame of objectivism, value-neutrality, and *stand-point-free-ness*.[281] Many authors who write about the world of work do not fail to mention issues such as the *standpoint* of the researcher, *positivism, post-modernism, or language*. However, a comprehensive or substantial discussion of these, at times, hotly debated issues in contemporary social science is largely absent. The vast majority of research into the world of work is conducted via linguistic tools, such as questionnaires, surveys, interviews, or other qualitative methods. However, the issue of communication, language, and language use remains absent when research into the world of work is concerned. Communication and language move into the background even more as *quantitative* rather than more *qualitative* forms of research such as language-based methods move to the front. Viewing the world of work in terms of functionality allows a statistical analysis of numbers supporting an orientation towards quantitative methods such as large surveys and questionnaires. These are often portrayed as particularly useful because many journals are especially likely to publish quantitative articles (Agger 1998). The presentation of collected data introduced by a literature survey (usually called *theory*!) has been labelled *journal science*.[282] In order to cater for the prevailing version of research output – *journal science* – research questions, research data, research discussion, and conclusions are linguistically framed in correspondence to the managerial perspective. Objective findings are formulated and reformulated and eventually presented in managerial language. Almost all academic journals have adopted this approach. It is part of those journals that have received the highly regarded label of *established, reputable, being an authority in the field, or having a good reputation*.[283]

Research trapped in *journal science* is often no more than a simple application of empirical-analytical science with the occasional excursion into hermeneutics. This occurs without any discussion, reflection or self-awareness of contemporary social science terminologies and methodologies. The complete absence of any inclusion of a critical understanding in this context is not surprising. In short, most research, methodology and understanding of the world of work can be summed up in the words by one of Great Britain's most recognised experts, Lord Bill McCarthy (2000): *I don't read high theory.*[284]

In conclusion, while our traditional understanding of the world of work seems to be obsessed with the avoidance of any theory, critical theory seeks the exact opposite. Consequently, any understanding that uses critical theory would include a significant theoretical content. Such an understanding would be supported by a hermeneutical and critical-emancipatory inquest into the world of work. Quite often the limited knowledge gained from studies conducted inside the empirical-analytical paradigm is highly restrictive. Rather than opening a wider understanding of the world of work it prevents any fruitful comprehension of communicative aspects. Therefore, a comprehensive understanding into the communicative aspects of the world of work needs the application of hermeneutical, communicative, critical, and emancipatory theories. The application of these enables a full understanding of the communicative element in the labour and management relationship that dominates the present world of work.

6
The Management of Labour at Work

Management and labour at work are in a somewhat difficult relationship as both have divergent interests and perspectives on what work actually is. Traditionally, the issue of work has been observed from at least two different viewpoints that reflect these interests. One view is enshrined in the field of labour studies, the other in management studies. At the overlapping point, the field of industrial relations research has traditionally sought to cover both views. Most of labour, management, or industrial relations studies are conducted within the positivist division between facts and values, the artificial separation between objectivity and subjectivity, theory and method, theory and practice, etc. A view that seeks to overcome these divisions calls for a new approach in which attitudes of domination, false social partnerships, and structural inequalities are replaced by a knowledge interest directed towards emancipation. Such a critical direction admits openly to a standpoint that includes an ethical and political interest. From this perspective, work is seen as an advancement of critique on domination thus fostering resistance. A critical understanding of management and work goes beyond social action that has been reduced to a scuffle *for* and the exercise *of* legitimate power at work. It recognises scientific consciousness as political consciousness and the scientific enterprise as a political enterprise.[285]

A critical understanding of management and work is forward-looking, dialectical, and utopian as it seeks the betterment of the human condition. It concentrates its analytical power on a critique of *what is* leading towards *what ought to be*. It is, however, not about creating blueprints for social engineering. A critical understanding of management and work favours theory development that is systematic and speculative. It is not satisfied with research driven by *busy empiricism* based on methodology and data-collection. Any investigation into a more critical understanding of management and work must be designed to go well beyond of simply '*what is*'. It can never stop at presenting merely socially constructed *facts*. A critical understanding of management and work does not eliminate reality-transcending thinking that goes beyond our present conditions. An exclusion of ideas that go beyond the present state of affairs would turn *men* into *things*. It locks thinking into the *Zeitgeist*. Human consciousness becomes a prisoner of the spirit of our time. Therefore, a critical understanding of management and work has to go beyond a mere *what is* and into *what ought to be*. Such an understanding needs to address the selective pattern of capitalist modernisation that has been so important to management and work arrangements. This means *social scientists are obliged to choose between repressive and emancipatory paradigms*.[286] A critical understanding of management and work can be summed up as building institutions of freedom that project communicatively structured areas in the area of work against the reifying dynamics of the economic system and system integrative forces via administration. A critical understanding of management and work depends on self-reflection to overcome suppressed forms of domination. It is directed towards emancipatory social science based on a critique of ideology joining epistemological and political questions. A critical understanding of management and work rejects the *depoliticalisation* of the elitist control project by technical or managerial intentions.[287] Essentially, three core areas of such an understanding of management and work are identified in Table 6.1:

Table 6.1   Understanding Management and Work

No.	Three Versions of Understanding
i)	a critical explanation of distorted and pathological forms of communication,[288]
ii)	the application of communicative action to the realm of management and labour, and
iii)	studies towards possibilities for social action based on communicatively established understanding that relies on the concept of ideal speech.

In order to expand on these three elements, a communicative understanding of management and work is essential. However it needs to locate communication inside present managerial ideologies such as deregulation, decentralisation, and the *free-market* myth.[289] All of them seem to have superseded *democracy* via the mystifying version of managerialism that pretends to master the productive domain as well as the public, propaganda, and politics domains.[290] The power of managerialism has enshrined the managerial ideology of free-market exchanges. It reproduces the hierarchies at production and forms of domination at work in society. A critical understanding of management and work seeks to re-establish the lost faith in critical reason as a method that uncovers these hidden ideologies of managerialism. A critical understanding of management and work is concerned first and foremost with reworking concepts of human beings and human doing, social reproduction and social transformation.[291] Such a critical understanding of management and work is not post-structuralist or *post-modernist* as it goes beyond the reactive idea of pure *interpretive-ism*.[292] It is an attempt to overcome domination. Unlike managerialism, a critical understanding of management and work does not seek to enhance the integration of working people into advanced capitalism. It would resist any attempts to integrate labour-management courses into the employment system where trade-*able* knowledge leads to *depoliticalisation*. A critical understanding of management and work within a given society cannot be ideologically neutral. Therefore, it is legitimate for a critical evaluation to be justified on the basis of Enlightenment's idea of critical rationality. Ideas from Enlightenment provide the guiding principle directed towards emancipation. But this can never be simply seen in a deterministic way. Although socially constructed definitions are often used and seen to be good and useful, they still set clear boundaries and justify one perspective over other perspectives or one way of looking over another. Definitions – almost by definition – exclude all other definitions or alternative ways of looking. The introduction of sharp boundaries and hard definitions often tend to close the window of understanding. They tend to block out alternative insights rather than opening up understanding. Definitions tend to kill rather than open up discourse, as the very meaning of definition or *definitio* is to kill or to make final. In sum, many definitions are more or less arbitrary in character and chosen rather arbitrarily, often representing a perspective that is directed towards system stabilising means promoting a certain political or scientific standpoint over others. In understanding work, often one definition is chosen over another already integrating work into a preset system of conceptual thinking. To conclude, a critical understanding of management and work cannot be definitial in character. Neither can it be restricted to a *piling up of mountains of facts on the plains of human ignorance*.[293] Without the development of a critical understanding of management and work in the realm of the so-called *linguistic turn* many issues linked to communication in management and work would remain hidden and uncovered.[294] The task of the following, however, is not only to uncover the hidden structures of management and its ideological expression of managerialism but also to position both inside relationships that define work. This accomplishes two things. Firstly, it highlights the relationship character of work overcoming a technical-managerial and rather one-sided view of work. Secondly, it highlights the two core actors at work: labour and management.

Relationships and the world of work

Before highlighting managerial and labour actors at work, a brief look at work itself should enable an initial understanding of the subject. Most commonly, work can be seen as *an interdisciplinary field that encompasses the study of all aspects of people at work*.[295] While a somewhat outdated view of work and labour or industrial relations at work still sees it as the study of collective bargaining and trade unions, this appears to be far too narrow.[296] To cover *all aspects of people at work*, any modern examination of *Communication and Management at Work* needs to include issues such as communicative action and instrumental communication. This can only be done when a broad understanding of '*all aspects of people at work*' has been established. To appreciate the significance of this definition, it is necessary to examine some of the key words used. Terms such as *labour or industrial relations* indicate a strong *relationship* character that is evident in any industry and in any industrial society.[297] Industry can simply be understood as a location where goods and services are produced. *Interdisciplinary field* relates to the academic fields discussed: communication, labour, and management studies. A full study of *all* aspects would exceed several library shelves. Consequently an investigation into *Communication and Management at Work* has to focus understanding to three core issues, communication, management, and work. Inside the definition *people at work,* the term '*people*' indicates the two core actors that together build the relationship at work: labour and management. The use of the term *work* translates into a place of work, a workplace. In sum, people and workplaces are the central core providing the very base for the rise of industrial capitalism. Concurrent with the rise of industrial capitalism was the rise of the *factory system*. Both led to two additional developments. Firstly, the factory system included the formal subordination of labour and, secondly, the invention of management.[298] The factory system and the invention of management resulted in three managerial ideologies supporting the factory system. These have been authority, obedience and the elimination of conflict.[299] While the early *factory* system of the 18th and 19th century established the basic parameters of domination, capitalism's advanced development in the 20th and 21st century has been marked by the rise of the modern *corporation*. The shift from the early factory to the modern corporation has coincided with *the disappearance of the entrepreneur* and the seemingly unstoppable rise of management (Marris 1966:1).

While early entrepreneurs were more or less able to communicate directly with workers, the rise of the modern corporation fundamentally changed that. The evolution of management and the rise of early companies also shaped language.[300] When the early factory systems became advanced corporations, language was reshaped. Unlike the conditions of early factories that saw an individual owner as boss, communication in large modern corporations has become systematically organised and shaped. The rise of communication and language use in the modern corporation has been followed by wealth creation but not by a wealth of good language use. The wealth that modern corporations create is neither reflected in their employees' wealth nor in the wealth of language. The art of communication and with it the aesthetics and beauty of language has been sacrificed on the altar of managerial language. Management has created wealth but it has impoverished the aesthetics of language.[301] Today workplaces such as the modern corporations may not be great places for the art of language, but they are great places of wealth (Watson 2003). More and more *people at work* find themselves inside workplaces that reflect tremendous wealth. Working in such large corporations positions people more closely to the centre of wealth and power than working or living in a specific country. More than ever before, many of these large corporations have overtaken nations and countries when measured and compared in terms of wealth. Adam Smith's idea of *Wealth of Nations* (1776) has moved towards the wealth of corporations.[302] Not only because of their wealth and being the workplace for many *people at work*, the event of the modern corporation also has a profound impact on the reproductive domain. People's daily lives are infiltrated by *corporate* communication commonly known as mass media. Corporate communication infiltrates their lives at as well as off work. While at work in any large corporation, corporate communication defines lives at the workplace. Once at home, it structures lives via corporate mass media and corporate mass communication.[303] The dialectic between communication at work and communication external to work is relevant.[304] It focuses on the role of communication at work and beyond the workplace. Workplaces, whether in large corporations or not, are locations where people spend considerable time, mostly as necessity rather than by free choice. But workplaces are also the location where – in some cases – most of our daily communication takes place.[305]

Similar to the non-democratic and rather one-dimensional character of corporate mass media that turns people into little more than passive receivers, patterns of communication created in work contexts similarly reflect non-democratic regimes that we take on uncritically. Workplaces remain exclusion zones of democracy constructing communicative discourses in non-democratic fashion based on authority, often reducing labour to receivers, passivity, and political apathy.[306] When compared to other areas of social life, places of work continue to be rather authoritarian, top-down, or dictatorial institutions.[307] The almost complete removal of democracy from the world of work enables management to simultaneously remove democratic language.[308] The artificial distinction between democratically constructed social lives and non-democratically constructed working lives creates a false dichotomy between work and workplaces on the one hand and social interaction on the other. This establishes managerial instrumental non-democratic rationality as a form of rationality that dominates workplaces and also infiltrates social lives external to workplaces. It justifies and legitimises the institutionalisation of managerial domination over work relations constructed as undemocratic and non-participative relationships. Managerialism has set in motion a systemic logic that operates with mechanistic routines based on engineering or mechanical, technical, and rational systems. Structured in this way, the capitalist enterprise became the physical, rational and non-democratic location where work is conducted. Habermas emphasised that it is only with the stratification of groups that power differentials can be used for the authoritative combination of specialised activities in organisations, companies, and corporations (Habermas 1997a:162).

What Habermas saw in the modern corporation has a very long tradition. The non-democratic, authoritative, and, above all, militarist origins of such business organisations, today called *com-panies*, can be traced back to feudalist Europe. Today's business texts tend to either neglect or even negate most of the true origins of the socially constructed institution of companies. But these origins still exist. Once the protective shield of textbooks' cloaking devices is removed, what comes to light is a fact that has been buried for nearly 700 years. The origins of the business term *company* reach back to somewhere between the year 1337 and 1453. Around that time privatised armies gathered together as groups and provided *employment* for soldiers and ex-soldiers alike. These groups or bands of soldiers saw themselves as soldiers ready to sell their services to anyone who paid. Their *modus operandi* was to rent out the *business* of war-making, killing, assassination and the like. But their employment organisation in gangs, cohorts, or groups specialising in killing and related war activities was subject to the infrequencies of organised warfare. During the unfortunate event of peace times they suffered.[309] Without money, food or career prospects outside the war business, mercenaries and ex-soldiers all over Europe – including the 14th-century infamous Englishman *John Hawkwood* – formed *com-pan-ies* (Saunders 2004). These companies or small communities derived from the Italian term '*con*' i.e. sharing and '*pane*' i.e. bread, linking bread to sharing.[310]

Among employed and unemployed mercenaries, private army members, ex-soldiers, and bands of soldiers, the bread that these members shared laid an organisational groundwork for early *half military and half business organisations*.[311] The 14th-century bread sharing as *con pane* became today's *company* as military warlike activities and modern business organisations merged. The war-business of plundering, pilfering, robbery, larceny, etc. of those *con-panies* could be compared to the profit-making activities of the modern *company*. The original *con-panies* of killers for hire from a distant past were employed in franchise arrangements as *franchising* provides yet another originally military term transferred into modern business methods.[312] These soldiers not only carried a weapon called *lance,* they also organised themselves as *free lances* creating today's business term of *freelance*. When war and killing was outsourced, these *freelance* operators provided *free lances* for those who hired them.[313] They were able to serve whoever paid, sometimes to the franchiser's detriment when one feudal lord who had hired *free-lancers* was murdered because another franchiser lord paid these franchisees or soldiers more. Essentially, 14th-century's Englishman *John Hawkwood* is today's Tim Spicer who is, well in line with a long tradition, governed by the 1870 *Foreign Enlistment Act*.[314] Mercenary and militaristic elements of a not-so-distant past such as hierarchical stratification became enshrined in today's companies. This is enhanced through strategic, militaristic, or business planning.[315] Past *con-panies* and today's companies operate very much with managerial orders conducted in instrumental means-ends fashions. Soldiers' bread sharing as *con pane* during feudalism as well as today's companies share militaristic, authoritarian, and non-democratic power stratification.[316] The authoritarian and undemocratic company and with it an equivalent workplace became the institutional nucleus of a system of *modern relations of power and dependence that arose with the capitalist enterprise* (Habermas 1997a:366). With the historical separation of owners and labour in companies came another separation, the split into a relationship between capital, management, and labour.[317] Inside this relationship labour has commonly been seen as *staff having no direct authority whatsoever. While managers are generally considered as those who have the major authority because they direct the major goal activities* (Etzioni 1959:45). No longer can the present workplace be seen as a location where direct conflict between capital and labour takes place. Only during the initial development of capitalism has labour been able to meet with capitalist owners directly. Overwhelmingly, this has only been the case during the early states of the development of capitalism. Today, it is almost exclusively management that represents the interest of capital in the workplace.

Consequently, it can no longer be assumed that clear lines of conflict run between capital and labour. These lines of conflict, while still there, are increasingly less visible as they tend to become more and more blurred. Once owners representing capital had been successfully separated from labour with the rise of management, lines of conflict between capital and labour became exposed not only to management but to its ideology as well. As the rise of management demanded the simultaneous rise of an ideology capable of supporting management, the idea of management went beyond its business function. In the modern corporation, management not only provides a hierarchy of directive power but also a hierarchy of communicative and ideological power. This is expressed in managerialism. Together with directive powers of management, the present corporate system is defined by a communicatively established elevation of management into the ideology of *managerialism.* The transitions from early to modern and eventually to advanced capitalism with the role of labour and the changes in the domain of management can be shown as:

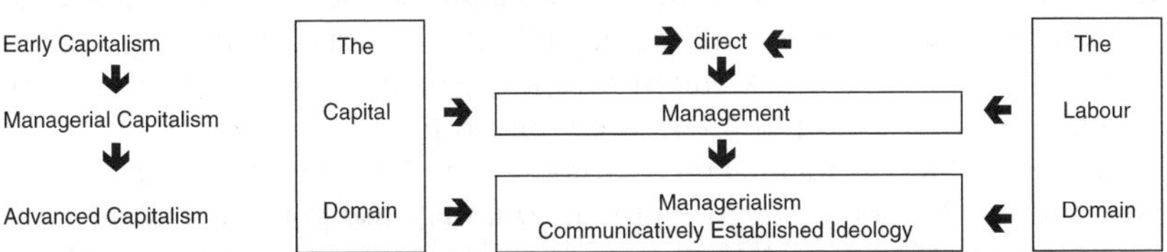

Figure 6.1   Management's Role from Early Capitalism to Managerialism

As Figure 6.1 shows, the move from a direct relationship between labour and capital to management and to manageri*alism* established a number of adjacent aspects. Firstly, manageri*alism* separated management from managers. A person that once just operated management has become a person designed to a role. The role that managers adopt is constructed inside the framework of managerialism and managerial knowledge. Only the adoption of managerial knowledge leads to the entrance into managerialism.[318] Managerial knowledge is designed towards *positional* rather than *personal* interest. It is the ideological context of managerialism that defines the position, not the person or a manager. Secondly, manageri*alism* exists in relation to historical changes. The rise of modern corporations demanded a more structured as well as a more ideological approach to management. Management no longer remained a simple technique as it moved towards the concept of manageri*alism*. It became an expressive system partly represented in the code of an *engineering ideology*. Using this code, management started to reach far beyond a simple control of a particular group of workers. Unlike management that can be seen as the operative expression of an ideology called *managerialism*, this ideology reaches much further. In the 1950s, Knowles' *Personnel Management* (1955) described the extended role of managerialism. This marked the beginning of the role of science in managerialism. According to Knowles (1955:156) *management uses scientific knowledge, particularly engineering knowledge, for making decisions.*[319] Management became managerialism and science was taken into the service of this new ideology. With the recruitment of science into the service of the ideology, science itself became part of this ideology. Managerialism, so it was announced, had to communicate its decisions inside the framework of managerial ideology that needed to be based on engineering, not on politics, even though more often than not, managerial decisions are no more than an expression of political decision-making. In short political issues had to be portrayed as a creation of evil men while management operates objectively based on the engineering code.

Unlike management that is confined to the workplace, managerialism does not stop at the factory gates. Once management had become managerialism and moved beyond the confines of corporations, society became exposed to the rules of management. Managerialism views society's true problems as engineering problems. Excluding the democratic domain of politics as malevolence, decisions in society should not be made democratically but objectively, according to the objectivity of managerialism. Decision-making problems in the domain of management and in the domain of society are engineering problems best solved by managerialism. Once the business function of management becomes an ideological function, its representatives do not only control production, they also practice this ideology. The ideology of *managerialism* has extended into extra-work or the reproductive domain located far beyond the corporation.[320] In society and at work, *managerialism* provides the conceptualisation of what society and corporations are, what goals ought to be achieved, what policies need to be created, what mission statements are presented, how the money and power code is applied, and which codifications are possible. *Managerialism* is best to solve or guide these problems as the engineering code is based on objectivity, value-freedom, and neutrality. Forester (1985:205) sees four ways in which objective, value-free, and neutral *managerialism* finds expression:

Table 6.2   Four Elements of Managerialism

No.	Description of Elements
(i)	to legitimate and perpetuate itself while it seeks to extend its power;
(ii)	to exclude systematically from decision-making process affecting the lives of particular groups such as workers' organisations, labour organisations, environmental groups, local citizen initiatives, etc. along economic lines;
(iii)	to promote the political and moral illusion that science and technology, through professional and experts (managers, HR managers, employee consultants etc.), can '*solve*' economic and political problems; and
(iv)	to restrict political argument, economic participation, and mobilisation regarding a broad range of policy options and alternatives which are inconvenient to and often incompatible with the existing patterns of ownership, wealth, and power.

As Table 6.2 shows, the orthodoxy of managerialism makes use of philosophy by trivialising philosophy's values of humanity, human dignity, and truth. In other words *business is not to do good but to do good business.*[321] The idealistic and humanist concepts of philosophy are reduced to a legitimising engineering instrument (i) geared towards means-ends systems with control as a prime motive. The claim to be efficient is one of the core elements enabling the legitimisation of managerialism.[322] Managers present themselves as the only institution capable of guaranteeing efficiency. The managerial idea of *efficiency* becomes standard managerial fanfare as decisions are made under the guise of efficiency removing all other forms of decision-making (ii). Even though managerialism has never offered a clear definition of *efficiency*, it has become the most common phrase. It is used as an unchallengeable and unquestionable almost *naturally* given term to legitimise one version of decision-making. Most importantly it directs attention towards the process of *creating* wealth away from the *distribution* of wealth. In the managerial means-ends concept, it directs attention towards *means* and away from *ends*. It negates the question of *what ought to be* reducing communication to *what is* and *how* – never *why* – to make a process more efficient. It is presented as a non-contestable element of managerial decision-making.

It can be applied in any form of communication without having to be exposed to any explanation or any need to account for. Without discussion, the managerial philosophy of mythical belief in efficiency collapses any aspect of humanised work. It turns any human element of work into a dehumanising project orchestrated by management. The managerial narrative of efficiency that started as a means has been elevated to an absolute and God-like end of managerialism. Once established, the *philosophy* of manageri*alism* adopts the logic of rationality making possible an articulation by owners and managers. This ideology presents managers as the sole experts that guard the technical process of managing a business (iii). Labour, while operating inside the managerial system, are relieved of cognitive instruments. Manageri*alism* adopts the power and money code to the needs of the corporation to negate any alternative view that is not presented inside this code (iv).[323] Managerialism establishes a one-dimensional line of communication and thinking that eliminates alternative, contradictory or non-supportive ideas. Only ideas that are supportive of management, business, and companies are deemed efficient and useful. Once they have received the managerial seal of approval these ideas are being communicated inside the companies.

But corporations are not simply systems of control *tout court*. They are deliberately designed social structures that collectively secure their capacity to operate through their organisational structure. This enables the corporation to ensure that decisions contain an authoritative character accepted by workers.[324] With the rise of the corporate system, corporations, rather than society or the state, increasingly determined the structure of society. The corporation remains capitalism's institutionalisation of purposive-rational economic and administrative action. Despite the significant energies of managerialism directed towards the ideology of *corporate governance*, corporations are not governed in a political or even democratic sense, they are directed by a board of directors. The idea of corporate governance is no more than an ideological cover for a deeply un-democratic form of rule. In short, the corporation does not have constitutive power but a regulative function. In legal terms the firm is presented as a *quasi-personal* institution socially constructed as a place of production and work with no particular status outside of its symbolic world that is communicatively established. However in an increasingly corporate-*ised* society, modern corporations have become one of the most important political decision-making bodies. As such they play a vital role in our identities and our public discourse. The *corporatisation* of everyday life determines to a large extent the ways in which people's discourse is structured and constructed. Individuals become corporate individuals. The corporate individual is reduced to a mere dot in an organisational chart that itself represents no more than lines of communicative authority and command structures. It is only valuable as long as it provides organising entities that legitimise hierarchies. The task of such charts has never been the presentation of hierarchies in solid or unchange-able ways. Organisational charts are an expression of the organising capac-ity and organising powers of corporations. They are less about the structure of corporations. To some extent, the organising model of corporations has been replicated in society. Society can be seen as an accumulation of sub-systems as shown in Table 6.3:

Table 6.3   Four Sub-Systems of Society

No.	Sub-Systems of Society
i)	the business enterprise (economy),
ii)	the public administration (political),
iii)	the law (integrative subsystem) and
iv)	the church and family (maintenance of cultural pattern).

The business enterprise (i) takes a special position in the historical develop-ment of these sub-systems (ii–iv). Unlike (ii–iv) that relate largely to the reproductive domain, the sub-system (i) relates to the productive domain. Even though sometimes portrayed as family, the modern corporation is detached from the family household thus depicting indifference between the organisation and those belonging to it who are often neutralised into organisational members with an employee number written on a piece of plastic with or without the picture of the employee on it. Unlike in real families, the managerial ideology of *we are all one big family here* needs a plastic card with a number to identify its members. Real families hardly ever have that. Families do not neutralise their members via identification cards and the like. Corporations, however, do not only neutralise their members via employee numbers, etc. they use the ideology of neutrality themselves. The four reasons for this are shown in Table 6.4:

Table 6.4   Four Reasons for the Use of the Ideology of Neutrality

No.	Four Reasons
i)	to escape the force of traditions;
ii)	to eclipse the shape of their own programmes;
iii)	to appear disconnected from morality and society; and
iv)	to neutralise their impact on society.[325]

Even though corporations play an important role in present societies and are inextricably linked to society, the ideology of managerialism portrays them as somewhat disconnected to the labour process. It seeks to discon-nect the results of the corporation, such as social stratification, as nonrelated. However, increasingly social stratification has been linked to the engagement in the corporate labour process. This process converts humans into labour. It turns individuals into a useful category for the factory system by creating the institutionalised individual. This is the transformation of a concrete person into abstract labour power as well as labour into a commodity. It is the abstract model of a very real process.[326] Unlike any other commodity that corporations produce, labour has some specifically unique characteristics attached to it. Therefore, it is bought and sold at a separate market, the labour market.[327] As Claus Offe (1984) noted, *the institution of the labour market and free wage labour is a fiction*. What is of interest positively and negatively in the commodity called labour power is what distinguishes it from all other commodities. This is in fact *living* labour power. Living labour power has three core values attached to it. These are shown in Table 6.5:

Table 6.5   Three Key Aspects of Labour

No.	Three Elements of Labour
i)	does not arise for the purpose of saleability
ii)	cannot be separated from its owner, and
iii)	can be set in motion only by its owner.

The unavoidable *subject-rootedness* (Offe 1984) of labour power implies that in wage labour the categories of action and functions as well as of social and system integration are inextricably intertwined. This has been the case ever since humans were converted from being peasants to being workers, from being owned by local lords to being exposed to the labour market. Humans have been forced into *industrialism* by entering '*The Evils of the Factory System*'. This has created several '*Social Problems of an Industrial Civilisation*'.[328] Individuals at work are still defined by two losses:

(i)   a loss of meaning through *alienation* and
(ii) a loss of freedom through *control* (Marx 1848; Weber 1924).

Marx and Weber have expressed the loss of freedom while engaging in work. *Marx had conceived a loss of freedom through 'monetarisation' and Weber as a loss of freedom through bureaucratisation to a categorical confusion of the provinces of different media* (Habermas 1997a:293). For Weber (1924) bureaucracy is a social tool that legitimises control using four central elements: (a) the division of labour and rational role selections (b) line versus staff distinctions (c) hierarchy, and (d) authoritarian structures such as *Herrschaft*.[329] But unforeseen by Marx and Weber, the loss of freedom that came along with instrumental rationality has not been restricted to work or to corporations. Bauman (1989) has described the height of the loss of freedom through bureaucratic means by arguing the *Holocaust* has not been a monstrous abnormality of modernity committed by hideous people. It was no more than the application of bureaucratic principles in four ways: Human subjects (i) are no longer treated as individual subjects but as mere objects having been converted into calculable entities that are seen as items inside a power relationship. Bureaucracies de-humanise humans in order to process them as objects. Rationality (ii) replaces societal and human links between social actors with spatial separation. Social distance is created intentionally, disconnecting actions and consequences by defining rule operators as technical entities and those to be ruled as dehumanised quantifiable objects. Bureaucracies separate human-to-human connections through systems of mechanical rule-based processes. Moral and human rationality (iii) is converted into pure formal rational-logical systems. These are applied routinely in computable procedures. Goal-achieving systems are directed strategically towards a means-ends rationality producing rules and regulations that are universally applied. Bureaucracies remove substantial or subjective rationality in favour of objective and purely rational systems. An object of bureaucracy (iv) is forced into a position of false choices. Such pre-set and managerially constructed objects are given choices allowing involvement in pre-organised sets of options. Whatever option the individual chooses has an adverse affect. Those who are '*to be ruled*' are disregarded in the options presented to them and they become objects of power. By participating in the process of bureaucracy, the dehumanised and de-individualised human supports the bureaucratic structure that works against the ruled. Rational choice is the preferred weapon of the ruler leaving the victim with faked choices such as '*to kill a few is less abhorrent than to kill many*' or '*sacrifice some in order to save many*', etc. Bureaucracies open up choices inside a bureaucratic framework organised and manufactured by the bureaucracy that is structured against the individual.

Bauman (1989) views these principles as an essential part of modernity. They guide today's societal organisations much in the same way as business organisations. This, as an example, is structurally reflected in the teachings in most business schools.[330] The *Holocaust's* strategic planning as a bureaucracy relied on modern business techniques. American Holocaust expert Paul Hilberg has exemplified this: *most bureaucrats composed memoranda, drew blueprints, talked on the telephone, and participated in conferences.*[331] *They could destroy a whole people by sitting at their desk* (Bauman 1989:24). Bauman's conclusion is that the Holocaust was rule without regard for persons *in extremis*. The key problem for modernity is that *ruling without regard for persons* is one of the core principles of bureaucracy. This is applied in everyday life as well as in the everyday workplace. The bureaucratic concept in line with the authority of an office and a formal bureaucratic structure represents domination at the organisational level.

The organisational form of work expressed in the labour process finds its clearest expression in the power relationship among actors at work, the use of instrumental rationality expressed in technical systems, and the organisational structure of individuals working in corporations. These three perspectives of the labour process are decisively necessary for any production:[332]

Table 6.6　Three Perspectives on the Labour Process

Level	Description
(i)　Power	the *labour power* of those active in production, the producers,
(ii)　Technical	*Technically* useful knowledge insofar as it is converted into productivity-enhancing tools of labour, into techniques of production,
(iii)　Organisation	*organisational* knowledge insofar as it is used to set labour power efficiently into motion, to qualify labour power, and to coordinate effectively the cooperation of workers on the basis of a division of labour.

As Table 6.6 shows, relationships of production take on meaning that goes far beyond the workplace. The way in which labour power (i) is converted into production is reflected in the structure of society where relations of production are expressed as a distribution of social power. Patterns of labour rewards are seen as the monetarisation of labour power. They are socially recognised determining the interest structure of society. Power relations (i) at work and in society are dialectically linked. At work, management's power can be seen as a symbolic concept without having an intrinsic value by itself even though the term *value-adding* has linguistically been levelled to new heights in modern economics. Nevertheless, the power code has structural features represented in management's interest that can potentially be mobilised towards the achievement of desired goals. Management's ownership of a power code, then, alters responses in a binary fashion by opening labour's option of either resistance or submission. Built into the power code is a structural force towards labour's submission. This submission aids management's position as power-holder. The managerial power code creates the opportunity to calculate success and to define outcomes. The operation of the managerial power code is closely associated with the hierarchical order of formal competencies. The owner of the power code is able to decide where the lines between top management, middle management, and line management are drawn. Hierarchies in organisations are established through linear strategic communication under conditions of instrumental rationality. Consequently, power is something that can be transferred. In management, the transferral of power relies on hierarchical structures establishing a command structure that allows top management to operate without having to give detailed reasons or demonstrating legitimacy. Management's ability to disconnect power from specific persons or specific contexts shapes managerial power, supplying a structural advantage to the power-holder as a rule-maker. On the other hand, power is needed to legitimise rule-makers. Therefore, it is necessary for management to establish a supportive ideological framework directed towards system integration. The need for an ideology that stabilises management makes such ideological structures vulnerable because management is in constant need to protect the ruler-legitimacy link from being exposed. Hence management needs to appear as having legitimate goals. These are set technically (ii), thus establishing organisational (iii) stability. All knowledge that is produced inside a company is subsumed under these two stabilising and legitimising principles.

One way of pacifying and incorporating labour into management's agenda has been participation in an attempt to neutralise labour by limited incorporation into a decision-making process (Ramsay 1977). Another way of achieving acceptance for the pretence of legitimate goals lies in the utilisation of techniques to formulate strategies that give the rule-maker the power to justify them and the *to-be-ruled* a catalogue of orders to be carried out. In society as at work, rule-makers do not only gain authority over the *to-be-ruled* through the ability to administer some form of sanction or through naked oppression. More often than not, authority over those *to be ruled* is established through recognition of office, bureaucracy, regulation and rules. Labour's recognition and acceptance lends undeserved legitimacy to management. In other words, the structure of management is resting on management's ability to create *interlocking interests,* and thus avoiding the use of sanctions. Authority established via sanctions alone *is hardly empirically possible* (Habermas 1997a:208). Therefore the relationship between management and labour at the point of production can never be solely based on sanctions, called disciplinary power in modern managerial *Doublespeak.*[333] Despite these managerial intentions the relationship of actors at work remains dialectical and is not a static top-down relationship. In order to function, management not only reserves its self-assigned right to sanction labour, but also more than sanctioning capacities, it needs the cooperation of labour.[334] Consequently, most managerial activities are not directed towards sanctions as it has been the case during earlier periods of capitalism (Figure 6.1) but directed towards system integration via ideology. For that reason present relationships at work depend on a dialectical relationship that includes four elements. At the vertical level, it includes an ideology relationship between sanctions and system integration. At the horizontal level it includes an actor relationship between labour and management. As a result, those who claim to rule in the world of work need those who they claim to rule over.[335] Figure 6.2 seeks to explain this further. It uses Kochan's definition of *people at work* but also emphasises the relationship character of people at work:

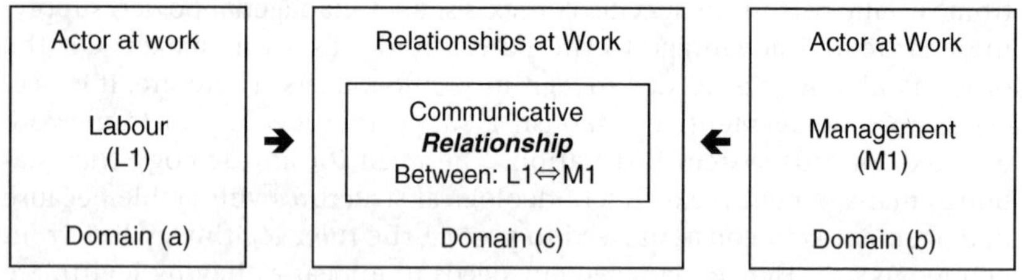

Figure 6.2   The Relationship Axiom of Actors in the World of Work

Figure 6.2 shows that the relationship between labour (L1) and management (M1) is not only a simple relationship that takes place inside their respective domains (a, b), but also has a communicative component (c). From a labour-management *relations* perspective a communicative *relationship* between the industrial actors (L1 + M1) is represented horizontally rather than vertically. A vertical representation implies a *top-down* approach inherent in managerialism.[336] A top-down view would position management on top as distinct from, but also dominant over, labour (down). A more truthful representation of communication at work would be horizontal as shown in Figure 6.2. The horizontal representation of the communicative relationship between labour and management still allows the distinction into those who manage and those who are managed.[337] It avoids showing a purely managerial point of view. The depiction of the communicative relationship of labour and management at work also avoids the shortcomings of several other fields that lay claim to the world of work. Firstly, is avoids a pure organisational studies (OS) viewpoint as this field, while being closely linked to managerial studies, tends to adopt the same perspective. OS' focus is on organisations as institutions; organisational behaviour (OB) studies predominantly discuss the psychology of behaviour or mis-behaviour of individuals in organisations.[338] Not surprisingly, the theory of organisations (OT) appears to be a theory of and mostly for management. Similarly, OT, OB, and OS are much less concerned with those who *are managed* than with those *who manage*. These theories are theories *for* those who manage rather than for those on the receiving end. Unlike management studies, HRM, and adjacent O-fields that seek to explain the how (means) rather than the why (motive) in top-down schemes, a true representation of people at work focuses on the *relationship* between labour and management as shown in Figure 6.2. Such a representation not only shows labour and management in their relationship to each other but also includes a representation of the two core domains in which they operate.

7
The Two Domains Defining the World of Work

The view that both the world of work and the reproductive world consist of two social actors goes back to the ideas of Adam Smith (1759, 1776) but it also found its expression in the philosophical discussions of Friedrich Hegel (1807, 1821) and was most prominently and analytically discussed by Karl Marx (1848, 1890). Frederic Taylor (1911) has *scientifically* introduced Smith's division between *labourers* and *capitalists* into the domain of work reproducing Hegel's and Marx' division between *labour* and *capital*. As the system of production advanced, the organisation of the productive domain demanded the introduction of a new actor (Marglin 1974). No longer was it possible to define the work domain by two actors as outlined by Smith, Hegel, and Marx. Advances in the productive domain demanded the establishment of management as an intermediate between capital and labour. From this point on, labour had to communicate with management rather than with capital directly.

For most of the past century, communicative relationships at work have been defined by the relationship between the two actors. But this defining feature of work is not locked in the past as present-day workplace relations are still defined by the two key actors: labour and management. What has changed however is the terminology attached to these two actors. While management remained as management in *Oldspeak* and *Newspeak*, labour underwent several, mostly ideologically motivated, changes. Today, *labour* (*Oldspeak*) has been renamed or *re-branded* (*Newspeak*) into organisational members, employees, or associates (*Newspeak*). Despite all attempts by managerialism and its entourage of affirmative writers, the structural imperatives of the present system still demand that work be conducted in order to realise profits. However, they have done the utmost possible to cloak this need. Even though the control of labour at work might have taken several different forms in the cause of development that capitalism took from its early stages to its present advanced stage, the combination of both labour (employees, etc.) and capital (machinery, etc.) still builds the foundation of the productive domain. The areas in which the two social actors meet are essentially: *work* as a physical, structural, emotional, and communicative activity, the *work domain* as a conceptual area structured by the productive and reproductive domain and governed by the code of money and power, and the *workplace* as the physical location where work is conducted. Today's work domain and workplaces are governed by two sub-domains, the domain of labour and the domain of management which not only contain different members but are also structured according to two different logics (Table 7.5 below). Due to the different structure of their relationship both sub-domains communicate in different ways.

The relationship between management and labour occupies some structural elements that determine their respective domains of activities at work. It also contains an exchange domain, a domain where labour and management meet. Inside this domain, any labour-management exchange relationship is by no means equal but asymmetrically structured against labour. Overall, management's power largely depends on its *willingness to set up institutional hierarchies of power* including support mechanisms by use of the steering media *money*. This is done in the form of wages and salaries. The use of the steering media *power*, on the other hand, resides in the potential for sanctions and disciplinary actions directed against labour. Labour's power largely depends on its *willingness to act collectively* against the asymmetrically designed power structure of the managerial system. Such action has to be taken *collectively* as individual action has a very limited chance of succeeding. One might argue that if individual actions or individual bargaining would deliver favourable outcomes for labour, their collective organisations would have never come about. The managerial power structure starts with the transformation of humans into labour under the labour process. While management can maximise its position and power through expansion, growth, outsourcing, downsizing, off-shore relocations, technical advances and the like, labour's options are more restricted. Labour's ability to optimise its situation is limited to improvements in wages and working conditions. To achieve this, labour is forced to seek extra- and inter-company organisational forms. The existence of such organisations provides the most visible evidence that humans are not just commodities to be bought and sold. It also makes visible that work in itself – without human intervention – is not only impossible but also useless as a theoretical category. It is not possible to limit the effects of work to workplaces as it affects humans well beyond the workplace and well outside the control of management.

Inside the labour-management relationship, however, labour is faced with additional problems. Unlike management, labour also faces the dilemma of size. This dilemma applies to the productive as well as to the reproductive domain. Internal democracy decreases with an increase in the size of the organisation. This occurs simultaneously with an increase of bureaucracy. The dilemma lies in the decrease of organisational size leading to an increase in democracy. In short, big organisations mean less democracy while small organisations are more democratic.[339] This represents an unsolvable dilemma because labour needs sizable organisations but with the increase in size, bureaucracy increases while democracy decreases. Hence either labour's organisation is sufficient in size and lacks democracy or labour's organisation is insufficient in size with a limited level of bureaucracy and good internal democratic structures. In contrast to labour, management is largely free of such concerns as it is not a democratic institution in the first place. Secondly, management does not face a bureaucratic dilemma. Rather than limiting its capabilities, an increase in bureaucracy enhances the power of management. Bureaucratic structures boost managerial power structures as both are based on hierarchy and domination. In short, while labour depends on internal democracy, management does not. At work, internal communication and discourses also suffer from the increase in size. This is potentially damaging to labour but not to management. Labour needs to organise communicative structures horizontally while management organises these structures vertically. Management's vertical structures reflect hierarchical power structures and the power structure of bureaucracy. Labour, on the other hand, needs to create a communication structure based on domination free forms of finding consent. For management consent-finding is less important as decisions are made inside hierarchical structures. Communicative asymmetry is a necessity, not a problem for management. For labour this asymmetry has potentially serious consequences. Unlike the singularity of management's profit motive, labour is faced with multiple interests. There are at least three identifiable core diverging interests. These are:

Table 7.1   The Three Universal Interests of Workers

No.	Interest
i)	an interest in high wages,
ii)	an interest in continuation of wages (employment security), and
iii)	an interest in working conditions.

In one way or the other, labour needs to balance these three interests. On the other hand, management and managerial activities are driven by the profit interest. Underneath the all-encompassing and one-dimensional interest directed towards profit maximisation lies a multitude of supplementary interests. Sometimes these managerial sub-interests that are all subsumed under the profit interest are merely designed to cloak the core interest of profit-making.[340] The asymmetry between management's single-interest and labour's three-dimensional interest has severe consequences. Members of the labour domain experience greater difficulties in defining their true interest. The difficulty lies in the four reasons as shown in Table 7.2 below:

Table 7.2   Four Difficulties in Defining Common Interests

No.	
i)	unlike interest formulation in the labour domain, the formulation of interest is largely unnecessary in the management domain because of monogenic interest,
ii)	there is a strong asymmetry in interest achievement between both domains,
iii)	the singular interest of the management domain is supported by a wide web of societal support mechanisms,[341] while
iv)	the labour domain faces multiple interests. It also faces ambiguity, alienation, mystification, and commodity fetishism directed against their consciousness much in the same way as the domain is affected by exploitation and deviations.[342]

Table 7.2 lists the four most common reasons that operate against labour's aim to find a common interest that unites labour. Most important is the fact that two conditions are operating in each domain. In the management domain a mono-logical or one-dimensional interest is directed towards profit (i). In the labour domain multiple interests come into play. Unlike management, labour needs to find an outcome between these interests. In short, the risk of experiencing problems is much higher when forced to engage in three interests rather than in one. The issue of interest mediation is uneven. It is asymmetrically distributed between managers and workers (ii). While management suffers much less from the problem of unity, labour has to balance a diverse range of interests and therefore struggles to keep unity among members of its domain. Management needs to make less effort in formulating unifying interest than labour because the transition from communicative action to social action is either lower or not even existent. To a much lesser extent, management needs to comply with the demands of social action. To a large degree managerial action receives meaning through power hierarchies, bureaucracy and intentional acts.

Thirdly, management is in a position to rely on a relatively large web of support mechanisms. These are not only to be found in the structural imperatives of present-day work regimes but also in the support that comes from the ex-work domain. While under previous forms of capitalism – which had largely been termed liberal or early capitalism – the working class possessed something similar to a milieu well alive in the reproductive domain (Gorz 1982), today's off-work living space has been successfully transformed. With advances in capitalism, the previously open, democratic working-class domain has been colonised by system imperatives coming from the structural impediments of advanced capitalism. With an increasing level of middle-class living, affluence and the commodification, privatisation, and centralisation of mass media, the reproductive domain changed significantly. This allowed managerialism to portray their ideas onto society. Consequently, the restructuring of the public domain in the image of managerial capitalism allowed management to rely on it as a powerful support mechanism (iii). The ability to infiltrate even the most distant parts of social existence by managerialism through mass-mediated reality-creating institutions has been powerfully described by Gadamer. According to Gadamer (1976:16),

> the mechanical, industrial world is expanding within the life of the individual as a sort of sphere of technical perfection. When we hear modern lovers talking to each other, we often wonder if they are communicating with words or with advertising labels and technical terms from the sign language of the modern industrial world. It is inevitable that the levelled life-forms of the industrial age also affect language, and in fact the impoverishment of the vocabulary of language is making enormous progress, thus bringing about an approximation of language to a technical sign-system. Levelling tendencies of this kind are irresistible.

In short, when managerial capitalism was able to penetrate previously open spaces of present-day society, it has definitely also been able to restructure the reproductive domain to support the managerially structured work domain. This has not only altered the reproductive domain in which labour is forced to live but also the productive domain. In both domains labour faces increasing levels of alienation.

Fourthly, the labour domain also faces the problem of a multitude of interests in both the reproductive and productive domain. Labour is increasingly confronted with a threefold dilemma because it is forced into the commodified world of work, into relentless consumerism in the reproductive domain, and previously open forms of voice and participative, democratic modes of social regulation are challenged from corporatised mass media portraying a managerial version of a mass-mediated reality. Labour is challenged in all three domains by system integrative forces that deny and negate its interests. At all three levels, socially constructed institutions communicate images that create ambiguity, alienation, mystification, and commodity fetishism all of which are working actively against labour's ability to establish a common interest. On the whole these forms of distorted realities are directed against labour's consciousness much in the same way as the work domain is affected by exploitation and deviations. While labour's ability to communicate its ideas and interests has been unsympathetically limited in the communicative domain as well as in the work domain, the reproductive domain is further eroded through relentless consumerism and commodity fetishism. Commodity fetishism is here seen in the Marxist understanding, not the Freudian sense. It relates to *use-* versus *exchange*-value and describes an overemphasis on exchange value when goods or commodities become purely exchange concepts without any real use. In other words, managerial mass production has created a massive amount of goods and services that overwhelms labour in its reproductive domain. As market saturation has occurred, mass production has more and more moved from *use*-value to the *exchange*-value of goods and commodities. In other words, most of today's goods are not consumed because there is an objective or real need for them, but because they have been marketed as goods that satisfy a demand which has been artificially created and that is a form of exchange-value. These goods, commodities, and services are not *use*-ful but satisfy artificially created needs for *brand* products, *status*-enhancing products and the like. Inside this mechanism, managerialism has created a working world that is geared towards the acquisition of the financial resources to enable labour to function in the off-work domain's consumerism. It has created an endless treadmill of work and consumption guided by the money code.

Managerial capitalism and the ideology of managerialism have been able to structure labour's social actions towards an interest that is system supportive. More than labour, management is able to take behavioural responses of other actors into account because it has more structural support mechanisms in place than labour. Secondly, instrumental action under means-ends constructions is less complicated when it becomes operative. Inside such a framework, management is able to anticipate labour's responses based on system thinking. In contrast, labour's ability to anticipate managerial behaviour is limited as it lacks system support and access to the communicative domain of management. These core differences between management and labour have been summed up by Offe and Wiesenthal (1980). They have discussed the domain differences between labour and management by reflecting more on their organisational expression in social and economic organisations and employer organisations. This analysis is shown in Table7.3:

Table 7.3   Two Modes of Operation of Management and Labour

	Management Domain		Labour Domain
i)	operating on the level of *system* integration	versus	operating on the level of *social* integration
ii)	power potentials without an external organisational need	versus	power created almost exclusively through organisational forms of collective action
iii)	Exercise of power through leadership[343]	versus	exercise of power through membership

Table 7.3   Two Modes of Operation of Management and Labour – *continued*

	Management Domain		Labour Domain
iv)	offensive use of power	versus	defensive use of power
v)	instrumental and technical rationality directed towards goals	versus	dialogical pattern of seeking to reach understanding for interest formulation and social action
vi)	communication in terms of technical imperatives	versus	communication in terms of demands and explicit normative claims
vii)	legitimacy through organised activity in terms of interest as a whole	versus	particularistic advocacy of specific interests of the prospective beneficiaries of demands

As Table 7.3 shows, any formulation of interest under conditions of the two modes of collective action is supported by an engineering ideology. Taylor constructed a division of work into management and labour. This social construction demands from management that it creates system integrative elements. The system is designed to integrate a – sometimes rather recalcitrant – workforce into a production process (i). On the other hand, labour needs social elements to be integrated as workers into a social organisation (i). Therefore, it needs to increase labour's *willingness to organise*. For management this is an outcome of the forces of the labour market. Secondly, management has no need for external forms of organisations to strengthen their position while labour needs such external organisational forms (ii). Managerial exercise of power rests not only in bureaucratic or organisational structures but also in their leadership (iii). On leadership, Watson (2003:32) notes, *under a general heading of, say, leadership, we see columns and dot points. One column is headed strategies and the other results. Under leadership we get windy summaries of ambitions* – while those who are *led*, those who are categorised as *followers* are almost completely absent. On the other hand, those leaders who are supposed to lead us take a relatively large slice of the cake in the so-called managerial literature because they possess a greater ability to exercise power.

Management's power use is offensive (iv). In the labour domain things are rather different. Its ability to exercise power rests not so much on organisational forms and bureaucracy but on workers' *willingness to act collectively*. All of this has profound implications on communication in each domain. In the management domain, communication is structured instrumental top-down, directed towards the rather commonly accepted goal of profit (v). To cloak the term profit behind so-called *organisational goals* is a reflection of Orwell's *Newspeak*. Wrapped up in the ideology of managerialism these *organisational goals* are communicated as part of a technical imperative linked to production (vi). Management only needs to communicate its socially constructed goals as technical goals. Every business report – usually there are two: one for shareholders (we made large profits pushing the share price up) and one for the tax office and other stakeholders such as trade unions, etc. (we made little profit and can't pay taxes, higher wages, etc.) – are often written in a highly technical language that fulfils a number of ideological tasks. Foremost, such reports need to portray the picture that business and profits are technically, not socially constructed activities. By doing so, management also portrays that the business of business is business. In short, only management represents its interest as the interest of the whole (vii). Simultaneously, labour's interest is portrayed as being partial, only representing a segmental interest of one particular interest group. In reality however, the opposite is the case because the managerial interest can be reduced to one single interest, the original profit interest (*Oldspeak*) or organisational goals, etc. (*Newspeak*). This reversal of the true state of affairs is almost universally supported by almost all corporate mass media. To portray the managerial interest as the interest of society shows the ideological content of the mass media. More than any other issue, aspects relating to work, the pathologies of business, inhumanities that have been created, and unethical conduct remain hidden behind the agendas of the mass media. To show the pathologies of corporate life and corporate business is not in the interest of corporate mass media. Preferably, it is better to cluster the human mind with petty crimes disconnected from society, individual disasters, stupid game shows, or just a bunch of teenagers who spend their time with gossip-mongering and expressing trivialities in a TV show called Big Brother.

In the labour domain, communication is more complicated. First of all, it is not part of a hierarchical structure. Secondly, it is not organised hierarchically but democratically. Thirdly, it needs to be geared towards finding common agreement on collective interests. Finally the role of communication inside the labour domain is to balance three interests. The result of this balancing act is to give preference, as one of the interests needs to be given preference over the other two. It is relatively hard for labour to accomplish all three interests simultaneously as some are not considered as of high priority. In whatever way these interests are balanced or given preference, there is a need to deal with all of them. On the other hand management in historical and in functional terms is largely free of such problems as its prime objective and historical mission is the achievement of organisational goals, usually profit. While Taylor's management ideology has had a profound impact on work in the 20th and 21st century, the role of communication for work has a long history. In the words of Hobsbawn (2004:11), *modes of production (or whatever we want to call them), based on major innovations in productive technology, communications, and social organisations – have been central to human evolution.* Work as a central category in the evolutionary development of human societies raises two important issues. Human action at work has always been directed towards a rational, instrumental, and purposive action. It is a planned element expressed in *strategic action*. On the other hand, work is never conducted as a planned, purposive and purely rational action only. Ever since the evolution of humans work has included a communicative element expressed in *communicative action* (Habermas 1979). Humans have always sought to communicatively establish organisational structures securing their own survival. Put simply, people make goods and services in a planned, structured or strategic process and they communicate while doing so. Historically and evolutionary, human development is the process of communicatively organised production and distribution of goods. The development of such communicatively established structures occurred in a three-stage development (Dux 1991:77):

Table 7.4   The Three-Stage Development

Stages	Development
i) instinctual	Gesture-mediated interaction at the sub-human state is followed by a stage of signals.
ii) signal	Language that is already symbolically mediated; here, action is further regulated and coordinated by means of instincts and/or instinctual residues, but the triggers no longer function in the same manner as with gesture-controlled action; they are replaced by signals that already have the character of symbols.
iii) symbols	Even if prepositional, illocutionary and expressive components have not yet been differentiated.

As Table 7.4 shows, the evolutionary development of human communication has developed from instinctual gestures (i) to a fully developed language (ii) necessary for the development of modern industrialism. Finally, modern means of production also demanded the development of symbols (iii). Without the human development of symbolic interaction, modern production and modern means of work and communication would be impossible. Language and symbolic interaction have been instrumental in the development of modernity.

This shift is reflected in a shift in language use. Visions expressed in older language related to a taming of capitalism when the state talked about security from cradle to grave. Today, the language of the market has replaced this with the language of the bottom line, throughputs, innovation, opportunity, and, above all, competition. Under conditions of modernity, the communicative and strategic-instrumental content of work has become more complex with the creation of two actors: labour and management.[344] Both are part of a one-dimensional system, the universally accepted market system. Like no other class, the entrepreneurial class has been able to position themselves as the clearest expression of the hegemonic powers of the free market system. This occurred as they gradually integrated corps of managers and technicians. Their relationship to the ruling system was at first unclear. But very soon it shifted only to become an instrument of order. It became a force that stabilised bourgeois rule at company and at society level. Subsequently, labour could not be separated from management. Both can only be discussed dialectically under conditions of *the two logics of collective actions* where comprehensive access to the world of work is linked to *theory* language. The idea of *the two logics of collective actions* is taken from Offe and Wiesenthal (1980). In simplistic terms, dialectics can be understood as a Hegelian/Marxian term. It has properties of inherent tensions between contradictory impulses. Of relative importance in any understanding of dialectics is Hegel's philosophy. He focused on contradictions and tensions such as those between object and subject, mind and nature, self and others, freedom and authority, knowledge and faith, etc. These tensions have an inherent dynamic that leads to further development in thinking and in human societies. *Observation* language, on the other hand, would restrict such a comprehension (Habermas 1997:336).

Two domains and two logics

The framework behind the idea of theory versus observation language is expressed in Table 7.5 below. In order to fully understand the world of work, an overall conceptual construction takes place at four levels ranging from (i) social action to underlying theories (iv) that explain social actions at work. At each of the four levels (i–iv) general theoretical (a) framework provides an umbrella under which specific work-related concepts (b) are located. At the first level (i), an understanding of the world of work can be seen as an understanding of emancipatory actions or as an understanding of instrumental actions (i-a). At the more specific level, understanding is directed towards positive changes at work or at instrumental actions at work (i-b). At the communicative level (ii), these are expressed as communicative action versus instrumental communication (ii-a). As a specific concept applies to the world of work (b), communication is directed towards either an understanding of work designed to reach social agreement for social action at work or towards managerial success (ii–b).

Table 7.5   The Concept of Two Logics at Work

Levels	a) General Framework	b) Specific Concept at Work
i) **Social action**	emancipatory action versus instrumental action	emancipatory action social change for positive versus instrumental action for managerial success
ii) **Communication**	communicative action versus instrumental communication	communication for understanding/agreement versus communication for managerial success
iii) **Conceptual perspective**	industrial/labour relations versus management studies	worker's logic for collective action versus management's logic for collective action
iv) **Underlying theory**	critical theory[i] versus traditional theory[ii]	traditional communication theory[i] versus critical theory of communicative action[ii]

Table 7.5 further shows how the idea of the two logics of collective action differentiates labour from management. The conceptual perspective (iii) shows that the world of work is often viewed from two perspectives. Either it is seen in terms of labour relations or as a subject of management studies (iii-a). At the work specific level (iii-b), this is expressed as a logic that governs labour's collective action and another logic that governs management's collective action. The last level is that of underlying theories (iv). These theories assist in understanding all the levels above (i–iii). The core theories that meet in Table 7.5(iv-a) are critical versus traditional theory. Here (7.5:iv-a[i]), all *traditional* theories explain the world of work in terms of empirical analysis or hermeneutics. These theories tend to focus overwhelmingly on Kant's idea of *what is*. In sharp contrast, *critical* theories (7.5:iv-a[ii]) do the same but they also go one step further. They include theory elements that allow social actors to end domination. This theory is deliberately designed and directed towards emancipation. Theories that explain the communicative aspect of the world of work (7.5:iv-b) are following *traditional* communication theories (7.5:iv-b[i]) or *critical* communication theories (7.5:iv-b[ii]). To a large extent a traditional understanding of communication is geared towards an understanding of *how* communication at work is

conducted. On the other hand, a critical theory of communication at work seeks to uncover hidden forms of domination and is directed towards understanding and common agreement leading to positive social change. The central question expressed in Table 7.5 remains the following: *How do labour and management communicate at the workplace and how can labour reach understanding for communicative action?* In order to understand the underlying theory behind this question, a critical theory standpoint needs to go beyond a traditional understanding of the world of work. Theory is understood as a human construction made up of a symbolic representation of phenomena. *The fact that theories are human constructions implies that they are neither objective descriptions of reality nor necessarily true. Instead, theories represent points of views* (Wood 2004:31). Theories are created from a standpoint. The starting premise of standpoint theory is that the material, social, and symbolic circumstances of a social group (such as labour and management) shape what its members experience, as well as how they think and act. A critical theory standpoint however does not stop at *describing* communication. It does not see communication as the neutral reflection of some objectified reality manifested in the belief that there is a singular truth. It believes that the singularity of one truth ends when many subjective interpretations come into play and succeed singularity. Truth cannot be reduced to an objectified truth where it is an object rather than something established communicatively and above all subjectively.

Secondly, a critical theory standpoint is able to deliver an *explanation* of *how* and foremost *why* communication between labour and management functions or does not function. Thirdly the underlying theory (Table 7.5:iv) is capable of delivering *predictions* on miscommunication between both actors and on the future of communicative action.[345] Lastly Table 7.5:iv includes the aspect of emancipation as a *reformative* content of the work, directed towards action en route for positive social change. The pursuit of social change is not founded on a law-based understanding of theory where a simple causal relationship between x and y is established. In this context, the term *law* is seen as a universal or physical law of human behaviour. Such law is an inviolate, unalterable fact that holds true across time and space. Unlike chemistry, physics, or mathematics, human society has hardly ever operated inside the confines of natural laws.

The aim is to show a *correlational* relationship where communicative action (x) and instrumental communication (y) go together but not to assert that one causes the other (iv-a, b). More accurately, such a link seeks to provide a *rule-based* – rather than a law based – explanation, articulating patterns of communication by describing and explaining what happens in work-based communications between labour and management. Rather than physical laws, such *rules* or *patterns* reflect the irregularity of human actors as rules are subject to change. Lastly, the issue of *parsimony* is aimed at *the best theory is the simplest one that is capable of describing, explaining, understanding, and instigating social change* (Wood 2004:43). This offers a practical usage of theory (iv) commonly expressed as: *nothing is as practical as a good theory*. Such a critical theory should be *heuristic*. It should provoke new ideas, insights, and thinking into the communicative relationship of labour and management at work (7.5:b). The advantage of a critical theory (7.5:a, b) for the world of work provides a new understanding of two sets of familiar materials by treating both in an original and stimulating manner. One set of familiar material is found in the *relationship* between labour and management. The second set is a link between communication and action. This enhances standard labour and management theory towards a critical understanding of the world of work providing a stimulating treatment of both areas. Communicative action theory (7.5:ii-a) is a contribution to the understanding of labour-management relations. A further enhancement shows how the communicative action aspect enables actors to understand the instrumental strategic content of communication. This takes place in the management domain (7.5:iii-b). The emancipatory power of communicative action takes place in the labour domain (7.5:iii-b). This rather complicated conceptualisation of communication in the world of work can be simplified. As a summary this is illustrated in Figure 7.1:

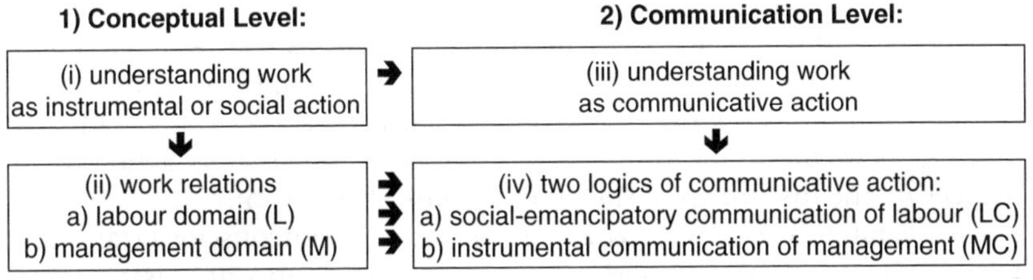

Figure 7.1   The Management of Communication at Work

Figure 7.1 explains how and why management communication is operating at work and where it meets difficulties in managing labour. This is illustrated first of all in two distinctive domains. One is the (1) conceptual domain of the management of labour while the second (2) domain shows the communicative aspect of it. At the conceptual level management tends to rationalise work only as instrumental action, as an instrument to get things done (i). By focusing on instrumentality, management has a tendency towards neglecting the social character of work (i). Therefore it tends to neglect the social-relationship character of work often leading to dire consequences. If management has a grasp of work as a social relationship at all, it is faced with the problematic of two distinctive domains of action (ii). One is its very own domain, the domain of managerial action (ii-b). Often it is faced with several choices on how to manage the labour domain (ii-a).

These choices range from ignoring the existence of this domain to trying to convert the (ii-a) domain into a substitute of the (ii-b) domain. Ever since the beginning of capitalism and managerialism these strategies have been applied. However, neither approach has proven to be successful. Management has not been able to either completely deny the existence of the labour domain nor has it been able to completely convert the L-domain (ii-a) into an M-domain (ii-b). As both strategies have so far failed, the continuation of two domains (L & M) opens up a space for collective action of labour. The problematic character of fully understanding the world of work inside (1) has subsequently been carried over to a communicative understanding (2). Given the instrumental character of a conceptual understanding of work the communicative view of work results in an instrumental communicative understanding of work. In other words, communication, in management's view, can be reduced to an instrument directed towards goal achievement in a means-ends framework (iii). This has severe implications for the management of labour at work. Communication (iv) follows two distinctive logics as much as social action follows two distinctive logics of collective action. The logic of communicative action differs for labour (iv-a) and for management (iv-b). For labour it results in social-emancipatory communication (LC), while for management the effect is instrumental communication (MC). The implications for labour and for management are that both tend to neglect the communication needs of the other side in their respective domain (L & M). Consequently (M) in (ii-b) tends to view communication as instrumental (iv-b) neglecting (iv-a) while (L) in (ii-a) tends to view communication in terms of social-emancipatory action (iv-a), neglecting the instrumental side of communication (iv–b).

The overall relationship (1 & 2) can be seen as an unconscious transferral from an instrumental understanding of work (i) into an instrumental understanding of communication (iii). Respectively, work relations (ii) are transferred into communicative relations at work (iv). Here the labour domain (L) in (ii-a) becomes the social-emancipatory communication domain (LC), while the management domain (M) becomes the domain of instrumental communication of management (MC). This domain specific conceptualisation of work and work relations governs to a large extent management's understanding of work and communication at work. Management's instrumental understanding of work has not only a long history but is also an expression of today's ideological interest of management to depoliticise relations at the productive level by pushing the idea of instrumentality. This follows a specific engineering logic used to justify and legitimise managerial existence. At first it was needed to legitimise management as an intermediary between labour and capital when the continuous rise of the factory system demanded order and control at company level. Later, when modern means of large-scale mass production under Taylorism and Fordism came into existence, management took science into service leading to the ideology of *managerialism*. Similarly, managerialism has a strong interest in burying its military origins and the *con-pane* among the rubbles of managerial ideology. It also buries Max Weber's idea of *Herrschaft* or domination in favour of a pretended neutrality of bureaucracy. It enables managerialism to hide the issue of power behind the equally neutralised issue of technology and organisation (Table 6.2). All of this is done to portray the world of work as technical, organisational, and instrumental. The adoption of the engineering ideology of managerialism denies the relationship character of work. Constructing the world of work as a one-dimensional world relieves it from any asymmetrical view that highlights the hidden power relations at work. These power relations come to light once relations at work are shown as domain specific relationships. The domain perspective also highlights asymmetries when it comes to communication. The denying of a domain perspective also hinders our understanding of the world of work in terms of communication. Communication in the labour domain is by far less trapped inside an instrumental framework. Inside this domain communication can be freed up of means-ends structures. It allows labour to direct communication towards common understanding as a preface for social action. The opposing domain, the management domain, is by far stronger determined by instrumental rationality. In this domain communication is directed towards domain specific demands such as instrumentalism governed via means-ends and goal-achieving structures. Unlike in the labour domain, communication is subsumed under the auspices of instrumental action. In other words, managerial instrumental rationality turns communication into instrumental communication at work.

8
Management and Instrumental Communication

The central task of purpose-driven communication is its strong reliance on instrumental rationality often expressed in strategic rationality. As a consequence, the issue of instrumental rationality or – in managerial terms simply called – *strategy* is a core issue of managerial functions in any larger company or corporation. It is also important for managerialism. Understanding the centrality of techniques, functionality, and instrumental means-end strategies by management also means understanding the strategic use of communication as a structuring device. To understand management's origin and the present use of instrumental or strategic communication, it is important not to neglect the core divisions prevalent in any workplace. Any view of work that blurs, obscures, or clouds the relationship between (a) *those who manage* and (b) *those who are managed* also blurs the borders of communication.[346] Despite all the rhetoric of managerialism, today's work is still defined by those two groups. The strongest reflection of the reality of work is Taylor's separation of planning, designing and coordinating from the execution of actual work by labour.[347]

Essentially, labour can still be seen as a human activity performed in a temporal process – usually nine-to-five – through which people form definite *relationships* among themselves at a place of work. Originally, this relationship was designed for the transformation of raw or natural material into manufactured commodities. Today, this is defined as *transforming* information into commodities or *creating* information as a commodity. Under modern conditions, communication and language gain importance. In the information-work-society process, management and managerial language become more important. In the words of Watson (2003:8):

> Managerial language may well be to the information age what the machine and the assembly line were to the industrial. It is mechanised language. Like a machine, it removes the need for thinking: this essential and uniquely human faculty is suspended along with all memory of what feeling, need or notion inspired the thing in the first place.

Even though manufacturing and machinery have been replaced by information, both have, nevertheless, one commonality. Common to the work of transforming nature or information is their social and material basis. Both need a functioning relationship among workers and managers to become operative.[348] Disregarding work organisation as material processing or information processing, production is always the production and reproduction of social relationships which are still divided into those who manage and those who are managed. Increasingly, this is no longer reflected in standard management literature. While standard management studies have a lot to say about those who manage, they are rather silent on those who are managed.[349] This silent part of management studies follows a common premise that any relationship aspect of *people at work* is best shelved into a box labelled industrial relations.[350]

The boxing-in of the relationship character of work has several advantages for management. It cuts off any link between management and society but above all, it shows management as a function of accounting, finance, marketing, and operations management. When the managerial process deals with humans it is shelved into a box labelled *Human Resource Management*. In this box, standard top-down methods from the other managerial boxes are applied and the relationship character of work is eliminated. Consequently, management can comfortably exclude those to be managed, those who are on the receiving end of Taylor's division of labour, or those who execute the actual work, i.e. labour. This is even more prevalent when managerialism transforms management into strategic management as it concentrates on the planning, instrumental, or strategic level. Within managerialism, the invention of a strategic level is particularly valuable in depicting management's true state of affairs. But the strategic level has also other advantages. It is safely located far *above* those to be managed, so one does not need to talk about them, include them in any way, or mention them.

The origins and use of instrumental strategies by management

The origins of management and strategic thinking date back centuries and can be found in their militaristic past. As much as the origins of business terms such as *company* as *con-pane* – the bread sharing among mercenaries – date back centuries, management itself goes a long way back to a very distant past. This past might be long forgotten but still holds important truths about management. It holds a truth that many would rather not see highlighted. Going back to management's origins means going back to a military past as business terms such as strategic planning in management are linked to military planning.

Originally, the term *strategy* was linked to *military* science that developed pre-planned warfare as an art of science by conceptualising warfare beyond the point of simple tactics (Clausewitz 1873). Strategy originates from Sun-

Tsu (600), a Chinese general setting forth 13 principles of war in 600 BC. While early concepts developed in Asia were unknown to Europeans, its European origins date back to more recent times. In Niccolo Machiavelli's *Art of War* (1520), he provided strategic advice to the wealthy corporations of the day. These were the Medici family of Florence and the Swedish military leader Gustav II Adolf (17th century). *The Art of War* uses metaphors of military, war, and strategy as a type of persuasion for war and for the management and business of war.

In French the term *strategie* derived from its Greek origin *strategia*, the art of *generalship*, as a prelude to the battlefield. *Strategos* or *stratagem* was a cunning plan or scheme developed especially in order to deceive an enemy. Strategy's modern development came with Prussian military strategists Carl von Clausewitz (1780–1831) and Helmuth Graf von Moltke (1800–1891) who saw war simply as a continuation of political intercourse with additional or other means. Modernity entered the business of military warfare with Clausewitz's book *On War*. His *bible of strategy remains the best general study of the art of war* (Howard 2003), emphasising modern mathematical, typographical, geographical and scientific principles aiming at the strategic destruction of the enemy's forces on the battlefield. Clausewitz' most famous dictum – *war was only the continuation of economic competition by other means* (Hobsbawn 1989:315) – can also be reversed. Under modernity, it appears as if the economic condition is a continuation of war by other means. This, of course, does not exclude the fact that massacres and torture have become standard operational procedures under the present system.[351]

Clausewitz and Moltke's development of strategic warfare also served to legitimise the quest of the Prussian military class. As the Germanic semi-royal and aristocratic class was severely under threat by rising capitalism rendering landholding worthless, a military career was often sought to alleviate a downgrading into poverty. A development of war-making themes – now called strategies – that could carry connotations of the ideologically neutral term *scientific* assisted this quest. The fabrication of a *strategic war* that could not be lost lent legitimacy to generations of Prussian and German aristocrats who formulated such strategies, not as value-neutral or scientific endeavours but as top-down relations between an officer class that strategically managed a battle and an operational class of foot-soldiers that were to die on pre-designed battlefields.

All of this is not just some kind of distant historical past, but an outcome of a military-scientific logic that prevails until today, a logic that can be summed up as follows:

i) warfare	+	science	=	scientific warfare
ii) scientific warfare	+	strategic planning	=	strategic warfare using science to win
iii) management	+	military strategy	=	strategic management
iv) strategic management	+	science	=	strategic management using science to win

Figure 8.1 The Militarist-Scientific Logic of Management

Figure 8.1 shows the transformation of warfare (i) into a pre-planned scientific warfare (ii) and the managerial use (iii) of military strategy resulting in strategic management. By taking militarist thinking (i) and combining (+) it with rational science, the result (=) is a scientific capability to wage war. Like the army, management has convinced itself that the application of science will lead to highly favourable outcomes. The use of scientific methods promises to win any war – no matter if these methods are applied to a real war or to the business of winning the market-share war. The somewhat irrational promise of a military war that can never be lost – something that hardly stacks up to the empirical evidence of Germany's WWI and WWII, America's Vietnam war or more recent Iraq war, etc. – is transferred to management and business. Similarly, the claim that the application of scientific methods to the strategic planning of business will lead to infallible outcomes is not supported when exposed to simple logic. If strategic and scientific planning are the key to managerial success why is it that so many companies – that have used these techniques – simply fail? Many of these companies have been relatively large and renowned, ranging from Chrysler, Enron, Netscape, E-Toys, Pan Am, Rover and Rolls Royce to Germany's AEG and Mannesmann, Italy's Parmalat, etc. Most – if not all – of them have followed the newest, best, and most scientific management strategies available to transform their business into a strategic business.

The application of strategy and science promises the transformation of *ordinary* management (iii) and business into *scientific* management and business and of scientific management and business into strategic management and strategic business (iv). According to this managerial belief system (Figure 8.1[i–iv]) only the use of science enables to arrange war or business in a pre-planned or strategic way. Planned scientifically and strategically it will not only enable management to win any war or business but – and perhaps more importantly – assist management in rationally, and even scientifically, justifying their managerial decisions. In this framework scientific methods have been used to construct and legitimise war-making and managerial choices which, now covered up by science and rationality, have scientific methods as a common denominator. Once these methods are applied to the planning of war or business activity, both are infallible as they are scientifically based. They promise military action and business activity that cannot fail. Management just needs to apply the strategic planning techniques that are found in almost any standard management textbook. Despite a relative large amount of discomforting evidence that renders management's claim as a promise that has largely been unfulfilled, the legitimising element in this construction cannot be underestimated. Even though these planning methods have failed, they are consciously or unconsciously part of today's business folklore.

The idea of *war = management* and *management = war* reaches deep into today's corporations. Not surprisingly, Max Barry writes in his novel *Company* (2006): *yes, some of us must play on the business battlefield.* The management = war link maybe historical, but its presence is felt in any modern corporation. Above that the science-military strategic link shown in Figure 8.1 also serves management and managerialism in another way by connecting military's anti-democratic and authoritarian structures with those of management. Historically, it also linked the military class structure of Prussian society to authoritarian business structures and vice versa. The Prussians viewed politics as an anti-democratic enterprise and war as an endeavour that could be extended into business. Their anti-democratic and militaristic thinking separated two core ideas. It divided military strategy from battlefield tactics. *Tactics* or the theory of fighting is in reality the principal object pre-designed via strategy. Battles are decisive actions comprising tactical elements that could be taught beforehand yet are somewhat limited as such actions depend on situational factors. Strategy is fundamentally different.

In contrast to battlefield tactics, *strategy* is the theory of the combination of separate battles towards the objective of the campaign. It is, according to Clausewitz and Moltke, a subject of natural and matured power of judgement and non-democratic *decision-making*. This is expressed in three core components: actions, states, and outcomes. Action is an episode under control of the strategic planner. Minor states or situations of warfare are seen as episodes outside the control of the strategic planner, and an outcome is created by a causal interaction between action and state. The target is the separation of action planning and operation. In the *strategic* versus *tactics* model, the decisions of other actors are relevant insofar as they secure their success. The tactic-strategy model has strongly influenced management thinking.[352] The strategy part of the model assumes three meanings:

Table 8.1   Three Core Meanings of Strategy

Meaning	Description
Military Positional Action Plan	the management of an army or armies in a campaign, the art of moving ships, troops, aircraft, etc. into a favourable position, and a pre-constructed, intentional, and strategic plan formed according to a rational and instrumental scheme designed for action or policy in business or politics, especially economic or management strategy.

As shown in Table 8.1 with its anti-democratic and militaristic background, the concept of strategy can successfully be transferred to management. It provides ideas for an attempt to find ways in which a business can plan its role in market places before engaging in a planned battle over market share

(Ohmae 1983:37–38). As Parks et al. (1994) emphasised in their *Marketer's guide to Clausewitz: Lessons for Winning Market Share:*

> *Clausewitz promoted the use of simple plans and their execution to achieve military success. Marketing managers can use the same strategies to be successful*

Figure 8.2   Clausewitz and Marketing Management

Simple planning and setting ends is viewed as no more than a mere function of knowledge that an actor has of a situation. This has been detected by one of the most eminent writers on the function of strategy for the rise of managerial capitalism, Alfred Chandler (1962:9). In his writings the warfare terminology changed microscopically when military *field-units* stayed as business *field-units* and a *general's camp* became *general office* reproducing the army's terminology, authority, and hierarchies for management.[353] In short:

Table 8.2   Clausewitz and Chandler: Military and Managerial Language

Clausewitz Military Language		Chandler Management Language
General's Camp	⇨	General Office
Field Unit	⇨	Field Unit

As Table 8.2 shows, a reflection on the military is clearly expressed in management's language, design, and differentiation of top-down hierarchical positions. Generals became CEOs and soldiers became workers. One thinks strategically while the other operates tactically.[354] The centralised decision-making as a *unit of command* enforces a scalar chain of communication producing an orderly and predictable flow of behaviour. Simon[355] (1965:154–156) have highlighted the military-management connection as:

> sometimes the organisation has its own sensory organs – the intelligence unit of a military organisation; not only is communication absolutely essential to an organisation, but the availability of particular techniques of communication will in large part determine the way in which decision-making functions can and should be distributed throughout the organisation; military organisation has developed especially elaborate procedures for accomplishing the gathering and transmittal of information.

This information gathering assists military decisions and is essential for the military and for the commander's estimate to combat units in the field. The combating units reappear in Chandler's (1962) famous *field units*. In the military as in management, command of and over information, according to Simon (1965:154–156), supports *the security of command* and the security of management. Information gathered by the military and the *intelligence divisions* of business is located close to the general's or CEO's staff.

The commanding military and management structures have an even wider range of common aspects that both share intimately. They share several core identities that define both, one of which is (i) the battlefield where enemies or companies respectively meet in friendly or unfriendly take-over fights over market shares and the like. Both are (ii) rather undemocratic and tend to be even monocratic when it comes to decision-making. The battlefield and decision-making are divided into those who manage and those who are managed (iii). Both operate very strongly with connotations (iv) of *The Order of Things* (Foucault 1994). Military, business, and management also operate in a dehumanising fashion (v). Both have rather strong similarities when it comes to internal structures (vi). Essential to military and to management is subordination (vii). Finally both rely on power (viii).

i) Horsemanship and the battlefield

While strategy was derived from armed warfare, management originated in *the craft of horsemanship*. In regard to management techniques both have common origins in the study of how to slaughter men on the *battlefield* or how to manage or domesticate a horse. The earliest evidence of written managerial instructions dates back to about 5,000 years when the Sumerians developed a script in order to manage their first developing cities. The oldest completely preserved text is the Instruction of *Ptah-Hotep* written by the vizier of King Issis around 2,700 BC.[356] Even today, the origins of management can still be traced back to the *manége* (now: workplace) as the location where a *horse-trainer* (now: manager) domesticates (now: manages) horses (now: labour) with sticks (now: power) and carrot (now: money) techniques. This is shown in Table 8.3:

Table 8.3   The Managerial Language of the Horse Trainer

Horses Trainer's Language				Management's Language
manége	⇨	now	⇨	workplace
horse-trainer	⇨	now	⇨	manager
domesticates	⇨	now	⇨	manages
horses	⇨	now	⇨	labour
sticks	⇨	now	⇨	power
carrot	⇨	now	⇨	money

The language similarities between horse trainer and management shown in Table 8.3 relate to many linguistically expressed ideologies that served the horse trainer over the horse and the manager over the worker. The language enshrined in these techniques strongly relates to many Machiavellian power principles which governed feudal top-down order as much as they govern today's top-down order found in all corporations. In the past, these principles found their application through feudal rulers such as princes, lords, monarchs, and religious orders and, in those days as much as today, the productive domain has been and is governed by these principles. But it is only the world of work which today remains governed by these principles. The domain of society is structured differently. Today the reality of the *power and money* code that governs the societal *Überbau* or superstructure is paved over by mass democracy mediated through powerful corporate mass-media interests.[357] The mass media that present and represent democracy are not governed *demo*-cratically but *mono*-cratically.

ii) Monocratic and democratic affairs

A second aspect that links the terminology of *strategy* to the terminology of *management* is their non- or anti-democratic value system. Strategy is an undemocratic concept much in the same way in which management is an undemocratic agency. Not surprisingly many writers on organisation and management have uncritically and unreflectively accepted the undemocratic tradition and have exempt the field of management and organisational studies from democracy (Mumby 2000:85). An excellent work on Max Weber can be found in Marcuse's (1968) article *Industrialisation and Capitalism in the Work of Max Weber* that positions Weber's work in the historical context of Bismarck's Germany providing a *value-free* and above all supportive analysis for capitalism during the rise of this system in a country where an emerging capitalist class was under strong pressure to keep up with France and England. It was first published during World War I. For Weber and the capitalist class of Germany only the development of large-scale industry could guarantee the independence of the nation in the ever more intense international competitive struggle. Imperialist power politics require intensive and extensive industrialisation, and vice versa. Weber defined himself as *bourgeois* and identified his work with the historical mission of the bourgeoisie.[358] Non-democratic or mono-cratic *companies* are considered to be more effective than democratic forms of organisations as their goal is to make profit in the market war. If one considers the original meaning of the term democracy, then today's companies could not be further removed from democracy. The etymology of the word *democracy* – from the Greek *demos*, people, and *kratein,* to rule – makes it clear that democracy means people are governing themselves. In modern business this is nowhere to be seen as non-democratic or *monocratic* managers – much like past generals or their military predecessors of feudalist *freelance* soldiers and mercenaries who were organised in bread-sharing *con-panes* or today's *com-panies* – demand at least three forms of *monocratic* authority. According to Etzioni (1959:48–49) these are:

Table 8.4 Three Forms of Monocratic Authority

No.	Forms of Authority at Work
i)	a general or major as goal-setting authority,
ii)	an institutional authority of heads or CEOs,[359] and
iii)	a self-maintaining and system preservative *autocracy* with authority over organisational structures.

Managers enact these three roles (Table 8.4) in a non-democratic way hidden behind the purposive rationality while at the same time portraying themselves as sole representatives of managerial authority. They uphold an observable masquerade of being in control and need to constantly control themselves never to let the mask slip. They need to ensure never to be exposed to the reality of power behind the shield. Rather than democratic values, managers represent order, command, and directive power relations and are constantly vigilant to prevent chaos from taking reign. They provide an authoritarian structure in an unstructured world. They signify modernity's non-democratic superiority over democracy by virtue of position and instrumental-scientific knowledge taught at business schools and represented in textbooks and managerial degrees such as MBAs and the like.

Academics in business schools, more than others, subordinate themselves to the anti-democratic ideological demands of managerialism as they show a willingness to accept the notion that businessmen perform a useful function. While their academic writings are highly supportive to managerialism, they increasingly behave accordingly as universities are transformed into businesses. Watson (2003:29) illustrates this in the following way:

> James and J. S. Mill wrote books that changed the course of history while working for the East Indian Company, a multinational. Today they wouldn't. Today they would be attending countless meetings, seminars and conferences to update their knowledge of work-related subjects, all of them conducted in the mind-maiming language of managerialism.

Today's academics – those who work in business and management schools more so than others – are no exception to this. They gain academic standing and satisfaction from being part of non-democratic decision-making mechanisms and managerialism. They practice good human relations as long as democracy does not get in the way and as long as it favours the profit imperative. They accept the anti-democratic corporate *culture* and structure of managerialism. Even terms such as organisational culture are an aberration of what they actually mean. True culture is reduced to a mass-produced commodity. Often such cultural objects of art are nicely framed posters in the foyers of corporations or meeting rooms. As there are hardly any writers, poets, novelists, or artists employed in such corporations, culture and art is, however, turned into equivalent industries, the so-called *art industry* or *culture industry*. They, like management, strive towards value-added, continuous improvement and total quality management to become world class in a benchmark process. In the arts and culture industry, managerialism sets its ideas in motion just like in any other industry as it forces its believe system onto it.

Most commonly, such non-democratic managerial ideas are *authored* in popular journals such as the *Harvard Business Review* and so-called academic journals, none of which is openly democratic as market forces and other structural determinants govern the so-called production of scientific knowledge of management. All too often a close circle of internally determined academics who uphold similar views referee each other's publications. Sometimes core managerial ideas are authored in quasi-popular management books but the core part of non-democratic management literature derives from a never-ending stream of management ideas published in reputable journals that have demonstrated their capacity for non-democratic system integration. Most importantly, however, ideas are frequently re-authored and re-authorised in standardised and mass-circulated textbooks.

The volume of management literature that clutters colleges, universities, airports, and bookshops is designed to cloak the prevalence of a non-democratic order in management. In it, a non-democratic management science and scientific findings are made easily digestible. These books are formatted in quasi-scientific and, above all, in non-democratic scientific language[360] that is designed to produce and reproduce a managerial class that has accepted their fate and operates non-democratically without ever questioning it. But no management textbook will ever state that being anti-democratic is good for business; hence a way had to be found to keep the illusion of democracy alive. While management literature promotes a democracy in the world of work that has largely been diluted, it has not totally vanished. It is an empty shell.

The linguistic maintenance of managerial authoritarianism and non-democratic hierarchies at work is achieved through the language of quasi-participation and quasi-involvement. In short, democracy is, first of all, downgraded to simple involvement or participation. Once re-configured in this way, it is, of course, subject of many managerial or MBA conditioning or training courses whether taught explicitly or implicitly. This is an important function as it secures the pretence of human agreement as a foundation of managerial facts. It is, in fact, a rather one-sided business school creation represented through the power established by assigning a thing (office) to a human being, thus creating the manager. This is secured through functional training. The merger between office and human being that allocates power to management includes status symbols such as stocks and bonds, as well as credit cards whether gold, platinum, or black, and the company cheque-books.[361] Any business-school training does not only guarantee access to such status symbols, it also allows for *speech acts to be self-identifying for those who know the language* (Searle 1996:119). Those who know the language are the *managers* and those who do not are the *to be managed.*

iii) Manage and to be managed

A third commonality can be found in management's emphasis on techniques seeking to exclude the agency component. Consequently, the literature of management *has much less to say of and for those who are managed* (Marsden & Townley 1996:660). Naturally, this is separated from the invention of *managerial authority and employee obedience.* The role of those who manage – management – over those who are managed – labour – is clearly defined, even though management experienced some problems in defining their role. The American economist, Galbraith (1969:80) saw management as *a collective and imperfectly defined entity.* While Mills (1951:80) defined it as *management is something one reports to in some office* and *Corporal Klinger* expressed his understanding of management in the US comedy series MASH 4077 as:

> *Management is when those who can't manage those who can.*

Whatever management is or might be, it plays a crucial role in the profit and market-share *war.* It establishes its legitimate role in capitalism and increases its standing by adopting the word *strategic.*[362] For those who manage, the affix strategic is a huge support in legitimising their very own existence and similarly portraying their rule over those who are managed. The usage of the term *strategy* has been illuminated in Hamel's (1996) ten principles of the strategy revolution:

Table 8.5   Ten Principles of the Strategy Revolution

1. strategy making must be democratic;	2. strategic planning may be planning but it isn't strategic;
3. strategy making must be subversive;	4. anyone can be a strategy activist;
5. the bottleneck is at the tip of the bottle;	6. perspective is worth fifty IQ points;
7. revolutionaries exist in every company;	8. top-down and bottom-up are not the alternatives; and
9. change is not the problem, engagement is;	10. you cannot see the end from the beginning.

Table 8.5 shows a number of advantages for management to transform itself into strategic management. Firstly, management prefers to attach the term *strategic* rather than *democratic* to themselves. Secondly and despite of using the term *strategy* management's prime task is not so much allocating resources, planning, strategic thinking, organising, and leading *but* their construction as managers to manage over non-managerial staff. Establishing the highly opaque use of core managerial terms, managerial language, and code words creates, more than anything else, the institution of management. This *managerial language* portrays the body of *managerialism* as knowledge that assists the modern manager in constructing themselves as managers.[363] It linguistically constructs managers as masters over all else. They are needed to manage and must be seen to be the masters over the order of things and over humans. The role of humans is reduced to those who are managed, a manageable entity. Humans are turned into *things* and reconstructed as human *resources*. This reduces humans to objects of managerial power relations within an administration that creates order, the order of those who manage over those who are managed.[364]

iv) The bureaucratic administration of the order of things

A fourth commonality between strategy and management is the *bureaucratic* aspect of both (Weber 1924). Here the agency of management creates strategies as courses of actions or orders to be followed by other agencies, usually lower in the hierarchy.[365] For Weber a business was not just business but it had wider implications that reached deep into society. He also saw strategic and managerial thinking related to cultural disenchantment thus establishing the basis for an extension of institutional coercion combined with an unstoppable expansion of discipline and strict obedience creating *specialists without spirit and sensualists without heart*.[366] These *specialists without spirit* create strategic plans through managerial means. This occurs through means of rationally structured functions called *bureaucracy*.[367] Bureaucracy derives from the French term *office* (bureau) and combines it with the Greek term for *to rule* creating the rule of an office as office-rule, the rule of the bureau or *bureaucracy*.[368]

Bureaucracy provides not only administrative means for the *Order of Things* at work; it also *Manufactures Consent* thus creating an *Affirmative Character* expressed in a conformist *Organisation Man*.[369] It is not so much bound to the *authoritarian* character as it is directed towards the *affirmative* character.[370] The overemphasis of individuality within management is in reality dissolved by the administration of people through HRM. It forces the individual into high levels of adoptive behaviour. This is mediated through HRM's bureaucratic powers.[371] Bureaucracy is an essential element of the reproductive domain as well as of the productive domain. Both are organised under the ideological determinants of managerialism.[372] Bureaucracy's ability to manage distant and complex systems reduces unpredictability and systematises everything. A high potential for system integration and an application of power relations inside a rational order turns *subjects* into *objects* of power. Inside the world of work, companies tend to become the object of total administration, which absorbs even the HRM-administrators.[373] The HRM web of domination is constructed as the web of reason itself. Workers and managers are fatally engaged in it. However, it will never completely succeed in total organisation and is therefore deemed to endlessly organise against disorganisation. Through bureaucracy, people at work as in their private lives have become mere instruments of a mechanistic and instrumental organisation of capitalist dehumanised pseudo-community.[374]

v) Dehumanisation and pseudo-community

A fifth commonality between management and strategy is language itself. The *dehumanising bureaucracy* outside of work and at work can be seen as functional only through communication corresponding to the demands of management and bureaucratic needs (Bauman 1989). Before Bauman (1989), Weber (1922) extensively discussed the de-humanising aspects of bureaucracy. While Bauman (1989) related bureaucracy to the Holocaust, Weber (1922) saw bureaucracy as an operation *without regard for persons* as it reduces people to abstract functions and exposes them to impersonal rules.[375] Communication and language establish legitimacy for management through shared goals and the vision of the firm. Above all, the faked language of *vision* and *mission statements* seeks to legitimise management and managerial strategy. Such *mission statements* can be summed up as, *you can smell it in his prose, which is equally adept at capturing the vacuity of a corporate mission statement or the back-and-forth of neurotic middle-management weasels crunching in the vice of mandated staff cuts* (Bing 2006:27). Despite all the corporate nastiness, mission statements are done – not *for* you! – but *for* the firm by creating a faked community among workers that Gouldner (1952:347) once labelled *pseudo-Gemeinschaft*. Located at the core of such a counterfeited *Gemeinschaft* is what Weber (1922) called *Gehäuse der Hörigkeit,* a cabinet (Gehäuse) or shell based on bondage or serfdom (*Hörigkeit).* Apart from management's control function exercised through the implementation of strategy or simply by giving *orders*, the application of managerial language produces an additional feature. It produces hegemony and the hegemony of meaning in organisations. By doing so, it adds legitimacy to management.[376]

vi) Structure over meaning

A sixth commonality between the military and management is their shared structural form. Both have structure as a defining feature. This gives meaning to a business entity as it is structure not substance that stabilises a corporation and with it management. The military and the management structures are explicitly stated and recorded, available for any authorised person. Structure is seen as prescriptive. It tells what the organisation looks like and these prescriptions have authority. As Weber (1922:76) once noted *no special proof is necessary to show that military discipline is the ideal model for the modern capitalist factory*. Structure involves statements that apply to members of an organisation defining their role, relationships and rewards. Structure is analytically separated from work processes or technology. Military, business and managerial strategies serve to structure, to organise and to give meaning to the complex operations of business companies. In both – military and business – strategies are not about *what should be* but rather *what is*. Such structures are one of the clearest expressions of managerial instrumental-rationality functioning as an element creating legitimacy for management.

In addition to structure, managerial authority is manifested through the management of meaning thus creating managerial legitimacy. As management is the prime institution of communication inside the world of work, it possesses a privileged position in determining communication and defining the meaning of it. Therefore, management is the main source of creating symbols, images, euphemisms, and metaphors representing power structures in sometimes very straightforward ways (Bolinger 1968, 1980). Management not only creates such symbols and images, it also has the prime objective in defining their meaning. Establishing such meanings can be of greater importance than creating a symbol. Most of all, managerial creation of symbols and the defining of meaning attached to it serves a prime purpose, the purpose of creating managerial authority, assigning responsibilities and maintaining the subordinate relationship at work.

vii) Authority, responsibility, and subordination

Authority, according to Max Weber (1922), is a guiding principle of management. But authority comes from a variety of sources. Traditionally, management did not evolve from *charismatic* authority such as Nelson Mandela or from *traditional* authority like the birthright of Prince Charles. It rather developed from *rational-legal* authority that is similar to militarist authority which is hierarchically established through a position.[377] According to early management writer Henry Fayol (1841–1925), military and managerial authority and responsibility share the following five aspects: planning, organising, commanding, coordinating, and controlling. Both have a division of work based on specialisation, authority and responsibility, discipline, unity of command, unity in direction, subordination of individual goals, centralisation, scalar chain of communication, social order, and collegiality and cooperation. Military and management also share a common interest in the use of power and the structure that supplies power to them.

viii) Power and power-relationships

An eighth and final commonality is the issue of power as both – military and management – strongly operate with power and power relationships via a range of power relations. These are: *reward* power, *coercive* power, *referent* power, *expert* power, and *legitimate* power. At the level of *reward power* 'A' has power over 'B' via some form of formal or informal reward. At the level of *coercive power* 'A' can issue punishment and disciplinary action against 'B'. At the level of *referent power* mentors or charismatic leaders have referent powers over 'B' when 'B' is willing to do what 'A' asks in order to be liked by 'A'. At the level of *expert power* 'B' is willing to do what 'A' demands because of knowledge and expertise. Finally, under *legitimate power* 'A' has positional power over 'B' by virtue of hierarchical ranking expressed as general (military) or general manager (business). Common to the use of power in the military as well as in the world of work is that power works best when seen least. To receive legitimacy, power almost does not need to do anything as too many people readily seek to comply with the will of the powerful and do what is expected of them. To encourage this behaviour, managerialism relies heavily on two ideological instruments at their disposal. These are technical domination and engineering ideologies.

9
Technical Domination and Engineering Ideology

In its quest for legitimacy management establishes a link to the term *strategic*. It lifts management from being a rather simple activity into a strategic activity worthy of academic attention. Managerialism is also legitimised through the acknowledgement by academics and universities. As a result, the issue of strategic management receives high popularity in fashionable and academic management literature such as the *Harvard Business Review, Academy of Management Review, Academy of Management Journal, Administrative Science, Quarterly,* and other management journals as well as numerous books.[378] The concept behind all that literature is to show how to win a war conducted on the battlefield of markets by operating strategically. Most importantly, the glorious promises to win the market-share war is issued to all and believed by all, even though not all can win or have ever won these battles. But they carry on believing it – almost by some form of inner logic. Strategy entered the literature of management with Chandler (1962:13). He defined strategy *as the determination of the basic long-term goals and objectives of an enterprise, and the adoption of courses of action and the allocation of resources necessary for carrying out these goals.* All strategic action is guided towards a goal under conditions of rational planning. This is not something terribly new. Aristotle had discussed such teleological action. At its core remains the following assumption (Habermas 1997:85):

> The actor attains an end or brings about the occurrence of a desired state by choosing means that have promise of being successful in the given situation and applying them in a suitable manner. The central concept is that of a decision among alternative courses of action, with a view to the realisation of an end, guided by maxims, and based on an interpretation of the situation. The teleological model of action is expanded to a strategic model when they enter into the agent's calculation of success the anticipation of decisions on the part of at least one additional goal-directed actor. It is this model of action that lies behind decision-theoretic and game-theoretic approaches in economics, sociology, and social psychology.[379]

In other words, strategy is a form of *rationality that can be measured by the success of goal-directed intervention* (Habermas 1997:15). One can call action *instrumental* when technical rules of action and assessments of efficiency are involved as an intervention into complex circumstances or events. For the planning of battles (Clausewitz) or *objectives of an enterprise* (Chandler), purposive instrumental rationality dedicated to hierarchical *means-ends* chains is crucial in the strategic planning of a business battle.

Instrumental rationality is closely linked to the army as well as to management as both transfer organisational principles to business or war *organisations*. Located behind both are also ideologies that conceal their political character. Principally, war is not called war but defence. Profit is not called profit but organisational goal. Conveniently, profit-making corporations are just called organisations which sounds much more neutral. It has an almost *value-free* appearance. Originally the term *organisation* stems from the Greek *organon*.[380] It means tool, apparatus or instrument. Organisations carry connotations of a formal system with them that has a teleological orientation towards achieving goals. Such organisations can be seen in a number of ways. This is shown in Table 9.1:

Table 9.1   Four Forms of Organisations

No.	Four Forms
i)	as *member-beneficial* organisations such as cooperatives, or as
ii)	*client-beneficial* organisations such as schools or hospitals, or as
iii)	*public-beneficial* organisations such as public postal services serving all members of a community. When the term organisation is used it is the
iv)	*owner-beneficial* or business that is meant in the world of work.

The standard business-management literature prefers the term organisation as it carries connotations of being of benefit to members, clients, or the public (Table 9.1:i–iv) even though *owner-beneficial* organisations (iv) are meant. The positive image of Table 9.1(i–iv) is most welcome as it diverts attention from the real purpose of the exercise, i.e. making profit. It is able to hide the profit motive behind a neat ideology of benefits to members, clients, and the public. Ideologically, the more neutral-sounding term organisation is appreciated as it even includes members, clients, and public associations. All have positive connotations. The partly positive term organisation also eclipses a much harsher reality of benefiting one group over another. It hides the fact that corporations exist to benefit its owners over its members, i.e. workers. It also benefits its owners over its clients and most of all its owners over the public.

In the world of work, the organisational communication idea eclipses a division of *those who manage* and *those who are managed.* They are not seen as workers but as organisational members. All of this is not only hidden behind the supposedly neutral term of *organisation* but also behind an *engineering ideology*.[381] A term such as *organisation* fits neatly to engineering. Organisations are seen to be in need of being engineered and engineering ideology matches the managerial use of rationality. The creation of the term *managerial rationality* provided management with a powerful code that legitimised its very own existence and at the same time politically neutralised a socially constructed reality by referring to an impartial and unbiased conduct at work. This all-embracing code has been presented as the one and only rational way towards modernity. It links progress and the benefit of all people to modernisation and management. Management, engineering, and managerial rationality were made synonymous with the advancement of society under modernity and *Enlightenment*.[382] In this project engineers like Frederick Taylor played a vital role as they supplied an engineering ideology to the process of establishing managerial control over production. While originally used for the organisation of production, in the hands of management engineering ideology became a useful tool that instrumentally and strategically supported management. This was established in a number of ways. Firstly, management has been able to turn engineering concepts such as technical solutions into technical problems via the transferral into social relations at work. Hence, social problems became technical problems and management used engineering solutions to solve problems in the area of work.

Secondly, the influence of technical problem-solving mechanisms is customary in textbooks used to educate managers. Scavenging teaching material from technical colleges and transferring it into business schools created the perception that issues at work can be solved by applying a few rational steps.[383] Instrumental rationality as applied by engineers has now entered business-school teaching in an attempt to redesign work that is totally subsumed under the encompassing engineering ideology of efficiency. To achieve profitable efficiency work has to be totally surrendered to managerial rationality in a taken-for-granted approach that claims to be universal.

Management has literally managed to represent itself as a TINA-institution. There Is No Alternative! Only the institution of management can guarantee effectiveness and efficiency.[384] Following that, management has increased its legitimacy dramatically. Overwhelmingly, all this is necessary for management to construct itself as an apolitical and neutral endpoint, serving only the common good of managing wealth creation.[385] Thirdly, along with a traditional understanding of engineering problems through the containerisation of problems in boxed-up versions came an equally boxed-in understanding of issues in the world of work. Such compartmentalisation of work issues into narrowly defined subject areas enables managers to disconnect work issues from the social existence of labour and management. Management is able to live inside the square it has created for itself. Issues adjacent or even outside such boxes can conveniently be excluded. By definition such managerial approach already excludes certain forms of knowledge and prevents any thinking outside a pre-defined subject area. Hence, non-managerial issues such as politics, economics, political economy, issues of a reproductive domain, etc. remain outside the comprehended realm of management and its standardised literature.

A neatly defined box of knowledge that selects issues for management and disregards those which can be ignored or neglected is mirrored in a set of accompanying literature that is constructed in the same way. As a consequence, there is no need for a managerial *Index Librorum Prohibitorum*. An index of forbidden books for management does not exist. Management scientists, management writers, and journal editors themselves closely guard and protect an equally closely defined body of knowledge.[386] The purposively built-in selectiveness of management and management literature is part of managerialism. It is one of the core guiding principles that enable one-dimensionality and exclusion. Because of the self-serving ideology of managerialism, there is neither a need for sanctions nor for external forms of punishment.[387] The French philosopher Foucault (1995) had correctly predicted that external forms of punishment are dissolved by internalised self-discipline.[388] Management's self-disciplining restrictions to issues regarded supportive of managerialism as predicted by Foucault has been achieved.

Fourthly, the application of engineering concepts also supports managerial issues by appearing to be *neutral* and disconnected to any historical understanding. Managerial history, the historical origins of managerial rationality, instrumental thinking, and the history of military-strategic thinking remain untouched or reduced to mere footnotes. Hence, academic texts are structured along engineering lines that cut off rather than provide historical origins of concepts such as managerial rationality. They negate historical origins through the reduction of managerialism to technical correlations. This diminishes the social, political and economic history of management and the world of work. Any issues related to the world of work are trimmed to the simple issue of pure application of neutral instruments or tools that can be used to fix any problem.

Fifthly, the individual as an active agent has been replaced by system rationality. This seeks to standardise the world of work via institutions, organisation, system planning, and strategy. Neutral organisational charts and graphs are produced and reproduced in order to eliminate the political and historical role of actors. Those who have been made the object of management are hidden inside a neglected historical understanding of mass production. Their historical suffering is also concealed. The history of this is covered up by an engineering ideology that is applied by management. Consequently, labour as an actor has been removed. This actor has been suitably deleted from the conscience of modern managers who are conditioned to think in simple engineering terms: 'A' leads to 'B'; □ ⇨ □; apply human resource 'A' to computer 'B' and it(!) will compute 'C' efficiently.

Such process of anti-agent system thinking fits to the standardisation and engineering of production. In human terms, this is the embodiment of social engineering. When management began to view labour as *engineer-able* the lines between worker and machine became blurred. In this way, *labour as a social actor has been reduced to a functional auxiliary to the machine*. Today, this labour-machine attachment has changed. The *engineering* logic of the information age works as follows: apply a human resource (A) to a computer (B) and *it* will compute information (C) efficiently. What has changed is not the engineer-ability of labour or the reduction of labour to a supplement. What has changed is the machine: the computer of late capitalism has replaced the machine of early capitalism. In early as in late capitalism, the social actor *labour* suffers the same fate – the reduction to a functional additive of an engineered production and socially constructed work system. The process of an engineered machine treatment of workers extends beyond simple engineering of the work processes. This process is able to re-engineer humans seen as upright-walking humans (*erectus*) into deformed or *fabricated* humans. The upright-walking *homo erectus* bends over to the system of production and is converted into *homo fabricatus* linking humans to the self-stabilising system. With this move a social system of fabricated humans that exist in fabricated workplaces has been established. Once exposed to the inner logic of a pre-fabricated machine existence, workers become objects of power as the rationality of irrationality takes its course.[389]

In this process the irrationality of converting humans into functional additives is covered by the instrumental rationality of the engineering process. According to Marcuse (1966:163), *the machine is only a means, the end is the conquest of nature, the domestication of natural forces through a primary enslavement: The machine is a slave that serves to make other slaves. Such a domineering and enslaving drive may go together with the quest for human freedom.* Inside this domineering system it is a challenging task to liberate oneself by converting previous slaves into human beings. The rules of the machine that turns humans into machine-slaves are accepted as a way of life in work as in society. While appearing neutral, socially constructed technology and engineering has been used to force workers into acceptance of their machine status serving specific management ends (Gouldner 1976). In the engineering and management discourse workers and machines have to be directed towards the same end. This has a long history. As the *American Machinist* wrote on 23rd March 1900 (p. 208), *hiring a man and buying a machine are very much alike*. Both are functions of an instrumental rationality that is directed towards measurable outcomes while the individual is merged with a machine or a system and subsequently ceases to exist as an individual. The individual vanishes into technical rationality via neutralisation of humans in production processes which are relieved of any humanity. The system metaphor became the system imperative based on standardisation and systematisation of work.[390] It is one of the clearest expressions of managerial rationality. It guides production as much as today's service, information, or knowledge industries. Standardisation and progress are equated. This system paradigm pretends to end domination and power relations and relocate them away from management in neutral systems.

These supposedly neutral systems operate independent of management who as the designer of these systems can move into the background only to observe how the system converts actors into system conforming in- and output functions. Management is even freed from control functions as system functions built into the system guarantee control. Such managerial system thinking establishes a cybernetic model of work.[391] In a hyper-mechanised machine society even management becomes entrapped in system mechanics. Management as much as labour represents its own alienated work situation. Being part of a system reduces the agent and creates a lack of spirit and aesthetics. This is reproduced in the managerial myths of equality, liberation, progress, and reason.[392] Once engineering ideologies that had been locked into the system narrative of the mechanisation of production exceed the domain of management, they start to colonise the economic, societal, moral, cultural, and political domain.[393]

The construction of labour and society as system auxiliaries occurs inside and outside the productive domain. This is communicatively expressed as a system only measuring in- and outputs. Only measurable entities are included.[394] The system is geared towards conformity in which the individual agent is alien unless it conforms to the system as defined by managers. These managerial work systems rely on engineering ideologies. Human elements are transformed into engineering elements, the result of which is needed to make the engineering or managerial system work. In such an engineering project only universally quantifiable forms of communication enter into a cost-benefit or means-ends analysis. They are a prerequisite for the system conforming domination of workers. The often-claimed individual, individuality itself, and non-quantifiable qualities only stand in the way of a business organisation designed to systematically dominate workers and material things inside a concept of measurable power relations. To further explain the role of the *agent* in the production process inside profit-oriented organisations, two economic concepts are called upon: *agency theory* and *transaction-cost analysis*. Agency theory includes three key assumptions:

Table 9.2   Agency Theory at Work

No.	Explanations
i)	workers – now re-named *organisational members* – are only interested in the maximisation of their own self-interest,
ii)	working life is reduced to contractual existence under conditions of self-advancement, and
iii)	organisations encourage self-interest behaviour and opportunism.

Table 9.2 shows that *agency theory* takes on three forms in which a worker – now more neutrally labelled *agent* – is reduced to a functional element inside a highly structured system. This is complementary to a relative high degree of system thinking that is used to justify and legitimise managerialism. It assumes that workers only act inside a given system without acknowledging that management designed the whole system. This system constrains and confines labour's action to a mere function that is part of the pre-conceived system. Forced to exist within these system precincts labour's behaviour is bound to include elements of system conformity that can be used by management and its entourage of willing management writers to support the ideas of agency theory. Workers, willing writers, and agency theory itself have become no more than a supporting tool of the system of managerialism. The other managerial tool is the *transaction-cost* analysis where a controlling hierarchy establishes internal company control of workers through the introduction of market forces. It operates via the introduction of supplier-*customer* models into a company.[395] By doing so, management has been able to effectively neutralise two issues, its own responsibility and the consequences of its action. Once the management of capitalist production has been set up in this way via the transferral of responsibilities and accountabilities into a neutral system process based on engineering ideologies, managers are free to act at will. All consequences have been offloaded to the system.

The impact and consequences of the Taylorist engineering ideology

As important as the ideological support through concepts such as instrumental, technical or *engineering ideologies* are, they still are *the major enemy of the workingman* (Morgan 1986:22). Apart from *agency* and *transaction-cost theory* it has been Taylor and with Taylor the outgrowth of Taylorism that has supported managerialism. As a technical-rational engineering ideology Taylorism has fundamentally reshaped labour's active participation in socially constructed decision-making processes at work. It did so by reducing all knowledge questions to the issue of technique, resulting in a cult of *the managerial expert*. Ever since Frederick W. Taylor (1911) it has commonly been assumed that the *managerial expert* only needs to apply a few simple law-like steps and tools to achieve his pre-determined goal of winning the market-share war. In order not to uncover the socially constructed management ideology of Taylor, Taylorism is presented as a scientific-neutral and technical-engineering project. The non-scientific and non-neutral character of Taylorism is hidden in just three of Taylor's (1911:59) own statements:

Table 9.3   Taylor's Value-Neutrality Exposed

No.	Three direct quotes from Taylor's work on scientific management
i)	*he [worker] should be so stupid and so phlegmatic that he resembles the mental make-up of the ox*
ii)	*to train an intelligent gorilla,*
iii)	*he is so stupid that the word 'percentage' has no meaning to him.*

Table 9.3[i–iii] shows that once exposed as *stupid worker*, *gorilla*, or *ox* the truth hidden inside the so-called *Scientific Management* of Taylor is less scientific and more ideological than the title of his work lets one believe. What is portrayed in standard management literature appears rather different from what Taylor actually wrote. Rather than being scientific the term *Scientific Management* seeks to eclipse the ideological content of Taylorism. Behind the screen of a supposedly scientific approach to management lies a rather unscientific but highly ideological form of managerial domination. Taylor's so-called scientific engineering steps seek no more than the conversion of labour – under Taylor scientifically called *an ox, a gorilla,* or labelled as *stupid* – into an unhistorical and socially disconnected element of production. Taylor's ideological statements and ideas are depicted as a techno-managerial project enabling management to appear neutral. The falsity of management's claim to *Scientific Management* through reliance on engineering and technology has been exposed not only in a few direct quotes from Taylor himself but also through a deeper analysis of technology. Technology is one of the core issues that management uses. It is particularly used when managerial processes have to pretend to be neutral. With technology in its neutralised form management is able to represent itself as neutral. There are a number of critical points against the technology-as-neutrality project. This is summed up in Table 9.4:[396]

Table 9.4   Critique of Technology-as-Neutrality Project

No.	Managerial Use of Technology to establish Domination over Work
1	Scientific-technical rationality as such has become an organisational principle at work supporting domination and managerial hegemony.
2	Operational techniques have moved to centre stage of the modern enterprise
3	Organisational techno-rationality has become the method for production and control over workers forcing them to comply with managerial methodologies.
4	Technical planning, formalisation of technical rules and technical functionalism occurs prior to its application at work.
5	Technical processes function as rational instruments for bureaucratic control.
6	Technical regimentation of work processes are used to eradicate workers' non-compliance as it is made to appear anti-technical, irrational and non-logical.
7	Affirmation to a technical process enshrines affirmation to managerial domination of production.[397]
8	Technology as means is not politically innocent because, even as it serves generic ends such as increasing the productivity of labour, its specific design and application in the existing industrial society forms the bias for a way of life that involves the domination of man by man.[398]
9	Technology as a total system or a cultural formation takes the place as an ideology that legitimises the existing society.
10	Scientific-technical rationality is *a priori* adapted to the maintenance of social domination.
11	Technological choice, like all other aspects of production, is determined by the fact that the pursuit of efficiency involves the impositions of effective control, not only over nature, but also over human beings at work.

The essence of Table 9.4 can be summed up in Marcuse's (1968:224, 225) words, *technology is always a historical-social project: in it is projected what a society and its ruling interests intend to do with men and things. The machine is not neutral; technical reason is the social reason ruling a given society. It can be changed in its very structure.* In order to hide the socially constructed character, its asymmetric power structure, introduction and application have been hidden behind the neutral claim. Similar to the use of Tayloristic social-engineering technology and domineering production arrangements is the application of Taylor's un-scientific, value-biased, socially rather than technically created *Scientific Management.* Taylor's idea of science is reduced to the application of a few technical steps. Depicting Taylor's project as non-historical engineering steps masks the historical, political, economical, and social context that influenced the creation of Taylor's ideas. Once freed up of its historical context and its socially constructed content, Taylor has been reduced to four key steps. These are shown in Table 9.5:

Table 9.5   Four Key Steps to Accomplish Taylorism

No.	Steps needed
i)	developing a science of work,
ii)	scientifically selecting and training labour,
iii)	combining a science of work and selecting and training labour, and
iv)	management and labour must specialise and collaborate closely.

These four steps shown in Table 9.5 depict that Taylor's engineering ideology is not directed towards an engineering problem but towards the social organisation of labour and management. His ideology is based on social theory, not technical theory. It creates a socially constructed reality, the reality of a separation between *techne* and *technology* as a socially introduced re-organisation of work under the division of labour.[399] Once technology was seen as a liberating force directed towards an instrumentalisation of things. Today this is no longer the case as we know that *even technological progress can be used for the diminution of human liberty* (Orwell 1949:201). The relentless application of engineering ideology turns the human mind into a shackled mind that prevents the liberation of thought. The instrumentalisation of workers at work represents the instrumentalisation of workers' minds at work and beyond. Shrouded as a technical or engineering process, this social re-organisation of work was done by taking or stealing knowledge from the craftsman's *techne*. Here, *techne* can be understood in its Greek origin of a traditional value-charged craft practised in pre-Taylorised times when craft, production, and art were one element. Under Taylor, the artistic *techne* of the craftsman is transferred to management who resides over the knowledge of *techne*. Eventually, it was converted into *technics* as an apparatus of industry, communication, transportation and other areas of production and extra-productive domains.

Eventually *techne* and *technics* became *techne*-ology or *technology* as the scientific version of *techne* via horizontal and vertical division of labour. Technology and social change altered the old ways of the crafts*man* significantly. They stripped the crafts*man* of his *craft* tools and with it he lost his productive power (Marx). It also stripped his *craft* knowledge away by transferring it as *techne* (Taylor) to management. Stripped of *craft*-tools and *craft*-knowledge, management was able to divide labour in two ways:[400]

Table 9.6 The Horizontal and Vertical Division of Labour

Division	Description
Horizontal	The *horizontal* division of labour enshrines the fragmentation of skill knowledge previously *owned* by crafts*men* by dividing work into an endless amount of tasks. This created a further level of alienation as the producer [worker] is further disconnected from the product of his work while it enhanced the social domination of labour at work.
Vertical	At the *vertical* level, the second division of labour allows the social re-organisation of work dividing production into in a managerial top-down fashion where the *top* designs tasks and the *down* operates them.

As Table 9.6 shows, management established itself as guardian of technology completing its socially constructed domination over labour via *horizontal* and *vertical* division of labour. At the horizontal level, this led to an acceptance of managerial task-oriented functions that split workers into little closed-up compartments on the one side and on the other side allowed social domination engineered through a technical process that has been sold as value neutral while in fact enshrining the horizontal division of workers. At the vertical level, management's *techno-ideology* allowed the extraction of long-established guild and craft knowledge from workers under the shroud of Scientific Management, the science of extracting labour's craft knowledge from them only to be converted into management knowledge and used as a weapon of domination. It transferred knowledge from one domain into another, from labour to management. This managerial operation sealed the fate of the workers. At the lowest level, it reduced workers to mere operators. The divisions of labour can be shown as:

Figure 9.1 Horizontal and Vertical Division of Labour

As Figure 9.1 shows, the hidden status of Taylor's engineering and technical ideology becomes visible through Taylor (1911:33) himself. He demanded that *management must take over and perform much of the work that* used to be done by the craftsman. Once the knowledge was taken from workers and transferred into the realm of management, workers could be downgraded. *He should be so stupid and so phlegmatic that he resembles the mental make-up of the ox.*[401] These words are neither scientific nor value-free. Taylor's non-value-free idea of social domination *applies not only to mechanised plants, tools, and exploitation of resources, but also to the mode of labour as adoption to and handling of the machine process, as arranged by scientific management* (Marcuse 1966:25). Instead of being a purely scientific and value-free process of material handling, Taylor's own words on *gorilla and ox* uncover it as *Un-Scientific Management*.

While viewing workers as oxen or gorillas, Taylor also realised that animals cannot run factories *scientifically*. For Taylor, the workman cannot be totally reduced to an ox. Therefore, he designed a system in which someone *more intelligent than a workman must train him.* In short, Taylorism is more about a *social* engineering ideology than *mechanical* engineering. *The very concept of technical reason is perhaps ideological* (Marcuse 1968:223). More relevant than the cloaking is its ideological character under the title of *Scientific Management* and a not-so-neutral and scientific application of laws to work is the creation of an adequate ideology for management. The ideology of the neutral *(management must take over!)* and value-free *(mental make-up of the ox!) Scientific Management* allowed Taylor to cloak a social reorganisation of work that provided for management. Its real relevance can be found in an ideological content that could be carried from manufacturing to the service industry; from the primary to the secondary and to the tertiary sector; from industrial to post-industrial work. At all levels, Taylor's engineering ideology legitimised managerial domination of labour. It became a dominant theme of managerialism.[402]

This domination had to be sold to the *workingmen* (Taylor) so that the value-biased engineered technical practice of social domination found acceptance among those who were on the receiving end. Modern production processes were linked to technology and communicated as a civilisation and *engineering* project and not as a *domineering* project. It was presented as an expression of pure rationality and modernity seeking to integrate humans into dehumanising work arrangements that start with separation.

> In modern industrial society, the separation of the worker from the means of production has become a technical necessity requiring the individual and private direction and control of the means of production,

that is, the autonomy of the personally responsible entrepreneur in the enterprise (Marcuse 1968:212).

The system integrative elements had to be communicatively established. Technology can never achieve this by itself. Only a technical system that is communicated in such a way that Taylor's *value-neutral gorillas* were willing to participate in their own domination can achieve this. Domination via technological means represents a universal mediation of modern working life. Using Feenberg's concept of *The Dialectics of Technology* (2002:178), acceptance, legitimacy, and willingness to participate have to be communicatively achieved. This has been done through eight key elements:

Table 9.7   Eight Communicative Elements of Technical Domination

No.	Form	Description
i)	Decontextualisation	Through technology the subject becomes an object of a technical process that hides the context of work process disabling a comprehensive understanding.
ii)	Systematisation	Work processes are presented as part of a rational – and therefore unchangeable – system with in- and outputs and self-regulatory mechanisms.
iii)	Reductionism	Workers are valued only via a reduction of exchangeable and functional qualities and quantities in a dehumanising process directed towards productivity.
iv)	Mediation	Interfaces between workers and the productive system are mediated through technical processes and communicatively established system integration.
v)	Automatisation	Factory automation (mass production) and automated offices (IT) communicate domination via positioning workers as functional additives to automation.
vi)	Vocationalism	Vocational training's domination-hiding qualities are communicated as a necessary system demand that excludes aesthetics and ethical qualities.
vii)	Positioning	Technical domination is established via a positioning of labour in a pre-designed work arrangement setting narrow boundaries for workplace life.
viii)	Initiative	Technical domination demands participation beyond passivity as demands encourage system-conforming initiatives that lead to self-domination.

Table 9.7 shows how communicatively established domination via technology is engineered. The ideology of technology converts a subject – the person – into an object of technology. The process of social engineering using specific techniques leads to a *technification* of a previously social process. A social process is turned into a technical one and becomes *technified*. Taylor's engineering ideology directs the objectified human at work towards a working world that is disconnected from work which could establish context. The individual is to perform a task detached from any meaning of work. Individuals are reduced to mere functional additives to a pre-designed system inside which they experience their own reduction. This is strongly expressed by Marcuse (1968:223):

> Under the compulsion of reason, the fate is fulfilled that Weber foresaw with remarkable clarity in one of his most telling passages: Joined to the dead machine, [bureaucratic organisation] is at work to erect the shell of that future bondage to which one day men will perhaps be forced to submit in impotence.

The technically driven work process *joins* workers *to the dead machine* creating a kind of *bondage* as well as a *submission to impotence.* But the system still depends on a domineering mediation between worker and machine. These mediations are communicatively established via an automated or computerised workplace that demands vocational training to be directed towards functionality and not towards critical reflection, aesthetics or ethical qualities of work.[403] The process of functional *socialisation* is directed towards pre-conditioning and pre-domesticating humans.[404] It stabilises the pre-designed work system inside which labour operates in a pre-engineered work context created by managerial experts and communicatively legitimised through the ideology of a value-neutral engineering project.

The role and socially *constructed-ness* of management, managers, and managerialism has been intentionally reclassified and reframed so that it appears almost synonymous to the term *engineer*. In this view a *managerial expert* is seen as: *man is an engineer too, a social engineer, engineering social consent* (Whyte (1961:29–30). Whyte is not alone. Celebrated philosopher Karl Popper has added his *piecemeal social engineering* to the managerial project (Birnbaum 1969:81). In short, engineering ideology is used to cover the social content of the enterprise. It is also used to cover the historical reality of management's role in establishing hierarchy, discipline, control, and supervision, all of which have supported the emergence of capitalism ever since human society left the dark ages of feudalism (Marglin 1974). Historically, management has achieved its historic mission to set up control over work via three essential control mechanisms:

Table 9.8 Management's Control Mechanisms

Control	Description
i) Nature	control over nature as engineering and production control;
ii) Humans	control of human beings via processing labour through primitive methods of surveillance and drill that did not mean that labour goose-stepped into factories but more significantly they were drilled in obedience to managerial rules;
iii) Organisational	control over organisational abilities via hierarchy and bureaucracy.

Table 9.8 shows that control over nature (i) and over organisational abilities (iii) has been less challenging for management than the establishment of control over humans (ii). Control over labour is strongly manifested in a structure of control over material and authoritative resources that allows management to generate command over labour. Control over labour also incurs the dialectic between labour resistance, hegemonic and consensual *domination* on the one hand and forms of control on the other (Mumby 1997:349). These do not operate independently of each other as they have developed historically.

Managerial, organisational and labour control are closely linked to the historical development of capitalism (Edwards 1979:177–183). This development has led to fundamental changes in occupations with the development of employment linked to routine production services, in-person services, and symbolic-analytical services.[405] As shown in Table 9.9 below, capitalism and communicative control not only changed in the world of work but both have also developed fine-tuned methods.[406] With changes in control instruments, communication has also undergone several changes. In Table 9.9 these changes are shown with their adjacent communicative metaphors able to exemplify these changes. They range from early capitalism based on (i) owner-worker relationship to mechanised production systems relying on Fordist and Taylorist concepts (ii). The shift from manufacturing industries towards service industries (iii) brought new forms of control. As society and work moved into the stage of a (iv) *Post-Industrial Society* and eventually into the (v) *Information* or *Knowledge Society,* shifts in communicative control mechanisms changed again (Bell 1973; Stehr 1994). Each of these five communicative stages of controlling work is shown through stage-specific metaphors.[407] The metaphors used in table 9.9 below symbolise each stage to a large extent. They are taken from fiction literature as such literature sometimes portrays reality better than reality itself:

Table 9.9   Metaphors for Five Stages of Communicating Control

Stage:	Early Craft-Based Workshops	Manufacturing Ford & Taylor	Service Industry and Bureaucracy	Post-Industrial Society	Information or Knowledge Society
	→ i) →	→ ii) →	→ iii) →	→ iv) →	→ v)
Metaphor:	Steinbeck's *Grapes of Wrath*[408]	Charlie Chaplin's *Modern Times*	Franz Kafka's *The Trial*[409]	The BBC's *The Office*	George Orwell's *1984*

Table 9.9 starts with *Early Craft and Workshop based Capitalism* (i) during the rise of the private enterprise system. These were workshops with capitalists as owners and bosses on the one side and workers on the other side of a production system dominated by craft. Supervision was direct and related to master and worker. Communication was direct. At the second stage (ii), the agency of owner started to separate from labour via the rise of management. Owners were no longer able to operate *direct* control over labour. With movement from such craft based workshops towards the rise of the *factory system* under Taylorist and Fordist principles, control shifted more from the agency of the owner towards technical structure. Rising technical structures have led to the use of technical processes as a controlling instrument. The form of *technical* control is expressed in Charlie Chaplin's *Modern Times* movie.[410] Managerial control over the use of technology such as Taylor's task and Ford's assembly line enabled management to establish control over the domain of labour (ii).

With the move from manufacturing towards the *service industry*, managerial *bureaucratic* control mechanisms were established (iii). Bureaucratic control shown as a *Kafkaesque* metaphor (iii) moved towards the so-called post-industrial society. The British BBC's TV series *The Office* (iv) became the defining metaphor.[411] Core to communicatively established control under *The Office* metaphor is the development away from strictly bureaucratised personnel management prevalent at stages (ii) and (iii). Control moved towards a more flexible Human Resource Management relying foremost on elements of knowledge management. It encompasses all knowledge entities and measures these against so-called *Key Performance Indicators* (KPI) at corporate level. It converts knowledge from something needed in production into something more definitive for industry. It turns knowledge into something that is managerially constructed, to be managed, and manageable. Hence management was quick to occupy the word *knowledge* for itself. It located knowledge literally in front of itself. By colonising the term knowledge it turned management into *knowledge management. Knowledge management is one more mutant form of managerialism that walks blithely over a whole tradition of Western philosophy, crushing all subtleties and distinctions* (Watson 2003:27).

The information or knowledge economy can be signified in the most dramatic metaphor of all, George Orwell's *1984* (v).[412] While Orwell saw the future of society only as dark and grim, the future of work might not be so. Unlike Orwell's vision, the future is not a dark and grim nightmare where workers are trapped in a communicatively constructed horror and where managerial language defines every human thought. Like all other stages before, this stage also includes the dialectic between control and potentials for emancipation and resistance. Hope may only be created for those without hope. Orwell himself had acknowledged this. Orwell (1949:174) wrote, *with all their cleverness they had never mastered the secret of finding out what another human being was thinking.* Deleuze (1995:182) has also expressed the dialectics between control and resistance:

> new ways of manipulating money, products, and men, no longer channelled through the old factory system…one of the most important questions is whether trade unions still have any role: linked throughout their history to the struggle against disciplines, in sites of confinement, can they adapt, or will they give way to new forms of resistance against control societies.[413]

The future might, according to Deleuze (1995) show who will be the agent struggling against Orwellian mind-control.[414] To establish the latest version of control at work, management has become more reliant on communication. Here, communication is neither neutral nor enabling as it is used to establish and, above all, to maintain control and hierarchies at work. Increasingly, managerial system maintenance is less achieved through direct, mechanical or bureaucratic control mechanisms at work. As core elements of the work regime become more and more internalised in the minds of labour, management has been able to utilise other forms of control. This newer version of control relies to a much greater extent on communication than it has in the past.

10
Control and Communication at Work

Regardless of the way control is administered, it is often communicated in some form. These forms can be depicted inside a framework that is however not sufficient to assess today's workplace. The traditional and sequential view of control developed by Edwards (1979) is most widely used. This idea asserts that with the advanced development of capitalism and its subsequent restructuring of work, control of work also changed. Any extension of communication must go well beyond Edwards' (1979) original concept of control. The three known forms of control no longer serve as a sufficient explanation of control at work. With advances in work organisations Edwards' original model of control must also be advanced to reflect today's workplace. This is shown in Figure 10.1:

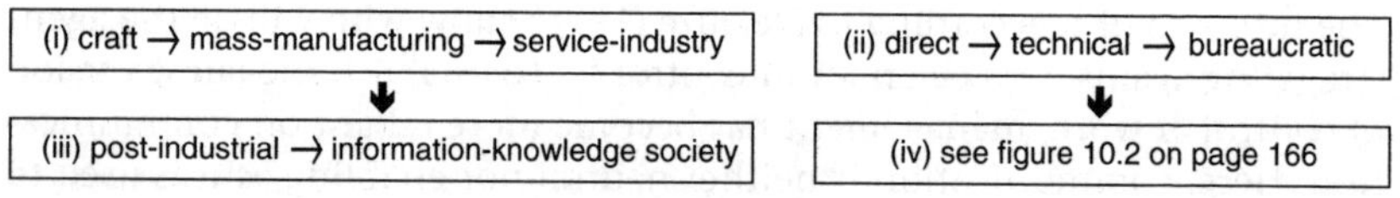

Figure 10.1   Workplace Control in the Post-Industrial and Information-Knowledge Society

Figure 10.1 shows that as modern production and society have advanced from (i) accurately reflecting Edwards' original stages of control (ii), industry has progressed towards post-industrial and eventually into an information-knowledge society (iii).[415] Management has established new forms of control coinciding with these developments (iv). The developments strongly exposed the demand for an extension of the forms of control. The additions of new versions of control are shown in Figure 10.2 below. Somewhat overlapping and often mutually supporting control instruments at stages beyond Edwards' (1979) traditional forms (A–C) are forms of control that appear in (D) and (E) in Figure 10.2 below. These two additions reflect the two new stages in capitalist development shown as new stages in the development of managerial control.

Controlling a post-industrial workforce beyond (A–C) relies firstly on what Barker (1993, 1999, 2005) has labelled *concertive,* indicating a *concerted* management effort to control which is not *coercive* in character. Here, new work arrangements such as teamwork created new control systems. These are enshrined in systems such as *neighbourhood-watch* or *peer-group* control (D). As these forms of control affect mostly workers organised in teams, functional groups, separated units and the like, they have been seen as an overall control instrument somewhat limited to these groups or teams of workers. Therefore, a fifth version of control was necessary to secure overall control. Increasingly, this is the task of the socialised form of control (E).

As working societies move increasingly into non-manufacturing work arrangements (figure 10.2:E), such control mechanisms are increasingly supported by an internalised form of *social-ised* control (Wills 1977). Today's workforce is well-conditioned or socialised for the demands of industrial work settings. This process started when workers entered industrial settings more than 200 years ago. Workers have been forced to internalise work regimes for several generations and work regimes have been part of a tradition that has been handed down from generation to generation. Social mechanisms of work have been inherited almost like any material inheritance. This social-inheritance process of converting *humans* into *labour* occurred in most advanced industrialised countries over several decades. In short, today's workforce has been exposed to the managerial structure of work for a very long time. As a result, it has not only internalised work mechanisms but also a concurrent work-support system external to work. Both work and its external support system have established workers' socialisation or system integration. Working inside the confines of the present work regime today is not challenged. Instead the present confines are widely accepted based on a long history of socialisation. Deleuze (1995:177) has expressed the internalisation process that leads to the socialisation of an individual:

Table 10.1   Steps of the Socialisation of an Individual

first	an individual is socialised through	all of the family,
then	an individual is socialised through	the school (*you're not at home, you know*),
then	an individual is socialised through	the barracks (*you 're not at school, you know*),
then	an individual is socialised through	the factory, hospital from time to time, maybe prison, the model site of confinement

Table 10.1 shows that after years of confinement in family, school, and barracks, humans adapt to the managerial machinery with ease and domestication at work is less necessary. The brutality that characterised early capitalism during the 18th and 19th century when whips, floggings, punishment, rape, beatings, etc. were used extensively, excessively, and sometimes sadistically are mostly gone.[416] All of these are no longer necessary in advanced countries. As Orwell (1949:220) put it in his *1984*,

> ...but in any case an elaborate mental training, undergone in childhood and grouping itself around the Newspeak words crimestop, blackwhite and doublethink, makes him unwilling and unable to think too deeply on any subject whatever.

In other words, an elaborate schooling, work training and conditioning starting with kindergarten in childhood and extended throughout schooling places workers within the system supportive language of working hard, be on time, follow instructions, etc. This sort of *doublethink makes him unwilling and unable to think too deeply on any subject whatever.* Orwellian doublethink prevents any deeper thinking about work, work regimes and the reason behind them. Today's workforce is domesticated through *elaborate mental training* linked to the generational inheritance of working experience that is passed on through traditions of working families. Functional schooling systems and mediated access to reality during *primary socialisation* accompany it in ever more sophisticated ways.[417]

This is not something spectacularly new. Rousseau diagnosed this in the year 1755. More than 250 years later Rousseau's words have not lost their significance. The process of *primary* and *secondary* socialisation still has the same goal. Rousseau wrote in 1755 (p. 12), *by becoming domesticated, they [the workers]...become sociable and a slave, he grows weak, timid and servile.* A mere 211 years later, Marcuse (1966:36) expressed this in a more modern way when saying:

> The slaves of developed industrial civilisation are sublimated slaves, but they are slaves...slavery is determined...neither by obedience nor by hardness of labour but by the status of being a mere instrument, and the reduction of man to the state of a thing. This is the pure form of servitude: to exist as an instrument, as a thing...as reification tends to become totalitarian.

To achieve such an all-encompassing level of societal status of totalitarianism, all workplace-based – *secondary* – socialisation seeks to create the modern *Organisational Man*.[418] This is established via a linkage between *primary* and *secondary* socialisation.[419] As a human being moves from primary to secondary socialisation, the *Organisational Man* comes into being (Figure 10.2:E). With a move to (E), control mechanisms external to the workplace gain importance. Consequently, HR managers receive an already-formatted *human* who only requires minor adjustments to be converted into a *resource* and *managed* to the benefit of the corporation.[420]

Table 10.2   Forms of Socialisation and Conditioning

No.	Forms of Socialisation and Conditioning
i)	*external* and *internal* conditioning or
ii)	*primary* and *secondary* socialisation

Table 10.2 shows how the complete adaptation of workers to today's work regime can be achieved by the interplay between the forms of socialisation and conditioning. External and primary socialisation engraves the ideology of upward movement into workers who will need only minor support to also flourish at work. Upward mobility is communicated from kindergarten to the school league table. HRM only extends this in an organisational perspective centred on *upward mobility*. It hides any a priori socialisation preserved in endless league tables, rankings, grading, and the like.[421] These rankings represent no more than the hierarchical structure of society that represents the hierarchical structure of work. In both the work and the society domain hierarchies support the social relations constructed by management at work and capitalism at society level.

Any view of social relations at work based on Edwards' (1979) original forms of control that are established at work via *secondary* socialisation needs to be enhanced. As Edwards' original forms for work-related control lose in relevance, advanced industrial societies' adaptation to work occurs via a combined effort of primary and secondary socialisation. Any understanding of current work regimes needs to include two things – firstly, two additional forms of secondary socialised control mechanisms at work (Figure 10.2:D&E) and secondly, the interplay between primary and secondary socialisation.

While Edwards' control model was able to operate with three stages, today two additional dimensions have to be added as only these two can truthfully reflect the current methods of controlling workers. Without them control at work cannot comprehensively be understood. In today's version of advanced capitalism managerial control via socialisation mechanisms combine *external* social relations with *internal* work relations. Only a combination of both can lead to a better understanding of the socialising and controlling mechanisms. A dialectic relationship between reproductive ex-work and productive in-work relations shows its system maintaining character. Both are directed towards establishing and maintaining domination and control via communicative means. Here, the system affirmative character and one-dimensionality of both parts become evident.[422] Inside the ideology of managerialism, the system stabilising affirmative character removes conflict and negates conflict's inevitable link to the economic domain. It shifts this link from an inherent issue of labour and management to mere problems of maladjustment of a few misguided workers. With a successful exclusion of conflict from the society and the work domain, social relations at work and ex-work are made to appear as a mirror image of each other. The elimination of conflict and contradictions in the reproductive and productive domains releases mutually enforcing elements of system integration.

At the point of work communication and control are achieved through socialisation. Socialisation at the point of *ex-work* provides a support function that maintains work relations. Otherwise forms of socialisation would lose their functions serving no purpose in the present system. The purpose of socialisation shown in Figure 10.2 below depicts how the support function of socialisation has supported the system. At its first stage of *direct control* (A), rules of engagement at company level were enforced through the classical instruments of an authoritarian state. These forces socialised workers into obedience, accepting the industrial way of life. The supporting institutions for secondary socialisation were police, military and militarised forms of schooling for the working class of the 18th and 19th century. When capitalism changed by using Taylorism and later Fordism, forms of protest changed as well. As the industrial work systems advanced, the use of direct state instruments directed against workers' protest and industrial action started to decline. At the same time, new forms of control mechanisms that are external to work gained importance. Direct state action moved from *send in the army* to liberal forms of *Manufacturing Consent* (Burawoy 1979; Herman & Chomsky 1988). Supported by the rise of mass democracy and *consumerism,* a totally *administered life* was made *comfortable,* appearing even as *the good life* (Marcuse 1966:53). Technology elevated through the mechanistic image of work and society became the metaphor for control systems enshrined in technical machinery and a technical production process. This increasingly reflected control mechanisms external to work. At the same time rapid developments of technology and technical systems altered work settings.

This move towards a techno-*sation* of society where a substantial area of human existence became technical and mechanised also affected the way people communicated. Even *modern language has been colonised by the technological mindset.*[423] Huge sections of human communication have been moved into technical language expressed in engineering language. Today, politics, morality, and ethics have to add value to the business process benchmarked via a transaction cost analysis seen as input-output factors. As capitalism moved from Fordist mass manufacturing towards a post-industrial society, this kind of language became deeply engraved into human society. With the rise of the post-industrial society, the technical, legalistic, and bureaucratic language at work supported social relations at work (C).

With the rise of work organisation via teamwork during the 1990s, control was increasingly communicated as *in-person communication*. New forms of persuasion from the ex-work domain began to colonise the world of work. Under neo-liberalism bureaucratic and organisational forms of regulation that had previously supported work systems moved towards post-industrial self-regulation cloaked as de-regulation. System integrative forces of market dominance were utilised to enforce control at work. Control moved from regulated capitalism to the power of the deregulated market. Changes in the rules and procedures at work were strongly communicated via a freeing-up of now deregulated market forces. The return of the *invisible hand* of capitalism showed workers the bad finger, once again.[424] This created a form of communication that could not be missed or misunderstood.

Finally forms of communicative control via socialisation at level (E) have been supported powerfully via the restructure of ex-work relations through the establishment of a mediated society.[425] Unregulated and non-invasive forms of communication became increasingly corporatised and used instrumentally. Open and democratic debate – in fact democracy itself – became increasingly a routine-*ised* practice mediated by a commanding mass media directed towards *giving one's vote* so that others could rule.[426] Today, neither representative nor participatory democracy is an internal factor of work. Democracy has been constructed as an ex-work only affair.[427] It has successfully been reduced to a routine that is repeated over and over again. With a mass-mediated public domain, democracy has been routine-*ised*. It has been safely located in the ex-work domain rendering work free of democracy and managerial autocracy.[428] So-called democratic ex-work relations have become structured under the premise of instrumental communication and have enforced system integration. Work processes are off-limits for democracy as voting is relocated to the off-work domain. As the steering media of democracy is excluded from work, another steering media covers the steering needs of work. This steering media is management and its ideological expression is managerialism.

The anti-democratic ideology of managerialism that establishes control over the reproduction and the production domains developed alongside capitalism's move from its early state to its present stage. During this process five (Figure 10.2.A–E) distinctive forms expressed in-work and ex-work relations. The ideological apparatus of managerialism established in the reproductive domain supports managerial operations inside the world of work. The first stages of this development can be expressed as a *direct*-power structure prevalent in early and small enterprises grouped around an individual boss (A). The steering power also operates in task structure operative in Taylorist/Fordist production (B).[429] It also works as rule structure based on bureaucracy with functional specialisation (C). Fourthly, commanding powers are also inhibited in personalised or individualised structures forcing the ideology of individualism and converting individuals into workers under pre-structured work regimes (D).

Finally, mediated socialisation structures with system-adapting forces have been established (E). With the non-democratic communicative systems in the productive and reproductive domains the adapting forces come into existence. The five stages of communicatively established control over work are shown in Figure 10.2. Domains of production are shown as work domains and domains of reproduction as ex-work domains. These two domains work together in stabilising the current system. The ideology of managerialism under advanced capitalism increasingly demands both domains to operate towards the combined goal of system integration. External and internal forms of control over the labour domain can be communicatively expressed via the following development:[430]

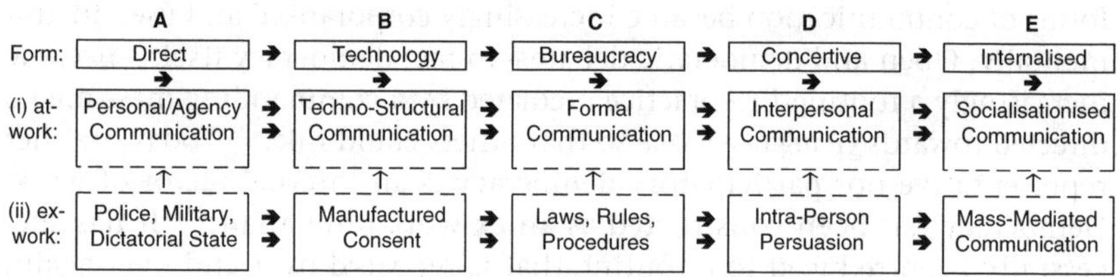

Figure 10.2   The Communicative Foundations of Control at Work

Figure 10.2 shows how forms of direct, technical, bureaucratic, concertive, and internalised control functions at work relate to (i) relationships at work and (ii) societal relationships that support the control of individuals at work (i). The supporting relations of the reproductive or societal domain are indicated via '↑' and a broken line between (i) and (ii). These supportive relationships are shown as a progression moving forward from (A) to (E). At each stage of capitalist development, control has been communicated inside work (i) and external to work (ii). As the system advanced, forms of control and the way it has been communicatively established have undergone changes. The first version of control was established when industrial capitalism came into existence. Control was communicated through a direct relationship between labour and owners. The following five sections will discuss the process of communicatively established control in more detail.

(A) Communicative control via a direct labour-owner relationship

Figure 10.2 shows that under direct or unmitigated forms of control (A) the agency as owner of capital has been able to exercise immediate control in small mercantilist like manufacturing establishments where communicative elements have been manifest in a spatial closeness. Relying on hierarchical owner-labour relationships the commanding authority of *illocutionary speech acts* have been directed towards instrumental action. These speech acts are directed towards *performative* and purposive activities. They use *warnings, estimates, verdicts, statements and descriptions* (Habermas 1979:51). The communicative element that established control over the worker has been direct. Top-down power relations at work are communicated directly. Control is established via direct order-giving instruments in a strongly hierarchical setting supplemented through authoritarian and non-democratic forms of ex-work support. This support came from an early authoritarian state and regional governance.[431] Such strong non-democratic but despotic work relations have been supported via quasi-dictatorial state institutions during early periods of capitalist development.

(B) Communicative control via manufactured consent

The rise of Taylorist and Fordist manufacturing principles (B) established a new domination, the domain of management. Here intellectual labour was established over manual labour. This form of domination gave privileges to management but also demanded justification for the managerial claim of domination.[432] To achieve this, management claimed to be legitimate and supportive of capital. The managerial claim states that management is *original*, the *first*, and *foremost* relevant institution. But management is also just an *ordinary* function. It is no more than a conversion of *intellectual labour* into what is today called *management.* One of management's prime roles is to drive communication towards making labour forget the origins of management. This is absolutely necessary otherwise management's claim to dominate the workplace would collapse. Since its self-establishment management has required a communicative shield. This shield is directed against any challenges that could expose management as a mere auxiliary function for capital. The auxiliary function of management also became a system imperative because capital itself could no longer conduct the domestication of labour (Marglin 1974; Albert 2006).

The ability to hide its origins has been provided through the claim of instrumental rationality expressed in technically structured work processes and communication. The management of Fordist and Taylorist production replaced direct communicative control with a task-division and a technically structured system of production. Control could be communicated via a techno-structure based on an engineering ideology. Management's so-called *scientific* method led to rapid increases in the effective domination of production. This claim could hardly be disputed. Linking itself to the rise of the affluent society became a conceptual model that provided a scientifically driven set of communicative instrumentalities directed towards an effective domination of workers.[433] Scientific and instrumental reasoning entered into managerial control services.

Directly communicated control became a techno-structured matter of *each man receives in most cases complete written instructions, describing in details the task which he is to accomplish...they were seated so far apart that they could not conveniently talk while at work* (Taylor 1911:39, 92). Taylor's (1911) rather un-*scientific*(!) but thoroughly ideological work rule stated: *they* [workers] *could not conveniently talk while at work*. This effectively hindered workers' communication among each other. It also ended any direct control of a boss over a worker as control was made part of a pre-planned rule of work. The new form of communicative control was expressed as *each man receives in most cases complete written instructions*. In the domain of labour, this severely hindered any attempt to establish a communicative domain among workers while working. It moved communication to meal breaks, union meetings, and into the ex-work domain. Inside such a Taylorised workplace, workers were discouraged from interacting with anybody in a company unless they had received permission from a supervisor. These supervisors wanted to control communication by knowing *what* they were talking and with whom. Communication was reduced to a pure instrument. It established one of the most immaculate forms of instrumental communication. The Taylorist notion of communication inside a company is that talking to people is not what your job is. Any communication among workers is excluded. Supervisors only permit communication when it is related to production. Any other communication – most of all communication among workers – was viewed as an interference with production. Henry Ford's assembly line of manufacturing enforced communicative work rules that ended worker-to-worker communication.

First of all, Henry Ford extended the fragmentation of tasks with an automatically driven assembly line communicating control through new techno-mechanical structures. The transferral of communication into the domain of management via the *division of labour* had already largely extracted communication from the production processes. The task fragmentation combined with strict cycle times enshrined in the technology of the assembly line enhanced the techno-structured control of communication even further. Control communicated via techno-structures became preserved in Taylor's *task* fragmentation and Ford's *mechanical* structure (Gouldner 1976). As capitalist economies moved away from industrialism and mass manufacturing shifted towards the service industry, not only the role of Fordism changed but new forms of communicating control replaced old ones.

(C) Communicative control via bureaucratic rules

The move towards the *service industry* accompanied a diminishing ability of techno-structural control. No longer was it sufficient to communicate control through technique and machinery. The new form of *bureaucratic control* (C) demanded new forms of communication. These were found in rules, policies, procedures, codes of conduct and others and established not as direct forms of communication but as formalised versions. These rules, procedures, and codes of conduct enshrined communication in administrative rules that were administered hierarchically.

These codified rules were established as a new form of control over communication. With it came a new form of language that influenced relations between the managerial and labour domains.[434] The communicative activity of *organisations frequently imposes a language of a certain shape on members and employees* (Watson (2003:10). The introduction of a more codified and more bureaucratic management language also introduced a highly formalised version of communication. Whether or not labour follows the rules that are frequently imposed on them, consciously or unconsciously, there are several aspects attached to these communicatively established rules:

Table 10.3   **Communicating Bureaucratic Rules of Control**

No.	Form
i)	managerial or bureaucratic, implicit or explicit, codified or non-codified official or non-official, etc. rules are human creations inside a socially constructed reality;
ii)	managerial rules are never self-interpreting as they always need someone to interpret them from one or the other perspective;
iii)	thirdly, managerial rules are never exhaustive as there is always room for more rules governing the non-democratic workplace and despite managerialism's rhetoric of deregulation;
iv)	even without managerial rules, workers, in fact, know what to do as we are conditioned in how to deal with situations at work, hence we apply rules even when there are no explicit managerial rules that establish bureaucratic control over work and labour;
v)	lastly, workers often behave in a rule-conforming way because managerially set structure of working life exposes them to behave in that way with or without knowing the bureaucratic rules.

Table 10.3 shows some of the core elements that shape the communicative aspects of bureaucratic rules directed towards control. Management has applied specific techniques to make these rules appear technical rather than socially constructed. This process is a technical-*isation* of managerially constructed rules. Rules have been *technified* and appear in a technical language within a technical ordering-system and take on the appearance of being technical rather than socially constructed. This tech-ni*fying* managerial process is the first step. In a second step and often conducted by others, these socially constructed (i), fundamentally human rules need to be interpreted and applied by other human beings (ii), adding a further level of human intervention into supposedly technical or purely bureaucratic rules of control. Both the rules and their interpretation have to be communicated. Controlling the labour domain is never exclusive (iii) even though the bureaucratic rules have existed for many decades (iv). Control over the labour domain is not only conducted via communication of these rules. There are additional supportive structures in place (iv). Finally, this is enhanced via a set of non-communicative rules that are implicit in the work process. For example, a simple thing like an employee number – the epitome of bureaucracy – is already a powerful and, above all, non-communicative sign of management control[435] even though it is already a rather old instrument of bureaucratic control. Modern instruments of communication are able to control even more effectively.

One of the defining shifts towards control communicated via a more sophisticated bureaucracy is that *the key thing is no longer a signature or number but a code: codes are passwords* (Deleuze 1995:180). By simply applying a barcode or password, labour becomes a prisoner of managerial vocabulary. Access to rooms, gates, and doors as well as to computers not only requires a raft of passwords, it also requires employees to have code-supplying managers. By issuing access codes, superiors establish subordinates. The managerial act of providing access gives management a superior position. It is cloaked in managerial vocabulary with workers believing that it is *their* access code. In reality, the access code is a managerial invention and only used for managing purposes. Managerial codes assign jobs tailored to specific, detailed, and narrow tasks. Codes, passwords, and organisations *have* (!) – are made to have – access levels. This in turn makes it possible for chains of command to become operative. It spans control because the guiding metaphor of all this is the military. Different levels of codes and access reflect hierarchies. Enshrined in these is the view that management is the superior and the worker is the subordinate. This relationship is also part of *open-door policies* and meetings.

These so-called *open-door* policies serve as another control mechanism. Managerial control is exercised in pretending to have an *open-door* policy or to have *information meetings* (Alvesson 1996). Once communication is framed as *open-door* policy or highly structured meetings, managers treat communication with their peers and subordinates as a kind of *market place of ideas*. Inside such market places of ideas individuals critique others' perceptions in an attempt to win the *argument* and elevate their own point.[436] To *win* an argument is as important as it is to win in the market place which for management is the same. Managers exploit the market to gain profits. The idea of exploitation is also used in communication because managers exploit arguments to maintain their superiority. So-called open-door policies and meetings do no more than ensure the managerial structure of work. The managerial ideology of a company as a market place of ideas establishes communicative forms of domination.

Similarly superior-subordinate communication establishes and maintains domination through down- and upward communication. Communication is structured as upward reporting and cascading information downward. This takes on three forms: firstly, it subordinates labour into *individuals* by denying it its collective character. By atomising workers it seeks to destroy the social organisation of labour and end solidarity. Secondly, it subordinates labour into a faked but often successfully pretended *plurality* of the institution of a corporation, workplace, or work team. Via system integration of now atomised individuals, workers are incorporated into a managerially organised group or team presented as a new but always unauthentic form of an artificial *collective*. The plurality-individual dilemma is covered by a teamwork ideology that legitimises the managerial re-organisation of the social organisation of work. The collective character of the labour domain is sub-divided and made to appear as a plurality of divergent interests represented as a plurality of interests inside a corporation.[437] Finally, it subordinates labour to a one-dimensional *principle* of profit communicated as *the company's goal*. Such goals and missions establish communicative control without having to be coercive as they establish control that is *concertive* (Barker 1993).

D) Communicative control via concertive interpersonal relations

Figure 10.2 shows how formal communication that once underpinned bureaucratic communication changes during the move to *concertive* control (D). This occurs as service industries move towards *knowledge* or *information* industries. In contrast to the formally established communicative domination under bureaucratic control, *concertive* control relies much more on closely supervised interpersonal relationships, teamwork, super-Panopticon hyper-surveillance, neighbourhood-watch systems, computerisation, digitalisation, and *iron cage* like self-management.[438] Inside the iron cage of a neighbourhood-watch system of group- or team-work, *what you think and what you are become one, which is the team, where everyone has learned to think the same thoughts, or at least with the same parameters* (Watson 2003:27).

A near perfect image or metaphor for concertive control is the *Panopticon*. More than anything else, the Panopticon communicates this new form of control. As an architectural structure or managerial design the Panopticon *makes work visible* through self- and mutual *super-vision*. The Panopticon creates a *super vision* of others and oneself. It is the perfect exercise in managing *subordinates' visions*. To manage labour's visions, ideas, mental pictures, imaginations, and insights the Panopticon's form of vision-management relies less on being watched by a supervisor but on a possibility of being watched. Labour is not constantly watched. Instead it never knows when but is always at risk of being watched. The *Panopticon* establishes an asymmetry of managerial super-vision based on seeing but not being seen so that labour knows it could be watched but never knows if. In addition, the *Panopticon* creates an image of a possibility of being watched not only by super-*visioners* but also by all others.

Deleuze (1995:178) has viewed the power of the Panopticon as metaphor for *confinement*. It is seen as the core principle of controlling rather than a disciplining system. Confinement can be seen as moulding the behaviour of workers who are forced into or subjected to different mouldings. In such confinements control elements are seen as *modulation*. The process of self-trans-moulding continuously changes from one moment to the next. This can best be understood as a sieve with the mesh varying from one point to another. Similarly, a *panoptical* control system alters its controlling ability through constant fluctuations. It operates between variances of controlling mesh sizes to allow the controller to control narrow aspects or a wider range of elements. A controller can adjust the control mechanism to whatever is deemed necessary. This self-controlling system is a much more flexible instrument of control than the narrow sets of bureaucratic control. Unlike a bureaucratic control system that operates as a narrow and stable set of controlling instruments, *concertive* control operates as a more flexible system of control.

In contrast to communication that establishes bureaucratic control, forms of *concertive* control rely less on explicit written rules, policies, regulations, process diagrams, etc. but more on a managerially driven and defined understanding of managerial values, company or team objectives, and hierarchical means-ends chains of achievements.[439] Mission statements and *company cultures* powerfully communicate a profound understanding of the labour place.[440] Accordingly, objects for management control are shown in Table 10.4:[441]

Table 10.4   Main Objectives of Management

Forms	Two main objectives
i) decreasingly	labour's organisational power, autonomous behaviour, communicative self-determination and
ii) increasingly	labour's mind-power to adapt to managerialism and the subjectivity of employees

Despite these strong tendencies towards Foucault's rather pessimistic visions of a post-modernist panoptical world, the world of work is not a vision of complete horror that lacks human possibilities for emancipation.[442] All social and work-related relationships can never be completely based on the Foucaultian horror of a panoptical prison. All social affairs always include options directed towards hope and emancipation. Both the horrors of the Panopticon and the liberating forces of emancipation are part of the way control is communicated under (D). However managerial control remains to be established communicatively through self-controlling instruments that are directed towards attacking the soul rather than the body of the worker.

Communication at level (D) has been viewed as communicating *the soul of the new organisation* (Tompkins & Cheney 1985:184). While bureaucratic control mechanisms are largely externally controlled, control mechanisms communicated under (D) are substantially assisted through internal forces. They attack and utilise the human soul in a psychological rather than bureaucratic way. Rather than being simply enforced and maintained by management, *concertive* control (D) relies much more on mechanisms that are *internal* to humans. Teams and groups, for example, are constructed by using both mechanisms. They are externally constructed by using work set-ups, rules, and procedures but also internally by using the psychological make-up of humans. In sharp contrast to earlier forms of control, they rely on self-controlling mechanisms that are internal to humans.

Table 10.5   Communicating External and Internal Control

Form	Transmission	Communication is directed towards
(i) external control	= communicating	rules and procedures (A-C)
(ii) internal control	= communicating	via the beliefs individuals hold about themselves using their own capacities

Table 10.5 shows that control is no longer simply communicated via plain bureaucratic rules and procedures (A-C). In more sophisticated forms of soul- or mind-control, it is enshrined in the *group-internal* communication process. This process is, of course, *externally* monitored but *internally* controlled in two ways. Firstly, humans are controlled through the self-controlling conduct of the subject population of a group. Secondly, control relies much more on the internal psychological make-up of humans. Self-control is communicatively established through pre-structured, pre-conceptualised, and pre-established power relationships. They exist through the application of social and communicative techniques.

Social control that is internalised by labour is a necessary condition for management's *coercive* control. Communication is distorted at the personal and the social level when *communicative action* is replaced by *system-supportive communication.* Unlike *communicative action* system-supportive communication is geared towards self-manipulation and enhanced through pre-structured communication. Management has been using pre-structured communication to control labour. Here, labour is constructed as self-managing and self-manipulating. This self-control is supported through the application of psychological methods. Labour's self-management and self-manipulation prohibits self-differentiation, self-reflection, and critical evaluation. It forces labour into a one-dimensional mindset, the mindset of production. It obstructs communicative action directed towards truth and mutual understanding and hinders any detecting of a common understanding of interest unity among co-workers.

Just like under Tayloristic work, communication inside work teams is pre-structured and strategically organised by management to achieve an instrumental goal, the internal self-regulation of labour which is communicatively established by labour within a strategic framework set by management. In addition to self-controlling work forms, *unobtrusive* control is strategically communicated through collaborative procedures such as normal working hours, time-setting for meetings and the like. All this is part of social relations through unacknowledged rules in an organisation. As values they motivate labour through money, time, accomplishments, sense of teamwork, etc. While originally labour was constituted as needing to be controlled and management was constituted as needing to establish control, labour is now constructed as self-controlling with minimal external control by management. In this managerial scenario, managers are free to take on the role of a communication expert. They can give expert advice on communication because control is established inside a self-controlling communication system. This is portrayed as a form of communication *for* labour while hiding its power to self-control and self-manipulation. When management moved from being *originator* to becoming *assessor* of communicative control, the value-laden ideology of '*we*' became even more instrumental.

The '*we*' becomes a *we-ness* as self-control becomes a necessity. Management can no longer reasonably insist on treating its employees as individuals even though this might be HR-Management's ideological intention. As management seeks to establish a corporate '*we*', it simultaneously joins other forms of managerialism to discipline labour. Confronted by an overwhelming organisational power of management and managerialism, the individual employee is reduced to atomised helplessness. Hence, *individualism* becomes an ideological tool that eclipses the organisational power of companies, management, and above all managerialism. However, the pretence of individualism provides a re-enforcing relationship between bourgeois ideology established in the re-productive domain and the productive regime put in force via managerialism. In both domains it has only one dimension, the dimension of monetary gain as a *be-and-end-all* of a concurringly designed career system.[443] In both domains, the myth of the individual labourer is kept up through the communicative means of a mass-mediated society and managerialism.[444] Labour is reduced to a vulnerable *identity-less individual* constructed as a self-controlling individual as *we*-ness takes over. This *we*-ness is preserved in the process of socialisation.

E) Communicative control via socialised communication

In the final stage (E), a self-controlling we-ness is largely established – not through direct control that is communicated via a supervisor but through two communication processes that led to self-controlling individuals. It is not mechanical control communicated via a machine-type structure where communication is enshrined in a production process nor is it communicated through bureaucratic means via rules, procedures, etc. or self-watching work groups and surveillance techniques. At stage (E) control mechanisms reach well beyond Foucault's *Discipline and Punish: The Birth of the Prison* (1995) as control is no longer based on forms as outlined under (A–D) but is part of a communication process that starts well before humans are converted into workers.

Under (E) system integrative control is communicated in two processes: *primary* and *secondary* socialisation. With an increasing sophistication of societal mechanisms that provide system integration of humans into the present structure of societal reproduction, these mechanisms become more refined. Surprisingly, this is nothing new as Mills (1951:110) had, already in the 1950s, summed up this process:

> Many whips are inside men, who do not know how they got there, or indeed that they are there. In the movement from authority to manipulation [A–D], power shifts from the visible to the invisible, from the known to the anonymous. And with rising material standards, exploitation becomes less material and more psychological.

No longer are demands towards secondary socialisations necessary as humans experience system integration via a pre-adaptation to working life before they even become workers. Through the process of *primary socialisation*, mechanisms of industrial life have been internalised leading to a reduction of secondary socialisation mechanisms.[445] This can be described as a movement from:[446]

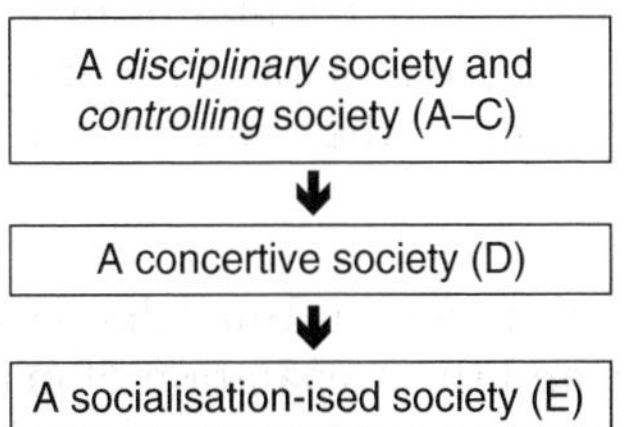

Figure 10.3 From Control and Self-Control to Control via Socialisation

Figure 10.3 shows how the world of work has been moved from being controlled towards a self-controlled environment. Eventually this has reached the stage of control through socialisation. Today's work regime neither needs external control nor strong elements of organised self-control (A-D). Today's controlling instruments are deeply incorporated into everyday life. Never before in human history has the need for A–D control been so low. Today's control is predominantly established as version (E). Current work regimes in operation can sufficiently rely upon human self-control established in (E). Increasingly this is accomplished in the reproductive domain. Controlling systems at work are established as a system that gains and is supported by societal control systems.[447] They provide a sufficient base of already internalised control structures that can be called upon when humans enter work regimes. By the time humans are converted into human resources by human resource managers, the human material to be processed has sufficiently been domesticated and conditioned. Their minds are filled with system integration imperatives that assimilate workers into the present economic apparatus. Deleuze (1995:179) has explained this as a conditioning system in which

> the stupidest TV game shows are so successful, it's because they're a perfect reflection of the way businesses are run...even the state education system has been looking at the principles of getting paid for results, in fact, just as businesses are replacing factories, school is replaced by continuing education and exams by continuous assessments. It's the surest way of turning education into a business.

While time-keeping is of high relevance for any TV game show, it is also particularly able to illustrate the point of moving towards control that is communicated via socialisation. Today's supervisors do not need whips to adjust workers to, for example, time-keeping regimes and punctuality as they did in 19th-century capitalism (A). Post-industrial societies have moved beyond time set by a technical apparatus. Time-control in the service industry (B) is disconnected from technical time-control. It has become part of a bureaucratic mechanism with policies and rules. Nor do today's managers need to communicate time-control mechanisms via bureaucratic means (C) or through peer pressure in work groups (D) as time-keeping control mechanisms have been communicated effectively to humans during primary socialisation well before they are converted into workers. Wills (1977:176) has explained the socialisation of time-keeping in the following way:

> Just as the school and its formal timetable lies tangential to the real processes of learning and the preparation of manual labour power, the particular meaning and scope of the role of institutions in reproduction

may be less to do with their formal nature and manifest communications than with the unintended and often unseen results of their relationships and habituated patterns.

In creating habitual patterns of time-keeping, primary socialisation through schools and other institutions prepares people in industrialised countries for a smooth transition between primary and secondary socialisation as the time-keeping adjustments have been established during primary socialisation. Secondary socialisation at work (E) can comfortably build on these already established patterns of human conduct. Above all, workers, once adjusted to time-keeping during primary socialisation, will unconsciously assume it to be normal and do not need to be adjusted to time-keeping over the next 40 years of working life under a 9-to-5 time regime.[448] Workers adjust to it not only because they have been conditioned that way for all their pre-work existence but they do it without rebellion and, above all, without questioning or reflection.

More than any other adjustment method, time-control during *primary* socialisation is a powerful descriptor. However, as much as Wills (1977:176) was correct, time-control does not begin with school. It begins long before entering kindergarten or school. Real time-keeping starts immediately after birth when the newborn is adjusted to the rigidities of hospitals and regular feeding times. Primary socialisation starts to take place in one of the first forms of communication between mother and baby. This communication is directed towards regular eating and sleeping times in order to control human will under a socially constructed time regime. Days are divided into the arbitrary – but commonly accepted – numbers. Without being logical, mathematical or natural, a day has twenty-four hours, not 10, 20, 30, 50, or 100! A baby's daily life-structuring time sequence with meals every three or four hours is unconsciously adopted much in the same way as a working day, structuring sequences of nine-to-five with a lunch time break of one hour between 12:00 and 1 o'clock. Kindergarten and schools also operate on strict time regimes. Both start at 8am and finish at 4pm. Both institutions encourage not only the institutionalisation of humans, they also continuously communicate time-keeping over many years. This process renders the individual highly adaptive to the 9-to-5 working-time regime set by management. This not only defines a worker's and a child's time but also two additional domestication issues. Perhaps even more importantly it defines at *what time* an individual has to be interested in *what* and secondly, it forces a child into adjusting to a school curriculum. This is established from above just like the managerial task system. The time-keeping regimes communicate very powerful messages.

At school, a child has to learn to be interested in biology, for example, on Tuesday mornings between 9:45am and 11:15am. The child is told to be interested in a particular pre-set subject – biology – on a particular pre-set day – Tuesday – and at a particular pre-set time – mornings. A child is made to adapt to them as ordered from above. It has to accept that it is Tuesday and not Monday and it is mornings not afternoons. All this is organised and communicated to the child by a so-called super*vising* authority. Children are made to accept that mathematics, sport, language or any other tasks are set in time sequences. They have to be accomplished much in the same way as work tasks in a post-school life. The accomplishment of mathematical tasks in a pre-set time frame is no more than the Taylorised task at work. Effectively communicated in this way, time regimes are established so that children and later workers get up when a little plastic lever switches from 6:59 to 7:00 on a $10 clock. They move into the bathroom, get dressed, have breakfast, and go to work without ever questioning the artificiality of time regimes that establish control over them through a long process of primary socialisation. Any secondary socialisation process at work hardly needs to focus on time regimes. They have been established during primary socialisation and also made to appear normal and as natural as possible.[449] Communicative relationships at work only need to build on primary socialisation to shape the individual in their interest. In sum, today's workplace and today's relations between labour and management are determined by a wide range of structural forces that have been communicated to labour. Inside these forces, labour is encapsulated by at least five versions of control. These are shown in Table 10.6:

Table 10.6   Communicating Control between the Management and the Labour Domain

	Managerial Domain	Labour's Acceptance of Control
(A)	owner/management	labour is conditioned to accept ownership
(B)	mechanical structure	labour is conditioned to accept structures
(C)	managerially formalised rules	labour is conditioned to formal rules
(D)	managerially set group-work structures	labour is conditioned to function in groups
(E)	primary and secondary socialisation	labour is conditioned to today's workplace

Table 10.6 shows how the five control instruments used by management enshroud labour. After decades of adaptation to a range of managerial and societal control mechanisms, labour is sufficiently conditioned to accept and even self-enhance the present work regime. This has been communicated to labour in society, at educational institutions, through corporate mass media, and eventually at work itself. In today's workplaces, communicative control has been established. When establishing communicative

control over the labour domain, management and managerialism utilise two different approaches:

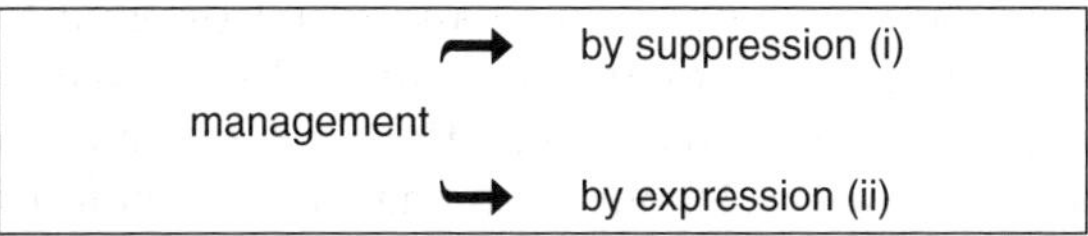

Figure 10.4   Management by Supervision or Expression

As Figure 10.4 shows, management has two options when controlling labour as it can either suppress labour (i) or – somewhat more complicated but also more successful – it can manage labour by allowing it to express itself (ii). Under (i), communication is directed towards the perceived role of managerial order directed towards the establishment, while (ii) is directed towards the incorporation of labour by seeking agreement with management. While communication at (i), often superficially called *theory X*, believes that labour dislikes work, in (ii) communication is based on a more benevolent view of labour, called *theory Y*. Here managerial communication takes on a non-threatening and non-coercive form. However, management has more forms of communication at their disposal than theory X and Y seek to make us believe. The range of managerial forms of communication operates at four controlling levels (Figure 10.4). These forms of communication are directed towards labour. Managerial communication directed towards labour subscribes to what Likert (1961) has labelled as four basic modes of communication:

Table 10.7   Communicative Control Systems

	Managerial	Styles	Modes of Communicative Strategies applied
(i)	Exploitative Authoritarian	Tells	Does not think much about communication except expressing desire clearly and forcefully to labour. Communication is $M \rightrightarrows L$ based.
(ii)	Benevolent Authoritarian	Sells	Labour can communicate feedback to management who listens to needs but retains its authority. The degree of distorted communication is high $(M \rightarrow L)$.
(iii)	Consultative System	Consults	Consultative communication is established between labour and line supervisors. Communication moves towards $M \leftrightarrows L$.
(iv)	Participative Management	Joins	Communication flows upward and downward and is accurate and clear. Distortion potentials are lowered: $M \leftrightarrows L$

Table 10.7 shows how Likert's four modes of managerial communication reflect on different levels of system integration of labour into the managerial process. It also shows the range of managerial versions of communication at an ascendant scale between (i) and (iv). Common to all forms of communication is that it preserves the hierarchy between management and labour via top-down system integration. It shows a communicatively established dependence of labour on management's guiding superiority. Labour's illusion of being listened to, consulted, involved, informed, or being part of joint processes creates a dependent relationship worth exploring and exploiting for management to the fullest extent. The masked inclusion of labour's voice into a pre-planned managerial process provides an ideal forum for making labour dependent on management (Barker 2005).

Today's system integration via involvement processes that create dependency carry connotations of Rousseau's (1755) 18th-century diagnosis of *man is weak when he is dependent*. Dependency-creating forms of communication can be seen as a slight shift from management control towards a tight managerial framework of so-called labour's discretion. Such discretion always occurs inside a prefabricated managerial system which allows limited discretion. This has been expressed as *Cycle of Control* (Ramsay 1977) where management widens the circle of control when in need for legitimacy and otherwise tightens it. These management fashions often appear in cycles. They rotate between more and less control, reflecting a *Cycle of Control*. Overall, the widening and tightening levels of control always remain inside what is necessary for management. They are always communicated inside a framework directed towards managerial goals, i.e. profit.

Such *Cycles of Control* are a constant interplay between managerial need for instrumental communication and labour's interest in *communicative action*. One is directed towards profit while the other is directed towards reflection and emancipation. The relationship between both can be seen as one that increases one side while the other side declines and vice versa. Communication based on management's instrumental rationality declines when labour's communication directed towards understanding is increasing. For management it is crucial that the *Frontier of Control* remains unchallenged. Managerial system integration must prevail. Management can never allow communication to go beyond the frontier of control. Labour's participation has to be confined to a pre-set circle. Management has a strong interest in ensuring that communication is not converted into social integration and into communicative action that might lead to positive social change at work (Goodrich 1920). For management, communication must remain firmly inside the circle of participation it created. Under any of Likert's four modes (Table 10.5), communication is not freed up from the constraints of instrumental rationality and strategic means-ends goals. Overall, all four forms of communication between labour and management remain socially constructed toward different levels of system integration under conditions of strategic rationality.

Eclipsing the true motive for a *socially constructed* division between workers and management, reason is constructed as managerial reason. Even though communicated differently as Table 10.5 shows, managerial reasoning is used to assert control. It also increases efficiency, makes it possible to calculate the future, and enables to achieve any proximate goals. The use of managerial rationality is always designed as instrumental or formal rationality (Weber 1947). The critical and communicative elements are excluded as rationality is reduced to managerial rationality. The complexity of human interaction at work is reduced to a mere instrument and is often highlighted in a few easy steps to follow. All management has to do is to administer the so-often assumed *one best way* through *planning, organisation, command, coordination, and control.*[450] Management's communicative function is no more than communicating a *hierarchy of control* (Habermas 1997a:239). The managerial ideology of *one best way* is no more than the basic task of management to balance control over social relations at work with the changing character of production.[451] This is called functional or *system integration*. Such functional integration relies on mechanisms that regulate work as an interaction between a firm's *structure* and its *function* in a never-ending attempt to find a perfect organisational design. The objective of the hierarchy of control is to control input and output that guide an internal transformation process combining machinery and labour.

The whole process of functional or system integration is oriented towards the same goal. Increased market share – in Weberian terms: *the determination of profit* – becomes central and measurable because *profitability serves as the measure by which success is calculated* (Habermas 1997a:264; Hyman 1987:28). The imperative of profitability in business leaves its mark on actions of a firm that must be followed by the operating staff. This is achieved by eclipsing the *socially constructed* aspect of the market. At the same time it provides a socially constructed set of rules for transactions. Simple techniques such as the application of *ceteris paribus* – everything else being equal – successfully eclipses the social construction of markets. The market also provides legitimacy to management as managers take the position of mediators between production and market by appearing to apply non-social, non-political, non-human, value-free, neutral, objective and instrumental-rational techniques, such as strategies.

Inside this scenario of management, companies have to adjust their internal structure and policies towards the external world, i.e. the market. The relevance of management can be found exactly at this point where it became a *mediator of standing between the producer and a wider market* (Marglin 1974:71). At the gateway between the market and the producer, management assumes its central role and remains unchallenged. Its role is part of a system that depends on primary socialisation to ensure that managerial functions are seen to be legitimate.

External determinants such as strategic goals of profit maximisation legitimise not only management behaviour, but also demand that HRM is structured accordingly. Despite its humanising claims, HRM is inherently a concept that views people at work as *means* to achieve strategic or corporate goals rather than *ends*. By converting humans into human resources it not only fulfils its function at corporate level, it also fulfils the part of secondary socialisation carried out at work. HRM's task in reducing people to mere *human resources* departs from Kant's dictum *never to treat people as a means but rather as ends only* (Cheney & Carroll 1997:596). While primary socialisation has shaped our understanding of work before work starts, HRM has – via an instrumental content and linkages to general management – a strong influence on work as it fits into a *means* rather than an *ends* view of work. Above all and as primary socialisation has not yet established a human who is already completely transformed into a human resource when arriving at the office, HRM's task is still needed in the transformation process. Secondary socialisation is exclusively conducted at work and exclusively conducted by HRM.

11
Control and Communication Through Socialisation

Control and communication are intimately linked to society. The task of socialisation is the introduction of an individual into a society. As we sustain our society largely through paid work, socialisation is foremost linked to the world of work. Socialisation mechanisms in such societies contain elements of control. This links control, communication, and socialisation to society and the world of work. As capitalism and modern production systems have moved from early craft workshops towards Fordist mass production and the Taylorist division of labour developed into horizontal tasks and vertical structures, forms of control have also changed.[452] While early forms of control could be communicated directly – worker and boss – or occurred through a technical apparatus – the assembly line – modern industry, especially since the move to post-industrial work regimes, executes control increasingly through the link between *primary* and *secondary* socialisation. Control mechanisms such as direct supervision or peer pressure under panoptical arrangements are no longer required. Modern work regimes have managed to largely free themselves from the direct, technical, bureaucratic, and group based peer-pressure systems of control of the past. This move has been supported by an increasing level of system integration of workers via socialisation and mass media. However, even though the *corporate-ised* mass-media domain provides a powerful support mechanism, control of workers has not yet been completely moved into this domain. Due to inefficiencies and the still incomplete colonisation of the communicative domain by corporate mass media, the mass-mediated ideological apparatus alone provides only partial powers of system integration. This issues severe system demands from the work domain towards socialisation institutions in order to assimilate today's workforce into advanced capitalism. Despite all efforts to structure the communicative domain as an ideological support mechanism for managerialism, there are still pockets of resistance to be overcome.[453]

Apart from some remaining gaps in the ideological apparatus of privately owned mass media, the institutions of primary socialisation still supply vital functions. Even after more than 200 years of development, capitalism still requires primary socialisation to supply functions for the system integration of workers, supported by an increasing body of ideologically oriented mass media. This is most manifest in the functional structures of today's schools and conditioning institutions but also in present forms of secondary socialisation.[454] The process of converting human *beings* into *useful* human *resources* at work – from *I* (human being) to *it* (resource) – always includes the process of secondary socialisation that links work regimes to previous experiences. Building on these two core mechanisms – the support management gains from a) the corporate mass media and b) the primary socialisation institutions – secondary socialisation's first task is to link previously conditioned knowledge to the actualities of the work regime. Rather than having to induct workers from a non-work domain into a work domain that does not relate to their previous experiences, today's secondary socialisation can rely on internalised structures that have already been communicated to the to-be-converted *resource*. Instead of habituating human beings to a totally new work regime, secondary socialisation only needs to build on an individual's mindset that has to some extent already been adapted to the expected and managerially created realities of working lives. Modern HR managers do not need to adjust a newcomer to a totally new and somewhat unfamiliar world; they only need to ensure that pre-work conditioning is sufficiently linked to the socially constructed realities at work.

At the very beginning of every employment relationship that converts or processes humans into workers or labour, Human Resource Management's role is evident in its function as a *secondary socialising* mechanism. Here socialisation means, if nothing else, the socialisation into an already existing order. At the core is a communicatively established identification of the subject – now turned into an *object of power* – with a profit-making organisation.[455] On the *subject* to *object* conversion, Adorno (1944:28) noted *in a phase when the subject abdicates before the alienated hegemony of things, its readiness to vouchsafe what is everywhere positive or beautiful, displays a resignation of critical capacity as much as of the interpretive imagination inseparable from such.* The organisation becomes an employing whole that seeks to smother all critical capacities by converting human consciousness into resignation in front of an overwhelming apparatus. Foremost, it seeks to exclude all critical forms of socialising identifications and engineers a predominantly one-dimensional mindset where TINA – There Is No Alternative – rules over critical alternatives, utopian speculations, and other forms of imaginations.

At work, the 'to be *socialisation-ised*' subject experiences a new identity constructed from the reality of work and corporate images. Secondary socialisation merges work-*reality* with *corporate* images into *corporeality*. The corporate sign-value becomes an integrative force. Similar to the physical meaning of *corporeal* that deals with the nature of the physical body or the nature of material and tangible matter, managerially constructed *corporeality* also seeks to create the perception of it being a natural process: the *natural* character of the corporation or firm. In short, *corporeality* must appear normal and natural. Hence, secondary socialisation means system integration into a pre-constructed and already existing regime, the regime of work, by merging human beings with *corporeality*. But before secondary socialisation can take place, *primary socialisation* needs to pave the way. Primary socialisation as the *first* socialisation process occurs when an individual undergoes childhood training to become a *process-able* member of society. Training that produces processable results is functionally related to the demands of industrialism through core elements such as time-keeping, order maintenance, obedience, respect for authority, use-knowledge servicing managerial demands, and the like. One of the foremost results of conditioning for primary socialisation is the adoption to an alien life. As an eclipsing method, people are trained to forget the authoritarian character of education and society by eradicating humanity and replacing it with domestication and the unconscious acceptance of domination.[456]

To bridge the gap between *primary* and *secondary* socialisation at an advanced level, special conditioning institutions have been installed. These are socially constructed institutions such as training colleges, apprenticeships, and special habituation and taming schools that are positioned in more direct support of system demands. They not only mirror the demands of business but increasingly operate as – and in fact are – real business.[457] Often the conversion of a human being from primary to secondary socialisation has been shrouded in ideology and expressed in a *we-help-you!* language.[458] At the educational level, this is principally expressed through the managerial textbook. It is the single most important tool when it comes to ideologically reconfiguring knowledge.

From the conversion of knowledge into ideologically adapted textbook knowledge to the standard business school, this kind of functional learning is designed to bridge the gap between the educational and the work domain. The bridging institutions, located between ordinary schooling and the work domain, represent a further and, above all, highly specialised form of domestication and conditioning. They most directly transform the individual to adapt to present authoritarian work regimes by converting what has been *learnt* in foremost special schools such as management schools (primary socialisation) to the functions, domestications, and regimes at work (secondary socialisation). The hierarchies learnt at pre-work schools and colleges are subsequently affirmed at work. While pretending to *help students bridge the gap*, tertiary business school conditioning seeks to establish three core elements: a) to simulate that there is a gap between ordinary schooling and work, b) it needs to be bridged by attending a specialised school, and c) we – the business college or management school – will help you to do so.[459] This largely cloaks the process of conditioning and domestication. In short, these institutions are a highly valuable (re)source in an un-critical continuation of present pathologies experienced in ordinary schools and at work. The linking bridge between social and working life had already been established during the times of early capitalism. Once established, the connecting bridge between primary schooling and secondary socialisation at work became the focus of capital, academics, and supportive educators. Already in 1876 *Horatio Alger published the book 'Ragged Dick', which was aimed at teaching the virtues of enterprise, responsibility, patience, hard work, honesty and ambition to juveniles.*[460]

More than a century later, Noam Chomsky (2002:258) has expressed what happened between the time of Horatio Alger and today as *one has gone through the ideological control system of the schools*, the goal of which is socialisation by providing *objective* use-value education and functional knowledge tailored to system demands. What has become more and more prevalent in ordinary schools has been part of standard managerial conditioning for a long time. Schools and managerial training institutions cloak their intentions behind the ideology of *objective* and *scientific* learning. According to Anthony (2005:23) *much of the ideological element in management education appears to be concerned with objective, scientific, research-based conceptualisation of practical managerial problemsolving.* In the more direct words of Watson (2003:152), *an airhead is no less an airhead for having a command of grammar, and a liar is no less a liar.* However, the functional education of an *airhead* provides *exchangevalue* education that allows participation at a monetary level. Watson's expression reflects on one of the core values of present-day educational institutions which is the ability to condition human beings towards their usability in the after-school world of work. In order to do this, educational schooling systems need to establish a link to the demands of the production process.

The link between supportive educational structures and the system imperatives of the present mode of production[461] is not only functional, it also represents a value system conducive to the work regime. The school's task, apart from knowledge transferral, is the integration of the young generation into the post-school system. Every newborn child needs to be regarded as raw material or a future *human resource* by the system. Its attitude has to be manufactured through schooling. The manufacturing of consent and affirmation occurs through public and private schools. Increasingly these schools are driven by the imperatives of profit and domination expressed in the power and money code rather than by human needs.[462] Democratic values such as assuring maximum participation in the democratic process, the protection of minorities against prejudices, support of the weak and disadvantaged, etc. are cast aside in favour of assuring *minimal* participation in school's decisions, in societal-democratic decisions and above all in work decisions.[463] Democratic as well as ethical values are sacrificed on the altar of efficiency, learning outcomes, measurable achievements, and KPIs (Key Performance Indicators). An unconditional adoption of core ideologies such as the so-called free market with the subordination of labour to management and managerialism are fostered. Structured in this way, the educational system has become a core part of the reproductive domain with direct links to the productive domain. One system *corresponds* to the other.

Bowles and Gintis's (1976) have established the link between the educational and the productive systems in their *Correspondence Principles*.[464] They link three key modes of the educational system to three key demands of the present productive system. These are firstly system demands for an affirmative and submissive workforce, secondly, the acceptance of hierarchies and managerial domination, and finally motivation based on external rewards. Based on these demands, schooling has become one of the fundamental institutions that transfer forms of use-value training – useful for the system while not being useful for personal development – and exchange-value – degree and certificates in exchange for jobs – to humans.[465] These conditioning institutions predominantly adapt us to future work regimes that almost immediately follow the end of schooling. A gap that could be utilised for self-reflection is painfully avoided. The bridge between primary and secondary socialisation needs to lock the individual into an uninterrupted chain of conditioning mechanisms. Schooling and work are two forms of alienated lives because both hardly allow the individual free self-development, autonomy, and individuality. As Gardner noted, *most human societies have been beautifully organised to keep good men down.*[466] Instead, behavioural adoption of regulations and rules ensure not only conformity but also success. This form of behavioural control is exercised over students at school as well as over workers at the workplace. A successful adoption of these control regimes allows the student as well as the worker to be channelled through hierarchies at school and at work. How educational elements conditioned at school correspond to the system imperatives at work is shown in Figure 11.1:

Schooling	In Correspondence To	Working Life
compliance and dependence = success in school and grades	→	compliance and dependence = success in reward and promotion
aggressiveness and independence = failure and exclusion	→	aggressiveness and independence = punished and unwanted
failure is failure of an individual student, not the school system	→	failure is failure of an individual worker, not the company system
at school one learns obedience	→	at work one needs to show obedience
teacher says – student does	→	supervisor says – worker does
teacher, subject head, department head, principle	→	supervisor, middle-management, top-management
motivation is conditioned via external rewards (brownie points)	→	motivation is conditioned through external rewards (money)
pass examination = reward by family and peer	→	performance review = reward via money and status symbols
teacher makes decisions	→	management makes decisions
students are not allowed to participate in decision-making	→	workers are not allowed to participate in decision-making
the promotion of system conform values	→	the use of system conform values
value system stresses certainty over ambiguity and innovation	→	value system stresses certainty over ambiguity and innovation
hierarchical authority and dependency	→	hierarchical authority and dependency
educational leader-follower orientation	→	business leader-follower orientation
student values: not a quitter, responsibility, orderly, no day-dreamer, determined, persevering, punctual, dependable, externally motivated, self-control, neatness, honesty, manners	→	work regime values: not a quitter, responsibility, orderly, no day-dreamer, determined, persevering, punctual, dependable, externally motivated, self-control, neatness, honesty, manners
unwanted behaviour: temperament, aggressiveness, frankness, unpredictable, etc.	→	unwanted behaviour: temperament, aggressiveness, frankness, unpredictable, etc.
private school ownership and no ownership by students	→	private company ownership and no ownership by workers
market exchange between school and student	→	market exchange between company and worker
teaching time controlled by a teaching system	→	working time controlled by a work system
law takes out attractive alternative to school	→	economic system takes out attractive alternative to work
student is commodity to be processed	→	worker is commodity to be processed
pyramidal structure: school captain (up) + students (down)	→	pyramidal structure: managers (up) + workers (down)
control emanates from top via principle and school board	→	control emanates form top via CEO and board of directors
teaching is determined by system needs, not students' needs	→	work-tasks determined by system needs, not workers' needs
students must be properly supervised at all times	→	workers must be properly supervised at all times
diligent in carrying out assignments and tasks	→	diligent in carrying out work assignments and orders
internalise school values and mission statements	→	internalise company values and mission statements
students must be methodical and predictable	→	workers must be methodical and predictable
fundamental change of school system is not feasible	→	fundamental change of work system is not feasible
creation of a consciousness of inevitable system imperatives	→	use of a consciousness of inevitable system imperatives
token gestures towards participation via student councils	→	token gestures towards participation via trade unions
conditioning through reinforcement and punishment	→	conditioning through reinforcement and punishment
legitimise and accept inequality via different grades	→	legitimise and accept inequality via different wages
education directed towards measurable outcomes, not interest	→	work directed towards measurable outcomes, not interest

Figure 11.1   The Correspondence between Schooling and Work

Figure 11.1 shows a somewhat incomplete list of items that the educational system enforces upon its students. They correspond most directly with the system demands of present work regimes. Fundamentally, the educational system fosters an early acceptance of hierarchies into those who govern and rule – teachers and principles – and those who are governed and ruled over – students. This corresponds directly to the workplace with supervisors, managers and workers. Both are hierarchically established institutions. A second core trade of schooling is the conditioning of students (Skinner 1953). As much as the domain of work has been converted into *Scientific Management,* schooling has also been managed scientifically. The conditioning process based on *carrot and stick* has become a scientific enterprise. Under Skinner the *carrot and stick* model has been replaced by a more sophisticated reward structure containing positive and negative reinforcement as well as punishment. Like Skinner's white rats, students are forced into a box – the classroom – and conditioned in a place that is removed from the real world. They are not encouraged to learn as an engagement with the world in order to understand it and become a fully developed mature person. Instead learning is measured and directed towards use- and exchange-knowledge that can be used in a work regime and exchanged for a job, i.e. for money. Learning is not directed towards individual needs but towards system needs. Success in this conditioning process that relies on *positive reinforcement* (e.g. good grades), *negative reinforcement* (e.g. denial of a school trip), and *punishment* (e.g. detention) can be measured.[467] Today's measurement of learning outcomes reflects a measurement of performance manifested in *performance-related pay* systems at work. Above all, however, it ends virtually all forms of non-measurable education. Today's school regimes increasingly reflect the exact opposite of the sign that Albert Einstein had hung up in his Princeton University office. His sign expressed the following core message of all human understanding and knowledge: *Not everything that counts can be counted and not everything that can be counted counts!* Finally, system demands cannot be better assured than when schooling itself becomes part of the privately owned system. Above all, this guarantees that supportive ideologies are not only enshrined in school curricular but schools, colleges, and universities themselves have become the actual carriers of this ideology. This preserves the determining power of the money and power code in systems (schools) and agents (children and students) from an early age on. Conditioning experienced through years of conversion from primary socialisation (school) to secondary socialisation (company) is predominantly a relocating process from one conditioning institution into another.

Structured as a pre-work enterprise, education means domestication into the system demands. It is a domestication process that turns anyone into a commodity bought and sold at market price. Education itself has become such a commodity. It is part of consumption and consumed like a commodity. It has left the idea of Enlightenment behind and moved from the humanist image of a self-aware, self-conscious, self-reflective, and self-critical human to the business image of a *double-functional* entity – functional at work and functional at consumption. Consumption of goods as well as education is industrialised like any other commodity. Vital human needs and services have been converted into productive industries with the fast-food industry, health industries, education industries and the like. Food-products (sic), health or even education are produced at industrial scale and with industrial methods. Dining is converted into an industrial process of a Taylorised and Fordist fast-food hall much in the same way as the sick and ill are processed in profit-making hospitals. Not surprisingly, children and students are similarly manufactured in the education industry: they are enticed by school ads, recruited and selected, processed (name tag and ID number), conditioned through KPIs, and measured by examinations. Eventually, the training is positively reinforced through a degree that has all the *sign-values* (BBA, MBA), all the *exchange-values* – degree-job exchange – and the *use-values* for corporate consumption. All this is ideologically reframed as *what one needs in life*! But the industrialisation of education not only conditions the individual to corporate consumption, it also creates divisions and inequalities. Education systems have remained class institutions and this not only due to the fact that there are inequalities of social or educational character but also in an economic sense. Only some people are allowed to achieve a higher level of mastery of the rational-logic system elements of the managerial environment directed towards functional use and organisational assimilation (Baudrillard 1998:59). In this sense educational institutions are more than just points of sale for functionally tailored exchange- and use-knowledge reduced to system demands. They also provide useful screening devices for employers seeking to select future employees formatted into *rule-obedience*. While the labour market turns its participants into a sort of sameness – the sameness of being forced to sell their labour – the world of work is made to appear highly differential. In addition to minutely detailed job descriptions, job titles, and entitlements there are – in accordance with Taylor's *vertical* division of labour – two large categories of workers to be found at today's workplaces. Inside the *rule-obedience* model they can be seen as a) *rule-makers* and b) *rule-abiders*. *Rule-abiders* combine two subsets, those of *rule-interpreters* (b^i) or *rule-appliers* (b^{ii}) at the lowest level. Those who create and invent rules are usually called managers, while those who have to interpret and live by these rules are called workers. Consequently, *rule-inventors* need a different set of training than *rule-abiders*. For one group the core value is *creativity* while for the other it is *conformity*. This division of labour inside the system of production is mirrored by the system of education. It has been expressed in Figure 11.2:

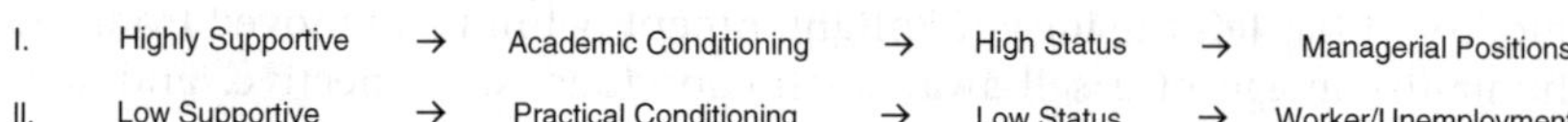

Figure 11.2   Functional Education and Socialisation

Figure 11.2 shows how the bridge between primary and secondary socialisation is structured, starting from a highly or low supportive environment through family and school and leading to a harsh selection process into academic or non-academic educational institutions.[468] The outcome is defined as *high* versus *low* status followed by respective positions in the hierarchy of capitalism. At the lower level (Figure 11.2^{II}) the conditioned subject is turned into an *object of power* during primary and secondary

socialisation (Bauman 1989). The imposition of high or low status functions to educational systems occurs according to a well-defined formula
generated in educational policies and creating not only constitutive rules
but also acquiring normative status. These functions provide a code of
conduct for those on the receiving end of such educational status systems.
They enter into a game that is not simply designed with the idea of playing
in mind. It is designed to turn players into *being played*. Managerial effort
is directed to those who are *'being played'*. When they play badly, or realise
that they are being *'played with'*, or even refuse *'to be played with'* then
they are disciplined or sanctioned. Having lost the game designed by
management, they are forced into a lower status.

At the lower level, but more so at the higher level (Figure 11.2[1]), failings
by individuals in being conditioned according to positivist science and its
corresponding educational conditioning system means individual failure,
not system failure. The ideology of value-free science eclipses the system's
inherently ideological content that drives towards system integration. The
educational player should not be aware that he or she is played (with).
Being educationally *played with* reduces the complexities of real life
through an anti-theory stance in support of practical problem-solving
solutions. Players should play without ever reflecting that they are being
played with. During primary socialisation, any reflection on what is to be
expected during the subsequent working life should be avoided. What is
emphasised is a functional practice and problem-solving skill, not reflective
theory directed towards a deeper understanding of society.

Assistance to endeavours that seek to disconnect functionally related
education from critical or reflective theory is provided through intellectually inferior methods such as case study methods – the *Harvard Business
School Case Study Method* – and storytelling in conjunction with anecdotes
and practical use-value-related exercises. This sort of quasi-scientific literature gives privilege to managerial stories, anecdotes, and invented cases
rather than providing critical understanding. Writings are cluttered with
practical examples to avoid any deeper understanding of the managerial
process. Theory is avoided, especially a theory that could explain the *why*
rather than the *how*. In Orwellian terms (1949:83), participants in this educational system should be able to think *I understand HOW!* But they should
never be able to even contemplate: *I do not understand WHY!* This sort of
education (sic) is based on the *How-favouring* positivist science of mechanics
and instrumental rationality that uses neutrality to cover its ideological
tracks, thus deflecting any critical understanding of the power relations at
work. It essentially smothers any tensions between asymmetric power relations. Use-value directed training and conditioning suppresses any tendencies towards critical reflection. People with so-called good research
credentials – usually acquired through a business school that is attached to
a university to conceal the ideological character of what is done – are

assigned to conduct such system-functional and highly ideological training (Figure 11.2[l]).

Their judgement – whether something is system-supportive or system-destabilising – is of value, not the knowledge of science. Industry credentials, long lists of functional publications, impressive titles, and well-regarded institutions and universities – *famous for being famous* – support their value judgements. These system-supportive institutions are ranked according to self-fulfilling and circular mechanisms of attitude and hearsay league tables published in commercial media outlets that are highly supportive of their teaching methods, goals and above all their level of subscription to managerialism. These institutions not only need to have shown to be worthy of the praise of managerialism, they have to adopt the ideology of managerialism themselves.[469] Their operations need to reflect the complete internalisation of managerialism. They have to prove their allegiance to management in at least two ways. Firstly, they need to show their ability to teach the essentials of managerialism and secondly that they have adopted managerialism in real existing teaching and educational structures. In the words of Watson (2003:166),

> managerialism came to the universities as the German army came to Poland. Now they talk about achieved learning outcomes, quality assurance mechanisms, and international benchmarking. They throw triple bottom line, customer satisfaction and world class around with the best of them.

While managerialism influences the tone for education at university level, management schools, training colleges, educators and trainers have to *operationalise* it.[470] Educators or trainers for conditioning provide *technical,* not *critical* knowledge. This enables primary socialisation to function via the learning of a discipline that conforms to the rules of managerialism. The most direct form of pro-managerial socialisation in pre-work learning is the textbook. It transfers *use*ful knowledge indirectly – via a mediator called academic, management writer, textbook author and the like – into socialisation-able knowledge.[471] Such *textbook* knowledge is neatly packaged, easily accessible, and written in a style that is of

> an overwhelming concreteness. The thing is identified with its function...this language, which constantly imposes images, militates against the development and expression concepts. In this immediacy and directness, it impedes conceptual thinking; thus, it impedes thinking...[such a] functionalised, abridged and unified language is the language of one-dimensional thought.[472]

This describes the one-dimensional thought of functional managerialism and its human expression of Human Resource Management.[473] Apart from constructing instrumental knowledge as one-dimensional, the fabrication of managerial language and communicative techniques services the task of binding humans into a pre-designed life inside a productive work- and consumption-society. In both domains they are deemed to be functional.[474] Functional knowledge used in the productive domain is not critically reflected upon. Instead it is simply *acquired* via pre-arranged clusters efficiently boxed up as *academic subjects* and passively delivered rather than actively discussed. Knowledge acquiring occurs in equally pre-arranged boxes called lessons where the educational customer has to purchase the correct box of functional and instrumental knowledge.

The *educational customer* is increasingly asked and ever more willing to purchase an educational box-set of *fast-forward functional (ff)* knowledge that is of no private, personal, or individual meaning to her or him.[475] While being low on *meaning* content it is highly *ff*. Such *ff* is only accessible by the *educational customer*. The content of *ff*-knowledge is not designed as education but as a functional toolbox. Constructed in that way, *ff* can only really be used by one *user,* which is management. The *ff*-consumer solely needs to be sufficiently and efficiently conditioned and to *consume* and *internalise* versions of knowledge. Through the purchase of *ff*, the customer takes part in primary socialisation and adapts to a pre-arranged and pre-formatted existence so that, for example, *learning OB [organisational behaviour] has come to mean associating the names with the theories and the theories with a list of key terms* (Harding 2003:24).

Increasingly socialisation into managerialism via *associating names* is done in a way where the consumer links models with names, memorises, and rehearses their content rather than critically studying it. To a large degree, academic studies conducted at today's colleges and universities are reduced to Pavlovian and Skinner-like conditioning[476] which present rewards at the end of each lesson, tutorial, or chapter in the form of core questions and achievement points. At the end of each text an easy to memorise summary is to be found. The end of each term or semester is marked by an often rather senseless examination designed to test a candidate's ability to memorise a text in a pre-set sector of knowledge. At the end of each degree a certification of achievement is handed out. This is the achievement *of* and *for* a formatted existence that comes with the commonly agreed and standardised *sign-value* of MBA, MA, or BA.

The standardisation of agreed and accepted knowledge represents the standardisation of managerial knowledge indicated by a sign (MBA) that signifies adaptation and affirmation. It is manifested in a highly standardised curriculum and standardised textbooks. This conveniently leads to a standardised educational consumer resulting in a standardised existence. Today's work societies started long ago to internalise standardisation as expressed in demands for effectiveness, efficiency, mechanisation, functionality, and specialisation of educational systems. This has created the obsession or *fetish* of effectiveness, efficiency, mechanisation, and functionality. It is the fetish of being an efficient learner that carries con-notations of being useful to society. The fetish of being useful has been encouraged by managerialism. It involves aspects of repression, authoritarianism, fragmentation, and domination[477] and is designed to obstruct critical and self-conscious education. It also prohibits any development towards substantive awareness of oneself. Finally, it is designed to hinder any reflection on the role we are designed to play inside today's work relations. Meaning, critical reflection, emancipatory potentials, and fulfilment are exterminated from a society that is highly engineered. Educational systems result in socialised humans ready for corporate consumption.

Subjects are primarily conditioned into being willing participants in the process of secondary conversion. Pre-work conditioning enables an in-work conversion into an *object of power* (Bauman 1989). Trained that way humans who are converted into *objects of power* have adjusted to an invisible set of organisational rules, work-related rituals, and organisational procedures. All of this runs by a distant but equally invisible master plan that builds a bridge between primary and secondary socialisation and that is certified via a paper – a sign-value – that acknowledges the successful conditioning into the functional rules that govern both forms of socialisation.

Academic studies and degrees certify the mastering of a functional training manifested in de-theorised, unreflective, and uncritical use-knowledge. They also certify a non-reflection on emancipatory knowledge. Filled up with use-knowledge, such training succeeds through a sufficiently organised process directed towards primary and later secondary socialisation. Markets, power, and money guide the regulation of both versions of socialisation. Education during primary socialisation is no longer a human right but a commodity exposed to markets. This organisational system has subverted critical knowledge that came from Enlightenment into commodity knowledge. Deeper insights, utopian speculation, humanity, critiques, personal interest, art, ethics (unless it is business ethics), culture (unless it is organisational culture), and imagination are no longer required.[478]

Tools and methods for secondary socialisation

While *secondary* socialisation provides the tools for induction into the world of work, primary socialisation lays the groundwork and must always precede secondary socialisation. It cannot be constructed *ex nihilio*. Most problematic for secondary socialisation is that a reality, once internalised during primary socialisation, persists in secondary socialisation. Therefore, managerial socialisation as secondary socialisation demands *structuration* of primary socialisation to provide a structural basis for secondary socialisation. The world of work under conditions of secondary socialisation is a mirror image of primary socialisation requiring the acquisition of work-supportive forms of behaviour but also of role-specific vocabularies through adapting, adjusting, and conforming to managerial norms and terms. In secondary socialisation workers (Orwell's *Oldspeak*) or *human resources* (*Newspeak*) are referred to as *others* to be acted upon, communicated to, ordered, and controlled, rather than as participants in communication or socialisation. Commonly the process of secondary socialisation has been described as *finding one's feet, learning the ropes, getting up to speed,* and *enduring trial by fire, sinking or swimming.*

Primary socialisation is constructed as role-specific acquisition of knowledge and communicated as a state or increasingly privatised function. This is manifested in curricular demands for primary socialisation that colonise schools and colleges. These curricular developments have been shaped by demands emanating from secondary socialisation. In that way, higher-level primary socialisation is directed towards tertiary institutions and business schools (Figure 11.2[1]) that seek to condition certain sections of labour by a *familiarisation* with highly specialised vocabularies used to distance them from workers and to appear to be the sole occupier of superior knowledge. This extends to the *internalisation* of semantic language fields. Once conditioned in this way the world of work becomes accessible via interpretation. This sort of interpretation occurs when humans find themselves in a new environment – the world of work – linking pre-learned knowledge to this new world in order to understand it. Pre-learned or pre-conditioned primary socialisation provides a meaning framework in which *Organisational Sensemaking* takes place (Weick 1995). It structures routines of interpretations, meaning-creation, or sensemaking by providing a pre-trained framework to understand work in the way it is designed to be understood.

This process also requires the adoption of the rudiments of a legitimatising communicative apparatus that seeks to stabilise labour-management relations. Human Resource Management provides such an apparatus. Unlike other management functions such as marketing, finance, and operations management, it is the task of HRM to conduct secondary socialisation. HRM is the area where individuals are made to walk across the bridge that links primary with secondary socialisation. Human Resource Management is the instrument that moves individuals towards secondary socialisation. The subsequent process of secondary socialisation *inducts an already socialised individual into the new sectors of the objective world of work* (Berger & Luckmann 1967:150). Whyte (1961:12) has summed up the social aspect of socialisation:

> Man exists as a unit of society. Of himself, he is isolated, meaningless; only as he collaborates with others does he become worth while, for by sublimating himself in the group, he helps produce a whole that is greater than the sum of its parts.

For management, managerialism and their subservient entourage of management writers it is only the organisation that makes the *human*. Only through the process of secondary socialisation can an individual become *worthwhile*. Secondary socialisation as the adoption of a company structure uses system integrative elements and turns them *against* newcomers who are passively made to sublimate themselves into a pre-set organisation. Newcomers are not actively participating in a socially integrative *group* via a conscious process. They are deliberately and intentionally made to enter into the pre-structured system called the workplace. The managerial conversion of *humans* into human *resources* creates a worthwhile *resource*. Only by partaking in the capitalist process does an individual become a human *worthy* to the managerially guided society. In short, only the successful completion of secondary socialisation turns humans into something *worthwhile*. Without it humans are unworthy and undeserving.[479] But secondary socialisation is by far more than just *organisational assimilation*. It is absorption, incorporation, and system integration into a one-dimensional world. This is attained by structuring people's behaviour in a pre-designed socialisation process to alter patterns of behaviour adapted to the system needs of a company. It targets a communicatively established creation of four identities (Table 11.1) relevant to the *organisational use* of human subjects now turned into objects of managerial power through secondary socialisation. These are:

Table 11.1   Four Communicatively Established Identities for Corporate Use

No.	Identity	Target
A	**Individual**	Personal interest that had put the individual above the profit interest has to be defeated and turned into profitable use.
	Target I:	Conversion of non-supportive attitudes into organisational attitudes (profit).
	Target II:	Conversion of individual identity into goal (profit)-achieving identity.
B	**Work Group**	Any group identity originating in ex-work experiences has to be converted into work-related group experiences that replace ex-work leaders with work-related leaders (CEOs, etc.).
	Target B-I:	Conversion of identity as group member (school team, sport, social) into work-group member.
	Target B-II:	Conversion of obedience to work-leader (team leader, supervisor) needs to be seen as natural.
C	**Corporate**	Identity originating in primary socialisation through voluntary organisations (sports club) or involuntary organisations (school, family) need to be converted into a corporate identity.

Table 11.1 Four Communicatively Established Identities for Corporate Use
– continued

No	Identity	Target
	Target C-I:	Conversion of voluntary or involuntary institutional identity into corporate identity.
	Target C-II:	Conversion into corporate identity through the cloaking of involuntary character of corporation.
D	**Professional**	The creation of previously established identities through professional association needs to be carried over into the framework of the corporation.
	Target D-I:	Conversion of professional identities into professional identities supporting the corporation.
	Target D-II:	Conversion of goals of professional associations into corporate (profit-achieving) goals.

Table 11.1 shows the use of these four identities (A–D) to create mechanisms that convert previously socialised identities into corporate identities or corporate supporting identities. In the process of *corporate identity creation*, communication gains vital importance for secondary socialisation. Instrumental communication sets up clearly defined goals or targets for system integration. Corporate communication targets specific areas of incomplete primary socialisation as primary socialisation has never been able to deliver totally affirmative humans to companies and is unable to totally pre-format individuals in the way demanded by managerialism. Therefore, any new subjects still have to be integrated into work. This makes secondary socialisation necessary which targets the four main areas shown in Table 11.1. First of all it targets the area of individuality (11.1^A). While supporting the ideology of individualism, individual attitudes have to be converted into standard corporate attitudes. These attitudes also need to be directed towards fellow workers and work groups (11.1^B). As the modern workplace is often composed of pre-defined units of workers or permanent groups, newly recruited subjects need to be converted into effective group or team players. While managerial ideology favours individualism on the one hand, the ideology of being a team player is unchallenged and unquestioned as much as adopted by everyone. The contradictory expectations of being a team player and at the same time being exposed to individualised performance management through performance-related pay systems and the like is cloaked by corporate culture and a highly ideological language.

At level (11.1^C), all institutional arrangements that have been deemed non-supportive of the corporate identity have to be diluted or diminished. Secondary socialisation instructors seek to delete or convert them into an organisational identity. This organisational identity is one-dimensional and directed towards the corporation.[480] Finally, any *professionalism* (11.1^D) that is not work-related or unable to create an identity supportive of corporate goals or managerialism has to be converted into a useful professional identity. The individual is made to belong to a *professional association* that is supportive rather than one that is critical or even against corporate goals (profit). The purpose of these professional associations is the provision of an additional support mechanism for managerialism. They should not be *Against Management* (Parker 2002). The conversion of subjects into *objects of power* is directed towards pre-set targets (11.1^{B-I} to 11.1^{D-II}) seeking the integration of humans via an extension of once learned behaviours. Building on primary socialisation, corporate socialisation uses earlier socialisations as a platform to re-construct and re-shape human identities to the company's interests. All identities are directed towards *organisational goals* (*Newspeak*) or *profit* (*Oldspeak*). Therefore, behavioural adjustments and identity conversion are mere tools along the way to achieve this goal.

Human Resource Management's task is set to convert an individual into an organisational goal achiever. By doing so it turns the individual into someone who achieves. In order to fulfil this task, HRM has developed instrumental-rationally guided goal-achieving mechanisms. These are developed strategically as they set targets for the realisation of secondary socialisation. The people-processing element of secondary socialisation or *organisational assimilation* applies two forms of secondary socialisation strategies to induct the newcomer into the work regime in a codified and highly structured process. *Informal* socialisation occurs on the job through communicative devices such as replacing an individual identity with a corporate identity. Both are thoroughly one-dimensional processes geared towards a one-dimensional identity to achieve corporate goals. Often, this is communicated through simple ideology-laden statements such as:

> *we are all in the same boat* **or**
> *how things are done around here.*

Figure 11.3   Two Common Statements for Assimilation

Particularly, the '*all in one boat*' metaphor (Figure 11.3) is used to manufacture consent and gloss over divergent interests between labour and management. Most interestingly, it hides the fact that some have to *pull the boat* while others sit on the upper deck at the steering wheel. While hiding the true social relationship at work – managers are steering the boat while workers are pulling it – the boat metaphor implies a naturally given order of an artificial relationship that does not exist in reality. To create a willing *boat-puller, sequential socialisation* seeks to move a newcomer through clearly defined stages of accomplishments measuring the success of conditioning. But non-sequential and unstructured strategies are also applied. Both are vital parts of any transitional induction period. *Organisational assimilation* through sequential/non-sequential and formal/informal processes are communicated through an official company message. Induction occurs through co-workers and peers, supervisors and other company members, such as secretaries, department heads, etc. or even through customers and other outsiders to a company. The task is the assimilation of the *self* with a company.

All secondary socialisation strategies are instrumental-rational, providing communicative tools directed towards a goal under a means (secondary socialisation) – ends (assimilation) dictum. The goal is the assimilation of the newcomer. Assimilation is achieved when a newcomer has become an integral part of the corporation and an individual-organisational relationship has been accomplished. Common to all socialisation strategies is that they are communicated through management and Human Resource Management. They establish meaning and socialise labour within an organisation. They also create power relationships and dominance. Human Resource Management is assigned with the task of creating and providing system maintenance for these asymmetrical relationships.

Finally, today's HR managers can rely on powerful support mechanisms when converting newcomers into work regimes. This assistance comes from two main sources. The first source that enhances and supports the process of converting human beings into human resources comes from the communicative ex-work domain. This domain provides powerful ideas supportive to management. It tells the unsuspecting human to mentally adapt to the code of *corporate life* (sic). This is portrayed as a given and stated as *'this is the way it is'* or *'these are the facts of [working] life'*, and so forth. It conditions the human being into a thing or an instrument with the appropriate forms of behaviour ready to be used up by the work regime.[481]

The communicative domain plays an important part in converting humans into obedient *things* because the privately owned media provide daily images of a commodity life and forms of existence characterised by obedience. This started to appear in conjunction with the rise and increasing dominance of internationally *oligopol*-ised corporate mass media[482] which has resulted in robust support mechanisms for images and system integrative behaviour patterns on which today's HR managers can rely. When seeking to work towards secondary socialisation, HRM's task is to link their requirements to forms of ideological content that have already been planted in the minds of the newcomers. The process of secondary socialisation, induction, or adaptation to the work regime is accomplished when the linkage between mass media and worker is completed. This will ensure that assimilating ideas conditioned through this link have turned employees into willing resources that support the so-called *organisational performance* (*Newspeak*) or *profit* (*Oldspeak*) on a daily basis. This is obviously not done through brutal '*in your face*' methods but in a much more sublime and settled process that targets underlying values and behaviours which need to be shaped and directed towards the creation of an affirmative character supportive of the work regime.

But it is not only the ideological conditioning that an individual has received before entering a work regime that provides valuable support for HR managers. It is also the restructuring of primary socialisation under advanced capitalism. The area of primary socialisation has made significant advances during the last decades. Unlike during the years of early capitalism when human resources were allowed to be *educated* in public institutions rather than *conditioned*, advanced capitalism has ended this. A child in today's world can go through kindergarten, pre-school, school, college, and university without having to enter any form of public education as privatised training facilities provide much more tailored training regimes. While public institutions have been – almost by definition – somewhat removed from the market forces of capitalism, private training facilities are much more geared towards the needs of capitalism. More than in public education, these private institutions are steered by the two most powerful codes advanced capitalism can provide: money and power. Not only do they cater for the system demands of advanced capitalism, they are also able to convert children into goal achievers, competitors, future leaders, and success stories. This is done primarily through teaching what is highly valuable to today's parents: discipline and social affirmation. These privatised institutions are able to delete any critical or even recalcitrant behaviour by converting youthful energies into *affirmative* and *useful* characteristics. The early and constant adoption of affirmative and system-supportive values allows the end product of this commodified training regime – the fully functional human resource – to internalise the system imperatives of advanced capitalism. System imperatives govern the educational domain by providing primary socialisation that is linked to secondary socialisation. As these primarily functional training regimes guarantee middle-class success – depicted in the sign-value of the status symbol and *Affluenza* – equally conditioned and system affirmative parents seek to ensure early entry of their children into these conditioning facilities. In this way, the interplay between primary and secondary socialisation is handed down from generation to generation, slowly but surely adapting the mind of the human to the conditions of working life.

Today's human beings are able to be conditioned towards acceptance and support of managerialism by going through privatised institutions which all communicate the same message: privatisation is good, private industry is good, and private consumption is good. The imperatives of the corporate workplace are made to appear as an unchangeable necessity.

What is portrayed is an unbroken chain of private institutions from private kindergarten to privately owned companies. This is made to appear normal. The uninterrupted chain of private or privatised educational institutions of primary socialisation is shown in Figure 11.4:

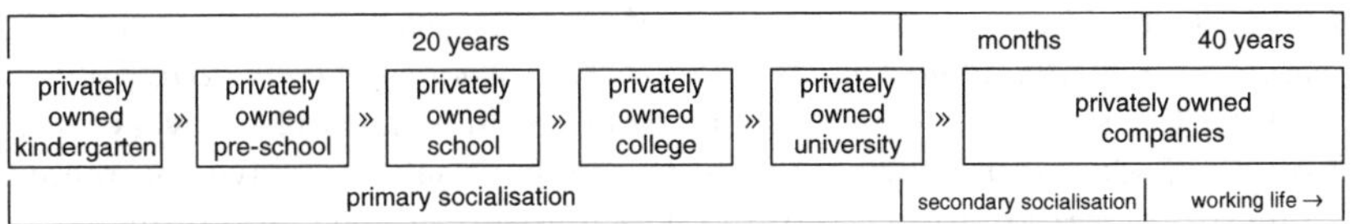

Figure 11.4   The Uninterrupted Chain of Privately Owned Institutions

Figure 11.4 shows that an individual of today's society can go through primary and secondary socialisation and working life without having to receive any form of public education or any experience of *not-for-profit* institutions. In that way the ideology of the *Privatisation of Everything* (Mandell 2002) is supported by the fact that the real existence of educational institutions is based on the same ideology. This delivers – socially created – factual evidence for the prevailing ideology.[483] The ideology-evidence link is of utmost importance to the upper-level consumer of such an education system. Upper-level (Figure 11.2[I]) conditioning of future resources demands extensive training. This can take 20 or more years of primary socialisation, while the process of secondary socialisation takes no more than a few months. Because of the extended primary socialisation the period of so-called in-house (corporate) induction is relatively short as most of the affirmation to the work regime has been done beforehand. This enables the end-user of socialisation – the company – to off-load expensive induction costs to the pre-work domain. Having undergone minor adjustment processes (of a few months), the human resource is sufficiently conditioned to survive an extended period of exposure to the work regime (40 years). It appears as if an individual that has been conditioned during the first $\frac{1}{3}$ of life inside primary socialisation institutions is ready to accept the imperatives of working life for the next $\frac{2}{3}$ of his life.[484] The ideology cloaked as *facts of working life* is turned into a fact of unconditional surrender. The individual is *invited* (*Newspeak*) to adjust to work regimes after successful completion of primary socialisation. Individuals are offered so-called *educational choices* (*Newspeak*) making them believe that they are able to *select* (*Newspeak*) a private school, college or university (*Newspeak*) or a conditioning institution (*Oldspeak*) that links educational value systems to the system demands of working life.

Reflecting on the needs for today's work regimes, the to-be-converted newcomers are conditioned at two levels (Figure 11.2). Some are conditioned to conduct *routine* and *monotonous* work while others are being accustomed to conduct *managerial* work. Sophisticated HRM techniques are used to adjust those two groups to the socially constructed realities of today's work regimes. The first group has been sufficiently prepared through *monotonous* and *routine*-ised primary socialisation to conduct their assigned and equally *monotonous* and *routine*-ised work tasks. As Albert (2006:96) emphasised, *eighty per cent of us are presently taught in schools to endure boredom and to take orders, because that's what capitalism needs from its workers*. The second group usually receives a somewhat higher-level conditioning. Today, most newcomers to the managerial class have completed some sort of tertiary formal training. Decades ago, colleges and universities were seen as training institutions for the upper class. Access was only provided to the selected few. During the post-WW II years this changed dramatically and these developments have definitely ended earlier forms of access arrangements. As advanced capitalism demanded a better-educated workforce, colleges and universities had to be opened up to a larger population. This led to a significantly increased student population that had access to critical knowledge and critical forms of thinking. Accessing previously non-accessible forms of knowledge in newly opened mass universities provided a fertile ground for the student revolts during the late 1960s. Shocked by these movements that provided workers with critical and emancipatory knowledge through radicalised students, the establishment sought to curb critical thinking by restructuring colleges and universities. Today, this restructuring process has been completed. Privatised colleges and universities are colonised by managerialism.[485] They have been converted from the educational facilities of Enlightenment into institutions that resemble the modern corporation with *achieved learning outcomes, quality assurance mechanisms, international benchmarking, triple bottom lines, customer satisfaction,* and *world-class performances* (Watson 2003:166). Today, instrumental rationality has almost completely replaced critical rationality.

In conclusion, the process of secondary socialisation is today – given the support from primary socialisation and mass media – ready to replace the identity of a newcomer with four new identities. Foremost, this occurs at the level of the individual that is still told to be an individual. However, the *individual* has now been issued with a six-digit staff number identifying the new human resource inside a pre-constructed code system. This resembles the identity and individuality of a number on a corporate ID swipe card. The individual identity has become a *corporate number* identity. Secondly, the process of secondary socialisation often includes the induction of an individual into a work group which is not *natural* as it is *managerially* organised, nor are these groups *self-managed* as management manages them. These groups only allow often severely limited access to a *getting-involved* process. Getting involved however means nothing more than the exclusion of all issues that have any significance, such as real participation, co-decision-making, and most definitely workplace democracy.[486] The managerial ideology of self-managing work groups is designed so that a newcomer does not need to be concerned with decision-making issues. They remain in the safe hands of management. Fitting into such work groups is made to appear as *natural* as possible, precisely because it is utmost *unnatural* to work in a pre-constructed and managerially guided work group. All this is designed to *manage* the conversion of an individual to a work group identity without any realisation of what is being done.

Thirdly, the managerial process of secondary socialisation also demands that a newcomer adapts to corporate values in order to become a corporate member. Today, this process is supported by the assignment of a new term to an individual. In the *Newspeak* world of managerialism workers are no longer called workers. They have become *corporate citizens* – without voting rights, of course! – or *organisational members* – just like a membership in the local gym! The hidden purpose of the renaming and re-creation of a new identity is twofold. Firstly, it seeks to reframe any association of the individual with work, workers, or even the working class. It is designed to end all forms of class solidarity among workers. Any connotation to class is to be avoided. Now the association is with the corporation, creating the illusion of *corporeality*. Secondly, instead of having a worker identity, *your* new identity is now connected to a profit-making institution. This form of identity shift allows the self-definition of an individual with the company rather than with fellow workers. It shifts the worker identity towards a *corporate* identity which is further enhanced through a professional identity.

Finally, HRM has a seemingly endless number of professional statuses in its cache that can be attached to any individual.[487] The assignment of a professional term to human beings is done for two reasons. Firstly, the assignment locates the individual inside the managerially constructed hierarchy.[488] The structure of corporate hierarchy is an extension of deeply enshrined previous institutions. Years of living and adapting to hierarchies have shaped our hierarchy-accepting identity. Life means to live inside hierarchies from early forms of primary socialisation in educational institutions to secondary socialisation in companies. The conversion from primary to secondary socialisation is predominantly a conversion from one hierarchy into another. All of these hierarchies are socially constructed while they are made to appear as natural as possible in order to hide their social and managerial constructiveness. They are designed to pretend it were a *fact of life* that cannot and, above all, should not be challenged. Secondly, attaching a profession to an individual also increases the illusion that this human resource is a *valued* and *needed* member of the organisation. It turns a *human* being into a *functional* being that defines itself through an imaginary link to a function. The secondary-*socialisalised* human resource is made to believe that their status depends on a professional function, not on their individuality. Identity, individuality and the professional functions are made to merge in the minds of workers.

Professionalism is linked to behavioural functions and patterns of conduct which are not only supported through the function-identity linkage but also through the bureaucracy-identity link. Any newly inducted human resource is also linked to a bureaucracy. In this process, the *individual* identity is converted into a *bureaucratic* identity that can be managed from above. But functioning in a bureaucracy does not only mean to accept the imperatives of hierarchies and power, it also means to accept an identity that is linked to a bureau. The newly created identity depends on the *bureau* or office and the resulting *power* that comes from this office. It is not the *demo* [people]-cratic power but the power of the office – the *bureau* [office]-*cratic* – power that creates the identity. Management – not the people = *demos* – is the sole agency that allocates this power, the power of the office-holder. This form of corporate identity creation merges a personality with a position in a hierarchy. The position holder has power as long as he holds the office. Once the office-power link is broken, the power of the holder ceases. The establishment of powerful organisational individuals who are powerful due to the office that has been allocated to them is of vital importance to management. It turns the power-holder into a willing instrument of managerial prerogatives. Obviously, a newcomer should not be aware of this process. Professions and the assignment thereof are made to appear as if they were part of a natural process. They should be perceived as something that cannot be taken away by those lower in the hierarchy. In that way the carrier of the bureaucratic identity is able to rule over those lower in the hierarchy as an untouchable which further enhances the status of the bureaucracy–identity linkage. The fact that all professions are socially or managerially constructed and therefore socially assigned or non-assigned is cloaked behind the façade of value-neutral and objective Human Resource Management. In sum, the conditioning that binds the individual to hierarchies throughout primary socialisation is continued during secondary socialisation. But the conditioning of the individual to hierarchies does not only derive from primary socialisation, it is also powerfully mediated through the daily ritual of a mass-mediated reality that controls the content of what is being communicated. The task of both primary socialisation and mass-mediated control is to pre-design the conditioning of individuals so that system imperatives are deeply engraved into the minds of humans long before they become aware that they have to enter an equally pre-designed work regime.

12

Human Resource Management and the Control of Communication

Overall, Human Resource Management provides the most vital support function in aiding the transformation of humans into workers. This is a form of *system integration* under instrumental rationality because it seeks to integrate labour's *compliance* into a system of goal-achieving objectives. Such a process creates two kinds of persons. This somewhat pathological split in personality is shown in Table 12.1:

Table 12.1   The Personality Split

i)   one is a person like you and me, called natural person;

ii)   while the other person is an intangible person which by law was once called fictional person but is now called *corporate person* also expressed as conformist *Organisation Man* (Whyte 1961).

The relationship between (i) and (ii) is asymmetrical because the natural relationship among *natural* persons has been displaced. This replacement takes the form of relations between *corporate* person and *natural* person. This can be shown as:

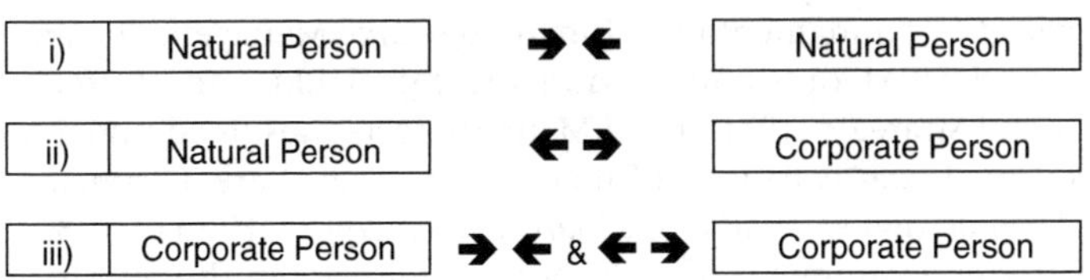

Figure 12.1   Natural and Corporate Persons

As Figure 12.1 shows, one of the consequences of the secondary socialisation process is the creation of a partly conflicting multitude of personal identities. Starting with 12.1[i], the relationship among natural persons is of a natural character relating naturally to each other. It brings people together naturally: →←. At the corporate socialisation level of 12.1[ii], the natural person is split into a natural and a corporate person. This split creates conflict and contradictions, shown as ←→ as both persons do not necessarily have the same attitudes. They are naturally and corporately constructed. This is neither natural nor do these persons relate to each other naturally. Finally, corporate persons relate to each other not in a natural way but in a corporately constructed way (12.1[iii]). This somewhat artificial relationship is defined by two opposing elements, the element of solidarity among workers and co-workers (→←) and the element of conflict and competition among workers (←→). These three relationships created at corporate level between natural and corporate persons can never be overcome or solved but they can be temporarily eclipsed via powerful managerial ideologies.

As the shifts (i–iii) are not without conflict and contradictions, an ideology is used to cloak them. One of the preferred ideologies capable of concealing inherent contradictions between *natural* and *corporate* persons is the creation of *occupant roles*. Management has to endure a somewhat never-ending contradiction between *human* or *natural* persons and between a *labour* identity and an identity of a managerially created *Organisation Man*. The annihilation of a natural person and the subsequent conversion into a *corporate* person is largely assigned to Human Resource Management. This has been made possible through the application of certain instruments or techniques in a *strategic fashion*.[489] In the world of work as in the fashionable world of strategic management and strategic Human Resource Management it is often no more than *fashion* that dictates the introduction of a new language, of new words and phrases and subsequently also the demise of old ones. Management and HRM tend to create and follow these fashions habitually.

With the ending of personnel management the very term *person* ended. Just like the fashion industry ended a certain style. The ending of personnel management led to the *fashionable* creation of Human Resource Management and completely replaced the old-fashioned rhetoric of *Personnel Management*.[490] Fundamentally, Human Resource Management can be split into *tactical* HRM or standard non-strategic HRM and strategic HRM. Tactical and Strategic HRM or SHRM are subjects subsumed under management's drive towards its goal of increased market share *determined by economic forces or laws external to the individual enterprise* (Hyman 1987:28–29). The reality of economic forces has been hidden when the term strategy is placed in front of Human Resource Management. A proliferation in book titles shows that the term *strategic* is placed in front of almost everything remotely linked to management. This also testifies to a trend by removing Human Resource Management from its classical domain of tactics oriented towards day-to-day activities towards a more strategic role.[491] In this new and much more fashionable version of *strategic* HRM planning is linked to strategic management by seeking to align a company's strategic business plan with strategic HRM planning.

Instrumental rationality reaches into the management of people. HRM becomes SHRM. While the issue of instrumental rationality and strategy has implications well beyond HRM, HRM remains functionally linked to the success of strategic management.[492] It provides a base for hierarchical relationships at the point of work. HRM has taken on a specifically important role in being able to operate as a steering function:[493]

Table 12.2   HRM's Steering Function over Power, Influence, and Values

Medium Components	(i) Power	(ii) Influence	(iii) Value commitment
Standard situation	Directives	Advice	Moral appeals
Generalised values	Effectiveness	Loyalty	Integrity
Nominal claim	Binding decisions	Authority via explanations	Authority via admonitions
Rationality criteria	Success	Consensus	Pattern consistency
Actor's attitude	Towards success	Mutual understanding	Mutual understanding
Real values	Rationalisation of collective goals	Reason for convictions	Justification for obligations
Reserves	Means of enforcement	Cultural traditions	Internalised values
Form of institutions	Organisation and official position	Prestige orderings	Moral Leadership

As Table 12.2 shows, HRM's functional task at work can be made transparent by examining HRM in relation to the media of power relations (i), influence (ii), and the creation of value commitments (iii). By doing so, HRM's role in relation to the eight components becomes clear. Its power to communicate directives and orders is of particular relevance. It influences behaviour through communication as evidenced in guidance, advice and moral appeals. At the level of value commitment, HRM strongly communicates corporate effectiveness and the creation of *loyalty* and integrity. Bing (2006:27) has emphasised that *the corporate world is a world without loyalty, friendship or trust, where a missing doughnut can engender a paranoia-fuelled department reorganisation.* This affects labour-management relations. *Labour-capital relations today because of its linkage to loyalty-ensuring* managerialism are made to appear unconnected to *exploitation and oppression* (Eagleton 1994, 1999). In other words, the power of loyalty allows managerialism to eclipse exploitation and oppression. Loyalty created in this way ensures that binding decisions and authority remain unchallenged.

At the level of rationality, HRM seeks success through achieving consensus and pattern consistency among employees. HRM supports managerial goal achievement by influencing employees towards understanding and acceptance. HRM's value system is based on realisation of management's goals influenced by a conviction to support management. This is based on the value that managerial decisions are justified, thus establishing an obligation to act. HRM supports this by hierarchical means-ends chains and enforces managerial decisions that influence employees on the basis of cultural values and internalised corporate values. Finally, HRM takes an official position within a company. Its prestige is established by enforcing managerial hierarchies and appealing to management's moral leadership whenever necessary.

Strategies to control communication

Overall, HRM assumes a power position inside companies by influencing strategic decisions based on a strong moral commitment towards company values as well as the ability and capacity to control labour's contribution towards a company goal. In many cases, this is achieved through simplified communication that reduces managerial strategies into simple statements. It also replaces them with symbolic generalisations of negative and positive sanctions. Inside the repertoire of HRM, at least six different levels of people management can be identified which operate in order to mediate between the corporate profit goals and the interest of workers. To cover these contradictions, the HR manager adopts a range of strategies deemed necessary to manufacture consent among human resources. Here, HR management takes on six roles as strategic planner on the human resource side of management (Forester 1989:88):

Table 12.3   **Six Forms of Strategic Communication used by HR Managers**

Strategy	Role of HR Manager
strategy 1:	strategic HR manager as regulator;
strategy 2:	strategic HR manager as pre-mediator and negotiator; strategy;
strategy 3:	strategic HR manager as a resource;
strategy 4:	strategic HR manager as a shuttle diplomat;
strategy 5:	strategic HR manager as an active interest mediator;
strategy 6:	strategic HR manager as job-splitter – you mediate and I'll negotiate.

As Table 12.3 shows, there are different strategic levels serving different organisational needs. From strategy 1 to strategy 7, HR managers see their role as representatives of organisational goals. In the attempt to service these managerial goals, HR managers take on different roles, communicating differently with labour in order to achieve compliance, acceptance and legitimacy for themselves and above all for management and managerialism.

Strategy 1

In strategy 1, HR managers communicate technical and bureaucratic rules and procedures seeking to regulate communication rather than enabling it. As such the field of HR activity is strongly linked to organisational profit goals as any corporation depends on regulation. These regulations always benefit those *who regulate* over those *who are regulated*. They favour those who manage over those who are managed. As much as HR mangers are entitled to be unfettered and creative in their expressions, they tend to see subordinates as working best when they are regulated and forced into efficient work regimes under rule-following measures.

The power of today's HR managers to regulate is expressed in their ability to issue a raft of policies as well as numerous codes of corporate conduct. In this work, they are able to apply a highly *reductionist* language. This form of communication reduces language to simple how-to-do manuals. As creators, inventors, regulators, and communicators of these rules, HR managers shape the working lives of millions of workers. They do so as they seek a fast comprehension of *their* rules. This way, they are enforcing strategies to cope with organisational complexities. Such regulations include organisational designs and diagrams, job descriptions, procedures, remuneration, performance measuring, and compensation systems. Often these kinds of regulations are issued not only in a language reducing fashion but also in communication reducing devices. The idea is to protect the *regulation* as well as the *regulation-maker* from challenging discussions. It relieves HR managers from the necessity to justify their action. They are able to hide behind pre-set regulations that neutralise them as regulators. They are also able to transform communication into an instrument of rule obedience.

Strategy 2

In strategy 2, pre-mediations and negotiations move to the top. In its pre-mediation version, HR management seeks to anticipate workers' responses to HR initiatives as a pre-calculative exercise. Negotiating as well as pre-mediation takes labour into account but with an attempt to pre-structure communication and discourse. Under negotiations, HR management seeks to classify issues. This pre-definitional exercise divides any negotiable issues into either *integrative* bargaining of win-win situations by increasing the share of a pie or into *distributive* bargaining seen as win-lose strategies. The latter is not based on an expanding pie but bargaining takes place over the win-lose or lose-win *distribution* of a pie. This classification seeks to achieve preparedness before any negotiation takes place. Labour is incorporated into corporate structures via participation. This occurs in disregard of *distributive* or *integrative* bargaining. Both versions of participation tend to incorporate employees into a managerial framework that does not construct people in their own right but as an individualised worker inside an HR framework. This framework entails the submission of workers through involvement. The ideological illusion of being involved inside a pre-set framework occurs inside a pre-conceptualised and controlled form of workers' attachment to managerial goals.

Strategy 3

In strategy 3, HR management sees itself as resource acting at a professional level. HRM pretends to be neutral adopting a facilitator role to assist with problem-solving solutions between labour and management. But information gathering, analysing, discussing, framing, storing, etc. of labour for management becomes a source of power itself. In this way, information about people at work is converted into a resource. In this process humans are collapsed into pre-existing and pre-designed categories. Labour at work, once extracted and converted into HR models and systems, is removed from its context and presented as resources ready to be used by management. The starting point of any conversion of people into objects of HR's power is a number, the employee number. Allocating a number to a person is a rather simple process that is often located at the very beginning of entering a firm. It reduces human individuality to numbers and assigns certain seniority qualities to people, thus transforming individuals into a resource for HRM, a resource *to-be-ruled* and *to-be-regulated*. This process is further enhanced through the categorisation of certain groups and a respective labelling process that can be – at will – extended to occupational groups or other categories.

Such a process of de-individualisation, de-personalisation, and de-humanisation becomes the guiding order of any HR regime. It successfully distances itself from any realm of moral or ethical considerations while pretending to be ethical at the same time. Any good HRM textbook will have a section on business or HR ethics and any good HR manager has an *Ethics Policy* ready to be shown. In most cases, however, such ethical considerations play a somewhat lower level role. For many HR managers and for HR ethics policies, ethical values are surface structures. It is something one has to have rather than a form of deeper value. Ethics is seen as having a somewhat *higher dignity* in *moral* and *spiritual* terms. In that way managers are able to conceptualise it away because ethical values are *not real* and untenable. In fact, they are not even necessary or connected to the business needs of the enterprise. Obviously, ethical values are not measurable and therefore not prevalent in any managerial database. Therefore, ethics and moral values *count* less in real business. Constructed in that way, ethics and business – sometimes officially announced as *business ethics* – enter into a reciprocal relationship. The *higher* the moral value, the *less* it counts in business and vice versa. Once management is able to elevate ethics by attaching high values to it, ethics become remote issues. The higher ethics are elevated *above* reality, the more irrelevant they become for real business, for the real business world and for the real world, and the more likely they will be disregarded. In short, humanitarian, religious, and moral ideas are seen to be only *ideals*. They are not allowed to disturb the established way of corporate life.[494] This construction enables management to relief itself from all ethics while at the same time being able to claim to have business ethics.

Above all, these moral ideas are *not invalidated by the fact that they are contradicted by a behaviour dictated by the daily necessities of business* (Marcuse 1966:151). Individuality, morality, and ethics are cast aside as *nice in theory but in reality…* are irrelevant to corporate life. Overall, HR at level 3 occurs as a process of de-contextualisation. This process separates issues from their context so that they can be understood in a way deemed beneficial to management. But the context needs to be so far removed that a real or even critical understanding is avoided. In this process all issues that enable humans to understand the socially constructed character of work arrangements is lifted out of a social, historical, and economical context. People are transferred into a *useful* resource. At the height of such treatment is the reduction of workers or sections of work to mere *overheads* once their transformation into HR accounting methods is completed.

Strategy 4

In strategy 4, HR management sees its role as an extension of strategy 3 but with a more engaging and active role in interest mediation. HR managers are concerned with suggestions, queries, and arguments that are taken up by both sides. Here, HR not only conveys information but seeks an active diplomacy role in *face-to-face* discussions. By shuttling between contradictory interests of labour and management, HR managers pretend to be the *honest broker* needed to solve conflict even though their organisational task is directed towards managerial goal achieving. The *art* of HR management lies in successfully pretending to be neutral. The role demands the assumption as an independent agent. The HR manager needs to be seen as a neutral negotiator or an unbiased mediator. This strategy dictates the presentation of being no more than a skilful diplomat with the interests of both sides at heart.

Strategy 5

In this version, diplomacy is superseded by active interest mediation, leaving more and more roles such as that of facilitator and resource supplier behind. HRM shows a keen interest in solutions by taking part as a positional agency. Communication is not seen as a neutral activity that provides a forum for discourse but as a tool to bring one's interest into force. The interests of workers are taken seriously and seen as legitimate. The role of management is to take care of them. Before they are taken care of, HR managers reformulate workers' interests into business functions through the division into *value added* and non-value added interests. Sometimes workers' interests are also labelled as legitimate or non-legitimate interests. By reformulating, categorising, and labelling them, HRM decides which interests are legitimate and value adding. The portraying of workers' interests in this way allows HRM to create the impression that workers add value. The interests of workers become synonymous to workers themselves. Both are constructed as adding value to organisational goals. In this way, the process of adding value is linked to a person. In order to become a better person they must, of course, contribute value to the corporation and to corporate goals and add value to profit goals. To communicate what a better person means and how to become one is HR management's task.

Strategy 6

Finally in strategy 6, HR management adopts a *split the job* attitude seeking to divide communicative roles into either a manager *mediates* or a manager *negotiates*. Strategy 6 is adopted when HR management is faced with an organised oppositional interest. This is the case when workplace organisations such as trade unions support labour in their interest formulation. Overall, managerial counter-strategies are applied in an instrumental and strategic way, directed towards the achievement of pre-determined organisational goals. Under the conditions of these strategies, communication is reduced to an instrument enabling HR management to achieve certain goals. Here, HR management presents itself as a mediator or negotiator with central management on behalf of workers while at the same time their language use seeks to incorporate workers into a pre-fabricated managerial viewpoint. Often this viewpoint is the viewpoint of *economic necessity, cost-benefit analysis, market determination, downsizing, rightsizing, outsourcing, re-engineering* and so on. All of these – including a sheer endless list of managerial terms – expose HR as being part of a managerial discourse. What is crucial to these terms is not only that they expose HR's true role inside the managerial process but instrumental and depersonalising language also removes real people behind such decisions.

Hidden behind the language of structure are de-personalised managerial decisions, managerial intentions and actions. In this instrumental language, top managers and corporate leaders are absent as terms such as *downsizing, rightsizing, suizing (!),*[495] *outsourcing, re-engineering* imply the myth of corporations as natural forces and not as socially constructed reality. When top managers and corporate leaders fire workers, HR managers re-label this as *resource re-allocations,* or *de-growth* or *pay-roll-adjustment.* The use of these terms *enhances* the people-less character of decisions made by managers.[496] Decisions are made to appear non-people-related to hide that real people – CEOs, CFOs, and other top managers – are behind these decisions. The decision-makers are effectively removed from the scene of corporate nastiness, while *downsizing, rightsizing, outsourcing, re-engineering* is presented as an inevitable consequence of higher forces that are often portrayed as external to the organisations and beyond managerial control. There are a number of higher forces upon which management can call. These are liberalisation, deregulation, globalisation, market forces, market fluctuations and so on.

HR managers are able to communicate this in a raft of different ways. They exercise power through the communicative application of a wide range of different genres, contents, and styles. These are often applied to express regulations and rules which limit access to communication. HRM often controls messages in reports, newsletters, and other company documents. An example of a report of Ford, Chrysler, and General Motors illustrates this point: In *the* [American car companies] *Big Three's annual* [business] *reports the entire pattern of arguments – selectively presenting data, focusing attention on favourable aspects of the organisation's operations, and projecting claims of increased efficiency, improved productivity, and enhanced allocation of resources in the future – supports the rationality myth. The effect of this approach is to place management's claim of efficiency beyond critical analysis* (Conrad 1992:202). Managers often determine who may speak about what in meetings. They set or invent pre-structured agendas for meetings. During meetings, they control expressions of criticism, information, and the tasks of meetings. They even control the participants of meetings. Managerialism establishes not only a managerial elite but also a communicative or information elite as an elite that communicates inside corporations and structures communication of the non-elite. Forester (1989:29–31) has expressed the *information as a power* relationship relating to five levels at which HR managers use information at a strategic level:

Table 12.4   HR Managers and Communicative Expressions

HR Manager as	Description of Communicative Expression
The Technician:	HR manager views information as technical; information supply solutions to technical problems; tradition of problem-solving.
The Incrementalist:	HR manager uses information as a source of power as they are related to organisational needs; workers that need to know will get information.

Table 12.4   HR Managers and Communicative Expressions – *continued*

HR Manager as	Description of Communicative Expression
The Liberal-Advocate:	HR manager sees business as a pluralist organisation with diverging interests, information help to bring these into bearing.
The Structuralist:	HR manager sees information as a source of power because they assist a legitimisation process that maintains existing structures; relates to conservative functionalism; keeping labour in their place to preserve structural power relations.
The Progressive	HR manager gives information to enable limited criticism to avoid being seen as a pure tool for managerial legitimacy.

Table 12.4 shows the *information-as-power* form of communication within the framework of strategic management and strategic HRM. It further shows how communication is used towards purposive activities directed towards goal-achieving action. Communication is pre-set in a narrowly defined usage under the strict guidelines of instrumental rationality.[497] By pre-structuring communication it not only assumes the appearance of rationality, it also pretends to be logical, neutral, scientific, non-contradictory, and it subscribes to an engineering ideology of impartial technology. Social action is seen as a process of rational adaptation to pre-created conditions. The involved role of an actor is reduced to understanding a situation and forecasting the future course of development. An inherent bias towards a binary logic is hidden inside an engineering process. The managerial construction of binary codes or binary choices engineered as a choice between A or B, left or right, up or down, plus or minus, etc., date back to Aristotle (384–322 BC). Today, they have entered managerial thinking. Even the four choices of the SWOT model – strengths, weaknesses, opportunities, and threats – enforce a binary logic of two opposing aspects:

Strength and Opportunity	*versus*	Weakness and Threat

Figure 12.2   The SWOT Strategy

Figure 12.2 sums up one of the most common managerial ideologies known as SWOT. It narrows thinking to four *managerial* issues. It is humanly constructed but designed to take on the form of neutrality. It should be seen as a tool not as an ideology. Behind it resides the managerial idea of cost leadership versus differentiation. The managerial ideology of a binary logic deletes all alternative ways of thinking. It negates any thinking about dialectical relationships. It bars the *thesis-antithesis-synthesis* thinking as this might lead to a challenge of managerialism. This way of thinking might be able to highlight contradictions inside managerial ideologies.[498] In contrast, a bias towards binary logic presents managerial ideology as a neutral engineering logic.

In such an engineering ideology social actors are constructed in strictly utilitarian terms as atomised actors. The utility of rational, linear and means-ends causality is emphasised. These are the practical and technical concepts of instrumental rationality. Technical mastery is cloaked as rational choice even when it reaches pathological levels.[499] Technical rationality is disconnected from *communicative rationality*. Rationality is designed to appear technical and without human intervention so that an instrumentality can be portrayed that hides the true communicative character of any form of rationality. Actors' choice so-called *rational choice* is either seen in economic terms as strategic choice of rational actors or in sociological terms as choice governed by internalised normative constraints.[500] In both cases the choices presented reduce and limit any freedom of decision-making to simple choices between prefabricated options. In managerial terms these choices are faked alternatives presented as alternative *means* for given *ends*. Such *means* are no more than goal-directed interventions directed towards the same *end*. Essentially, such strategies are means-ends structured actions. Among the endless array of examples for *means-ends* strategies that pretend to give workers some level of *means*-choices always directed towards the same *end*, the *end-purpose* of profit-making, of course, starts with the invention of the division between a) work for labour and b) *strategic* planning for management:

As Table 12.5 shows, there is an always incomplete but still extensive selection of communication tools directed towards achieving competitive superiority as well as the contradicting notion of *one best way*. Table 12.5 provides a glimpse into the extremely wide range of strategic choices that in fact is no more than a set of alternatives none of which

Table 12.5   Easy Steps for Strategic Management

• 5 topics for work analysis and planning (Taylor 1911:117),	• Whittington's four generic perspectives (1993),
• SWOT or strength, weakness, opportunities, threats,	• Salaman & Asch' E-S-C model (2003:25),
• 7 easy steps to corporate success (Peters & Waterman 1982),	• Spulber's 5 transaction cost strategies (2004:252)
• Miles & Snow's *defender, prospector, analyser, and reactor model* (1978),	• Biegler & Norris' 6 strategic growth factors (2004:65),
• Ohmae's *identify, group, evaluate, solution* (1983:23),	• Whittington's 4 strategies model (1993),
	• Whittington's 7 strategic questions (2003).

Table 12.5   Easy Steps for Strategic Management – *continued*

• 4 strategic Bs: bigger, bolder, better, broader (Biegler & Norris 2004:64),	• Mintzberg's *5-Ps* (1987; cf. 1973, 1987a),
• Harrison's 4 culture-strategy model (Hartley & Bruckmann 2002:77),	• McKinsey's 7-S model (Biegler & Norris 2004:35),
• 1st, 2nd and budget level strategies,	• Porter's *5-forces* (1980),
• Boxall & Purcell's 1st, 2nd, and 3rd order strategies (2003:13),	• Porter's Cost, Differentiation, Generic model (1980),
• Biegler & Norris' 10 operational strategic factors (2004:5),	• Dynamic, profit and turnaround strategies,
• Biegler & Norris' 11 strategic change patterns (2004:93),	• Formal, Flexible, Attribution Strategy,
• Legge's start-up, growth, maturity, decline (1995:105, cf. 2005),	• Target, guide, direct, and running,
• Develop, control, administer, scanning strategies,	

can ever prove to be successful. Even though there may not be *one best way* to communicate, SHRM's demand for it is insatiable.

In order to integrate workers into the system of instrumental rationality of strategic management, HR managers are expected to communicate cleverly and effectively.[501] As a result, communication becomes a core activity of any HRM function conducted today. Under the auspices of strategic management linked to SHRM, such a link is orientated towards fitting SHRM to managerial goals that have to be communicated to workers. Not surprisingly, many HRM textbooks spend considerable time on communication *with* or rather *to* workers. Here, communication is presented as *cascading down*.[502] Such textbooks are not designed as a critical discourse on communication or HRM. They are written with the intention to convert the *negatives* of HRM and communication into *positives*. Commonly, they neglect or simply hide negatives or critical viewpoints. What occurs is a sweeping readjustment of concepts, theories, and thought itself as a non-critical, one-dimensional and highly affirmative exercise, designed to adjust the individual to a hierarchical work regime (Baritz 1960). As a result, intellectual thought and research are codified into operational terms directed towards system-functional operations. This reflects, according to Marcuse (1966:111), on a *functional analysis enclosed in the selected system which itself is not subject to a critical analysis transcending the boundaries of the system towards the historical continuum, in which its functions and dysfunctions become what they are. Functional theory thus displays the fallacy of misplaced abstractness*. He described this process as follows (Marcuse 1966:110ff.):

The therapeutic character of the operational concept shows forth most clearly where conceptual thought is methodologically placed into the serve of exploiting and improving the existing social conditions, within the framework of existing societal institutions – in industrial sociology, motivation research, marketing and public opinion studies. If the given form of society is and remains the ultimate frame of reference for theory and practice, there is nothing wrong with this sort of sociology and psychology. It is more human and more productive to have good labour-management relations [italics, TK] than bad ones, to have pleasant rather than unpleasant working conditions, to have harmony instead of conflict between desires of the customer and the needs of business and politics. But the rationality of this kind of social science appears in a different light if the given society, while remaining the frame of reference, becomes the object of a critical theory which aims at the very structure of this society, present in all particular facts and conditions and determining their place and their function. Then their ideological and political character becomes apparent, and the elaboration of adequately cognitive concepts demands going beyond the fallacious concreteness of positivist empiricism. The therapeutic and operational concept becomes false to the extent to which it insulates and atomises the facts, stabilises them within the repressive whole, and accepts the terms of this whole as the terms of the analysis. The methodological translation of the universal into the operation concepts becomes repressive reduction of thought.

What Marcuse had expressed in 1966 relates directly to a classic of modern management thought and HRM. This is a study on the *Hawthorne Works* of the Western Electrical Company widely popularised by Elton Mayo. Marcuse (1966:110ff.) commented on this study, *this mode of thought has since not only spread into other branches of social science and into philosophy, but it has also helped to shape the human subject with whom it is concerned. The operational concepts terminate in methods of improved social control: they become part of the science of management, Department of Human Relations.*

Workers' complaints about working conditions are – guided by the principles of *human relations'* operational thinking of management and HRM writers for textbooks – reformulated and translated. The importance of the human relations school to capitalism has been summed up by Henry Ford II (1946) when he stated *if we can solve the problem of human relations in industrial production, we can make as much progress towards lower costs in the next 10 years as we have made during the past quarter century through the development of the machinery of mass production.* For example, when a worker complained that *the piece rates on his job are too low* (Marcuse 1966:113), he was interviewed and it was uncovered that his wife was in hospital resulting in medical bills. In modern HRM textbooks this reads as: the fact that B's present remuneration is insufficient is due to his wife's illness as he is unable to meet his current financial obligations. The low-wage issue has successfully been translated away from wages and into a personalised realm of the individual, just as HRM's individualising ideas demand. Systemic conditions are individualised. In other words, something *general* – wages of workers – is converted into something *particular, the wage of one single worker*. A *collective* issue is translated into a *single* case that can be presented as case study to be served up in a textbook and rehearsed by HRM students.

The collective pay system of piece rates is reduced to an individual issue eliminating the power of the collective by replacing it with the relative helplessness of the individual. The individual in turn is reduced to an organisational *object of power* (Bauman 1989). Issues of a worker, work, and working conditions are converted into an issue of consumption. Unrelenting consumption linked to the idea of consumerism focuses economic activities on the free choice of the consumer as a guiding *leitmotiv* for all economic activities as well as society. It leads to people's tendency to identify themselves with consumer products and brand names where unhealthy product relations replace healthy social relations, thus creating pathologies in modern societies. Humans no longer behave towards each other; they behave towards products and commodities. Their behaviour is altered towards economic behaviour. This somewhat irrational economic behaviour that follows consumerism has been called *conspicuous consumption*. It is not locked up in the private domain of consumption but impacts on the world of work as well. The issue of a workplace is converted into an issue of ex-production. The conditions at work are exchanged with conditions of, as in the example above, private health insurance. The worker is no longer a worker as he is reduced to "B" eliminating the worker and the work issue altogether. The wage earner has disappeared. Similarly the job is eradicated – in the same way as it is not the job but his wife's hospital bill that is at fault here. Managerially created job problems are converted into problems of the worker.

As a result gained from the example above, the HRM researcher and textbook writer displays an *arrested* or *asphyxiated* experience. It pretends to display *fixed* models on which to train future mangers. This is what they are trained for. This is what they do. It is not their *function* to think in terms of critical theory but to train HR managers and supervisors in more human and effective methods of dealing with their workers. In this realm of thinking, the only term that seems non-technical, non-operational, and non-systematic is the term *human*. Even this term may be analysed away or converted into a technical, operational, and systematic term. As this managerial mode of thought and research spreads into other dimensions of the intellectual effort, services that are rendered become increasingly inseparable from their scientific validity. In fact, scientific knowledge cloaked in scientific terms is not only appropriated by managerialism, it becomes a central part of management terminology provided by numerous functional academics working in the so-called management studies trade in various management or business schools attached to the modern university which is functionally attached to the demands of managerialism via market forces. Consequently, there is a *growing tendency for universities and their scholars to treat knowledge like a commodity* (Washburn 2005:151). These management *scientists* (sic!) engage in an endless production of scientific language. What they do has been successfully described by George Orwell (1946:3): *words, phenomenon, element, individual (as noun), objective, categorical, effective, virtual, basic, primary, promote, constitute, liquidate are used to dress up a simple statement and give an air of scientific impartiality to biased judgements.* George Orwell could not have expressed this any better. What has been done is the torturing of language by managerial writers and management science. This is done in order to hide the true character of relations at work. It is done to hide the reality of work behind scientific language brought to functional use.

In the context of a managerially deformed language *functionalisation* takes on a truly therapeutic effect. *Once the personal discontent is isolated from the general unhappiness, once the universal concepts that militate against functionalisation are dissolved into particular referents, the case becomes a treatable and tractable incident* (Marcuse 1966:114). But they also testify the ambivalent rationality of progress. It is satisfying with its repressive power, and repressive in its satisfactions. The repressive character and satisfactions have eliminated almost all forms of meaning from the world of work. What has remained is a communicative representation of work in empirical HRM studies. As a result, all *unrealistic* excesses of meaning have been abolished. All meanings directed to critical rationality, speculative rationality, and towards *what ought to be* rather than towards *what is* have been abolished. Once this process is completed, all HRM investigation into the world of work can be securely locked inside the confinement of managerial language. These confinements establish a managerial framework that validates and invalidates every research, every form of social science, and every form of text. By virtue of its methodology, this empiricism is ideological. Any analysis of work issues is locked inside an ideological framework that pretends to be neutral but is in fact directed towards managerialism. In order to prove to be scientific, the range of judgement is confined within the context of managerial facts. These facts are made to appear neutral even though they are *man made, made-up* facts inside a framework in which their meaning, function, and development are determined. In other words, *it is power relations rather than facts about reality that make things true* (du Gay 1996:43). HRM can only become truthful to a humanly constructed world of work when it stops pretending to be value-free, objective, and capable of delivering neutral facts. The human constructed-*ness* of facts only serves to support an equally constructed concept, the concept of managerialism. At the same time it supplies scientific value while cloaking the ideological character that underlies these managerial concepts.

13
Conclusion: Communication, Management and Work

Like all other forms of human communication, communication at work starts with the premise that *'you cannot not communicate'*. Whenever and wherever humans assemble collectively, communication plays an important part. Coming together communally and communicating with each other is something that has been absolutely necessary to ensure human survival. It has been essential for all forms of human life from early tribal societies to modern times. Human life occurs predominantly in association with others, such as families, play groups, school mates, peer groups, neighbours, formal associations, work colleagues, and the like. In all these situations what is demanded from us is communication. But communication is more than just talking to each other because all forms of communication contain at least three elements. One element looks at the *semantics* and *construction* of what is expressed, the other at the *technical transmission* of messages, and the final element examines the *reception, appropriation,* and creation of *meaning* in messages.[503] Throughout the previous chapters, the semantics, construction, reception and appropriation of communication has been discussed. These discussions centred on the place where many people spend most of their time, the workplace.

Today's modern workplaces are governed by several key elements. First of all, the majority of workplaces are places of mass production as most activities related to work are not geared towards the production of individual goods and services. In a mass-production society the substantial amounts of goods and services are also consumed. This occurs in the same way in which they have been produced. The conveyor belt is as much part of every modern mass-production facility as it is part of any supermarket checkout. Modern society has turned those who produce these mass commodities and services into those who also consume them on a mass scale. Today, people have been constructed and attached to two domains. In the *productive* domain of work they exist as *workers* or *labourers* (Orwell's *Oldspeak*) or as *organisational members* and *associates* (*Newspeak*). At the same time, they have been constructed as mass consumers located inside the *reproductive* domain. Inside this dual system of production – the creation of mass goods and services – and reproduction – the consumption of mass goods and services – humans are often reduced to not much more than functional additives to a system. In both domains communication is essential to make them functional in a pre-designed way however the ability of people to communicate among themselves in both domains has been harshly limited. Management and the ideology of *managerialism*[504] have been able to structure communication in the *productive* domain while communication in the reproductive domain is structured by corporate mass media.[505]

In both domains, the overwhelming capability of communication does not lie with those who are asked to oscillate between the productive domain – nine-to-five – and the reproductive domain with seemingly unlimited hours of access to consumption. Most members of present societies have been made to accept these conditions as they are presented as *imperatives*.[506] These imperatives provide strong system integrative forces compelling societal members into a one-dimensional mindset. In both domains, system integrative forces have been able to integrate any opposition to the prevailing form of production and consumption. In sharp contrast to *feudalism* and *early capitalism,* the development of socially organised production and reproduction under advanced capitalism has allowed the splitting of the working class. What had previously been unified under proletariat or working class (*Oldspeak*) is now divided into a middle and a lower class (*Newspeak*). This division found its clearest expression in new *social* classes.[507] In the middle class it led to a distinctive pattern commonly known as the *Affluent Worker.* These workers are firmly located in the realm of the *middle class*.[508] In conjunction with a corporatised mass-media apparatus this system has been able to reduce any opposition to a minority. Resisting groups opposed to both domains are largely seen as irrelevant, obscure, and even obscene.[509] In the work domain, those who hold the view that life could have originally meant something different from sitting at a desk for eight hours per day, five days per week, 50 weeks per year, and for 40 years of their lives are successfully marginalised. In the reproductive domain, those who refuse to consume, those who do not see human fulfilment in the hunt for the newest mobile phone, the latest plasma screen, or the fastest internet connection are portrayed as pathological while in reality the exact opposite is the case. In both domains, the messages directed towards assimilation with the present work regimes and towards mass consumption are powerfully communicated to those who are designed to fulfil a functional necessity to the system.

The creation especially of the affluent middle class who is predominantly concerned with their next shopping trip or the newest products has received unlimited support through the private mass media that communicates nothing other than consumption. This has most successfully ended any revolt against consumption and most obviously any revolution against the system. It has also ended any revolutionary character of those institutions that used to present opposing interests and with it most forms of *working-class* or *proletarian* existence ended altogether. Today, these institutions as much as *proletarianism* itself have been successfully integrated or annihilated. The few revolting or revolutionary energies that remain have been re-directed into relentless consumption, channelled into system stabilising forms of conflict resolution, or marginalised and isolated. Present societies are stabilised by powerful enforcement mechanisms that support a rather one-dimensional view directed towards managerialism at work and mass consumption in the off-work domain. The affirmative mass consensus that has been supported through managerialism at work and through corporate mass media is designed to create a managerial conception of reality.

However this has not resulted in what George Orwell has described in his book *1984*. Today's world does not resemble the setting of Orwell's *It was a bright cold day in April, and the clocks were striking thirteen* where BIG BROTHER IS WATCHING YOU and the *thought police* is looking for *thought crimes*. The harshness of Orwell's *Department of Love* that tortured people is not necessary today as more sophisticated systems of mass loyalty in conjunction with *Affluenza* – a form of affluence that has pathological traces – have been able to integrate today's society into the mechanisms of the present system.[510] The mass integration of society carries stronger connotations with the final words in Orwell's 1984: *but it was all right, everything was all right, the struggle was finished. He had won the victory over himself. He loved Big Brother.* In sharp contrast to Orwell's novel, today the struggle over capitalism has, at least in the industrialised world, largely ended. Most people do not love Big Brother but they love shopping and silly TV shows and above all have accepted the imperatives of present work regimes. In those societies where forms of advanced capitalism combined with the welfare state have been established there are no signs of mass revolt anywhere to be seen. *We have won the victory over ourselves* as we have successfully adjusted ourselves to life as a commodity in the world of work and to life as a consumer in the off-work domain. Today, we may not be asked to *love Big Brother* like in Orwell's novel but we are made to believe that we should love consumption and that we should also love *'our'* work, both of which are being communicated through sophisticated methods in advertising as well as through primary and secondary socialisation at work. In the reproductive domain, this is supported through a gigantic marketing machinery while at work the latest and most sophisticated Human Resource Management techniques are brought in which are applying the very same techniques used to make us *love* consumption.[511] We have been successfully conditioned to engage into what has been termed *retail therapy*.[512]

Above all, what we do at work and in our private lives today is portrayed as rational. The idea of rational behaviour and rationality might have originated in *Enlightenment* but it has successfully been captured by the present system. Rationality has been freed of its *critical* character and is largely understood in the equation of *rationality = rational capitalism = management's instrumental rationality = instrumental communication*. Originally the idea of rationality has been important as a theoretical and methodological system separating modernity from a feudalist past where concepts of God and church governed society. Freed from the Kantian *Enlightenment* idea on *critique,* present society has established rationality as instrumental rationality.[513] It has disconnected rationality from critique directing it only towards instrumental rationality as enshrined in means-ends, system theory, cost-benefit, transaction analysis, and other system integrative ideas.[514] The annihilation of the critical character that had been part of rationality since *Enlightenment* enabled the present system to isolate or restrict critical thinking. What remains is a rational link between rationality, instrumental rationality, and instrumental communication which are highly system integrative forms of thinking and communicating.

In this way, the socially constructed domains of consumerism and work regimes can be made to appear as rational *facts of life*. Today, socially constructed *institutional* facts have been constructed so that they take on what Searle (1996, 2002) has termed *brute facts*. The social character of *facts* that can only be established through human intervention has been separated from their social *constructed-ness* and made them appear as facts that do not require human intervention. In the world of work, this is achieved through the pretence that work is *natural,* rational, logical, scientifically organised, and *deterministic*.[515] This pretence is further cloaked through managerial metaphors culminating in *we are all in one boat* and *this is the way things are done around here*. Managerial language predominantly expresses this in a way that converts socially constructed facts into independent and so-called scientific or rational facts that are naturally given. All of this is directed towards the acceptance of the world of work as natural and unavoidable. The underlying message is one from Star Trek's Borg: *assimilate or be annihilated – resistance is futile!*

The restructuring of the three domains

System integrative messages such as *resistance is futile* are not exclusively found in the world of work. They are also a reoccurring feature of the non-work domain. Similar to the productive domain, system integrative communication can also be found in the communicative public domain which gained importance because it communicatively assisted exchange processes between the work-productive and reproductive domain of private consumption. When societies moved from feudalism to capitalism during what has been called *The Great Transformation*, the communicative domain played an important role. Its role was to provide an open and democratic forum for the exchange of *Enlightenment* ideas as much as the regulation of societal steering needs through the idea of *representative* democracy (Canfora 2006). In this setting, access to the communicative domain was open to all members as it provided a forum to share the concerns of all members of a society. With the emergence of advanced capitalism, the commodification of access to the communicative domain took a largely non-democratic turn. Increasingly, the communicative domain became a domain relevant for the exchange of consumer goods. Eventually, the communicative domain itself took on elements of commodification as access to it was increasingly gained through private ownership of media. Today, the communicative domain has been successfully restructured. It is no longer a domain for the democratic exchange of social and political ideas of the way society conducts itself but has been converted into a mass-media guided transmission system for affirmative managerial ideologies. The restructuring of the communicative domain has been largely completed and this has significantly altered the original idea of this domain.[516]

There are two forces that establish control over the communicative domain. They stem from the corporate mass media as well as from the state. One force is the collusion between state, government, and bureaucracy. It operates largely through administration of state and governmental *control* as well as *censorship*.[517] Adjacent to state and government control a far more important form of control can be found. This force originates from the private corporate system. Its version of control operates through five key activities. Firstly, the private ownership of mass media guarantees interest similarity between the owning of media companies and the broadcasting of affirmative messages. Secondly, the global scale of international mass media provides almost unlimited access to the media markets of all advanced countries. Today, even the previously democratically organised *communicative domain* itself is relabelled and restructured as *media market*, turning it into the famous *market place of ideas*, a place where exchange-value is attached to information that is purchased and sold on a market. Thirdly, the alignment between media and corporate interest has advanced significantly. The previously open communicative domain is no longer an open place for the *free* exchange of ideas but a market place for advertising. Fourthly, the process of exchange has been reduced to a mere advertising of commercial goods and political ideas. Pretty much in the same way in which toothpaste is sold to us, political advertising sells us political ideas, often wrapped up in 20-second sound-bytes that follow the advertising format. The democratic mass consumer only has to *vote* for toothpaste A or B or for political party A or B. Lastly, advertising toothpaste or politics is done in a way not to upset any commercial or political consumer through challenging or critical ideas. In order to increase the market acceptance of toothpaste A or party A, the socially accepted and affirmative status quo is maintained. Conservative values are called upon and the KISS – keep it simple, stupid! – doctrines are applied.[518] These elements build the guiding principles for the integration of people into mass consumption and mass democracy. They turn a once critical character into an affirmative character, thus creating a vital element for mass loyalty.[519]

To be able to function in the prescribed way, today's societies can no longer be understood as a dialectic relationship between the reproductive domain (13.1[i]) and the productive domain (13.1[iii]) because the creation of mass markets, mass production, and mass consumption demands a fully functional communicative support domain. The reproductive domain (i) cannot be organised as a simple market without communication. The steering needs of the communicative support domain (ii) can only be organised through the communication of the two most powerful steering medias, *money* and *power* (13.1[iv]).[520] While players and conditions of the communicative domain have changed over time, the basic principles of the domain have remained. Already the medieval world was able to structure the communicative domain through mysticism, God, religion, and the institution of the church to guarantee mass loyalty and an affirmative society. This system, while working for thousands of years, temporarily broke down during the time of the *Great Transformation*. The temporary lapse occurred when the old communicative regime of church and lords broke down and the modern communicative domain was not fully established. This was only achieved when capitalism, affirmative mass consumption, and representative democracy were successfully established (13.1[v]). During these brief moments of human history, unwarranted elements had access to the communicative domain. They were able to significantly destroy the belief in church, religion and lords. But they were also, at least temporarily, able to have access to those on the receiving end of both feudalism and capitalism. The relationship between these three domains is shown in Figure 13.1:

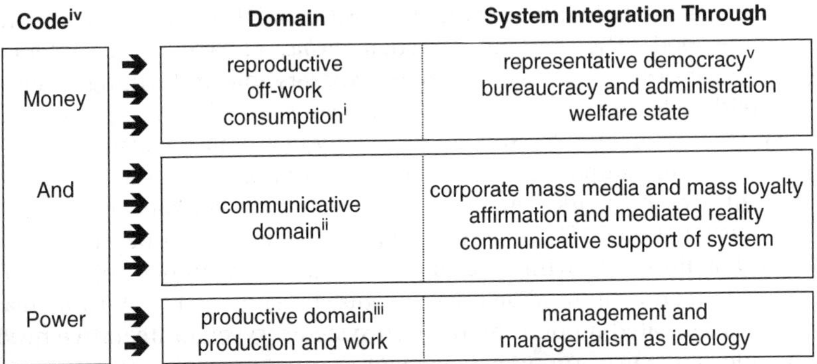

Figure 13.1　　The Three Domains that Define Society and Work

During the brief moment of revolution the democratic forces were able to temporarily alter the relationship between all three domains (figure 13.1[i–iii]).[521] As corporate system integration grew stronger, the relationship returned to the master–worker dialectic. According to George Orwell (1949:210), *from the point of view of the low, no historic change has ever meant much more than a change in the name of their masters.* Even though the names of *the low* (Orwell) might have changed, the revolutions that took place during the move from feudalism to modernity did not alter the fundamental relationship between the *low* and their *masters*. Barons and landlords became capitalists and managers while peasants became workers. Their relationship remained intact despite the fact that a number of revolutions against both systems – feudalism and capitalism – occurred during the temporary breakdown of the ideological domination that structured the communicative domain.[522] Subsequently, these revolutions provided not much more than minor interruptions on the way to early and eventually advanced capitalism.

The changes from feudalism to *early* capitalism and subsequently to *advanced* capitalism altered the reproductive domain (13.1[i]) as well as the communicative domain (13.1[ii]). Most fundamentally, they also altered the world of work (13.1[iii]). While early capitalism was able to operate in a direct relationship between labour and capital, managerial capitalism positioned the institution of management between labour and capital (Marglin 1974). At the more advanced stage, management moved on from being a functional necessity of mass production to become an ideological apparatus. At this stage management was able to transform itself into an ideology, the ideology of managerialism. No longer was it sufficient to exclusively communicate system imperatives to workers at the world of work. System imperatives demanded a stronger link between the domains to provide the ideological support mechanism necessary for the maintenance and survival of the system.

The managerial system could no longer restrict its ability to structure the world of work to the sphere of companies and corporations; they needed to extend their realm of influence into the communicative domain. The rise of Fordist mass production altered the position of those who actually produced the goods. They became the actual *producers of wealth*. The system of Fordism not only demanded compliant workers able and willing to suffer 55-second cycle times under the inhumane constraints of mass production, the system also demanded something totally new – mass consumption.[523] The production-supportive system of consumption had to be communicated into the off-work domain to effectively turn workers at work into consumers at home. Therefore, the reproductive domain became a consumer domain (13.1[i]) while the communicative domain developed into a restructured and commodified mass-media domain (13.1[ii]). With increasingly sophisticated modern production systems, system integrative needs demanded an expansion of management in order to ideologically colonise the communicative domain. During the early stages of mass-production systems, management's ability to assimilate workers into the modern apparatus of production proved to be sufficient. But with the rise of more complicated production methods and especially with the conversion of mass production into post-industrial settings, previous control mechanisms that had been largely restricted to the world of work provided insufficient means to integrate workers into the advanced systems of post-industrial work regimes. Increasingly, management found that non-communicative control mechanisms such as technical or bureaucratic control had to be supplemented by an overarching ideology.[524] This ideology, like all ideologies, issued strong demands directed towards communication, thus converting management into the ideology of managerialism.[525]

In sharp contrast to previous forms of management that were able to organise Fordist and Taylorist production methods, the transformation of management into managerialism demanded a number of elements to be put in place. Previously, management's task had been to legitimise a production system and their role as guardians of this system. Managerial capitalism and managerialism had to restructure the communicative domain in order to enshrine its values and ideology in this domain. This has been supported by the *money* and *power* code (13.1[iv]). The restructuring of the communicative domain under conditions of managerial imperatives rendered representative democracy as unnecessary. Domain specific steering needs could now be allocated to the money and power code.

Secondly, the managerial ideology of instrumental rationality and instrumental communication has isolated all forms of direct democracy and mechanisms to find participative consent. Decisions that affect people at work and in the reproductive domain are relocated away from democracy and solved through instrumental rationality. In the reproductive domain, these decisions are positioned inside the administrative bureaucracy. The instrumental rational organisation of society is only occasionally interrupted through ritualistically organised mass routines of voting. An increased linkage between the three domains demands that system imperatives such as *affirmation processes* are designed to integrate people into the production-consumption apparatus mediated through corporate mass media (Figure 13.1[i–iii]). While democracy has been firmly downgraded and secured as representative democracy, all forms of direct participative or *deliberative* democracy have ended.[526] This not happened in the off-work domain but also in the world of work.[527]

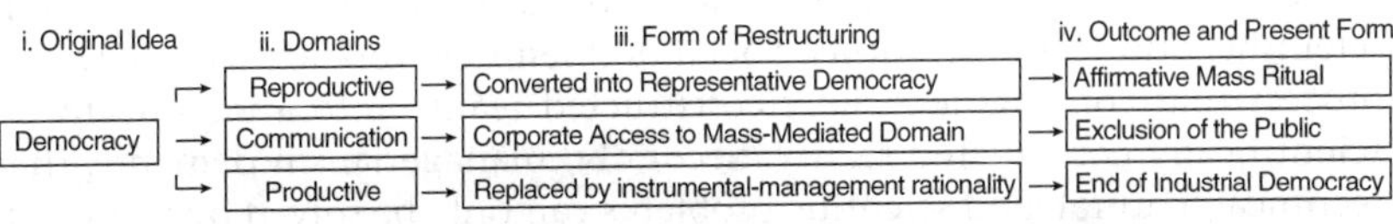

Figure 13.2   The Restructuring of Democracy

Figure 13.2 shows the restructuring of democracy on the basis of general domains that define present societies as shown in Figure 13.1. The restructuring process starts with democracy's original conception as *'will of the people'* (13.1[i]) located in all three domains (13.1[ii]). During the restructuring process the concept of democracy has been significantly altered in all three domains in three different ways (13.1[iii]) with three different outcomes (13.1[iv]). In the originally participative reproductive domain, direct and deliberative democracy has been converted into *representative* democracy disconnecting the will of the people from the representation of the will, thus establishing a *double-mediated* form of democracy where democracy is mediated through the act of representation as someone represents *some* interest. The second mediation was achieved through corporate mass media. The outcome is a ritualistic and mass-guided affirmation process that has doubled the distance between voters and democracy. This process has ended the idea of an open and public domain idealised as a *market place of ideas.* While the original idea of a communicative public domain might have been conceptualised as a place for the free exchange of ideas, today it has been restructured towards corporate access to this domain. This has allowed significant transmission of ideologies through this domain. Simultaneously, massive information distortions take place, the outcome of which is the almost total exclusion of any democratic influence or control over the communicative domain. Finally the successful restructuring of the work domain has occurred under unlimited access of non-democratic forms of managerial instrumental rationality. A *technified* and managerial process of steering inside the world of work has not only replaced democracy but also made it appear as *inefficient* and *non-scientific.*[528] Today, any debate on industrial democracy has ended as system imperatives such as functionalism and *means-ends* doctrines are brought into play.[529]

Thirdly, managerialism promotes the political and moral idea that instrumental rationality, science, technology, and instrumental communication resolve all problems. Therefore the application of *scientific* means to socially constructed problems at work as well as in the reproductive domain has to be trusted. Neither society nor work depend on communicatively established mechanisms to reach consent; however, they depend on *non-communicative* forms such as non-democratic hierarchies and instrumental rationality. In this process, managerialism has converted itself into a science, the management science which operates in two ways. Firstly socially constructed forms of production are converted into natural, scientific, and technical forms. Social problems at work are *technified* in a process that converts a socially constructed reality into a technically or scientifically constructed reality. Secondly, managerialism demands that technical, natural, and scientific problems can only be solved by technical, natural, and scientific means. By applying this process, work as a socially constructed domain has ceased to exist. It is linguistically converted into a domain of managerial science and managerial techniques to solve problems. Non-democratic means are made to appear to solve problems. Only techno-scientifically university-graduated managers and managerial experts such as IR experts and increasingly HR experts are able to solve these problems. In the sub-domain of people management or HRM it is the trained HRM expert that solves *technified problems*.[530] The world of work is freed from all social, political, and democratic communication. It has successfully been converted into a *technified*, non-socially constructed, and above all non-democratic domain.

This process enables managerialism to construct the world of work as *business is the business of business*. The domain of work has been disconnected from all social and political influences that could come from the reproductive or communicative domain. This has distanced the world of work even further from economic participation and industrial democracy. Today, corporate mass media have been able to establish the separation between the democratic and the work domains firmly in the minds of their members. The work domain is freed from any challenges resulting from shifts or alterations in the reproductive domain. Alternatives to managerialism are not presented, the ownership of private property, and the managerial prerogatives of managerialism are not challenged. Managerialism has been able to install itself as TINA: there is no alternative. The one-dimensional mindset has been powerfully communicated at work as much as in the off-work domain while the communicative domain has been restructured to communicate this deeply into the work and reproductive domains.

Communication and managerialism at work and in society

With the rise of managerialism that could only find legitimacy when communicated to those who are managed, the communicative need at work increased as well. While the old conceptualisation of industrial relations at work was sufficient to discuss the relationship between labour and management, under modern managerialism elements of communication could no longer be excluded. In this respect, the relationship between labour and management has firmly become a *communicative relationship*. This is an important conceptualisation given the fact that standard academic understandings of the world of work had largely excluded communication. On the other hand traditional management literature on the world of work has reframed communication as instrumental and constructed it as *organisational communication*. The managerial image of organisational communication is based on the *pipeline* metaphor that focuses on *top-down* communication between *superiors* and *subordinates* constructed as *delegating down* and *reporting up*. In this standard managerial view, communication is seen as the direct transmission of information between managers and employees. This type of communication seeks to avoid any spillage. All non-managerial and non-supportive communication is portrayed as spillage and therefore has to be excluded. Hence communication is seen as an information flow that runs through a closed steel pipeline. This managerial model of communication focuses on narrowly defined hierarchical forms of top-down communication between *superiors* and *subordinates*. It neglects all forms of communication that take place among workers who were reduced to a *commodity* or a *resource* when they were converted from some*one* into some*thing*. Once reduced to some*thing, 'it'* has to be managed like a *resource*. Most importantly, the idea of a communicative exchange domain inside the work domain in which ideas between labour and management are discussed is basically non-existent[531] and is also largely excluded from standard management literature on organisational and business communication.

Consequently, the formulation of workers' interests, their communicative domain, and workers themselves are largely absent from the one-dimensional world of managerialism. The formulation of the one-dimensional managerial interest can be established without having to engage in communicative asymmetries between labour and management. Workers experience this form of one-dimensionality in the work domain quite differently – and this is often despite all the efforts of managerialism and its entourage of affirmative writers and publications – as workers still communicate among themselves. At work, managerialism has been able to infiltrate the communicative domain of workers by structuring workplace communication. Hence, consensus-finding forms of communication in the domain of the workers have been more difficult to establish. Management has been able to rely on asymmetric communicative capabilities to maintain their one-dimensional interest of a so-called *organisational goal* or *shareholder value* which can be summed up as profit.

In sharp contrast to the one-dimensionality of the profit interest, workers or the labour domain face a divergence of – at least – three interests: high wages, an interest in the continuation of wages or employment security, and an interest in working conditions. In order to formulate these interests and mediate between them, labour has to establish forms of communication that are non-instrumental. These need to be free from managerial colonisation attempts. Labour also has to find common agreement on mechanisms that give preference. This is necessary due to a multitude of interests that force labour into a choice-determining process between the three core interests. In contrast, management's interest formulation is aided by two factors. Firstly, structural forces such as the asymmetric distribution of communicative abilities that support management and secondly, management's one-dimensionality of profit that supports its very own interest formation. This occurs in stark contrast to labour's ability to formulate interests.

While labour is forced to communicate and find agreement on three interests, management can securely rely on the singularity of one interest. Unlike the discursive needs of labour, management can draw upon a monological form of interest that shows no need for interest mediation. Labour's multitude of, at times, divergent interests lacks the web of societal and communicative support mechanisms on which managerialism can rely (Figure 13.1). The restructuring of the communicative domain allows managerialism to receive support from the institutions of mass media which support the same values. There is an implicit and sometimes explicit coalition of interests between those who manage industry in general and those who manage the mass-media industry or the *culture industry* (Adorno 1944), at least in terms of supportive worldview, values, public, i.e. *publicised* opinions, and principles. The communicative domain provides a powerful support mechanism for the transmission of managerial ideas.

Finally, at work as well as in the off-work domain, labour is faced with principles that are often constructed against their own. For example, issues such as solidarity tend to be neutralised by managerialism's push for individuality, personal advancement, and competition.[532] Labour also faces additional problems as their interest mediation is exposed to ambiguities communicated to them through the communicative domain. Labour's consciousness about what is real in society is further eroded by its own alienation from production and from society through a relentless consumerism also advocated through the communicative domain. Lastly, labour's interest mediation is further complicated through the mystification of the production process that disallows any understanding of modern management. This is communicated as an identity that transforms labour into *organisational members* as if they were employed by an *organisation* and not by a company that has its origins in the bread (*pane*) sharing (*con*) of feudal *freelance* killers. Those who run these ex-killer organisations have also managed to eliminate their horse-domesticating (*manége*) past, presenting themselves as the guardians of modernity.

The organisational form of the company is hidden behind the ideologically neutral-sounding term *organisation*. Today's *associates* or *human resources* (*Newspeak*) are designed to associate themselves with the modern workplace which seeks to cloak the true character of profit-making companies or corporations even further. The *Newspeak* terms such as *associates* imply that people associate themselves with something or someone *freely*. Terms such as *resource* are invented not only to turn attention away from the profit motive but also to conceal the worker-management interest contradiction that is operative at work. The idea is to make workers believe that their relationship to management is similar to a voluntary cooperative membership. The enforcing demands of the labour market and work regimes are shrouded behind the illusion of free association and *voluntary* membership organisations. But the use of the term organisation goes even further. It also carries connotations to *client-beneficial* institutions such as schools and hospitals. This is designed so that workers are made to feel that *their* organisation provides a client-benefit to them. Finally, the last image of organisation calls upon truly *beneficial* organisations, such as postal services, etc. The idea is simply to make one believe that *their* organisation provides a good service to others or the community. All these forms of associations are established to hide the true character for the very existence of companies, i.e. to make profit.

In this concept the message that workers (*Oldspeak*) are organisational members (*Newspeak*) in the same way as management is an important equalising term. It communicates a false equalisation between labour and management that does not exist. Communicative constructions like this seek to hide the true origins of management as a horse training and domestication institution. It seeks to create an artificial equality where no such equality exists. Finally, it seeks to hide the profit motive behind the term *goal*, pretending there is a commonality of *goals* between labour and management. All this is designed by managerialism to mystify the profit motive. The money and power code allows the *fetishising* of socially constructed relationships at work.[533] This *fetish* is transferred into the reproductive consumption domain[534] where life is engineered towards the money and power code and expressed in consumption, thus leading to an overemphasis on commodity fetishism. Social life is reconstructed so that the money code infiltrates all eventualities of human life.[535] In order to fulfil yourself in such a commodified society, managerialism assists the individual to function according to a work-performance system where *performance-related pay* systems can be linked to individual remuneration, thus allowing the individual to fulfil their consumer function in the off-work domain.[536] Seduced and coerced into an endless treadmill of work and consumption supported through the communicative domain, incentives for workers to uncover the hidden structures of the present system are increasingly limited.

Workers are severely hindered in their project to understand the underlying structures of modern work processes. While managerialism has successfully cloaked these structures, it has not been completely successful in shifting the control at work into the communicative domain – where the daily communication of the advantages of capitalism and managerialism takes place – and into the reproductive domain where relentless consumption and the *fetishisation* of social relations are practised. It has not managed to completely eliminate the need for control at work, however, the issue of control has moved into more advanced stages as forms of management have moved from early craft production to post-industrial work settings. While under conditions of early capitalism bosses were able to exercise *direct* control, the management of large-scale mass manufacturing demanded controlling instruments to be linked to technology. The individual boss no longer had to communicate control to workers as this was exercised through the assembly line and other technical work processes. As we moved into the bureaucratic service industry control could no longer be communicated through the means of technical mass production but had to be established in a new way. When post-industrial settings superseded the administratively organised bureau, control became part of a new HRM regime at work. Unlike equalising bureaucratic and administrative means of control, social control at work started to be communicated through a more individualised approach. While the administrative form of control had moved the application of general formulas and bureaucratic rules to the centre, these were replaced in advanced work settings where control is exercised through a raft of new HRM techniques such as individual job descriptions, individual performance appraisals, performance-related pay systems, and individualised remuneration systems.

The individualisation of control, however, does not mark the end of controlling people at work. While communicative elements increased sharply with changes in control, the present stage of control relies more heavily on communication than previous forms. The post-industrial information and knowledge society is controlled by more sophisticated communicative techniques at work in conjunction with the completion of the communicative domain's restructuring process. Managerialism has been able to combine controlling elements at work with affirmative characteristics received from the communicative domain. But management can also call on other support mechanisms.

Already at the point of conversion of a *human being* into a *human resource, secondary* socialisation processes as an induction into a company can draw on *primary* socialisation processes. Even before individuals reach a new workplace, parts of the affirmative characteristics required at work have already been established in the minds of the workers. Primary socialisation carrying affirmative values has prepared prospective newcomers in a way so that the inductive function assigned to human resource management (secondary socialisation) has almost been completed. Managerialism has been able to restructure institutions of primary socialisation in its image. Long before individuals are converted into *useful* organisational members, they have undergone several institutionalised forms of conditioning during primary socialisation that starts with the family and continues with the school where the individual is conditioned to sit quietly on a desk for extended hours under the premise of *you're not at home, you know.*[537] In some cases secondary socialisation includes the barracks in the form of military service when one is told *you're not at school, you know.* But secondary socialisation can also include conditioning institutions such as hospitals, or even the prison.[538] Especially the schools, hospital wards, and above all the prison have been model sites not only for confinement but also for the panoptical version of control. These institutions sufficiently condition individuals to work regimes with minimal adjustment needs and even more negligible resistance during secondary socialisation. During the process of secondary socialisation the modern HR manager only has to establish a communicative link between a priori conditioned forms of behaviour and individual achievement to turn a human being into a productive *human resource*. The need for harsh *discipline and punishment* as exercised in the 17th, 18th and 19th century has largely vanished (Foucault 1995). It has ended with the mass-mediated rise of the highly system integrative affirmative character of today's individuals.

While older forms of control needed to operate with coercive methods that adjusted human beings to the production regime, today's *regime change* from primary to secondary socialisation occurs seamlessly. The brutality of working life is securely locked in the history of capitalism by corporate media that create a mass-mediated reality. Equally, there is no need for control via machinery and technical apparatuses as they are by and large not the determining factors of modern work processes. Today's adjustment process to modern work regimes can be found in a self-*disciplinary* as well as in a self-*controlling* society (Foucault 1995).

At the early stages of work regimes when firms and factories were established discipline and punishment were part of any induction into the work regime. Early forms of control were also communicated and supported through linking the factory regime to work-supportive institutions such as the police and the military. Mass production demanded new communicative links. Instrumental rationality, technicality, and mass consumption had to be communicated to the workers of the mass-production age. The system demand of mass consumption supported the rise of the corporate mass media domain that mediated the consumer realities of life. At this stage, managerial promises of material affluence not only domesticated workers, they also linked the reproductive consumption domain closer than ever before to the work domain. This communicative link further gained importance when bureaucratic rules increasingly governed the rising service industry and society in general. As work regimes became deregulated and individualised, managerialism linked *inter*-personal communication with *intra*-personal psychological techniques directed towards persuasion. Modern managerial techniques relied, similar to the techniques used in advertising, more and more on sophisticated psychological methods to adapt workers to the work regime.

As the commodification and the restructuring of the communicative domain reached satisfactory levels, managerialism was able to shift control needs towards the communicative domain. This is supported through the restructuring of the reproductive domain into an auxiliary domain to managerialism. Today, it is the communicative domain that supplies ideological values in support of the work regime. But managerialism is also able to increasingly rely on educational conditioning. Previously, this was experienced in traditional institutions such as schools and training colleges. With system demands for better-educated human resources, more recent adjustments to institutions of primary socialisation had to be made. In recent years the privatisation of schools, training colleges, and universities has reached satisfactory levels so that individuals who went through these institutions are sufficiently conditioned in the ways of managerialism. The inclusion of universities has been necessary as they increasingly provide an educated workforce demanded by modern production systems.

As mass production is increasingly relocated to developing countries, the remaining tasks of the post-industrial service and knowledge economy in the developed world have been reduced to two issues. One task is the maintenance of the remaining research and development facilities in the developed world, the second the maintenance of the service industry. The so-called service industry is primarily a distribution industry as it does not produce commodities but is occupied with their distribution. This relates predominantly to finance and marketing, the two most important departments of any business school and MBA programme. At the same time the other two core departments – people management (HRM) and operations management – have been reduced to minor status. Adjacent to these are located those sections of the workforce that do not need to receive tertiary-level education. Therefore, system demands originating in managerialism commanded that the educational part of primary socialisation was restructured so that access to it was guaranteed. Educational demands are a showcase for system contradictions directed towards the need for an educated workforce to ensure the survival of the system on the one hand and the unwillingness of individual firms to train their workforce on the other. Despite HRM's illusion of in-house training and development, most companies are deficient in workplace training. In-house or workplace training is seen as a cost. Under the profit maxim these costs have to be eliminated or at least reduced as much as possible. This is the first contradiction that plagues work-related training schemes. The second contradiction is the problem of retaining costly trained workers in the company. Once money has been *invested* into human resources, management has an interest in retaining *their* investment. Better-trained workers however often realise not only the *use-value* of their training but also its *exchange-value*. Gaining consciousness of this *exchange-value* often means changing jobs for employees and with it a loss of investment for management. These two core contradictions influence training at work.

Traditionally, off-loading functional education to the state where it was paid through the tax system had solved the contradiction between system interests versus company interests. With the rise of neo-liberalism, managerialism was able to go one step further. Increasingly the educational demands of the system were relocated to the private domain, turning primary socialisation into a commercial good that can be purchased. Under the old system both company and income tax paid for education. Under the new system capital has been relieved from its contribution, as functional education is now the responsibility of the individual consumer. Today, individuals finance their own occupational training and conditioning which has no *use*-value to the individual but an *exchange*-value insofar as it can be exchanged at the labour market for higher wages.[539] In short, the structure of the institutions for occupational conditioning institutions reflects the needs of the current system. As the complexity of capitalism increased, educational institutions such as universities and colleges that provide a sufficiently trained workforce have been incorporated into the managerial system. However the system does not only need academically but also technically educated workers. Academically conditioned positions with high status are required to conduct managerial work, while the low supportive group experiences practical and lower status conditioning necessary to conduct manual or routine-task work.[540] Supported by sufficient conditioning of both groups, secondary socialisation occurs today with almost no adjustment problems and no resistance to the modern work regime.

In today's work regimes, managerialism has achieved the previously unthinkable – the almost total system integration of labour. This has been done through an ideological apparatus that communicates the managerially constructed world of work as a system imperative to labour. System integration has further been achieved through institutions that structure the mind of individuals and condition them into accepting these imperatives as given and natural. Labour has been conditioned to accept the private ownership of the means of production, the prevailing structures of managerial capitalism and its pathologies[541] as well as the formal rules that govern the present system. It accepts its position and functioning in socially constructed and managerially controlled workgroups. Eventually, the establishment of labour's affirmative character leads to the acceptance of today's workplace that is assumed to be a given. Once inside the workplace and adjusted to the work regime, the individual is transformed from being a *natural* person into a *corporate* person.

Advanced capitalism and managerialism have been able to create primary socialisation institutions that support their agenda. They also managed to restructure the communicative domain to support their needs and they successfully set up work regimes that embed labour into their framework. But these communicative achievements have not been made without challenges. Despite asymmetrical communication between management and labour at work, workers have always been able to resist part of the communicative colonisation of their domain. The first and perhaps most fundamental communicative difference between management and labour is their communicative interest. While management and managerialism's interest is directed towards instrumental rationality and instrumental communication, workers' interest is directed towards critical rationality. This is shown in Table 13.1:

Table 13.1 Domain Specific World Views, Interests and Communication

Domain		World Views		Interest		Communication
Management	→	commodification of world	→	commercial	→	instrumental rationality
Labour	→	understanding the world	→	understanding and truth	→	communicative rationality

As Table 13.1 shows, the worldviews of management and labour are highly opposed to each other. While in the labour domain the view is directed towards understanding the socially constructed environment in which we live, management's view is directed towards an interest in the commodification of the world. While one view is based on a genuine interest in critical understanding and truth, the others' main focus is directed towards the utilisation of the world as a selling instrument for commercial profit. This leads, finally, to two divergent communicative interests. In the management domain, the communicative interest is directed towards the strategic use of communication, i.e. instrumental communication. In the labour domain, the interest in truth and understanding demands a different form of communication which is that of communicative rationality because truth and understanding cannot be established with the means of instrumental communication.

In sharp contrast to management, labour's communicative interest is directed towards establishing truthful content about the world. During the process of establishing common understanding among labour, the need to communicate does however not only deliver challenges to labour but also provides opportunities. In order to utilise these communicative abilities, labour needs to shield their communicative domain against all colonising attempts of management. In other words, labour needs to establish discourse forums that are structurally separated from management. It cannot rely on the communicative domain as this domain has been de-democratised and transformed into corporate mass media that guide the administrative and bureaucratic steering needs routinely reaffirmed through the mass ritual of representative democracy. While the communicative domain has been sufficiently colonised and restructured, the reproductive domain has been almost completely converted into a consumer domain which means that labour's options to establish a communicative domain are restricted to the world of work or to discourse forums that are linked to the world of work.

This is not to be seen in a revitalisation of previously established organisational forms of labour as these have been structurally impaired by the colonisation of managerial instrumental rationality and instrumental communication. Labour needs to create totally new forms of a communicative domain. This new domain cannot be based on instrumental communication. It must be based on communicative rationality. Inside this domain, open and domination free communication can lead to forms of communicative understanding, communicatively established consensus, deliberative democracy, and finally social action directed towards positive social change.

Notes

1   For example, Human Resource Management or HRM is – despite the illusionary claim of many textbooks that it is practical rather than theoretical – a highly theoretical concept. It is impossible to buy five pounds of HRM. HRM has no practical use-value; it provides a legitimising support function inside the equally conceptual idea of managerialism. In short, it is an artificially invented concept that only exists as long as enough people believe in it. When HRM replaced the old concept of personnel management, conceptual elements were added. Consequently, HRM is no more than conceptually advanced personnel management.

2   In his article on *From 1984 to One-Dimensional Man: Critical Reflections on Orwell and Marcuse*, Douglas Kellner (1984), assesses that Orwell's *vision of revolution, power, bureaucracy is quite similar to major conservative ideologies (Nietzsche, Pareto, Michels, etc.), Huxley's Brave New World provides deeper insights into the actual social process of post-1950s capitalist societies*, and that Orwell relies too much on the coercive character of dictatorships while today's consumer capitalism achieves affirmation with more subtleties. Furthermore, one might equally argue that in Orwell's '*1984*' society is controlled by state and bureaucracy while today the corporate mass media has taken on this function. Finally, in '*1984*', there is one TV channel while today we have hundreds, many of which broadcasting more or less the same system stabilising messages. In Kellner's words, *structurally, they [the corporate mass media] privatise, serialise, and depoliticise individuals by keeping them safely within the confines of their own homes rather than in public or social activity. That is, the very act of watching television privatises individuals, and often subliminally imposes images, role models, and values which shape individual thought and behaviour.* They are designed to *distract the individual from social and political issues and problems.*

3   From this point of view, an assessment on the importance of books that do not submit *everything to critique* can already be made. If one accepts Kant's words on *under modernity everything has to submit to critique*, then books that do not submit *communication, management and work* to critique do not seem to be too important for our understanding and for the advancement of modernity. Important, according to Kant, is critique or as Orwell would have put it, to understand the WHYs and not so much the HOWs.

4   Only most recently, in August 2006 the *International Astronomical Union* has decided that the planet *Pluto* is no longer regarded a planet. This has been a clear example on how scientific facts are established. They are established by common agreement among a scientific community and not so much based on *objective* facts. It has been more about the interpretation of facts and a show of hands during a meeting. This may be a hard pill to swallow for the believers in value-free and objective science.

5   Taken in capital characters from Orwell's original wording on the first page (1949:3).

6   On *how* and *why*, Orwell (1949:226) noted, *he had still, he reflected, not learned the ultimate secret. He understood how; he did not understand why.* In other words, the world can never be understood by endlessly – as many management texts

do – describing purely the *how*, the ultimate secret lies in understanding why and that is precisely the reason why standard managerial textbooks remain inside the domain of *how*, to prevent an understanding of the ultimate secret.

7 Two of management's core concepts are *effectiveness* as having a definite or desired effect and *efficiency*: the ratio of useful work performed to the total energy expended.

8 A book is not text that just *speaks to a reader*. Meaning does not come *from* a book. Meaning is created as we *engage* with a text. A book becomes alive during an engagement resulting in meaning construction. A text does not flow from one mind into another. Rather it is a dialogical process. *Your reading of this is not an instance of transmission, but an example of conversation* (Radford 2005:173).

9 Searle (1969, 1979, 1996, 2002) rejects the idea of interpretations in everyday communication as people seek to understand one another and do not conduct conscious and structured operations such as interpretations; Searle does not prefer the language use of interpretations in this context.

10 We can test this mechanism by simply going to the movies. Often, when people see a movie and have read the book of the story beforehand, they tend to say, *oh, the book was better than the movie*. What occurs here is exactly this mechanism. As we read a novel, we create quite individually – as Kant (1781) said a *necessarily* – subjective interpretation of a particular text. When we see a movie, we receive someone else's interpretation, usually the movie director's. As someone else's interpretation can never be as good as our own subjective image, we tend to view books as being better than subsequent movies.

11 Further examples see: Clampitt (2001) as well as Hartley & Bruckmann (2002).

12 We are conditioned to focus on *how* to achieve success while the secret of *why* we do it is hidden very much in the way Orwell (1949) has described. *Just do it!* as Nike tells us and don't ask *why*.

13 The meaning of life may not be fixable with an easy *how* but the secret of life might be found in why, as Orwell told us.

14 George Orwell writes in his 1984 (1949:83), *at one time it has been a sign of madness to believe that the earth goes round the sun, today, to believe that the past is unalterable*. While we acknowledge the former, we are weaker on the latter as we have created entire industries that alter the past. Today, there are virtually no movies on work, work experience, sweatshops, exploitation, alienation, etc. There are not many movies showing the pathologies of our present system of production either. Nor are there any movies about the ruthless path of capitalism establishing itself as the dominant system in a post-feudal world. Even great authors like Victor Hugo are dissolved into thin air. See also Chomsky's chapter on *Perspectives on Language and Mind* (2002a).

15 The encroachment of managerialism into almost every aspect of everyday life is made visible in the sheer endless number of book titles that tell us how to manage any part of human life. Today we do not enjoy a marriage, we manage our spouses; we do not educate our children, we manage them; we cannot simply have a sex life, we need to manage it; we can't find fulfilment and gratification in relationships, we are asked to manage our friends. By managing, we destroy living through the alienating idea of managing.

16 Thinking critically outside of KISS means engaging in something that Orwell (1949:220) has called *Crimestop* in his novel *1984*. *Crimestop means the faculty of stopping short, as though by instinct, at the threshold of any dangerous thought. It includes the power of not grasping analogies, of failing to perceive logical errors, of mis-*

understanding the simplest arguments if they are inimical [to the mainstream] and of being bored or repelled by any train of thought which is capable of leading in a heretical direction. Crimestop, in short, means protective stupidity. But stupidity is not enough.

17 Many of these texts pretend to be disconnected from a process that constructs reality. They live with an unconscious assumption of ordinary language. They take social facts at face value. A critical understanding is substituted with a prevailing and universal understanding of administered communication supportive of managerialism. This, of course, occurs not as their own doing and their own saying. It just happens to them as they are compelled by circumstances. They *identify their mind with the mental processes, their self with roles and functions which they have to perform in their society. If philosophy does not comprehend these processes of translation and identification as societal processes – i.e., as a mutilation of the mind (and the body) inflicted upon the individuals by their society – philosophy struggles only with the ghost of the substance which it wishes to de-mystify* (Marcuse 1966:208).

18 *Interdisciplinary* research and border-crossing are dangerous acts because the whole academic enterprise is set up to operate safely inside self-constructed boxes that reflect the division of labour prevalent in present society. One of the dangers of interdisciplinary thinking and publishing is that it falls between those boxes, often resulting in unpublished work. If unpublished research is research not done then the need to publish academically demands all too often to adhere to prescribed boxes. This means articles on *communication* are published in journals on *communication*, articles on *work* are published in journals on *work*; articles on *management* in *management* journals and so forth. Publishing outside the expected, respected, and respective boxes is one of the finest and maybe even hardest challenges for anyone who seeks to think and publish outside the borders of their prescribed box. These borders represent a division of labour, they enhance academic isolation, and prevent critical thinking. Even if these borders are crossed in what is called interdisciplinary research, this research and the resulting publications still maintain the borders. Interdisciplinary research crosses borders but does not dissolve them. It fosters techniques that cross borders but are not directed to overcome them. Only a *supra-disciplinary* approach can end these borders (Kellner 2006:1).

19 According to Marcuse (1966:128), *the achievements of advanced industrial civilisation lead to the triumph of the one-dimensional reality over all contradictions.* As there are many areas of the human condition that display one-dimensionality, managerialism is certainly one of them as almost all thinking is submitted to this ideology and contradictory or even critical thinking is shelved into boxes labelled as CMS (Parker 2002:115–133).

20 Mendieta (2002:150) and Quotations from philosopher *Berlin*:
http://berlin.wolf.ox.ac.uk/lists/quotations/quotations_from_ib.html

21 The German philosopher Gadamer (1976:14), came to the conclusion that the term *standard* carries connotations of *coming to a stand* (zum stehen kommen) as it cements a status quo hindering the development of any thinking, above all critical thinking.

22 Traditionally, people at work are not called people. They are labelled as staff, workers, employees, colleagues, shop-floor workers, or increasingly *production associates* (assembly line), *crew members* (at McDonald's), *associates* (CableTel), *cast members* (Disney World), *partners*, etc. The following text will rely on the traditional terminology of *labour* to indicate people at work in non-managerial functions.

23   The non-democratic tradition of management that feeds from militaristic vertical structures rather than from democratically and human-communicatively
horizontal relationships has been summed up by early management writer
McGregor (1960:31) *there is nothing inherently wrong or bad about giving an order
or making a unilateral decision.*

24   Standard textbooks on organisational communication such as Blundel
(2004:9) define it as a wide-ranging field that spreads across academic disciplines (e.g. psychology, anthropology, organisational studies) and professional
special-*isms* (e.g. marketing, public relations, and human resource management). Such books do not even mention: philosophy, history, political
science, sociology, political economy, industrial relations or labour process
theory.

25   Writers on the *Great Transformation* are Kant, Hegel, Marx, Weber, Polanyi,
Moore, etc. The human condition after *Great Transformation* has been described by French philosopher Deleuze (1995:181) as *one thing, it's true, hasn't
changed – capitalism still keeps three quarters of humanity in extreme poverty, too
poor to have debts and too numerous to be confined: control will have to deal not
only with vanishing frontiers, but with mushrooming shantytowns and ghettos.* Even
though this has largely been exported to the developing world, areas of
extreme poverty ranging from small pockets to large regions can increasingly
be found in the developed world.

26   Many present-day managerial writers on organisations and organisational
communication pretend there are just *organisations* without identifying them
as profit-making capitalist companies. Equally, they pretend that there are
vanishing borders between workers and management who work happily
together towards *organisational goals* (in reality: profits for one and work for
others). In reality, any step into almost any aircraft in almost any country
makes the symbolism of business class for one and economy class for the
other visible. Similarly, managerial status symbols extend not only to a pin-
striped suit for the one and the casual Polo-shirts for others but also to the
business class, the status company car, the secretary (nowadays called Personal
Assistant or just PA), etc, but also to status enshrining language use (Searle
1996). There is a managerial language and a workers language. There is the
power-point presentation for the one and the shop-floor language for others.

27   The *reductionist* view tends to condense communication in labour-management
relationship to *voice*. However, the communicative content in a labour-
management relationship goes far beyond the somewhat simplistic issue of
voice or a discussion of communication during a collective bargaining process
(Hirschman 1970; Putman 1995).

28   Furthermore, the subject is not participation, trade unions, works councils,
collective bargaining, etc.

29   See: Tompkins, Wanca-Thibault (2001); Bundel (2004); Wood (2004); Penrose,
Rasberry & Myers (2004); Grey & Willmott (2005); Alvesson & Deetz (2005);
Krizan, Merrier & Jones (2005); Merrier (2006).

30   The neglect or denial of a contradictory existence of labour vs. capital/
management at work is well-hidden behind the language of *organisational communication* when Putnam & Fairhurst (2004:83) note, *from a socio-linguistic perspective, language becomes a system or code in which organisational communities
define their identities and relationships.* When deconstructing their language use
of *organisational communities,* connotations of rural and unspoilt living communities surrounded by green hills can be found. This is the instrumental use

of language to gloss over a harsh reality of corporate profit-making (Mander 2001). Even in more critical organisational communication perspectives, profit-oriented companies inside the prevailing economic system are reduced to neutral-sounding *organisations*. Economic contradictions between *workers* (wages for cost of living = purchasing power) and *management* (wages = cost factor = reduced) have been discussed ever since Karl Marx. Secondly, managerial divisions of labour have been discussed ever since Taylor. Both have been reduced to the metaphor of *communities* such as the business community. It portrays an image of a *community* park where mothers and children play ball games, far removed from the suppressive pathologies of capitalist affairs.

31   For many traditional labour relations experts communication is a largely unknown field. A search at AASAP-Plus Databank conducted during May 2006 on the six most important journals (Industrial Relations, Canada; Industrial Relations, USA; Industrial Relations Journal, GB; the British Journal of Industrial Relations (GB), Industrial and Labor Relations Journal, USA; and the Journal of Industrial Relations (Australia) on *communication* found just 18 references to communication. Issues on *communication* ranged from *Spanish trade unions* to *Internet for Employee Organization* or *Using Computers for Communication in the UK Workplace*. Similarly, an investigation into books did not produce more promising results. Books on communication in the area of IR can be divided into three groups: a) books that do not mention communication, b) books that mention communication as a minor issue, and c) books that discuss communication comprehensively in a chapter or as part of a book.

32   Theory language is abstract language. According to Marcuse (1966:138), *nobody really thinks who does not abstract from that which is given, who does not relate the facts to the factors which have made them, who does not – in his mind – undo the facts. Abstractness is the very life of thought, the token of its authenticity.* Observable science is often linked to a technical-scientific project that *tends to identify things and their function. As a habit of thought outside the scientific and technical language, such reasoning shapes the expression of a specific social and political behaviourism. In this behavioural universe, words and concepts tend to coincide or rather the concept tends to be absorbed. The former has no other content that is designated by the word in published and standardised usage, and the word is expected to have no other response than the publicised and standardised behaviour (reaction). The word becomes a cliché and, as a cliché, governs the speech or the writing; the communication thus precludes genuine development of meaning* (Marcuse 1966:90).

33   See: Francois Rabelais' *Gargantua and Pantagruel* (1532), www.gutenberg.org/files/1200/1200.txt. The Catholic Church banned his writings and later placed on: *The Index librorum prohibitorum* (the index of forbidden books).

34   Hegel (1770–1831) developed the first philosophical system that has historical change at its core. He argued that all of history is the progress of mind and spirit along a logically necessary path that leads to freedom. Kuhn has applied Hegel's historical progress to science. Kuhn's *The Structure of the Scientific Revolution* suggests scientific processes as no more than an endless replacing of paradigms inside institutional elitism that seeks to maintain the status quo constructing Kuhn's paradigm as a system integrative process (Fuller 2003).

35   The metaphor *standing on the shoulder of giants to see further* is often somewhat incorrectly associated with Isaac Newton but in fact goes back further. Originally coined by Bernard of Chartres in 1159, the term has been used ever since. Isaac Newton used it in a letter to Robert Hooke on 5th February

1676, *if I have seen a little further it is by standing on the shoulders of Giants* (http://en.wikipedia.org/wiki/Standing_on_the_shoulders_of_giants).

36   In Osborne's *Civilisation – a New History of the Western World* (2005), the values of the *Enlightenment* are defined as individual conscience, rational scepticism, and intellectual curiosity as a long tradition that has invoked civilisation as some unchallenged virtues enshrined in art, science, architecture, literature and philosophy.

37   Greek philosopher Plato (428–348 BC) once remarked that the highest pleasure, in fact, comes from intellectual speculation. Plato is regarded as the founder of Western Philosophy. What followed after Plato are mere footnotes to him.

38   Chomsky (1968:4) has summarised this, *the most meaningful contribution that an individual can make toward a more decent society is to base his life's work on an authentic commitment to improve values, such as those that underlie serious scholarship or scientific work, in any field.*

39   According to Marcuse (1966:200), *the desideratum is rather to make the estab-lished language itself speak what it conceals or excludes, for what is to be revealed and denounced is operative within the universe of ordinary discourse and action.*

40   Commonly, organisational communication on effectiveness covers three areas: a) the way in which communication processes have been conceptualised in formal organisations as mechanical communication or as a process of information gathering, b) the kinds of communicative interactions such as information flow or the use of manipulation, and c) the relationship between research theory and the symbolic interaction that they examine. In addition, if one defines *organisational communication* as *the process of creating collective, coordinated struc-tures of meaning through symbolic practices oriented towards the achievement of organisational goals* (Mumby 2001:587), then the term organisational communi-cation can no longer be used for a comprehensive understanding of com-munication at work as such an understanding cannot be directed towards *organisational goals.* Any understanding of communication at work demands to be freed up from the demands of any teleological and instrumental pre-direction that narrows and distorts such an inquiry.

41   In 1755, *Jean-Jacques Rousseau* formulated this in his *Discourse on the Origins of Inequality* as *I should have wished to live and die free.* 211 years after Rousseau, Marcuse (1966:132) applied his dictum to today's working society, noting *in the human reality, all existence that spends itself in procuring the prerequisites of existence is thus an 'untrue' and unfree existence.*

42   As Thompson (1990:25) observed *it may enable them to question or revise their prior understanding of a symbolic form [of communication], and thereby to alter the horizons of their understanding of themselves and others. I describe this process, the possibility of which is implicit in the interpretation of ideology, as the interpretative transformation of doxa – that is, the interpretative transformation of the everyday understanding, attitudes and beliefs of the individual who make up the social world.*

43   Such an illustration provides neither *descriptions* nor *prescriptions* but is directed towards truth. We do exactly that when explaining *prescriptive* ideas – laying down rules by custom as an imposition of authority – as *descriptive* ideas – seeking to describe or classify without comparing, endorsing, judging, or condemning. Both can no longer be used as an inquiry into communica-tion at work. It is not possible for this to be discussed under any imposing authority nor can it be presented as an illusionary tale of a value-judgment free approach.

44 As misunderstandings are contextual-based because meanings change as symbols move from one context (domain a) to another context (domain b). Hence specific IR/HR terms can change meaning as they move from a labour domain (a) through a communicative domain (c) into a management domain (b).

45 The term *law* is seen as a universal law of human behaviour. Ever since French philosopher *Comte* social science has had a strong tendency to *construct social reality* (Searle 1996) in terms of the physical world leading to attempts to search for social laws as physical laws govern the natural world. In this tradition, a law is an inviolate, unalterable fact that holds true across time and space. In the world of socially constructed reality no such thing can exist (Berger & Luckmann 1967).

46 According to Marcuse (1966:198), *if philosophy is more than an occupation, it shows the grounds which made discourse a mutilated and deceptive universe. To leave this task to a colleague in the Sociology or Psychology Department is to make the established division of academic labour into a methodological principle.*

47 Searle (2002:20) noted, *beginning in the seventeenth century, the area of systematic knowledge, this is, scientific knowledge, increased with the growth of systematic methods for acquiring knowledge. Unfortunately, most of the questions that most bother us have not yet been amenable to the methods of scientific investigation.*

48 Quoted in Blundel (2004:1)

49 In his novel *1984*, George Orwell (1949:226) identified one of the core principles that reduced and manipulated thinking in the Orwellian world as: *he understood how; he never understood why.* Keeping people's thoughts locked inside the *how* without ever telling them or even preventing them to simply ask *why* is a core element of corrupting *Enlightenment*.

50 While modern *Newspeak* uses the term *human resources* as in *Human Resource Management*, the following text will not adopt the term *human resources* every time *workers* are meant. It will continue to use the *Oldspeak* term *worker* as a rejection of an idea that reduces people to *resources. Human resources* also gives the appearance of being connected to nature – human nature – while in reality reducing *humans* to managerial *resources means* converting them into *objects of power* (Bauman 1989).

51 Albert (2006:1) has argued that *capitalism is also defined by corporate divisions of labour and authoritative decision-making. About 20 per cent of the employees of capitalist workplaces do mostly conceptual and empowering tasks, while the other 80 per cent do mostly rote and obedient tasks. The 20 per cent make many decisions and affect social choices. The 80 per cent make few decisions and mainly obey orders.*

52 Many have argued that the process of modern mass communication has started with *Johann Gutenberg, who invented a method for the replica-casting of metal letters and who adapted the traditional screw press to the purpose of manufacturing printed texts* (Thompson 1990:14). Adorno (1944:16) noted, *the invention of the printing press stood at the beginning of the bourgeois era.*

53 According to Marcuse (1966:193), *today rational and realistic notions of yesterday again appear to be mythological when confronted with the actual conditions. The reality of the labouring classes in advanced industrial society makes the Marxian 'proletariat' a mythological concept.* See also: Jones' 1983). *Languages of class: studies in English working-class history, 1832–1982.*

54 Hegel always saw the term *Zeitgeist* as thinking that is trapped into a certain *Zeit* or time. It is thinking that lacks historical understanding. It lacks the ability to position ideas into an historical context. It is unable to see that ideas

are connected to the historical development of society. This turns one into a prisoner of the *spirit* of time (Zeitgeist).

55   One of the harshest pathologies of our present society is *30,000 people die from poverty-related issues each day* that society could prevent but society carries on as usual (Brown & Kelly 2006).

56   Unlike a theory, the term *model* in this context is used as a more workable framework that reproduces and reduces the complexities of modern society and working life into more simpler, accessible, comprehensive, and understandable terms.

57   Like the *productive* domain, the *reproductive* domain can be understood as a realm in which system demands are issued that are directed towards consensus. To ensure an ongoing support for productive relations, social relations in the reproductive domain depend to large parts on a consensual belief and value system that is widely accepted and shared and binds workers to an established order. Core values that are shared are freedom, liberty, democracy, equality, equal opportunity, human rights, etc. In contrast to core values and beliefs that are commonly shared, there are also different values existent in different groups. For example, middle-class values differ from working-class values and upper-class values also differ as well. Equality and fairness score higher among member of working-class background while individual property rights score higher among members of the upper class.

58   For an historical overview of Critical Theory see: Jay 1974.

59   According to Marcuse (1966:130), a philosopher *subjects experience to his critical judgment, and this contains a value judgment – namely, that freedom from tail is preferable to tail, and an intelligent life is preferable to a stupid life. It so happened that philosophy was born with these values.*

60   Among many philosophical concepts, Kant developed a dualism of *thing-in-itself* and *appearance*. The ability to understand and think in both categories is a distinctive human's ability to think freely. *Kant described man's inclination and duty to think freely as the germ on which nature has lavished most care* (Chomsky 1976:128). On Kant's successor, Hegel, Gadamer (1976:76, 110) once commended that language is the medium through which the subjective mind mediates the external world of objects. *Language is the medium through which consciousness is connected with beings* and *Hegel's philosophy represents the last mighty attempt to grasp science and philosophy as a unity*. Decades after Kant and Hegel, Lukács' (1885–1971) sought to turn Marxian economic science into social-philosophical theory by posing the question of the consequences of the universality of commodity exchange (cf. Albert 2006:134ff.).

61   There is virtually no textbook on western or modern philosophy that does not start with Kant or has Kant as a core figure. It appears as if Kant is, more than many other philosophers, the utmost authority on modern philosophy.

62   *It seems that the persistence of untranslatable universals as nodal points of thoughts reflects the unhappy consciousness of a divided world in which 'that which is' falls short of, and even denies, 'that which can be'* (Marcuse 1966:214).

63   As the editor of Gadamer's work on *Philosophical Hermeneutics* (1976), David E. Linge (1976:xxviii) pointed out, *...there is no world in itself beyond its presents as the subject matter of a particular language community.*

64   In Kant's work on *Der ewige Friede* or Perpetual Peace the idea of *selbstverschuldete Unmündigkeit* or voluntary servitude is further developed.

65   Hegel's project has been to understand the history of philosophy and the world itself as a progression in which each successive movement emerges as a solu-

tion to the contradictions inherent in the preceding movement. For example, the French Revolution for Hegel constitutes the introduction of real freedom into Western societies for the first time in recorded history. Hegel developed a radically new form of *logic*. He called his way of solving contradictions *speculative*. Today this is known as dialectics. According to Marcuse (1966:130), *philosophical [thinking] originates in dialectics; its universe of discourse responds to the facts of an antagonistic reality*. Not surprisingly Hegel was very much concerned with what decades later Chomsky (1968:5–6) described as *the most important role of the intellectual since the enlightenment has been the unmasking of ideology* (Cf. Chomsky 1967c; Adorno 1944:3).

66   Hegel's Phenomenology argued for the historical evolution of reason, from lower to higher stages, which would absorb and compete the limited and alienated products of earlier forms of culture and education.

67   According to Kant's *Critique of Pure Reason* (1781), knowledge can be distinguished as *a priori* and *posteriori*. In contrast to a priori knowledge, posteriori knowledge is based on empirical evidence while the source of a priori knowledge is a form of universal rule. This can be expressed as: a man who undermines the foundation of his house might have known *a priori* that it would fall and he did not need to wait for the experience of its actual falling (*posteriori*). This idea of *a priori* and *posteriori* can be, like many others, linked to dialectics. Commonly, this way of thinking links a proposition (*thesis*) to a counter-proposition (*anti-thesis*) leading to a *sythesis*. It is designed to solve problems of contradictory nature (*immediate-mediate-concrete* or *abstract-negative-concrete*). One of the core thinkers on dialectic, Hegel, has applied this to the contradictions of capitalism with labour as *thesis* and capital as *anti-thesis*. The outcome (*sythesis*) of this contradiction shapes our present society (cf. Adorno 1944:2).

68   On the objectivity problem, Searle 2002:11) wrote, *since science aims at objectivity in the epistemic sense that we seek truths that are not dependent on the particular point of view of this or that investigator, it has been tempting to conclude that the reality investigated by science must be objective in the sense of existing independently of the experience in the human individual. But this last feature, ontological objectivity, is not an essential trait of science.*

69   Gadamer (1976:59) sees ...*man as the animal rationale, the rational being, distinguished from all other animals by his capacity for thought. Thus it rendered the Greek word logos as reason or thought.* Habermas agrees with Marxian theory's work-as-central-category theory but emphasises that work has not only an *instrumental* component but also a *communicative* component as human work has always been conducted not at an individual level, but communal. Hence, humankind has been defined as *zoon echon logon*, as talking animal.

70   Searle (1996:70) has described one of the crucial differences between *animals* and *human* society in the following way: *animals running in a pack can have all the consciousness and collective intentionality they need. They can even have hierarchies and a dominant male; they can cooperate in the hunt, share their food, and even have pair bonding. But they cannot have marriages, property, or money. Why not? Because all these create institutional forms of powers, rights, obligations, duties, etc., and it is characteristic of such phenomena that they create reasons for action that are independent of what you or I or anyone else is otherwise inclined to do. Suppose I train my dog to chase dollar bills and bring them back to me in return for food. He still is not buying the food and the bills are not money to him. Why not? Because he cannot represent to himself the relevant deontic phenomena. He might be*

able to think, 'if I give him this he will give me that food.' But he cannot think, for example, now I have the right to buy things and when someone else has this, he will also have the right to buy things. Anthropology texts routinely remark on the human capacity for tool using. But the truly radical break with other forms of life comes when humans, through collective intentionality, impose functions on phenomena where the function cannot be achieved solely in virtue of physics and chemistry but requires continued human cooperation in the specific forms of recognition, acceptance, and acknowledgement of a new status to which a function is assigned (Searle 1996:40).

71   *Lukács characterised the working class as occupying an epistemologically privileged position simply by virtue of their alienation from, and commodification by, capital* (Mumby 1997:354).

72   *In our intellectual tradition since the Enlightenment the whole idea of power makes a certain type of liberal sensibility very nervous. A certain class of intellectuals would rather that power did not exist at all (or if it has to exist they would rather that their favourite oppressed minority had lots more of it and everyone else had lots less). One lesson to be derived from the study of institutional fasts is this: everything we value in civilisation requires the creation and maintenance of institutional power relations through collectively imposed status-functions. Institutional power – massive, pervasive, and typically invisible – permeates every nook and cranny of our social lives* (Searle 1996:94).

73   Unlike Kant's, Hegel's, and Marx' philosophy of the 18th and 19th century, *twentieth-century philosophy has been obsessed with language and meaning, and that is why it is perhaps inevitable that somebody would come up with the idea that nothing at all exists apart from language and meaning* (Searle 1996:167).

74   There are so many affixes and labels, even very minor ones, to indicate variations on Marx. These cannot possibly be listed. However, it has been made feasible to insert almost any label one seeks to use or abuse. In some cases this has been a blunt misuse of Marx's ideas, in others an improvement, an abuse, or in some cases it has been done purely to distinguish between a certain trend or fashion. The final insult to Marx came when he was turned into an absolute God-like figure that destroyed his theory and theory development by turning it into a belief system – something Marx would have utterly detested.

75   *Pacification presupposes mastery of nature, which is and remains the object opposed to the developing subject. But there are two kinds of mastery: a regressive and a liberating one. The latter involves the reduction of misery, violence, and cruelty* (Marcuse 1966:240). Marcuse (1996:52) saw three rationalities governing the welfare state's un-freedom *because its total administration is systematic restriction of (a) technically available free time (b) the quantity and quality of goods and services technically available for vital individual needs (c) the intelligence (conscious and unconscious) capable of comprehending and realising the possibilities of self-determination.*

76   According to Marcuse (1966:195) *society is indeed the whole which exercise its independent power of the individuals, and this society is no unidentifiable 'ghost'. It has its empirical hard core in the system of institutions, which are the established and frozen relationships among men.*

77   *Describing to each other our loves and hates, sentiments and resentments, we must use the terms of our advertisements, movies, politicians, and best sellers. We must use the same terms for describing our automobiles, foods and furniture, colleagues, and competitors – and we understand each other perfectly* (Marcuse 1966:198).

78   If one envisages ideology as *meaning in the service of power and domination* that mobilises instrumental communication supporting and sustaining asymmetrical power relations at work and society, then the rise of corporate mass communication had unimaginably strong repercussion for the productive and reproductive domain.

79   Hobsbawn (2004:11) has emphasised *I would like to look forward to a time when no one asks whether authors are Marxist or not. But, as I also observed, we are far from such a utopia.* Still, texts are judged or rather pre-judged along these lines. Marxian, such as *Lukáscian* thinking, assumed the proletariat is a historically privileged class predestined to realise truth. This can no longer be assumed. Critical theory has overcome a sense of certainty that once prompted such a revolutionary agent idea. All of this, however, does not end the class system as socio-economical classes continue to constitute the fundamental axis of the present social structure.

80   Class should be seen as a *relationship*, not a *thing*. It started with the hegemony of capital as the new and principle force of organising society via its organising power over production and secondly, an uprooted class was driven from the countryside community and became a property-less and land-less proletariat.

81   Marcuse (1968:220) emphasised for the 20th century, *the affluent society [exists] in the face of inhuman misery and methodical cruelty outside its borders, squander its unimaginable technical, material, and intellectual power and abuse its power.* For the 19th century, Lafargue (1883) wrote, *the economists go on repeating to the labourers work, to increase social wealth* while keeping quiet on the distribution side of the equation. See also Mills (1951), Galbraith (1958), Goldthorpe, et al. (1969), Bell (1973), Gorz (1982:45), Marcuse (1966), Hamilton (2003), Hamilton & Denniss (2005). Above all, Marcuse (1969:8) summed up, *the obscene exposure of the affluent society normally proves neither shame nor a sense of guilt, although this society violates some of the most fundamental moral taboos of civilisation.*

82   Quoted from Baudrillard (1998:51). On democracy, Canfora writes in *Democracy in Europe – A History of an Ideology* (2006:5–10) that *demokratia* derived from *demokrator…these words clearly mean 'rule over the people' (or over the entire community). The belief that democracy is a Greek invention is rather deeply rooted a nonsensical formula and so schematic that, looked at in depth, it proves false.* Most crucially he states, *democracy was the term opponents of government 'by the people' used to describe such government, precisely with the aim of highlighting its violent character (kratos denotes exactly the violent exercise of power).*

83   A sentence such as *for relative large sections of the working class in most major industrialised countries…* should better read: *for relative large sections of human resources in most major industrialised countries…* to make the dangerous character of today's *Newspeak* in management and Human Resource Management visible.

84   After Marx, Lafargue (1883:13) was one of the first to detect the rise of consumption when *the capitalist class [became] relieved from its function of universal consumer* and Fordism led to the universal and standardised consumers consuming equally standardised products.

85   Quoted from Marcuse (1966:26): Baudrillard (1998:53) comments, *there is not in fact – and never has been – any affluent society…every society produces differentiation, social discrimination, and that structural organisation is based on the use and*

distribution of wealth (among other things)… growth neither takes us further from, nor brings us closer to, affluence. It is logically separated from it by the whole social structure… Commonly, the existence of social inequality in society is measured via the Gini-Index.

86 Quoted from Harding (2003:1): Definitions express the perspectives from which the creator of such definitions formulates them (Morgan 1986, 1993). Management has produced almost as many such definitions as there are different perspectives. There are, however, two reasonable definitions of what management actually is. After having examined many management textbooks Harding (2003:28) sees management as: *there is no more important area of human activity than management, since its task is that of getting things done through people. Corporal Klinger* of the US-television series MASH 4077 provided the second definition as: *management is when those who can't manage those who can.*

87 Most devastating for Horkheimer has been the failure of the German working class to stop fascism. In Horkheimer's 1934 article on *The Impotence of the German Working Class*, he shows the role of *integrated working-class elite* (Jay 1974) into capitalism and ultimately fascism. Apart from fascist developments of the 1st half of the 20th century, capitalist developments during the 2nd half of the 20th century showed new pathologies. The argument that social mobility increases with wealth appears to be a myth as *the rich have gotten much richer and the poor have gotten poorer – and the vaunted middle-class society seems to be disappearing altogether* (Nealon & Giroux 2003:182). This marks an end of the traditional Fordist compromise between labour and capital. Post-Fordism and neo-liberalism is opening up with an increasing gap between rich and poor.

88 Ideology is an unconscious tendency underlying technical, scientific, political, and managerial thought to make facts amenable to ideas and ideas to facts in order to create a managerial image convincing enough to support the collective and individual identity at workplaces. Ideology masks the fact that managerial images are credible even though they differ under different socio-economical conditions.

89 As George Orwell (1949:192) put it in his *1984* novel, *throughout recorded time, and probably since the end of the Neolithic Age, there have been three kinds of people in the world, the High, the Middle and the Low.*

90 Quoted from Nealon & Giroux (2003:180). The concept of *cultural capital* further enhances this view as is sees access to a certain way of speaking, a certain way of behaving, a certain cultural code, a certain taste, etc. as essential. Hence the designed and successfully mediated decline of *human culture* furthers inequality.

91 The sociological construction of society in *upper*, *middle* and *lower* class represents nothing more than a conscious or unconscious internalisation of societal hierarchies. The *upper* construct carries all the false connotations of superior, strength, being in command, elite, better instincts, higher values, etc. Above all, it locates a social class in a geographical or geometrical framework where it is safely positioned inside a neutral framework and away from a socio-economical framework that could highlight the true state of affairs (Bolinger 1980:142).

92 While this system replaces *the focus*, it does not delete wage labour. *The individual serves the industrial system not by supplying it with savings and the resulting capital; he serves it by consuming its products. The system needs people as workers*

(wage labour), as savers (taxes, loans, etc.), but increasingly it needs them as consumers (Baudrillard 1998:83). The triple character does not eliminate the wage-earning *workers* as many people sustain their lives by selling their labour on the labour market as they are not independently wealthy to sustain their lives through not working or non-participation in the labour market.

93 Apart from consumerism, politics provided another pacifying element as described in Orwell's *1984* (1949:74), *all that was required of them was a primitive patriotism which could be appealed to whatever was necessary to make them accept longer working-hours or shorter rations.*

94 This title is taken from a Mandell (2002) article. Like almost no other ideology, the ideology of privatisation has become a core panacea of today. It is the belief that privatisation is desirable as the market can do it all. It downplays *public* goods and even deletes them via a conversion into *private* goods. Now we have an Early Childhood Education *Industry*. Nurses in privatised health care assess our needs, firstly, in terms of monetary gains when entering a hospital and, secondly, into patient needs, etc. This conversion assigns enormous power to private corporations infiltrating almost every eventuality of human life. Resisting groups that fight privatisation are often – especially when compared to corporate media power – *poorly funded, not effectively linked together, frequently work across purposes, and have little leverage in mainstream institutions and the mass media. Lavishly funded pro-corporate think tanks, academics and public relations agencies, on the other hand, are significant propagators of the corporate ideology. Their influence is large and growing in the media system. Corporate interests also dominate electoral campaigns with their ability to fund candidates, thereby minimising the possibility of dissident voices entering the political debate* (Herman & McChesney 1997:37; cf. Chomsky 1967b).

95 *It is repressive precisely to the degree to which it promotes the satisfaction of needs which require continuing the rat race of catching up with one's peers and with planned obsolescence, enjoying freedom using the brain, working with and for the means of destruction* (Marcuse 1966:246). *Commodity fetishism is defined as social relations between men, that assume, in their eyes, the fantastic form of a relation between things...the famous replacement of men with things* (Zizek 1989:23).

96 *The proletarian of previous stages of capitalism was indeed the beast of burden, by the labour of his body procuring the necessities and luxuries of life while living in filth and poverty. Thus he was the living denial of his society. In contrast, the organised worker in the advanced areas of the technological society lives this denial less conspicuously, and like the other human objects of the social division of labour, he is being incorporated into the technological community of the administered population* (Marcuse 1966:28).

97 Quoted from Marcuse (1969:57). The *Lumpenproletariat* used to be a poorly dressed (Lumpen = rag) underclass of a highly stigmatised poor sub-class of workers exposed to poor houses, prisons, work camps, etc. Under welfare capitalism they are equally poor and often used as scapegoats for social ills (petty crimes, drugs, etc.) and largely kept in check via social programmes. They serve two purposes, firstly they are used to provide existing proof for a *'blame the victim'* ideology and secondly, they are used to remind the middle class of the dire consequences they face for non-compliance with the present system.

98 Criminalisation can be seen as a process of declaring even the tiniest property violation such as stealing bread from a supermarket into a punishable crime. It criminalises specific sections of society as such laws affect the poor discretionally

while at the same time so-called white-collar crime is largely seen as a mishap among gentlemen.

99   As Foucault (1995) has successfully shown in *Discipline and Punish: The Birth of the Prison*, prisons serve less as a punishing institution or as an instrument that solves crime. As the roughly 400 years of imprisonment shows, crime is still with us. If the idea of locking your door to prevent the Black Death and after 400 years of locking doors, the Black Death would still be with us, some might start questioning if locking doors is a good method in preventing the Black Death. Not so for prisons. As Orwell wrote (1949:83), *I understand HOW; I do not understand WHY…until they become conscious they will never rebel.* Hence, most have accepted that prisons are needed. They are, however, not needed for criminals, as Foucault has shown, they are need for those who are outside.

100   As large parts of the proletariat are converted into the middle class, some elements of the proletariat are carried over into the world of the middle class. Orwell (1949:219) has described them as *from the proletarians nothing is to be feared. Left to themselves they will continue from generation to generation and from century to century, working, breeding, and dying, not only without any impulse to rebel, but without any power of grasping that the world could be other than it is.*

101   Deleuze (1995:181) once noted, *markets are won by taking control rather than by establishing a discipline, by fixing rates rather than reducing costs, by transforming products rather than by specialising production. Marketing is now the instrument of social control and produces the arrogant breed who are our masters* (cf. Chomsky 1997).

102   See: Marcuse (1964a, 1964b, 1966), Offe and Wiesenthal (1980) and Offe (1985). Marcuse, once a supporter of the reigning party of Weimar Germany (the conservatively Marxist SPD, the Social Democrats, led by Friedrich Ebert), *severed his political ties to the SPD in 1919 when the SPD was implicated in the murders of the revolutionaries Rosa Luxemburg and Karl Liebknecht. Ebert struck a Faustian bargaining with General Wilhelm Groener, second-in-command of the German army. Groener would allow the SPD to rule if Ebert allowed the army to crush the massive, armed street demonstrations led by the revolutionary Sparticists, Luxemburg and Liebknecht. The army thus secured, betrayed the SPD to the Nazis* (Reitz 2000:17).

103   In an interview on his life and work, Lukács (1971:53–54), said on Max Weber: *You must understand that Weber was an absolute honest person. He had a great contempt for the Emperor, for example. He used to say to us in private that the great German misfortune was that, unlike the Stuarts or the Bourbons, no Hohenzollern had ever been decapitated…you must remember that Weber was a deeply convinced imperialist.*

104   *In a work, man is not only quantitatively exploited as a productive force by the system of capitalist economy, but is also metaphysically over-determined as a producer by the code of political economy* (Baudrillard 1975:31).

105   A dialectical view of the structure-agency relationship means that there is a constructive tension between them expressed in the term *dialectics*. Inside this, *structuration* rejects functionalism that generates clusters as key constructs to deal with structure-agency (Conrad & Haynes 2001:57). *Action* structuration focuses on how structure influences action while de-emphasising the process through which action influences structure. This occurs inside the structure-agency dialectic. Finally, *integrated* structuration is directed towards action research but does not fail in its critique on social action-*ism*. It always focuses on a dialectics between action and structure.

106   There are two basic models of such an asymmetrical power relationship: a) the power to impose *authority* on workers and b) the power to impose *requirements* on workers.

107   Agger (1979:206) suggests *workers' control of investment decisions and day-to-day logistics of production must be transformed into a process in which machines do not dominate people but people dominate machines.*

108   In the words of Orwell (1949:213), *every new political theory, by whatever name it called itself, led back to hierarchy and regimentation.* As much as hierarchy and regimentation are core necessities of capitalism, the historic task of democracy has been its support during the rise of capitalism via law and order. Democratic liberalism's task was to keep revolutionary forces in check while on the other hand opening up the illusionary option of Überbau-participation well removed from the basics of the capitalist order.

109   For the research on German workers, the Frankfurt School asked 3,300 respondents to answer a 271-item questionnaire (Bonß 1984). The Frankfurt School member Walter Benjamin noted *nothing was more corrupting for the German workers' movement than the feeling of swimming with the current* (Baudrillard 1975:36).

110   Gadamer (1976:16) has expressed the industry – language link as follows: *the relation of our modern industrial world, founded by science, is mirrored above all on the level of language. We live in an epoch in which an increasing levelling of all life-forms is taking place.* In Nazi-Germany, this levelling of language was turned into state-sponsored propaganda. Altheide and Johnson (1980:23) emphasise *the success of the Nazi programme unwittingly established the connection between propaganda, politics, and the mass media. What has been overlooked is the essential aspect of propaganda – the practical use of information, the strategic use of information or the instrumental use of information and knowledge* (cf. Bauman 1989; Albert 2006:138ff.). While Germans were exposed to propaganda, German industrialists were given clear directions on where the Nazis were going. On 20th February 1933 Hitler met German industrialists. *Hitler laid down the line to a couple of dozen of Germany's leading magnates, including Krupp von Bohlen, who had become an enthusiastic Nazi overnight, Bosch and Schnitzler of IG Farben, and Voegler, head of United Steel Works…He promised the businessmen that he would eliminate the Marxists and restore the Wehrmacht (the latter was of special interest to such industries as Krupp, United Steel, and IG Farben, which stood to gain from the rearmament)* (Shirer 1950:265). On Hitler, Adorno (1944: 41) noted, *Hitler…was the executioner of liberal capitalist society. He, who saw through the untruth of liberalism like no other bourgeois…*

111   Quoted from a good overview of Voltaire: http://en.wikipedia.org/wiki/Voltaire, see also his predecessor René Descartes' (1595–1650) *'I think, therefore I am'* or in Latin *cogito ergo sum.*

112   Power is seen as a discursive phenomenon located in the context of material interest representing different social formations. Essentially, power is the affirmation of difference. According to Dahl (1957), power has four properties attached to it: (a) *base* as the base of power expressed in resources, opportunities, acts, objects, etc. that can be exploited in order to effect the behaviour of others; (b) *means* or instruments such as threats or promises; (c) *amount* of an actor's power expressed in probability statements such as '9 out of 10'; and (d) *scope* that consists of responses that an actor receives during the application of power. Power relations can also be analysed at several levels (Krippendorff 1995): de-mythologies, de-abstract, colonising/admitting

participation, contesting, re-articulation, and enabling others as emancipatory dialogue. Power can be seen as machinery in which everyone is caught, those who exercise power just as much as those over whom it is exercised. However, Mumby (2001:588, 595) emphasised, *power resides not simply in relations of cause and effect (as Dahl suggests), but in structured relations of autonomy and dependence that are an endemic feature* of working life. Power's communicative aspect emphasises: *power is defined in terms of the ability of individuals or groups to control and shape dominant interpretation* at work. Finally, power is prevalent horizontally and vertically, in vertical relationships [management and worker] and horizontal relationships [management–management and worker–worker]. According to Zizek (1989:31), *money is in reality just an embodiment, a condensation, a materialisation of a network of social relations – the fact that it functions as a universal equivalent of all commodities is conditioned by its position in the texture of social relations.*

113   Perhaps the most misleading term is the phrase *market system* coined as a meaningless construction to avoid the use of the term capitalism. The market system has also been able to conceal the harshness of capitalist competition. Referring to capitalism, John Stuart Mill, one of the foremost philosophers of the 19ᵗʰ century wrote, *I confess that I am not charmed with the idea of life held out by those who think that the normal state of human beings is that of struggling to get on, that the trampling, crushing, elbowing, and treading on each other's heels, which form the existing type of social life, are the most desirable lot of human beings* (Albert 2006:2).

114   Anomie to use Durkheim's term or anomaly *runs from destructiveness (violence, delinquency), to contagious depressiveness (fatigues, suicide, neuroses). Each of these characteristic aspects of the affluent or permissive society raises in its way the problem of fundamental imbalance* (Baudrillard 1998:175; cf. Chomsky 1997).

115   As much as positivists claim that facts-can-speak-for-themselves, they tend not to speak (one can hardly hear them talk!). Instead, they must be read, interpreted, discussed, and analysed by human beings. Facts need human input in order to be facts and to be recognised as such. See also: Chomsky's *The Responsibility of Intellectuals* (1967a).

116   Popper (1999) has shown this for science, Kochan (2003:17) for work, and Putman (1995) for communication. In the collective-bargaining domain this relates to: process, conflict, information exchange, issue development, time phase analysis, boundary-spanning, coalition and inter-group relations, organisational structure, and negotiated outcomes.

117   Consequently and not surprisingly *no radical critique has ever been presented in an IRRA book* (Adams 1993a:141), IRRA is the international *Industrial Relations Research Association.*

118   Most instructive are: Watson's (2003) *Death Sentence – The Decay of Public Language;* Zengotita's (2005) *Mediated;* and Poole's (2006) *Unspeak.*

119   One of the most obscene versions of access, use, misuse and instrumentalisation of the public domain through corporate mass media has been the event of advertising that infiltrates every living room, every bedroom and every child's room telling all how delicious and healthy a *Happy Meal* is (Zengotita 2005).

120   In Roman mythology, *Janus* was the god of gates and doorways depicted with two faces looking in opposite directions being bipolar, deceptive, double-dealing, or double-tongued. *Janus* is marked by deliberate deceptiveness pretending one set of speech while being the other. *Janus* was popularised as

double agent in James Bond's *GoldenEye*. But already in Shakespeare's Othello, the double-crossing Iago utters the words *by Janus* when lying to Othello, a play on words considering his two faced nature.

121   *Under the repressive conditions in which men think and live, thought – any mode of thinking which is not confined to pragmatic orientation within the status quo – can recognise the facts and respond to the facts only by going behind them* (Marcuse 1966:189; cf. Chomsky 1968:2). Representatives of the problem-solving view are Dunlop (1958:vi–vii), Eldridge (1975), Barbash (1997:19) and many more.

122   Epistemological philosophy deals with theories that seek to explain how knowledge is created.

123   According to Gadamer (1976:21), the *sociological interest in reflection is basically a means of emancipation from authority and tradition.*

124   Enlightenment can be seen as containing the following: scientific development, the importance of reason, the rule of law, rationality, a secular state, progress in human rights, with representatives such as Kant, Hume, Voltaire, Locke, Adam Smith. There has been a view that actually four different versions of Enlightenment exist: a French, a Scottish, an Italian, and a German. There has also been a suggestion that our understanding of Enlightenment is distinctively European. It is a set of ideas possibly created during the 1930s to fight against the pre-Enlightenment ideas of fascism.

125   Rationality, rational, and rationalism carry connotations of a way of thinking that uses reason as a base. It rejects what is unreasonable or cannot be tested by reason. It is a theoretical construct that sees reason as a foundation for creating knowledge. Reason and not religion is the guiding principle in life and in human conduct demanding that *man* (!) must make public the use of reason.

126   Poole (2006:68) comments that *the natural/unnatural distinction is one of which few practising scientists can make much sense…[it] is senseless. It is part of the old idea that, since humans are part of nature, anything they do must be natural: it is in principle impossible for their actions to be unnatural.*

127   The question of *what ought to be* has been linked to '*What should be done?*', first raised by Russian socialist and novelist Nikolai Gavrilovich Chernyshevsky in a book *What should be done?*, written in Siberian exile in 1862.

128   As Adorno (1944:58) has shown, progress is not a simple linear movement forward. He noted that *the double character of progress, which constantly developed the potential of freedom simultaneously with the reality of oppression, has created a situation where the various people are ever more completely suborned into the control of nature and social organisation, yet are at the same time incapable of understanding how culture goes beyond such integration, due to the compulsion which culture inflicts on them.*

129   It exposes *religion and law, art and philosophy to the revolutionary consciousness that unhinged this tradition through emancipatory reflection* (Gadamer 1976:18). The philosophical problem of *idealism* (religion as God's creation) versus materialism (the creation out of matter) has been described perfectly by Searle (1996:190), *the simplest way to show that is to show that a socially constructed reality presupposes a reality independent of all social constructions, because there has to be something for the construction to be constructed out of.*

130   Reason is not enshrined in a simple logical system but is a historical dimension linked to the period of *Enlightenment*. Reason contradicted an old order of things and thought by uncloaking pre-modern myths as irrational. Modern reasoning establishes a mode of thought and human conduct that is directed

towards the reduction of ignorance, destruction, brutality, and oppression. Marcuse (1966:225) noted, *I believe that the very concept of reason originates in value judgement, and that the concept of truth cannot be divorced from the value of reason.* Alarmed by the proliferation of knowledge, *Francis I of France went so far as to forbid, in 1535, the printing of any book on penalty of hanging* (Simonds 1982:601). In modernity, the free market has replaced the banning of book. Today, prohibition is hardly necessary as system destabilising books that do not subscribe to dominant ideas are either not published by mainstream publishers or largely ignored. The *free* market pushes publications that are *handy, useful,* that stabilise our present system, and that manufacture consent while the free market simultaneously marginalises others.

131 The foremost example illustrating the link between social life and theory is that of Italian physicist and astronomer *Galileo Galilei* (1564–1642). *As he rose from this knees having confessed before the Roman Inquisition of the 'errors of his ways' in defending the Copernican system, he is alleged to have tapped the ground beneath him and to have muttered, 'And yet, it moves'* (Chalmers 1994:150). It took the Catholic Church a mere *359 years to admit, in 1992, that it had wrongly condemned Galileo for proving that the Earth moves around the Sun* (Habermas 2001:10; Marcuse 1966:161, 168; cf. Albert 2006:77).

132 Quoted from: Horkheimer (1937:188–243) and Habermas (1997:401).

133 Albert Einstein, while at Princeton University positioned a sign in his office that read *Not everything that counts can be counted, and not everything that can be counted counts.* Similarly, one of the most common mistakes is made when (sometimes unconsciously) correlations become causalities. These are used to explain connections in way where none exist. On this Adorno (1944:15) notes, *what is not reified, what cannot be counted and measured,* falls off.

134 Under advanced capitalism, science and technology take on new importance even though they have always existed under capitalism. As capitalism depends more and more on technical innovations rather than erratic innovations, the economic value of technical innovations increases. Consequently, modern capitalism creates large-scale industrial research and development facilities. It establishes a scientific-industrial complex spanning over private industries and state-funded universities and research institutions. As technology becomes more and more a production factor, state institutions are incorporated and subordinated to profit-driven engineering projects. Instrumental rationality infiltrates more and more institutions that previously had been designed to operate on critical rationality as they become vital to advanced capitalism (Albert 2006:77–98).

135 Quoted from Hobsbawn (2004:11). Crucial to the understanding of Max Weber is Herbert Marcuse's *Industrialization and Capitalism in the Work of Max Weber.* Furthermore, in *Negations* (1968) he argues Weber's value-freedom carries an undeniable political determination in the political context of the Wilhelmine German empire. In contrast to Weber, Marcuse argues that neutrality is dependent on self-reflection as neutrality can only be real when it has the power of resisting interference. Something Weber's concepts of bureaucracy and organisations failed to achieve. Rather than being neutral, Weber's neutrality and Weber himself became neutrality's victims. Neutrality became an aide to every power that wants to use it.

136 This development is partly expressed in an unconscious use of language even though *no one would deny that the practical application of modern science has fundamentally altered our world, and herewith also our language* (Gadamer 1976:35).

137 In standard management studies Max Weber has been used to legitimise hierarchical order. In reality however, Weber's core idea is linked to domination (Herrschaft). Even though this is the key to understand Max Weber, it has been suppressed by standard literature to convert Weber's idea into a legitimising ideology. Weber's idea is much less suitable to managerial ideology because it carries connotations of critique like the *Order of Things* (Foucault 1994). Today's affirmative management writers turned Weber into their *Godfather* while originally he may not have been the *Sugar-Daddy* of management writers who supply legitimacy. For a different view see Marcuse (1964b).

138 Watson (2003:2) emphasised that *managerialism, a name for various doctrines of business organisations, also comes with a language of its own, and to such unlikely places as politics and education.*

139 The German word *Herrschaft* means literally *domination by man* [as in *male!*] over someone or something [-*schaft*] (cf. Shenhav 1999). The term *Herrschaft* should be translated into domination, which for example C.W. Mills did correctly. However, Parson translated *Herrschaft* into *imperative coordination* and later into *leadership* (Shenhav 1999:15). Both terms are wrong. But the dominative content, as intended by Max Weber, drops off!

140 George Orwell's *1984* reads: *until they become conscious they will never rebel* (1949:74). These texts are produced to ensure that this shall not happen.

141 *Materialists…use the concept 'ideology' expressly to warrant normative claims regarding the exploitation of the 'proletarian class' by self-serving plunderers* (McGee 1980:3).

142 One really does not need something like ethics when the task is *getting things done*. Hence what is called *business ethics* [what ever happened to *management ethics?*] suffers in the fringes of standard textbooks and in extreme cases is reduced to something like: *how ethical is it for an employee to use an office copy machine to copy private notes?* This is done in full view of some of the worst excesses of management's unethical misbehaviour ranging from Bhopal to Enron (Smith 1759, 1776); Gandhi 1869–1948; Kohlberg 1981, 1984; Mander 2001; Cheney 2004, 2006).

143 To understand managerialism in modern society, *George Orwell* (1949:213) is most instructive, *what kind of people would control this world had been equally obvious. The new aristocracy was made up for the most part of bureaucrats, scientists, technicians, trade-union organisers, publicity experts, sociologists, teachers, journalists, and professional politicians. These people, whose origins lay in the salaried middle class and the upper grades of the working class, had been shaped and brought together by the barren world of monopoly industry.*

144 While Marcuse's *One-Dimensional Man* (1966) offers the bleakness of Kant's *what is*, his An Essay on Liberation offers more of Kant's *what ought to be*.

145 According to Marcuse (1969), Marx and Engels did not develop concrete concepts of possible forms of freedom in a socialist society. More than Marx could have ever imagined, Soviet-style socialism achieved almost the extreme opposite (see Marcuse's work on *Soviet Marxism: A Critical Analysis (1964a).* See also Albert 2006:145ff.

146 Pre-modern and modern modes of domination are fundamentally different just as much as slavery differs from free wage labour; paganism differs from Christianity; feudal slaughters differ from Nazi death camps. From then until today, the history of these relations is still the history of domination as the system of authority has survived from peasants and lords to workers and managers (cf. Cooke 2003).

147 This is extensively discussed by Marx (1848), Polanyi (1944), Birnbaum (1971:7) and more recently in Eric Hobsbawn's article on *History: A New Age of Reason* (2004:11).

148 A rather simple understanding of ideology is to see it as simply false, misleading, or mystifying reality. Ideology can be seen as *a discourse that always misrepresents concrete conditions and specific causes, trading concrete realities for murky, vague, metaphysical explanations* (Nealon & Grioux 2003:83). *If dialectical logic understands contradiction as necessity belonging to the very nature of thought (Zur Natur der Denkbestimmung), it does so because contradiction belongs to the very nature of the object of thought, to reality, where reason is still unreason, and the irrational still the rational* (Marcuse 1966:146). Francois Perroux in his *La Co-existence pasifique* (loc ct. vol. III, p. 631), quoted in Marcuse (1969:211), wrote, *they believe they are dying for the class, they die for the party boys. They believe they are dying for Fatherland, they die for the industrialists. They believe they are dying for the freedom of the person, they die for the freedom of the individual. They believe they are dying for the proletariat, they are dying for its bureaucracy. They believe they are dying by orders of a state, they die for the money which holds the state. They believe they are dying for a nation, they die for the bandits that gag it. They believe – but why would one believe in such darkness? Believe – die? – when it is a matter of learning to live?*

149 On the role of the state in modern society, Adorno (1944:17) noted, *the mechanism of the reproduction of life, its exploitation and annihilation, is immediately the same, and industry, the state and advertising are fused accordingly. The old exaggeration of skeptical liberals, that war is merely a business, has come true: the power of the state has given up even the appearance [Schein] of independence from particular profit interests and puts itself into the latter's service, which it always did in reality, now ideologically as well.*

150 Some have argued that the rise of the welfare state has been part of the so-called *social-democratic century* that ended with the neo-liberal takeover via economic deregulation, a reduced state, reduced taxes, and a socio-economic shift of wealth from the poor to the rich popularised in '*the rich are getting richer and the poor are getting poorer*'. As a result, it is almost universally accepted, the welfare state needs *reform*. Reform is a term originating in the reformation of the 16th century that carries strong connotations of purification. Ever since then the term *reform* has been seen positively. Today, the very word *reform* argues efficiently in favour of itself, whatever it actually is. In *Unspeak* (Poole 2006:34) no one wants to be non-reforming or anti-reform. Of course, neo-liberal's rollback of social welfare provision has used the word *reform* in the reverse sense. Neo-liberal *Newspeak* turns reform into a reactionary policy. Present reforms do not *conserve* the welfare state. They are not *conservative*. They go back, they are reactionary in character.

151 Rather somewhat romantically, Adorno (1944:39) noted on the language of workers and the proletariat, *in the speech of the subjugated, however, there is only the mark of domination, robbing them even of the justice which the unmutilated, autonomous word means to all those who are free enough to say it without resentment. Proletarian speech is dictated by hunger. The poor chew words, in order to feel full. From their objective Spirit [Geist] they expect the powerful nourishment, which society has denied them; they fill up their mouths because they have nothing to bite on.*

152 On mass consumerism, Adorno (1944:98) noted, *the unchanging uniformity [Immergleichheit] of machine-produced goods, the net of socialisation, which in*

equal measure catches and assimilates objects and the gaze at those objects, transforms everything which is encountered into something which has already been, to the accidental exemplar of a species, to the model's doppelganger.

153 Nietzsche had less faith in this ritual as he called democracy, *a political system calculated to make the intelligent minority subject to the will of the stupid* (Watson 2003:124).

154 Perhaps mass democracy is one of the most widely organised mass activity of our time as relatively large numbers of *pre*-selected people (foreigners, teenagers, children, and often prisoners are excluded) are told to arrive at a *preset* date at a *preset* place to mark a *preset* paper that lists a *preset* number of *pre*-selected candidates by *preset* parties (cf. Canfora 2006).

155 *An academic study that appeared right before the* [US] *presidential election reports that less than 30 percent of the population was aware of the positions of the candidates on major issues, though 86 percent knew the name of* [the president's] *dog* (Albert 2006:110; Canfora 2006).

156 It is most obvious, that neither steering needs of complex societies can be satisfied by a single voting exercise every three to five years, nor can the steering needs of the economic domain be satisfied by whatever is left of democratic workers' participation in the production process.

157 While the idea of efficiency has been applied to management, economists such as Harford (2006:61) have applied it to economy and society by saying, *as we'll see, taxes are like lies: they interfere with the world of truth. But I'll reveal one way in which taxes can be implemented, which is both fair and efficient. This could be good news for seniors struggling to pay their winter heating bill, but bad news for Tiger Woods.*

158 A good summary is Kellner's *Introduction to Marcuse's One-Dimensional Society* (1991).

159 This commodification goes well beyond the work domain, as Chomsky wrote, *in a well-functioning capitalist society, everything becomes a commodity, including freedom; one can have as much as one can buy, and those who can buy a lot have every reason to preserve an ample supply* (quoted from Poole 2006:215; cf. Albert 2006:145ff.).

160 While *Tocqueville predicted in October 1847 that the political struggle will soon be between those who have and those who do not, and the great battlefield will be that of property* (Canfora 2006:76), the conversion of large sections of the working class into an affluent middle class has sufficiently ended Tocqueville's prediction. Adorno (1944:75) noted on this, *the rich dispose over the means of production. Consequently the technical progress, in which the entire society participates, is accounted for primarily as 'their' progress, today that of industry, and the Fords necessarily appear to be benefactors, to the same degree which they in fact are, given the framework of the existing relations of production.*

161 According to Adorno & Horkheimer's *The Culture Industry: Enlightenment as Mass Deception* (1944:2), TV and radio programmes are no longer art forms. The ideology that they are just business is made into a truth in order to justify the rubbish they deliberately produce. Today they see themselves as cultural industries.

162 One of the more serious problems with the rat race is that even if you win the rat race you are still a rat!

163 Hamilton (2003), Hamilton & Denniss (2005) have used the term *Affluenza*.

164 Similarly, as advertising seeks to move consumers into the mainstream of consumption as this is easier to satisfy, democracy and the language that comes

along with it, does the same. It seeks to satisfy the mainstream. *If the language of politics tends to become that of advertising, thereby bridging the gap between two formerly very different realms of society, then this tendency seems to express the degree to which domination and administration have ceased to be separate and independent functions in the technological society. This does not mean that the power of the professional politician has decreased. The contrary is the case* (Marcuse 1966:107).

165   As mass democracy is sold as a choice that isn't a choice, only the end of mass-mediated democracy can lead to democracy. *It can become democratic only through the abolition of mass democracy, i.e. if society has succeeded in restoring the prerogatives of privacy by granting them to all and protecting them for each* (Marcuse 1966:249).

166   Which are, after all *freedom fries*, as US Republican congressman Walter Jones sought to re-christen French fries as the French did not participate in the *Coalition of the Killing(!)* during the Iraq invasion of 2003.

167   On the deformation of modern affluence Adorno (1944:12) notes, *what sort of condition must the ruling consciousness have achieved, when the binding proclamation of extravagance and champagne-inebriation, formerly reserved for attachés in Hungarian operettas, is raised to a maxim of the right life in brute earnest.*

168   See Zengotita (2005). On this Adorno (1944:5) commented, *every visit to the cinema, despite the utmost watchfulness, leaves me dumber and worse than before.*

169   Scientism is the triumph of science when all human concerns and problems have become mere problems of management and technical implementation.

170   According to George Orwell (1949:210), *from the point of view of the low, no historic change has ever meant much more than a change in the name of their masters.*

171   Thompson (1990:11) has emphasised the shift from religion to capitalism in the following way, *as religion and magic lost their hold on individuals caught up in the restless activity of capitalist industrialisation, the ground was prepared for the emergence of a new kind of belief system: for the emergence of secular belief systems which could mobilise individuals without reference to other-worldly values or beings. It is these secular belief systems which some contemporary theorists describe as ideology.* In capitalism *ideology, communication* and above all the *public* are intimately connected. *Until the idea of the public was recognised as a relevant audience to be communicated with, there was no need to develop sophisticated techniques for manipulation; rulers simply did what they and their supporters deemed necessary* (Altheide & Johnson 1980:6; see also Chomsky 1997).

172   Watson (2003:1) sees the *public domain* as structurally separated from the private domain. This assigns a separate language use to each domain. In the *public* domain *public* language is the language of *public* life. It is the language of political and business leaders, civil servants, and officials. It is a formal and sometimes elevated language. Public language is the language of *leaders* more than that of the *led*, of the *managers* rather than of the *managed*.

173   One might even argue that the ideological hegemony of the church largely prevented any revolutionary spirit during feudalism with a few exceptions such as the German peasant war and other minor revolts. When the old order of church and aristocrats ended and the communicatively established hegemony had not yet been successfully moved from church to corporate mass media, a window of opportunity opened. This brief period of an open window between the decline of ideology communicated by the church and the rise of corporate mass media communicated ideology opened a gap in the ideological armour between feudalism and capitalism. It was a moment of relatively un-

restricted free speech with unrestricted access to the public domain. It was undistorted, not infiltrated, and uncorrupted by either the feudal church or by capitalist corporate mass media. Only this moment allowed peasants and workers to find common interest. They could convert communicative action into social action that led to revolution. Once this window was closed via corporate media, revolutions ceased. Ideology had successfully moved from church to corporate media. Ideology and hegemony had, once again, established the ruler over the to-be-ruled. The ideology of ruler over the to-be-ruled however was no longer preached in churches once a week but reached into our bedrooms via TV every night!

174 Habermas (2006:8) commented on factors that dominate the democratic domain, ...*the political public sphere is at the same time dominated by the kind of mediated communication that lacks of defining features of deliberation.* The previously democratic domain has been successfully colonised by indirect or mediated communication that does not carry any notion of participative democracy.

175 On the issue of exchange value, Adorno (1944:29), noted, *if human beings were no longer possessions of any kind, then they could also no longer be exchanged. The property relationship in human beings, the exclusive right of priority, recalls to mind the old saying: Lord, they're only human beings, which one, doesn't really matter.*

176 The event of *The News* clarifies this. *The News* – a relative enlightening event during capitalism's early phase – increasingly became a commodity that could be sold. Rather than serving truth in enlightened discourse, the main purpose of news became a functional instrument that served the profit motive rather than the enlightened truth motive. Once converted into a commodity, *The News* is sometimes not only sold but also produced for the sole purpose of selling a commodity. Under advanced capitalism, *The News* is owned, produced, and sold by large mass-media corporations. Its role is reduced to a sellable commodity like a car or cheese. This is no more shown as in Fox-News' *we report – you decide*. This *Newspeak* gives the image of we report – unbiased – and you can make up your own mind. In reality more than others, Fox *makes* up the News – they decide, you watch – so that the viewer's mind is made up the way Fox wants it (see Violanti 2006).

177 Chomsky wrote (1997:37), *meanwhile the business world warned of the hazard facing industrialists in the newly realised political power of the masses, and the need to wag and win the everlasting battle for the minds of men, and indoctrinate citizens with the capitalist story until they are able to play back the story with remarkable fidelity.*

178 See Adorno & Horkheimer (1944); Marcuse (1966); Zengotita (2005); Albert (2006).

179 As the democratic and public domain has been restructured even democratic freedom takes on a new meaning. As freedom remains associated with democracy, corporations have only one use for the public domain and that is not democracy but the selling of consumer goods. Consequently, *democratic* freedom has become *economic* freedom. The one-dimensional ideology that comes along with it is the ideology of the free market, just like democracy needs to be free. Any intervention into the free market is portrayed as bad. It is an unreasonable burden on business. Any form of regulation hinders economic freedom. It also hinders, so the ideology goes, democratic freedom. Government should not intervene and restrict itself to maintaining law and order, protect private property, maintain economic growth, etc. (cf. Chomsky 1997; Albert 2006:20).

180   The one-dimensionality of the prevailing ideology is task of the globally oper-
      ative corporate mass media. The ideology of the one-dimensional consumer
      society helps laying the groundwork for the marketing of goods and a profit-
      driven economic and social order. It establishes the ideological link between
      happy consumers in India, Chicago, Sydney, or London. From Hollywood to
      Bollywood the acceptance of consumption is unchallenged. As the brain of
      the consumer is clustered with advertising slogans, those at the top of the
      hierarchy benefit exponentially from this ideology.

181   In some cases, in-depth, thought-provoking, meaningful, serious, and
      reflective or even self-reflective programmes are intentionally avoided. This is
      done so that the consumer does not recognise the trivialities served up in
      advertisements. The consumer should not reflect and definitely not even be
      reminded that critical reflection adds meaning to life.

182   Corporate mass media hardly ever show programmes that critically examine
      or even challenge their own media concentration. Neither do they rarely show
      programmes – apart from the token show here and there – that report criti-
      cally or even attack the corporations that guarantee advertising revenue or
      report about the abuse of their power resulting in many of the pathologies of
      our society.

183   Every day' life of commercially driven normality and happiness of the end-
      lessly consuming middle class is only interrupted by the two most powerful
      guarantors of viewing ratings, sex and crime. Even more than the commercial-
      isation of sex, the showing of violence achieves that goal. It is assisted via
      overemphasising crime, the use of violence, and weapons (guns, etc.) in
      society. It constructs the atomisation of society where every one is afraid of
      the other and the only outlet left for secure engagement with society is the
      shopping mall. A perfect match is found when sex and crime merge into child
      abuse, sex crimes, child-abductions from playgrounds, rings of child pornogra-
      phy, etc. While all of them exist, the likelihood that one becomes a victim of
      them is rather insignificant but the tabloid media is only too willing to
      portray them everyday occurrence, common, numerous, etc. as long as it leads
      to ratings increases.

184   Herman & McChesney 1997:7) take the example of *Procter & Gamble, the
      world's number one corporate advertiser* to show this. Procter & Camble *explicitly
      prohibits programming which could in any way further the concept of business as
      cold, ruthless, and lacking of sentiment or spiritual motivation.*

185   As social reality is always socially constructed so are attempts to place such
      social developments into boxes. Boxes like models serve as a shortcut to
      reduce complexities to more accessible levels. This is especially the case when
      multifarious complexities are an issue. While boxes assist clarification of social
      processes, they – by definition – also include severe shortcomings such as
      carry-overs from one box into another. One such carry over occurs at horizon-
      tal level impacting on vertical boxes. Despite these – and other – problems,
      Figure 3.2 is designed to provide an overview of social developments.

186   Habermas' (1988) concept of a *Public Sphere* is located here. It is seen as an ideal
      of unrestricted rational discussion of public matters providing a societal forum
      for *The Great Transformation* from feudalism to capitalism. The public domain
      has been important for early democracy, modernity, *Enlightenment,* new dis-
      coveries, modern scientific endeavour, revolutionary ideas (Kant, Hegel, Marx,
      Newton, Darwin, Freud, Einstein, etc.). Critical and scientific rationality
      rejected and ultimately ended the old order of feudalist mystic (Simon 2005).

187   *The rapid proliferation of institutions of mass communication and the growth of net-works of transmission through which commodified symbolic forms were made available to an ever-expanding domain of recipients* (Thompson 1990:11), weakened rational communication at the expense of ideological, affirmative, system integrative, and profit-driven communication.

188   According to Thompson (1990:15), *mass communication institutes a fundamental break between producer and receiver.* As rational communication became increasingly commodified, this fundamental break increased and became object to steering based on money and power. Money and power further distanced producer and receiver from each other. In Thompson's words (1990:16), *the development of technical media separates social interaction from physical locale.*

189   Even though there has been a strong move towards so-called *de*-regulation, in reality this has often been no more than re-regulation asymmetrically distributed between rich and poor. As Chomsky (1994:8) pointed out *it did advocate markets for the poor, but it went well beyond even its predecessors in demanding and winning a very high level of public subsidy and state protection for the rich.*

190   While standard theory suggests there are two domains, the *productive* and the *reproductive* domain, when focusing on communication, a third domain has to be added to address communicative developments. This is not meant to suggest that communication is disconnected from production and reproduction, it is rather the opposite. Communication is of high importance to both domains. However, the communicative domain has always existed as communication always played a role in society and work. System imperatives that stabilised feudalism (*it is the lord's will that you work from sunrise to sunset on the field*), early capitalism (*competition dictates that you work 16 hours*), and late capitalism (*9-to-5 is the normal work day*) had to be communicated. In sum, the increased importance of communication demands the introduction of a separated but never unconnected domain.

191   Quoted from Habermas (1997a:285). In historical development terms, the industrial revolution wasn't really a *revolution* as it was more of an *evolutionary* process spread out over several decades. The change from feudalism to industrialism did not happen within the time frame of days, weeks, or months. It is misleading to term it *revolution.* Rather than being a fast-moving revolution like those of France (1789) or Russia (1917), the so-called *industrial revolution* has been a rather slow process stretching from workshop mechanisation to stationary and mobile steam-engines to diesel engines (ship, trains, factories) and petrol engines (motor-car) to electric engines for today's factory machinery.

192   Even though, the modern humanity project has made significant progress, it is still unfinished as humans still have wars, with *The Coalition of the Killing(!)* against Iraq being the most devastating at the turn from the 20th to the 21st century. Humans still torture and still accept affluence for 1/5 and poverty and starvation for 4/5 of the world population. We accept the destruction of 25,000 km^2 of rainforest a year for cheap beef to be consumed in cheap fast-food restaurants or that 1,700 mobile phones are discarded every hour. We export misery to the developing world that is – apart from the occasional TV appearances – reduced to mere statistics. All according to Stalin's dictum: *one death is a tragedy, a million is a statistic.* There is environmental destruction, and human rubbish on the Moon and Mars. Marcuse (1966:248) has emphasised it as, *a new standard of living, adopted to the pacification of existence, also presupposes reduction in the future population. It is understandable, even reasonable,*

> *that industrial civilisation considers legitimate the slaughter of millions of people in war, and the daily sacrifice of all those who have no adequate care and protection, but discovers its moral and religious scruples if it is the question of avoiding the production of more life in a society which is still geared to the planned annihilation of life in the national interest, and to the unplanned deprivation of life on behalf of private interests.*

193　See: Habermas' *Modernity: An incomplete project*, in: Foster (1985).

194　One of the most interesting aspects of money is that without common agreement about what it actually is, money would be no more than colourful paper. Money has virtually no use-value. It is inedible, somewhat useless to heat housing, and similarly useless as a notepad. However, as the commodity money has one most decisive character, it has assumed the utmost universal exchange character.

195　Although the mass media has largely removed present pathologies created by the system out of sight for most people, these pathologies are still with us. For example, every day about 100.000 people die on hunger even though there is an oversupply of food – currently rather unequally distributed. The world can produce 2700 calories per person per day, enough to feed 12 billion people. There are currently about 6.4 billion people on planet earth. Every five seconds a child below the age of ten starves to death. Every four minutes someone loses his/her eyesight because of vitamin A deficiency. 856 million people – about one in six people on this planet – go hungry every day and are permanently undernourished. On the other hand, the 500 largest corporations control about 52 of the world's GDP (Metall 2006:30).

196　This has been expressed by George Orwell (1949:212) as *even if it was still necessary for human beings to do different kinds of work, it was no longer necessary for them to live at different social or economic levels.*

197　The concept of democratic citizens has been largely substituted by the concept of the consumer in a system that turns everything in to a sellable commodity in a process of *reification* or the thing-like character of all social, political, economic, private and public relations.

198　Quoted from Watson's *Death Sentence* (2003:49)

199　In the words of George Orwell's *1984* (1949:207), *it helps to preserve the special mental atmosphere that a hierarchical society needs* (cf. Olson 1971; Offe & Wiesenthal 1980).

200　European fascism was strong in Fascist Italy and Austria, Franco's Spain (1936), Poland, Hungary, etc. A classical view holds that the working class has an historic mission in a revolution against capitalism. Instead of the perceived revolution the opposite occurred. During the 1930s in Germany some sections of the working class supported German fascism. Hamilton's *Who Voted for Hitler?* (1982: 46), provides the following numbers for Nazi support (and class composition in % of non-farm labour): Upper Class 15% Nazi support (1% of non-farm labour); upper middle class 25% (14%); lower middle class 60% (25%); and working class 25% (60% of non-farm labour), see also Moore (1966). Lacking a majority in the January 1933 election, Hitler was made Kanzler through a coalition government when conservatives assigned power to him. Hitler was never elected by a majority of votes. After this assignment by conservatives, the mass media (Hugenberg) and capitalism (Deutsche Bank, Dresdener Bank, IG Farben, Krupp, Mannesmann, etc.), Hitler held another election in spring 1933 in which he *manufactured his election victory* (Canfora 2006:147).

201 While Anglo-Saxon countries (GB, USA, Canada, NZ, Australia, etc.) established special faculties for *labour relations* or *industrial relations*, European countries did not follow this segregation of work and society. More than Anglo-Saxon countries, Europeans view *work* as part of a social, political, and economic field where the social domain (social actors at work), politics (the reproductive domain) and economy (the productive domain) are linked.

202 *Since the first usage, probably in the school of Saint-Simon, the term positivism has encompassed: (1) the validation of cognitive thoughts by experience of facts; (2) the orientation of cognitive thought to the physical science as a model of certainty and exactness; (3) the belief that progress in knowledge depends on this orientation. Consequently, positivism has been important in the struggle against all forms of metaphysics, transcendentalisms, and idealisms. They represent obscure and regressive ways of thinking* (cf. Marcuse 1966:176; Adorno 1976).

203 Quote taken from Whyte (1961:31). This version views social affairs like a controllable property of physics. It assumes that any human element of thought can be scientifically organised just like in natural science.

204 On natural science, Searle (2002:16–17) observed, *natural science describes features of reality that are intrinsic to the world as it exists independently of any observers. But such features as being a bathtub, being a nice day for a picnic, being a five dollar bill or being a chair are not subject of the natural sciences because they are not intrinsic features of reality.* The world of language belongs to social domain, which is socially constructed and does not exist independent of us. We have created the world of work.

205 Quoted from Whyte (1961:28). *August Comte* (1798–1857) saw the scientific endeavour as a three-stage development: the theological or fictitious state, the metaphysical or abstract state, and the scientific or positivist state (Miller 2000:49). As the founding positivist, *Comte* believed that empirical scientific research can only improve the world by making better humans, but would enable them to control the ravages of nature. He was the first to use the term *consensus* in his attempt to find a source of legitimacy not founded in the feudal order but in secularism. *Consensus* also became handy as an ideology enabling the integration of society after the French Revolution. In the 19th-century conservative sociology used it to integrate a class-based society into their project.

206 As much as proponents of Comte have fallen victim of Hegel's *Zeitgeist*, some contemporary Marxists have also shown signs of falling into a similar *Zeitgeist* trap by continuing to operate Marxist tools developed in the 19th century in the 21st century without reflecting on the 150 years of social, political, and economical development since then. As much as capitalism has reconstructed the ways in which it operates, Marxist analysis needs to reconstruct their analysis as well. Remaining an unreconstructed Marxist carries connotations of Zeitgeist. It is no longer possible.

207 One of the most visible examples of 200 years of attention on *how* while neglecting the *why* has been manifested in US President Clinton's announcement on cloning. When challenged with the technical possibilities on *how* to clone a human being, Clinton set up an ethics commission to discuss the *why*. This episode seems to indicate that we have, as it appears, just spent 200 years developing how to clone but don't know why to do it. We might just have wasted 200 years of philosophical development.

208 On dialectical thinking, Adorno (1944:25) noted, *to think dialectically means, in this respect, that the argument should achieve the criticality [Drastik] of the thesis and the thesis should contain the plenitude of its ground within itself.*

209 According to Searle (1969:175), *one of the oldest of metaphysical distinctions is that between fact and value.* The underlying belief of the fact-value distinction is the perception that an individual has *values* and that they have nothing to do with the real world. Under managerial ideology, values are often portrayed to be *value-added* as if management is value-free and free to add value. It is the illusionary pretence that human action does not contain value but it can be added later on, like sugar in a cup of tea.

210 There are almost as many definitions on what management is as there are on what elements are part of management. The socially constructed idea of management qualifies for *Martinus Scriblerus'* advice of the year 1727. *The expression [management] is adequate, when it is proportionably low to the Profundity of the Thought. It must not be always Grammatical, lest it appear pedantic and ungentlemanly; nor too clear, for fear it become vulgar; for Obscurity bestows a Cast of the Wonderful, and throws an oracular Dignity up a Piece which bath no meaning* (Poole 2006:161; cf. Berger & Luckmann 1967; Searle 1996).

211 In the words of George Orwell's 1984 *until they become conscious they will never rebel* (1949:74).

212 For a detailed analysis see: Habermas (1976a:142), or Held (1997:148), or Deetz (2001:19).

213 *The system knows only the condition of its survival, it knows nothing of social and individual contents* (Baudrillard 1998:56).

214 This is visible in most modern universities and business schools. *The dominance of the positivist model of science had acted to exclude critical thinking from business schools* (Grey & Willmott: 2005:8).

215 This point has been highlighted in Mander's (2001) seven rules of corporate behaviour, by Kohlberg's (1981, 1984) stages of ethical behaviour, and by Ghandi's *Seven Social Sins* (1925).

216 Some valuable lessons can be learned from the Bhopal case where a US chemical company killed more than 10.000 people in India and more than two decades after it, victims (only those who are still alive) wait for compensation while the US company boss retired peacefully and shareholders did well. The victims are external, while the boss and shareholders are internal to the system. The system deals with those inside, not with those outside. Above all, the profit equilibrium has been restored.

217 Socially accepted norms are one of the most important elements for social cohesion. For example, the killing of humans by humans is largely not prevented by fear of prison but killing contradicts the fundamental and shared moral values and norms that state that killing is wrong.

218 Adopted from Eriksen & Weigard (2003:32).

219 Adorno (1944:57) noted on decision-making, *to paint the decision-making inside large-scale industry as the wheeling and dealing of crooked vegetable-grocers suffices for a monetary shock, but not however for dialectical theater. The illustration of late capitalism through pictures from the agrarian or criminal storehouse does not allow the mischief of today's society to emerge from its wrapping in complicated phenomena.*

220 Money and power are elements of system integration. Both are more relevant than those persons who have actual power or actual money. According to Orwell (1949:218), *who wields power is not important, provided that the hierarchical structure remains always the same.*

221 One could argue with Krippendorff (1994:79), that theory can emphasise limits in a representational sense. Theory *for* indicates an enabling character.

Hence, Habermas' book might better be called The Theory *for* Communicative Action. Of the 220 authors cited by Habermas in The Theory of Communicative Action, the top five are Parsons (180), Weber (140), Durkheim (76), Mead (75), and Marx (69).

222 According to Marcuse (1966:177), *Wittgenstein's assurance [is] that philosophy leaves everything as it is...one might ask what remains of philosophy* (183). Apart from a somewhat anti-philosophy stance by language expert Wittgenstein, a philosophical view of modern language comes from Dante. According to Karl-Otto Apel (Mendieta 2002:50ff.), Dante is perhaps the last medieval intellectual and the first of the modernity. As a person situated at the crossroads of two intellectual traditions, he gave expression to the momentous change then taking place. Dante was the first to develop out of theological sources a historical-generic and anthropological analysis of the origins of language and the nature of its plurality. He developed arguments for the valorisation of *mother tongues* that, coupled with his political views, contributed to the then-emerging nationalism of the nascent European nations. To this extent, the *De Vulgari Eloquentia* is the first manifesto of national independence from the *imperial* and *sacramental* Latin that ruled through the writings of Augustine, Ambrosios, Hieronimous, and Jeroome. Latin was, but since Dante no longer is, the holy language but a communicative tool that has, from now on, three aspects: a) a humanist tradition found in the formal education of the European elite, b) the technical-scientific version as an expression of mathematics, and c) linguistic mysticism (cf. Chomsky 1967c).

223 *The principle of hermeneutics simply means that we should try to understand everything that can be understood* (Gadamer 1976:31).

224 Language, according to Searle (1996:59), *is essentially constitutive of institutions' reality*.

225 These are somewhat similar to Morrow's (1994) three interests: a) ontology as the study of the nature of the world, b) epistemology as the study of knowledge, and c) normative theory as the study of how the world ought to be.

226 The empirical understanding important for human societies has been advocated by *John Locke* (1632–1704) extending the work of *Francis Bacon* and becoming one of the foremost thinkers of *Enlightenment's* understanding of the relationship between the state and the individual. In sum, *classical British empiricism arose in often healthy opposition to religious obscurantism and reactionary ideology* (Chomsky 1976:128)

227 Quoted from Popper (1965:97). On the idea of *pure science*, Marcuse (1966:158) commended, *pure science is not applied science; it retains its identity and validity from its utilisation. Moreover, this notion of the essential neutrality (H.M.) of science is also extended to techniques. The machine is indifferent toward the social use to which it is put, provided those uses remain within its technical capabilities.*

228 Quoted from Adorno (1976:116), see also Chomsky (1968:5) and Albert (2006:108ff.).

229 See especially, Marcuse (1966:154); Chalmers (1994); Morrow (1994); Searle (1996, 2002); Poole (2006:59ff.). According to Searle (1996:151) *complete epistemic objectivity is difficult, sometimes impossible, because actual investigations are always from a point to view, motivated by all sorts of personal factors, and within a certain cultural and historical context.* See also Albert (2006:77ff.).

230 Quoted from Marcuse (1966:187). Austin (1962:3) has also made this point by arguing it *is called the descriptive fallacy* when only facts are reported and the circumstances that create these facts (the factors) are left out.

231 For a comprehensive discussion of linguistics, linguism, and linguistic theories, see Chomsky's work on *The Logical Structure of Linguistic Theory* (1975:9; cf. 1968a, 1976, 2002a) and others works by the same author. In a recent *New Statesmen* poll (www.newstatesman.com200605220016/) Noam Chomsky was voted the 7th most influential hero of our times.

232 According to system logic, *an individual must accept and assimilate this system entirely* (Volosinov 1929:54).

233 Like all other social phenomena, language does have a history, even though system theory tends to construct communication and language as a discontinuity and disunity between the history of communication and the system of communication. It pretends that communication and language are ahistorical but have inner system logic. The relationship between sign and meaning is to be found inside a system deprived of its history but transferred into system logic with connotations of mathematics or algebra. While cloaking the ideological content behind objectivity, positivism creates ideology, the ideology of positivism.

234 As much as this is part of the repertoire of what is called *critical realism*, critical theory is different from critical realism (Rorty 1979, 1982). *Critical Realism* can be seen as a critical version of positivism as a critical expression of an empirical analytical interest relying strongly on *the connectedness of events and the causal sequences produced by generative mechanisms…causal sequences…may be multiple causes of a single event…identifies causal mechanisms* Ackroyd (2004:151). Notably absent from Fleetwood & Ackroyd's *Critical Realist Application in Organisation and Management Studies* (2004) and from Edwards' *IR & Critical Realism: IR's Tacit Contribution* (2006) are any attempts to direct theory comprehensively towards a critical-emancipatory interest.

235 In the world of work, management, and labour relations, frameworks inside which social facts are presented and interpreted are constructed in academic journals, books, textbooks, conferences, etc. In short, they are not scientifically based but communicatively established. These academic subjects are not science based but communication based.

236 In many cases, journal editors, conference organisers, academic supervisors, etc. are boundary-guardians of such research communities. These communities are established communicatively, not scientifically. In most cases, the maintenance of these communities is a job given to so-called respected journals, organising committees for academic conferences and the like. The idea of a *Robinson Crusoe* like existence of a researcher living on a tiny research island on his or her own is no more than a romantic illusion. Similarly, a researcher cannot have an indigenous slave called *Friday* (a working day) to do his work (cf. Cooke (2003).

237 Despite failing to lift the material conditions of all humans, rationalism occupies an important place in human history. It is a philosophy that asserts that truth can best be discovered by reason and factual analysis, rather than faith, dogma or religious teaching. It provided a framework for communication outside the domain of church and religion. The three main rationalists are: Descartes, Baruch Spinoza and Gottfried Leibnitz, while John Locke, George Berkeley and David Hume are considered to be empiricists. The former were distinguished by the belief that, in principle, all knowledge can be gained by the power of our reason alone. The latter rejected this. They believe that all knowledge has to come through the senses and from experience.

238 Linge (1976:xv) emphasised in his introduction of Gadamer, that *prejudices are the biases of our openness to the world. Shaped by the past in an infinity of unexamined ways, the present situation is the given in which understanding is rooted, and which reflection can never entirely hold at a critical distance and objectify.* This is the meaning of the hermeneutical situation as Gadamer employs the term.

239 Philosophers such as *Johann Gottfried von Herder* (an early supporter of democracy and republican self-rule) reasserted the idea from *Greek* antiquity that language has a decisive influence on cognition and thought, and that the meaning of a particular text was open to deeper exploration based on deeper connections, an idea now called hermeneutics (Radford 2005:155; Canfora 2006:8).

240 Gadamer (1976:13) emphasised that *the real power of hermeneutical consciousness is our ability to see what is questionable.*

241 *But for social facts, the attitude that we take towards the phenomenon is partly constitutive of the phenomenon* (Searle 1996:33)

242 The editor of Gadamer's work, David E. Linge (1976:xx) emphasised *the hermeneutical conversation begins when the interpreter genuinely opens himself to the text by listening to it and allowing it to assert its viewpoint.*

243 Hermeneutical understanding is less about the flowing of ideas from one mind to another as one does not receive meaning *from* a text but one creates *meaning* with a text. A text is alive in the context of such an engagement. Any text does not simply speak to us. To understand a text is to understand oneself and our relationship to a text.

244 More details can be found in: Flöistad (1970:178) and Lyddon & Smith (1996).

245 One study following the historical-hermeneutical approach is Kaufman's work on the *Origins and Evolution of the Field of Industrial Relations in the United States* (1993) and its chapter on *Industrial Relations in the 1990s and Beyond* (1993:157–185), or partly in David Lyddon's UK journal *Historical Studies in Industrial Relations.*

246 *Hermeneutics achieves its actual productivity only when it musters sufficient self-reflection to reflect simultaneously about its own critical endeavours, that is, about its own limitations and the relativity of its own position* (Gadamer 1976:93).

247 In its economist variant, instrumental rationality and instrumentalism has been introduced by John Dewey and put into prominence by the so-called Chicago boys, a neo-liberal school of economics trapped in a means-ends paradigm.

248 See also: Whipp (1998:51) and Whitfield & Strauss (1998). Statistical methods and the purposive use of statistics when driven to an extreme as outlined by Orwell (1949:43), *statistics were just as much as fantasy in their original version as in their rectified version.*

249 According to Orwell, *power is not a means, it is an end…the second thing that you have to realise is that power is power over human beings…power is in inflicting pain and humiliation…power is in tearing human minds to pieces and putting them together again in a new shape of your own choosing* (1949: 267, 277, 279).

250 Value-neutrality in the discovery of natural functions can only take place inside a specific set of *a priori* (Kant) assignments inside a researcher's mind as a value. Such a value-system includes the historical, social etc. existence of researchers as much as values that create purpose, teleology, and the ability to function (cf. Habermas 1976a:155).

251 According to Mumby 1988:51) *at the heart of both domination and power lies the transformative capacity of human action the origin of all that is liberating and productive in social life as well as all that is repressive and destructive.*

252 See Dunlop's (1958) *three-actor* model and later into Kochan, Katz & McKersie's (1986) *three-actor-three-level* model at the strategy level and into *pluralism-unitarism-adversarialism* model at the agency level (Fox 1966, 1973; Hyman 1989).

253 Ever since Descartes (1596–1650) western philosophy has been defined and confined to an *agency versus structure* and *object versus subject* dichotomy. With this, modern rationality was born.

254 In many books and especially in textbooks boxes are created to simplify reality. Knowledge is literally *served up*. It is knowledge for easy access. Knowledge is constructed so that it can be memorised and rehearsed in management seminars and lectures. Furthermore, the use of some *boxes* is often done to avoid theory. However, once removed from being central to a book and from being used as a supplement for theory, the use of boxes can still serve a threefold purpose: a) to critically sum up a given theme, b) to highlight, and c) to show the uncritical use such boxed-in thinking. Unlike the use of boxes in textbooks, boxes, tables, graphs, and figures are not designed to be memorised as simplified way of *what is* or to be understood as a completed set of knowledge. Here, they are designed on the background of Kant's dictum, in modernity everything is open to criticism.

255 Most likely most of these *managerial abbreviations* (Linstead, Fullop & Lilley 2004) became prominent in the management and business world through one single mechanism: *if you speak about it often enough it must exist* (Poole 2006:25).

256 More traditional viewpoints tended to divide the world of work into management and workers or into employers and trade unions. Attached to the relationship of these has been the state. Critical theory goes beyond the restriction of such a triangle as it reduces theory to the interplay of these three actors under a certain set of rules (Kelly 1998:55, 130, cf. Murakami (2000a, 2000b).

257 A critical understanding of the world of work would overcome disciplinary borders. Traditional writers such as Kaufman (1993:93) barely mention the term *interdisciplinary*. Critical theory sees itself as fundamentally *interdisciplinary* in rejecting the traditional division and artificial segregation of academic labour. On the lack of interdisciplinary thinking, Adorno (1944:3) once commented, *the departmentalisation of the Spirit [Geist] is a means of abolishing such.*

258 British academic Linda Dickens (2000) has highlighted this problem by arguing for research *from a critical viewpoint.* She emphasised, *I think it becomes a problem only when you have policy-makers who just want research to support the policy they have decided on, rather than wanting research that can inform policy development.* Marcuse's (1966) critique is more directed towards a commercial use of research arguing that the form and level of control over research has become commercialised in such a way that opposition and even reflection are automatically suppressed.

259 One of the problems of *value neutral* claims is that of the process of *valorisation*. In the process of *valorisation* certain values is ascribed. In this case the value *neutral* or sometimes *free* is ascribed to the term science. Only this linguist process can formulate science as value-*neutral* or value-*free* science. The process of valorisation can be ideologically determined by ascribing (a) symbolic value such as praise, denouncing, cherishing, or despising; (b) technical values when values are cloaked in technical language; or (c) as time and space distancing elements creating value attachment that appears to be distant in

time (as history) or distant in space (as spatial or location) via an insertion into a new context that has previously been remote to the term used.

260 This point has been elaborated by Giddens (1979:235), Hyman (1979:194, 1989:120), and Heath (2003:7).

261 *The idea that everything is now subordinated to what 'capital' wants to 'see' [is] stated clearly in public by those who minister officially to capital's desire* (Poole 2006:208).

262 As the rise of the factory system under early capitalism moved on to ever larger and increasingly multi-national corporations, they accumulated more and more power. They *have a greater proportion of power in the world today than they did 100 or 200 years ago (although the total amount of power in the global system has increased)* (Cheney & Carroll 1997:622).

263 According to Monbiot, G. (2005), *our quality of life peaked in 1976.* From this point onwards the quality of life has been in decline (cf. Gorz (1982).

264 See: Marsden (1999); Cornfield & Hodson (2002); Grint (2005).

265 In France, such philosophical or intellectual interest is defined as *someone who uses a reputation in science, the arts or culture to mobilise public opinion in support of causes that he or she regards as just* (Le Monde Diplomatique, eng. edition, May 2006:1). This is in sharp contrast to the American tradition of anti-intellectualism (Le Monde Diplomatique, eng. edition, June 2006:14–15).

266 *Johann Gensfleisch Gutenberg* (1400–1468) invented book printing and contributed significantly to the proliferation of knowledge. By doing so he also enabled *Enlightenment* ideas to flourish. If he were still alive, he might cry in his house in Mainz when considering the gross aberration books have undergone since his invention. The event of the textbook signifies this. Not surprisingly, a recent sign above a university bookshop read: *Real Books not Textbooks!*

267 Unlike real books that convey ideas, concepts, theories or even critical theories, textbooks are reduced to a function. Such functional textbooks are a form of technology that requires the mastery of skills and acquisition of managerial tools solely designed to enhance profit-maximising production, conveniently labelled *organisational goals.* Unlike real books that might serve as *Enlightenment* of thought, textbooks are consumed via an endless rehearsal of managerial terms and models until they become part of the managerial ritual that is uncritically adopted, rehearsed, and accepted by students around the world.

268 On the affirmative character of academics, Adorno (1944:43) noted, *those who link the critique of capitalism to that of the proletariat – which itself more and more merely reflects capitalist tendencies of development – are suspect.*

269 The managerial use of social science did not occur out of an interest in scientific inquiry. Neither did it occur because of ethical reasoning. It was solely directed towards a solving of two problems: (a) as an instrument of reducing labour costs and (b) as system integrative tool to increase worker's loyalty towards the company and away from other loyalties such as co-workers and trade unions. On the managerialism-science link, Adorno (1944:17) wrote, *those who are organised want intellectuals of prominence to issue proclamations on their behalf, but the moment they fear they have to issue proclamations for themselves, the latter are capitalists, and the same prominence on which they speculated is now ludicrous sentimentality and stupidity.*

270 *The intention, quite apart from the disguise of scientific language, is twofold: to provide a basis for the control of subordinates by facilitating their integration in work, and to reinforce the integration of managers* (Anthony 2005:24).

271   On objectivity, Adorno (1944:25) noted, *objective means the non-controversial side of the phenomenon [Erscheinung], its unquestioned imprint, taken as it is, the facade constructed out of classified data, therefore the subjective; and they call subjective, whatever breaks through such, emerging out of the specific experience of the thing, divesting itself of prejudged convention and setting the relation to the object in place of the majority decision concerning such, which they cannot even see, let alone think – therefore, what is objective.* If science, scientists, and above all scientific facts were objective and value-free then one wonders why *twenty American Nobel laureates were among the signatories of a 2004 report which detailed how the Bush administration, while appealing to 'sound science', had consistently falsified scientific findings in order to support its own politics* (Poole 2006:60). Most discomforting to many positivists, there might be a hidden link between science and politics.

272   On universities, Chomsky (1968:9) once remarked, *that the universities have betrayed a public trust by associating themselves with the government and the corporate system.*

273   *And so business people, usually in cut-throat competition with each other, will present themselves in a united front as the 'business community' when it comes to lobby against corporate tax rise or an increase in the minimum wage* (Poole 2006:27) or when universities have to be converted from truth-seeking establishments into functional entities closely linked to the needs of business. The business community takes over the science community. Ideologically, terms such as *science or business community* imply that there is no diversity of opinion inside such a community. In Poole's *Unspeak* terms: who would want to be anti-community or anti-science community or anti-business community?

274   Further examples are to be found in Agger (1998), Brown (1998), Murakami (1999, 2000c), Parker (2002), and Washburn (2005).

275   To cater for the market of external grants, some universities have already renamed themselves into *University of Applied Science*, telling potential grant-givers: here is value for money. We do research tailored to your needs. We deliver results for your money. In short, you get the best research result that not only serves your needs or legitimises your ideology but also the best research money can buy.

276   There are cases where academic workloads of researchers at universities are tailored to external grant-givers. Here research is measured not in *quality* but solely in managerialism's favourite: the *measurable quantity*. Every refereed publication is valued with 1 point. A book equals five articles. It is valued at five (5) points. If you reach 2 points, your teaching load is reduced by x hours. If you reach 6 points, your teaching load is reduced from 16h to 7h per week. Any further reduction is only possible via external grants. This is the border between pure research output measured in numbers of articles and books and the beginning of the ultimate steering media: money. The same managerialism is applied to career progression. Increasingly full or tenured professors are only those who can attract external grants or collect money. While scientific achievement gets the backseat, money moves into the front seat.

277   The idea of *objective research* is a fine example of Poole's idea of *Unspeak* (2006). The term *objective* research, in *Unspeak* terms, implies that no one really wants research to be non-objective. The term *objective* research has an implicit ideological connotation. It masks research's hidden ideology behind the veil of objectivism. In reality no research into the world of work or management can ever be objective as it is always driven by interest(s).

278 Despite Bell's notion in *The End of Ideology* (1960), ideology – as it appears – is still with us. Hence, the task of *Ideologiekritik* [the critique of ideology' is *not to announce truth and expose errors, but to identify and endeavour to eliminate constraints on communicative activity as they impede inquiry, comprehension, and consequently efficacious action on the part of historical subjects who are dominated* (Simonds 1982:594).

279 See Meltz (1997:3).

280 According to Rice (2003:3) this approach helps to identify problems and find solutions. Instead of focusing on systems, one needs to emphasise social rules. By identifying work with social rules and relationships, labour-management studies remain firmly locked within the framework of empirical-analytical theories, even when using *complexity theory* because it remains inside a rule identifying relationship matrix. The empirical-analytical matrix can be further observed in contemporary industrial relations literature. Rice (2003) has argued this point by outlining that the field as a non-substantial but social relationship can be theoretically developed by using '*complexity theory*'. A complexity-based approach can be summarised as complex, adaptive systems consisting of a number of components, or agents that interact with each other according to sets of rules that require them to examine and respond to each other's behaviour in order to improve their behaviour and thus the behaviour of the system.

281 Whitfield and Strauss' (1998) collection on research and methodology illustrates many shortcomings by pretending to go *beyond how to do* contributing to epistemology.

282 In the form of as collection of articles, Whitfield and Strauss' (1998) work serves as a good example of journal science. Their collection is reduced to ''understand work and work relationships' inside the empirical–analytical framework. A discussion on hermeneutics is absent. Even though contemporary feminist research methods such as Clough's *The End of Ethnography* or Smith's *Texts, Facts and Feminism* have been seen as *perhaps the most powerful source of interpretative theory today* (Agger 1998:32), such methodological approaches are never discussed in one of the most relevant publications on work research. The Whitfield and Strauss' (1998) collection carefully avoids mentioning contemporary social science and research such as the postmodernist contributions on language and hermeneutics, the critical theory's examination of the limitation of positivism, or feminist research methods. Experimental methods are described as *to determine if a causal relationship exists between two variables by manipulating one.* A critical discussion on the limitations of such research is avoided or reduced to *narrowly controlled* laboratory *experiments*. The type of research conducted in the way Whitfield and Strauss (1998) suggest can only result in a very small group of researchers operating as a relatively *isolated tribe carrying out their work either in ignorance of, or in deliberate disregard for, the work of other groups* (Adams 1993a:150). This has led to the exclusion of interchanges between social theory and work-studies. Unfortunately, contemporary discussions such as Rorty's (1979, 1982) critique on experiments as *enclosures* in his book on *Critical Realism* remain absent.

283 In some countries the state actively supports this by creating lists and classification of academic journals – unconsciously and unquestionably – representing useful journals. More often than not such classifications are no more than an indicator of a capitalism-science link.

284   On not reading or not understanding theory, Adorno (1944:14, 48) noted, *the fear of the powerlessness of theory yields the pretext of declaring fealty to the almighty production-process and thereby fully concedes the powerlessness of theory...* [the standard academic's] *resentment is socially rationalised under the formula: thinking is unscientific. Their intellectual energy is thereby amplified in many dimensions to the utmost by the mechanism of control. The collective stupidity of research technicians is not simply the absence or regression of intellectual capacities, but an overgrowth of the capacity of thought itself, which eats away at the latter with its own energy.*

285   On consciousness, Searle (2002:7), emphasised, *by consciousness I simply mean those subjective states of sentience or awareness that begin when one awakes in the morning from a dreamless sleep and continues throughout the day until one goes to sleep at night, or falls into a coma, or dies, or otherwise becomes, as one would say, unconscious.*

286   The presented choice between repressive and emancipatory scientific paradigms has already been taken once research is located in a specific area. Unconsciously, repressive structures are represented in repressive research and teaching programmes. According to Hyman (1989:17) today's *students...cannot avoid a similar choice* when determining to enter into an education programme that pretends to be technical, neutral and value-free while in reality representing nothing more than an enhancement of repressive structures. Albert (2006:95) has commented on this as: the aim of public education is not to spread enlightenment at all; it is simply to reduce as many individuals as possible to the same safe level, to breed and train a standardised citizenry, to put down dissent and originality. That is its aim...whatever the pretensions of politicians, pedagogues and other such mountebanks, and that is its aim everywhere else.

287   Eagleton (1994:200) notes on the process of depoliticalisation as follows, *the depoliticalisation of the mass of the population, which is legitimated through technocratic consciousness, is at the same time men's self-objectification in categories equally of both purpose-rational action and adaptive behaviour.* In other words, subscribing to technocratic mindset leads to self-objectification. It turns humans into objects of power and they do so by themselves. Step by step we turn ourselves into objects of power, a power that governs us.

288   In the 5th century a group of teachers, known as *Sophists* gained a reputation for deceitful or fallacious reasoning *making the worst case appear better* (Plato). They conceived the term *sophistry*. Similarly Orwell's *doublespeak* refers to the use of ambiguous or evasive language. Such euphemisms relate to offensive terms substituted for inoffensive ones. No one gets fired or laid-off. Instead companies downsize or right-size – much in the same way as *garbage collectors* are now *sanitation engineers. Salespersons* are *clothing consultants.* A dump for radioactive rubbish from nuclear power stations is no more than a *deposit park. Killing people* in war has become *collateral damage.*

289   *It is hardly surprising that despite their announced allegiance to unrestricted free trade many organisations in all sectors today are busy trying to avoid competition – by creating strategic alliances with other organisations, thus redefining some competitors as collaborators* (Cheney & Carroll 1997:620). Similar arguments can be found in Galbraith's work on *American Capitalism* (1952) and *A Theory of Price Control* (1952a). While today's large corporations seek to eliminate the market, the free market is – apart from being *the best* – not the only way to provide goods as Harford (2006:68–69) has shown. He argues that *yet any modern*

democracy provides goods outside the market system, and looking at the way such goods are provided gives us a hint of the strengths and weaknesses of markets. Think of your friendly local police force, which is paid for by a non-market system of taxation...government-provided schooling is another example of a non-market service that many of us use... the non-market system has the cosy advantage of concealing the fact that the poor don't get the same quality of education than the rich do.

290   Quoted from Marcuse (1966:194). If one accepts Gusfield's (1980:xi) definition of *propaganda* as *the making of deliberately one-sided statements to a mass audience* then managerial language at workplaces is not propaganda as they hardly address a *mass audience*. But they may still be *deliberately one-sided*. However, in contrast to political propaganda, *bureaucratic propaganda* is seen as being more specifically targeted. The target audience of *bureaucratic* propaganda is an individual, a group, or a specifically targeted segment such as workers in a company. Unlike political propaganda, which focuses on a mass audience to gain support, *bureaucratic* propaganda may be aimed at a specific group influencing their decision-making capacity (cf. Altheide & Johnson 1980:14).

291   On the reproductive powers of society, Adorno (1944:45) notes, *the mechanical processes of reproduction have developed independently of what is reproduced and have become autonomous.*

292   A most informative article on post-modernism is *The Sokal Controversy* by Thompson (2004:57).

293   As American labour writer John Dunlop (1958) has once famously pointed out in his work on IR systems.

294   The so-called *linguistic turn* that can be found in many social science areas has a long history as it links to the role of communication in understanding the world. *The origins of critical communication theory can be traced back to Plato's conception of Socratic dialectic as a method of attaining truth in the give and take of disputative interaction by asking questions that provoke critical reflection upon the contradictions that come to light in the process* (Craig 1999:146).

295   Kochan, Katz & McKersie (1986:1) has developed this widely accepted definition of work. He restated his original definition of IR at the Berlin World IR Congress in September 2003, personal memo.

296   Similarly, a reductionist view tends to reduce communication in labour-management relationships to *voice*. However, the communicative content in a labour-management relationship goes far beyond the somewhat simplistic issue of *voice*.

297   Originally, the first craft workshops that ended feudalist peasant work showed more features similar to craft-based manufacturing or early batch production industries than today's service industry settings. As with these early industrial settings new forms of social work relations appeared, the term *industry* has been linked to the term *relations* as the appropriate way to describe relations at work. During the first half of the 20th century – the height of industrial work – the term industrial was even more appropriate to describe what happened in non-farming work settings. Even though today's work is seen as service industry, it still shows strong signs of being industrially organised.

298   Even though the factory system has originated in England, the oldest continuously operating company is supposed to be the one of the *Weihenstephan* Brewery founded in Germany in the year 1040. Despite numerous textbook entries and often somewhat romanticised, modern factories have almost no resemblance to a craft shop of the 11th century. However, it serves as a managerial metaphor portraying an idyllic and romantic past of managerialism

and firms. In sharp contrast to such a romanticised past, today's firms are *pro-ductive monsters* [with] *individuals incapable of any independent act, stunted and crippled, governed by an entirely military discipline – in short, factories produced the opposite on the ideal proletarian able to master a totality of productive forces and find complete personal fulfilment in no longer restricted self-activity* (Gorz 1982:27). Such disciplinary acts took on form of beatings, rape, child-labour, monetary fines, etc. All this has been designed to create an *organisational life [that] requires a certain degree of subordination…departing from Kant's dictum never to treat people as a means but rather as ends only* (Cheney & Carroll 1997:596).

299 On authority, Richard Sennett (1980:18, 19) emphasised, *in English the root of authority is author. The connotation is that authority involves something productive. Yet the word authoritarian is used to describe a person or system that is repressive. Of authority it may be said in the most general way it is an attempt to interpret the conditions of power, to give the conditions of control and influence a meaning by defining an image of strength.*

300 Despite the common use of the term *management revolution*, management is not only anti-revolutionary but also has developed rather slowly over the past 200 years. The development of management was evolutionary rather than revolutionary.

301 More often than not, art is no more than pre-fabricated, mass manufactured, standard-designer, and shopping centre art to be hung up in equally standard-ised boardrooms or bleak corridors of large corporations, often put there to impress respective clients rather than as a contribution of art. Such art is boring, system-conforming, industrially manufactured, and essentially dead. It is an expression of industrialism rather than art that is alive.

302 According to Chomsky (1994:2) *there was only contempt for what Adam Smith called the vile maxim of the masters of mankind, all for ourselves, and nothing for other people.* Smith did not foresee we are *not free people who have a right to dignity and independence but* [that we are] *atoms of consumption who sell* [ourselves] *on the labour market, at least if we're lucky.*

303 According to Marcuse (1996:88): *in the same way the destruction of resources and the proliferation of waste demonstrates its opulence and the high level of well-being, the community is too well off to care!*

304 Dialectic (Greek) is seen as an exchange of *proposition* (thesis) and *counter-proposition* (anti-thesis) resulting in a *synthesis* of the opposing assertions. It is related to how we can perceive the world (epistemology) as an assertion of the interconnected, contradictory, and dynamic nature of the world outside our perceptions (ontology). See Hegel's project to take contradictions and tensions and interpret them as part of a comprehensive, evolving, rational unit that operates in different contexts.

305 This is supported by the relatively high viewing times of television showing predominantly TV programmes, game shows, movies, etc. produced by large corporations. A high level of daily TV viewing has been noted in all industrial and increasingly in developing countries.

306 Apart from the work domain, democracy in the public domain has not fulfilled most of the promises as made by the bourgeoisie. If democracy means self-government of free people, with justice for all, then the realisation of democracy would presuppose abolition of the existing pseudo-democracy. Hence under corporate capitalism, any fight for true democracy tends to assume anti-democratic forms as such fights are directed against the prevailing and ritualised forms of mass democracy. Such fights can only be fought from

without and not from within. System-integrative forces would prevent any success that is organised inside the system. On the other hand, the fight for democracy has led to an absurd situation. In established democracies the only sanctioned forum for non-violent – but largely cosmetic – options for changes are the ones that are limited to democracy. From an internal viewpoint democracy, as it appears, needs to be defended against all attempts to restrict democratic freedom. On the other hand, the preservation of current ritualised and quasi-mass democracy also preserves the status quo and along with it the containment of substantial change. This is further enhanced via a *democracy=capitalism* link. *The conscious and intelligent manipulation of the organised habits and opinions of the masses* [is the] *engineering of consent* [it] *is the very essence of the democratic process* (Chomsky 1997:37; cf. Canfora 2006).

307　As George Orwell put it in *1984* (1949:37), *to repudiate morality while laying claim to it*, to believe that democracy is only possible in society not at work is part of the standard fare of managerial ideology (see further details in Deetz 1992).

308　Democracy depends upon plain language and common understanding. The removal of democracy from the work domain allows management to reshape language. Today, language is deliberately ambiguous. It has removed meaning from language. It obscures language. It makes language incomprehensible and meaningless. Linguistically it erodes the trust needed for democracy to become operative. The depletion of the language of democracy becomes established as non-democratic forms of managerialism govern people's existence at work and at home.

309　There is hardly a better illustration of the war and peace situation than in Brecht's *Mother Courage.*

310　These mercenaries banded together and formed strong bonds in groups of ex-soldiers. They were bound together with a strap that holds an axe in the Italian *fasci* movement of mercenaries and ex-soldiers. See: http://www.fasciitaliani.it/& http://en.wikipedia.org/wiki/Fascism; Luca de Caprariis' (2000), Fascism for Export'? The Rise and Eclipse of the Fasci Italiani all'Estero, *Journal of Contemporary History*, vol. 35, no. 2, pp. 151–183.

311　Quoted from Singer (2004:10). The military work link has also been expressed in the *Communist Manifesto* (1848) stating *masses of labourers, crowded into the factory, are organised like soldiers. As privates of the industrial army they are placed under the command of a perfect hierarchy of officers and sergeants* (Canfora 2006:71). Today, this *command of a perfect hierarchy* is called Human Resource Management and their *officers and sergeants* are called HR managers. On the training of soldiers in Prussia, *Karl Liebknecht* (Canfora 2006:110) commended, *recruits are drugged, confused, flattered, bribed, pressed, locked up, disciplined and beaten. Thus grain upon grain is missed and kneaded to serve as mortar for the great edifice of the army, stone added to stone, calculated to form a fortress against revolution.*

312　The transfer of military concepts to the world of business includes an establishment of *deontic* powers relating duties and obligations to ethical concepts. Once derived from the military these ethical duties were transferred to business and workers just as soldiers before that were bound ethically to serve their masters. The point of having *deontic* powers at work is to regulate human relations between workers. Once human behaviour is secured in categories of deontic power, management is able to impose rights, responsibilities, obligations, duties, privileges, entitlements, penalties, authorisations, permissions, and others onto workers.

313 The military-management-language link existed in medieval times as it does today. Following the 2003 Iraq war and subsequent occupation, torture was *outsourced* [a management term!], known as *rendition* when captured victims were secretly relocated for torture. Whether rendered or not, torture via sleep deprivation was labelled *sleep management*, of course. *Management* used to mean the correct handling of affairs. However, enforced sleep deprivation induces severe cognitive impairment. A truer description would be sleep *mismanagement*. But who were the people being tortured? They were *like dogs*. And so threatening to attack them with dogs seemed quite appropriate. They were the raw material for *Human Exploitation Teams*. They were *human resources* to be exploited. They were enemy combatants (Poole 2006:173, 175).

314 Under a US$300m contract by the US army in Iraq, Tim Spicer's mercenaries or hired killers are now called *private security companies* (Monbiot 2005:15).

315 *Captains of industry* relate to captains of battleships and so employees can be fired like guns, cannons, or cannon fodder. After all *war is business* as usual.

316 One of the great illusions of our era is the *power grows out of the barrel. In fact power grows out of organisations, i.e. the systematic arrangements of status-functions. And in such organisations the unfortunate person with a gun is likely to be among the least powerful and the most exposed to danger. The real power resides with the person who sits at a desk and makes noises through his or her mouth and marks on paper. Such people typically have no weapons other than at most, a ceremonial pistol and a sword for dress occasions* (Searle 1996:117–118).

317 The capital-management-labour separation has been discussed by Marglin (1974). To operate such a capital-management-labour relationship elaborate configurations have been set up. This evolves around institutional structures by way of the collective imposition of managerial status function on top of social relations at work. The clearest indicator of the existence of such status function on top of social relations is to be found in a codification of rules by management. However, on the downside, when managerial institutions are primarily maintained by habits, they are in danger of collapsing easily when workers lose confidence in the managerial currency or cease to recognise management as management. Hence, the institution of management is under constant demand to justify their existence in order not to be exposed to the danger of being based purely on habits. One of management's preferred methods to maintain their status function is the use of power. This is enshrined in institutional facts. According to Searle (1996:94) *the structure of institutional facts is a structure of power relations.*

318 As much as managers can be defined simply as *servants of power* (Baritz 1960), managerialism reaches beyond that as it takes on an ideological content. The servants of power have managed to transfer their service into an all-inclusive ideology.

319 Knowledge for managers as well as for politicians is ever since US Secretary of Defence, Donald Rumsfeld, a dodgy concept. Rumsfeld said, *as we know, there are not known knowns. There are things we know. We also know there are known unknowns. That is to say we know there are some things we do not know. But there are also unknown unknowns, the ones we don't know we don't know* (quoted in Watson 2003:45).

320 Even with the transformation of management into the ideology of managerialism, managerial ideology still – after more than 100 years – seeks to entice worker's love for work. In 1883, Lafargue correctly described this. *A strange delusion possesses the working classes of the nations where capitalist civilisation*

hold its sway. The delusion drags in its train the individual and social woes, which for two centuries have tortured sad humanity. This delusion is the love for work, the furious passion for work pushed even to the exhaustion of the vital force of the individual and his progeny.

321 Watson (2003:2) writes that *marketing, for instance, has no particular concern with truth. Management concerns are relatively narrow – relatively. This alone makes marketing and managerial language less than ideal for a democracy or a college.* Whether selling for a college, selling democracy, or simply selling meat, the actual form of marketing comes down to the sales representative. On this, Barry (2006) comments *there is something wrong with the kind of person who becomes a sales rep. or if not, there is something wrong after six months. It isn't just the sales reps who are turned into meat in this dehumanised environment.*

322 Harford (2006:71) has applied the opposite of efficiency, i.e. inefficiency to economics as subjected closely related to managerialism. He argues, *remember that when economists say the economy is inefficient, they mean that there's a way to make somebody better off without harming anybody else. While the perfectly competitive market is perfectly efficient, efficiency is not enough to ensure a fair society, or even a society in which we would want to live. After all, it is efficient if Bill Gates has all the money and everybody else starves to death...because there is no way to make anybody better off without making Bill Gates worse off. We need something more than efficiency.*

323 Managerialism has found that Maslow's hierarchy of needs (1943) has been particularly helpful in support of the money and power code. Higher order needs are: self-actualisation, self-esteem, and social acceptance, and lower order needs are safety and security and basic physiological needs. Somewhat similar to workplaces, *Maslow's starting for the hierarchy of needs was in fact research on captive primates with regard to dominance behaviour [with an interest in] reproductive strategies of female primates. Based on this somewhat problematic study, then, Maslow concluded that the apes that were less aggressive and most relaxed about their dominance (and consequently the most worthy of their positions) had greater confidence in themselves. He carried his idea through into research on sexuality, which focused on women and what he called 'dominance-feeling' (later self-esteem)...* (Brewis & Linstead 2004:71). What can be seen is the usefulness of Maslow's idea for managerialism as it relates *to captive primates with regard to dominance* and to workplace *captivity* of humans with regard to *dominance* by management. Just as apes, humans at work should feel *less aggressive and most relaxed about their dominance.* This can be achieved by making them believe that they are *the most worthy of their positions.* Consequently, workers should not *feel* managerial *dominance.* This can be achieved by converting Maslow's *dominance-feeling* into the feeling of *self-esteem.* It appears almost self-evident that studies on apes in captivity should feature in most books on organisational studies, management, and HRM. Above that, Maslow's hierarchy of needs narrows human needs as it excludes, for example, the enjoyment of warm personal relationships and being free to peruse one's project without interference by others. These are human – but unfortunately management unsupportive – needs and therefore they are not mentioned in textbooks.

324 In his novel *Company*, Max Barry (2006) describes an organisation as follows: *the organisation bends and twists human characters...sociopaths [people with signs of social pathologies] are often the most successful at the game.*

325 Morality is seen in accordance of Kohlberg's (1971, 1981, 1984) morality model of: 1. punishment and obedience orientation, 2. instrumental relativist

orientation, 3. interpersonal concordance or 'good boy-nice girl' orientation, 4. law and order orientation, 5. social-contract legalistic orientation, and 6. universal ethical principle orientation.

326   John Locke (1689a, b) argued that labour not only is the origin of *property* but also puts the difference of value on everything. He considered labour important enough to account for nine-tenths, perhaps even ninety-nine hundredth, of the value of good, the rest being contributed by nature.

327   *In a free and democratic society*, Chomsky (1994:7) once wrote, [...] workers should be the master of their own industrial fate, not tools rented by employers.

328   See: Wing (1837), Mayo (1945), Habermas (1979:139) and Marcuse (1966:157) described the great transformation from feudalism to capitalism: *the hand-mill produces a society of feudal lords, the steam mill a society of industrial capitalists.* While American industry writer Sinclair wrote *it was as if mankind's history could be divided into two periods: before and after the invention of the steam engine. The achievements of civilisation are now being measured according to speed, size and energy* (Shenhav 1999:47).

329   As George Orwell (1949:198) put it in *1984, in the long run, a hierarchical society was only possible on a basis of poverty and ignorance.* As our present society and work arrangement are still hierarchical, Thompson's (2003:359) claim of *the substitution of hierarchies with networks* remains illusive.

330   See: Barry et al. (2001), Barratt (2003), Pfeffer & Fong (2004), Starkey et al. (2004),

331   The *Wannsee* Conference was the location where Eichmann and the Nazis planned the systematic and industrial destruction of whole sets of people.

332   See: (Habermas 1997a:168). Unfortunately, even the most developed stream of *Labour Process Theory* inside IR has been directed mostly towards *control* rather than on domination and resistance. It has never been directed towards *communicatively* guided resistance.

333   From *Orwell's novel 1948, written in 1948 and named in the same year as 1984. First published in 1949.*

334   The right to sanction labour is closely linked to the right to manage which derived from the right to own and the right to property: Property rights = sanction rights. *But the formulation is misleading. Property has no rights. In both principle and practice, the phrase 'right of property' means the right to property, typically material property, a personal right which must be privileged over all others, and is crucially different from others in that one person's possession of such rights deprives another of them. Person is broadly defined to include any individual, branch, partnership, associated group, association, estate, trust, corporation or other organisation. Corporations, which previously had been considered artificial entities with no rights, were accorded all the rights of persons, and far more, since they are 'immortal persons', and persons of extraordinary wealth and power* (Chomsky 1997:39).

335   Albert (2006:94) has described this as follows: *owners can't oversee their wide-reaching assets without assistance. The low number of owners and the large requirements of control propel the creation of an intermediate coordinator class.* The coordinator class has been able to define the corporate division of labour because they monopolise all powers at work. They also dominate daily decision-making. *The requisites of legitimising control by managers and other coordinator class members ensures that this class monopolises advanced training, skills, and knowledge – as well as the confidence that accompanies these. If an economy has 2 per cent of its members ruling its outcomes through their ownership of property,*

18–20 per cent administering and defining economic outcomes due to monopolising circumstances, and 80 per cent obeying due to doing only rote tasks, then each year's new recruits to the economy arriving from the educational system must be prepared to occupy their designated slot in one of these three classes.

336 Any representation of the communicative relationship between labour and management in a vertical version represents a managerial view. This is the *what is* management perspective. Seen from Kant's *what ought to be* perspective, a horizontal representation of a communicative labour-management relationship represents Kant's utopian *what ought to be* view. The horizontal view should not represent the ideology of managerialism as it often tends to misrepresent reality as a horizontal *partnership* between management and *associates* (in *Newspeak* terms). Managerialism, like all ideologies, contains some relationship to the true state of affairs. If it did not, it would cease to be an ideology.

337 The term *human resource management* (HRM) and especially the term *human resources* (HR) carries connotation of natural resources. This is a clear expression of Poole's (2006) *Unspeak* concept. Under *Unspeak everything in the natural world is there to be used by man, and is valuable only to the extent that it fulfils a place in the human economy* (Poole 2006:64). HRM does that by converting people into human resources (in Nazi-terms: *Menschenmaterial*) to fulfil that.

338 Surprisingly, publications in the area of organisational behaviour often carry the title *Organisational Behaviour* indicating that there must be some sort of organisational *mis*-behaviour in order to justify these titles. Maybe humans do not enter as willingly and as freely into organisations as managerialism tries to make us believe.

339 The relationship between size, organisational form, and democracy has been shown by Piven & Cloward (1971); see also Canfora (2006).

340 Walsh et al. (2006:95) have expressed this clearly in their book on *The Measurement and Management of Strategic Change – A guide to Enterprise Performance Management.*

341 According to Gadamer (1976:16), *the mechanical, industrial world is expanding within the life of the individual as a sort of sphere of technical perfection. When we hear modern lovers talking to each other, we often wonder if they are communicating with words or with advertising labels and technical terms from the sign language of the modern industrial world. It is inevitable that the levelled life-forms of the industrial age also affect language, and in fact the impoverishment of the vocabulary of language is making enormous progress, thus bringing about an approximation of language to a technical sign-system. Levelling tendencies of this kind are irresistible.*

342 Commodity fetishism is seen here in the Marxist understanding, not the Freudian sense. It relates to use- versus exchange value describing an overemphasis on exchange value when goods or commodities become purely exchange concepts without any real use.

343 On leadership, Watson (2003:32) notes, *under a general heading of, say, Leadership, we see columns and dot points. One column is headed Strategies and the other Results. Under Leadership we get windy summaries of ambitions.* While those who are *led*, those who are categories as *followers* are almost completely absent. On the other hand, those leaders who are supposed to lead us, take a relatively large slice of the cake called managerial literature. A quick search of the internet-journal databank for business (http://ejournals.ebsco.com) produced a list of *495* articles on *leadership* and 16 on *follower – a* 30:1 relation.

344 The creation of management is not a natural process but a social process (Marglin 1974; cf. Albert 2006:94,138ff.). Harding (2003:211) sees management as *a social construction that has rendered us incapable of dreaming of other ways of running the organisation in which we belong.* It is the triumph of TINA: there is no alternative.

345 Misunderstandings are contextually based because meanings change as symbols move from one context (domain a) to another context (domain b). Hence specific terms in the world of work can change meaning as they move from a labour domain through a communicative exchange domain into a management domain.

346 Until today, an article by Kerr, Dunlop, Harbison, and Myers in 1960 on *Industrialism and Industrial Man*, published by the International Labour Organisation's journal *International Labour Review* (vol. 135, no. 3–4, reprinted 36 years in 1996) remains one of the prime discussions on those who manage and those who are managed. See also: Marglin's (1974) *What do bosses do?* cf. Parker (2002), Watson (2003), Poole (2006).

347 There is virtually no modern textbook or modern management course taught at business schools around the world that does not have Taylor as a core concept.

348 Even though management can be seen as covering four functions: accounting and finance, marketing, operations management, and HRM, it is the human side that makes to whole enterprise work.

349 While management studies' critical wing of *Critical Management Studies* (CMS) may be an established part of general management studies, *CMS is predisposed to problematise everything and resolve nothing* (Thompson 2004:59). However, CMS appears to utilise some elements of Critical Theory to achieve some critical reflection on the field without questioning the underlying assumptions such as management's instrumental rationality expressed in strategic communication directed towards success, efficiency. At the same time CMS neglects possibilities for communicative action directed towards meaning and truth. CMS misses that managerial communication is not directed towards the truth of a *BMW* or a *McDonald's Big Mac* but how to sell it. CMS assists management in such discussion without challenging the meaning and truth of the managerial system (cf. Thompson 2004:65 on Adler's question to the US CMS' internet list).

350 The primary text on IR is Kochan, Katz and McKersie's (1986) *Transformation of American Industrial Relations*. While the book (1986:13) debates strategic choice, it is not specifically written as a strategic book. Nevertheless, it adds three vertical levels to Dunlop's *Industrial Relations Systems* (1958). The core is a threefold matrix consisting of three actors operating at three levels, rather than a systematic application of strategy.

351 Of course, in the management of business, the management of economic expansion, and the management of war substantial massacres were involved in conquering South America, colonising Africa and Asia, in battles over resources ranging from gold and silver to copper and eventually to oil.

352 Articles such as Kroll, Toombs, and Wright's *Napoleon's tragic march home from Moscow: Lessons in hubris* (2000) and Pringle and Kroll's *Why Trafalgar was won before it was fought: Lessons from resource-based theory* (1997) – published in the American Journal Academy of Management Executive – diminish border-crossings between military and management (Hyman 1987:28; Morgan 1993:14). The military-management link has clearly been expressed by

Fiedler's (1996:241) article for the 40th anniversary of the *Administrative Science Quarterly*: *brilliant military leaders have won battles against superior forces and managers have turned failing organisations around.*

353   See: Engels (1874), Weber (1947), Fayol (1949), Adorno et al. (1964), Marglin (1974:63).

354   Simon's *Administrative Behaviour* (1965:22–26) details the link between management and military and the relevance of *unity of command* for management and military.

355   Simon and Bernard's book (1965:154–156) is entitled *Administrative Behaviour – A study of decision-making processes in administrative organisations.*

356   See Morgan (1993).

357   See Zengotita (2005). A little cross on a paper every four years allows ordinary members of societies the bare minimum of participation in their own domestication. It maintains the illusion that the normal person can exercise some sort of influence over public affairs neatly separated from the private business domain which operates largely untouched by events in the political domain. See also Albert (2006:108ff) and Habermas (2006).

358   Quoted from Weber (1924:21) and Marcuse (1968:208).

359   The term *executive* in *CEO* dates back to *the 17th century, it had denoted the part of government – the executive branch – concerned with carrying out the law. The application of the word to employees of businesses, dating only from the early 20th century might thus have been an attempt to cloak commerce in a halo of associations with justice, law, and proper government* (Poole 2006:207). Today, the use of the term *corporate governance* carries similar connotations with similar ideologies attached to it.

360   Textbook writers are no more than minor writers. Nobel Prize laureate *Alexander Solzhenitsyn* once said, *a great writer is, so to speak, a second government in his country. And for that reason no regime has ever loved great writers, only minor ones* (Alexander Solzhenitsyn's *The First Circle*, quoted from Watson 2003:137). If Alexander Solzhenitsyn's words are transferred to management and to corporations, then no regime based on managerialism has ever loved great writers, only minor ones!

361   Just *consider the language of lending money. Credit, which means credibility, trustworthiness, or moral praiseworthiness (from Latin credere, to believe), was hijacked to mean either lending money or your bank. 'Interest', meanwhile, which originally meant either intellectual curiosity or a legal or moral claim to something, became the mechanism by which money breeds money* (Poole 2006:205).

362   Already Marx saw the similarities between real war and the market-share war (Marx 1848).

363   Long before management and managerialism came to flourish, French philosopher *Voltaire* remarked that *everything conspires to corrupt a language, merchants introduce into conversations their business terms* (http://history.hanover.edu/texts/voltaire/vollangu.html). Just like an attorney, physician, or president, manager names a status with a function imposed on it via collective intentionality.

364   The managerial sub-division of managing people has already re-invented itself during a conversion from Personnel Management to Human Resource Management. With new words come new meanings. Orwell expressed this (1949:53) as *we're getting the language into its final shape – the shape it's going to have when nobody speaks anything else. You think, I dare say, that our chief job is inventing words.* When nobody speaks any longer of capital and labour, the language of HRM has succeeded in annihilating all capital-labour contradictions. The end

result of all of this is, again, expressed by Orwell (1949:55), *in the end, we shall make thoughtcrime [the crime to see the world of work as a contradiction of interest between labour and capital] literally impossible, because there will be no words in which to express it.* Orwell (1949:311) closes *1984* summarising the final goal of HRM: *but it was all right, everything was all right, the struggle was finished. He had won the victory over himself. He loved Big Brother.*

365   As Holocaust-Administrator and German Nazi Eichmann put it, *I was just following orders* (Parker 2002:17; Bauman 1989).

366   Consequently, the specialisation and introduction of experts trained in functionalism into managerial curriculum reflects a conversion of ethical social science into managerialism when *academically respectable disciplines [were converted into] management and business more comparable to trades, like plumbing* (Grey & Willmott 2005:9).

367   Derived from *burel*, the coarse cloth that might cover a desk and later from *bureau*, the desk or *bureaucracy* (English), *burocrazia* (Italian) and *Bürokratie* (German). Bureaucracy's true *inventor* Vinvent de Gourney (1764) saw bureaucracy as an illness (Parker 2002:18).

368   An historic conjuncture between early Greek *rule* and French *bureau* resides Italian military thinker *Machiavelli's skill in using information for practical purposes. This was institutionalised and accepted as common sense by officials and bureaucrats within two centuries* (Altheide & Johnson 1980:6).

369   See: Foucault (1994), Burawoy (1979), Marcuse (1966), and Whyte (1961).

370   While Orwell (1949:214) saw *the possibility of enforcing not only complete obedience to the will of the Sate, but complete uniformity of opinion on all subjects (that) now existed for the first time*, the state is much less involved in this in the 21st century as corporate mass media have taken over to fulfil Orwell's predictions.

371   *The terrible phrases (and realities of) 'engineers of the soul', 'head shrinkers', scientific management', 'science of consumption', epitomise (in a miserable form) the progressing rationalisation of the irrational, of the 'spiritual' – the denial of the idealistic culture* (Marcuse 1966:239).

372   The role of bureaucracy in society and management has been described as bureaucratic propaganda by Altheide & Johnson (1980:5). They see bureaucratic propaganda at work when *a report produced by an organisation for evaluation and other practical purposes is targeted for individuals, committees, or publics who are unaware of its promotive character and the editing processes that shaped the report.*

373   Even for unconscious HRM-administrators the seductive quality of the term *human* in an often totally administered, bureaucratised, and rather inhuman work process creates the appearance of being a human and natural activity when in reality it is rather the opposite.

374   See: Galbraith's *American Capitalism* (1952) and *The Affluent Society* (1958).

375   In sharp contrast to the often claimed *abstract* thinking of philosophers and academics, Hegel argued in his *Who Thinks Abstractly*, that the opposite is the case. It is not the philosopher, the academic, etc. who thinks abstractly but the ordinary bureaucrat or the ordinary manager, the person on the street or in a managerial office. A person who uses concepts as fixed and unchangeable givens without any context thinks abstractly. It is the philosopher or the critical academic who thinks concretely because they go beyond the limits of everyday concepts and understand their larger context.

376   When workers use managerial language they also use managerial rules, concepts, and ideas that govern the use of this language. When actually playing

the game of managerial language to some extent, this *playing* turns workers into *being played* (with). In the managerial game, workers are not players but *being played* (with!) as the rules of the managerial language governs their *play*. But the managerial rules not only govern the use of language, they also govern the social behaviour of workers. Almost self-evidently, Krizan et al.'s (2005:651) textbook on business communication does not even list the word *strike* in its index. Obviously, social actions such as *strikes* should not even enter into a game played by management. Searle (1996:139) has described what occurs inside such language games. He emphasised: *so when the agent, for example, produces an English sentence, the unconscious internalisation of the rules is actually acting causally to produce that particular syntactic structure.* By playing the managerial language game, workers produce *English sentences and unconsciously internalise* managerial *rules.* In the world of business communication textbooks this means that such internalised sentences should not include terms like *strike.* All of this carries clear connotations of George Orwell's *Department of Word-Elimination resulting in thought elimination!*

377 However, military leaders have not all be in their positions solely because of rational-legal, i.e. hierarchically established leadership. Some also had charismatic authority, usually, those who have sacrificed thousands, if not millions, of human lives and have created uncountable human misery.

378 As Watson (2003:4) commented on *managerial cults or fashions* (Abrahamson 1996) *economic rationalism; dope-smoking; Knowledge Management – wherever cults exist the language inclines to the arcane or inscrutable.*

379 One should keep in mind that the real subject of playing is the game itself as a game creates its own place, movements, aims and rules cut off from the real world. *All playing is, in fact, a being played* (Radford 2005:170). While eclipsing the *being played* part, one of the most prominent theories behind playing is conveniently called *game theory.* Game theory assumes that bargainers are rational and able to calculate the best outcome from available information; the rules of the game are known in advance and remain fixed throughout the game; each player has perfect knowledge of alternative outcomes and values attached to these outcomes; contextual and outside influences do not affect the model and perceptions and expectations remain fixed throughout the game. In reality, however, these conditions hardly ever exist, even less so inside the world of work.

380 According to Mendieta (2002:142) *no one is deluded about the utopian promised by science as technology, bureaucracy as modernisation. Auschwitz, Hiroshima, and the gulags have rendered both suspect. Still, the question of the difficulty and necessity of an ethics for our modern societies remains a pressing issue.* The use of modern techniques in the gulags and Holocausts has been value-free. Some of the worst expressions of inhumanity have been created through the use of modern science and modern organisational methods applied without ethics (i.e. value-free) as an extreme aberration of ethics (Bauman 1989). This unsolved problem exists, often unquestioned, until today.

381 A study of engineering ideology serves to show how such an ideology has constructed meaning in the service of power and is able to sustain work relations of domination. Such ideological phenomena are only meaningful constructs insofar as they are able to create, service, maintain, and protect established forms of managerial domination in the domain of work.

382 According to Searle (1969:6), *synonymy is defined as: two words are synonymous if and only if they have the same meaning.*

383 *Put bluntly, business schools located in established universities which jealously guard their hard-won reputation and independence cannot simply appoint [management] consultants or [management] gurus as professors, even though it might be the wish of some corporate patrons and students to do precisely that. Instead, tenured staff is required to have a modicum of academic respectability* (Grey & Willmott 2005:7).

384 *Effectiveness* can be seen as a managerial action that has a desired effect while *efficiency* relates managerial action as a ratio of useful work performed to the total energy expended.

385 Institutions such as management are *institutions not worn out by continued use, but each use of the institution is in a sense a renewal of that institution. Cars and shirts wear out as we use them but the constant use renews and strengthens institutions such as marriage, property, universities* (Searle 1996:57).

386 One can await the time when managerial science is coined as *sound science* to create the appearance of a scientific programme that is beyond question, that according *Unspeak* (Poole 2006), can't be challenged as all challenging science would be un-sound science.

387 Sanctions such as differential rewards backed by force that restrict freedom are no longer required. *An increase in wages, in Marx's phrase, would be nothing more than a better remuneration of slaves, and would not restore, either to the worker or to the work, their human significances and worth* (Chomsky 1971:35). In other words, the acceptance and internalisation of wages and the wage system, not the level of wages, makes the slave.

388 In accordance with self-censorship, there are also forms of (self)-punishments in academic circles. A *why* and *what* to teach has long been overtaken by managerialism via learning achievements and the like. Only if an academic surrenders critical thought to the functionality of managerialism he/she has a carrier in academia. Only those management *scientists* (sic!) who *produce* journal articles conforming to the confines of a certain body of knowledge are allowed to publish in so-called *high quality* and *respected* journals. Academic careers are all too often made dependent on such publications. This is a quantity not a quality game. Furthermore, submitted articles are checked by a highly selective group of peers to ensure an article confirms to a restrained and well-defined body of knowledge. This process operates as an internalised *Index Librorum Prohibitorum* (the index of forbidden books).

389 On the *irrationality of rationality*, Marcuse (1968:207) wrote, *in the unfolding of capitalist rationality, irrationality becomes reason: reason as frantic development of productivity, conquest of nature, enlargement of the mass of good (and their accessibility of broad strata of the population); irrational because higher productivity, domination of nature, and social wealth become destructive forces.*

390 Systematisation is one of the clearest expressions of a capitalist order. It turns everything into a system or into a standard. The move to standardise everything was itself turned into a standard movement. *The general claim of the movement was that the adoption of universal standards would result in technical predictability, and would provide greater control over irregularities, anomalies, and uncertainties. This movement, which focused initially on technical matters, spilled over eventually to human affairs, social institutions, and the design of government bureaucracy* (Shenhav 1999:24, 49; cf. Bolinger 1968:111)).

391 A cybernetic model of work operates like a standard kitchen refrigerator. It checks temperatures, cools until a certain temperature is reached, stops cooling, measures temperatures and starts all over again. All this depends on

system demands. It is a never-ending system that demands each part work in favour of the system. At work such system of cybernetic engineering demands extreme conformity. As system complexity increases, demands for conformity increase as well.

392 Marcuse (1966:193) saw myths as primitive and immature thoughts that have been invalidated during the process of rational civilisation. Separating myths from reality has almost been as important as separating dreams and fictions from reality, science, and technology.

393 George Orwell's words in *1984* (1949:197) might sum up the false image of engineering ideology, *if the machine were used deliberately for that end, hunger, overwork, dirt, illiteracy and disease could be eliminated within a few generations*. Neither has been the case. Management, technology and the machine narrative of engineering solution have failed to deliver humanity ever since it was invented as an ideology. The so-called *Green Revolution* as a bio-technical solution to feed the world has failed, as has the promise of genetically modified foods.

394 Non-measurable entities such as *happiness* (Mander 2001; Hamilton 2003; Hamilton & Denniss 2005) are excluded.

395 *Not long ago the word customer was generally understood – with a few variations – to mean purchasers or clients, people who took their custom to a shop or some other kind of commercial establishment. Now libraries and universities have customers, just like the CIA and McDonalds. Do not be surprised if one day you hear an American general talk of enemy customers* (Watson 2003:145).

396 Feenberg (1988:230, 235) has enhanced Offe's (1988:216ff.) earlier critique through three elements that depict technology's fundamental bias towards domination (cf. Feenberg 2002, 2004).

397 As technologies and managerialism increase, *the declining labour power in the productive process means a decline in political power of the opposition* (Marcuse 1966:40; cf. Parker 2002:189).

398 Feenberg (1988:231) sees bias in two ways: a) as a result from applying different standards to individuals where they ought properly to be judged by the same standard and b) in applying the same standard to individuals under conditions that favour unfairly at the expense of others.

399 While *technology* consists of socially constructed relationships in an established society expressed in the mode of production, *techniques* can be seen in terms of a technical apparatus inside productive forces of such a society. Overall, the technical shroud covers the brute presence and the operation of the class interest in the modern corporation. When serving the class interests such a belief in techniques results in the production of technocrats. Those *who want us to believe that life is a collection of key issues that can be strategically managed into favourable outcomes* (Watson 2003:172) are the technocrats of an Orwellian future.

400 Apart from horizontal and vertical division of labour, capitalism relies on the third division of labour, the sexual division of labour. It forces women into a double exploitation of paid and unpaid work necessary in the area of reproduction to allow necessary system survival elements (Agger 1998:99ff.).

401 Quoted from Taylor (1911:59), Jaffee's (2001:42–63), Handel's (2003:28, 31).

402 *Marcuse's basic thesis, according to which technology and science today also take on the function of legitimating political power, is the key to analysing the changed constellation* (Eagleton 1994:191). A key access in analysing the world of work is the legitimating power of technology but also the power to communicate the

ideology of technology. This has to be communicated in such a way that managerial ideologies support a technical-instrumental rationality on which power and domination are based.

403   One should not fall victim of a dangerous thinking that sees present-day office life as exclusion zones. A mere computer is no more than an automat, an automatic processor of calculations and symbols, words, and signs in a digitalised +/– fashion. Called computer nor not, it is still a *dead machine* to which one is *joined* in a *bondage* relationship that creates *submission and impotence* (Max Weber).

404   *Human beings are conditioned, not directly to belief and behaviour, but to a vocabulary of concepts that functions as guides, warrants, reasons, or excuses for behaviour and belief* (McGee 1980:6). In its extreme end-form an Orwellian (1949:26) future can be: *what was worst of all was that by means of such organisation they were systematically turned into little savages, and yet this produced in them no tendency whatever to rebel against the discipline. On the contrary, they adored [managerial capitalism] and everything connected with it, the [advertising] slogans and the worship of [consumption]. It was all a sort of glorious game to them. All their ferocity was turned outwards, against the enemies of [consumption], against foreigners, traitors, saboteurs, thought-criminals.*

405   Even though Reich (1992) has developed these three forms of *service* it should not neglect the problematic construction of the term *service*. Already in 1919, a US *Ladies' Home Journal* introduced a new way of shopping as *self-service* as *the customer, not the store provides the service*. Today, we are sufficiently conditioned not to realise this reversal. The roles of those *who service* (store) and those *who are served* (customer) have been reversed. The customer remains largely un-serviced while walking through aisles, selecting items, putting them on a conveyor belt and collecting them from the conveyor belt after the only service the store provides – the collection of money – has been concluded. The so-called service industry increasingly appears like a *customer-service-yourself* (while believing to be served) industry. But *service* also aims at other purposes as customer-service relations are introduced in workplaces. Now, HR managers *serve* their *clients* (client = *Newspeak* while worker = *Oldspeak*) *in the same way, the service (the military) as a whole may be recast as a service industry. Missiles and aircraft are force packages and delivery systems, as though the US Air Force were just a branch of FedEx* (Poole 2006:113). The smoothness of the military language in management as in society is very much with us.

406   See Edwards (1979) and Reich (1992).

407   While these metaphors are indicators of situations found in each stage of development, they – quite often – also tend to be a portray of the disruptive character, the rebel, the artist, the prostitute, the adulterer, the criminal, the outcast, the warrior, the rebel-poet, the radical, the revolutionary, the dissenter, the mutineer. Even in the final stage of a post-industrial society with strong tendencies towards Orwell's *1984*, these characters do not completely disappear. Today's *culture industry* produces mass-*mediated* societies with *individual* heroes but no mass movement for the betterment of human society (Zengotita 2005; cf. Adorno & Horkheimer 1944; Bolinger 1968:111, 1980:17ff.). In mass-mediated reality *these characters are transformed. The vamp, the national hero, the beatnik, the neurotic housewife, the gangster, the star, the charismatic tycoon perform a function very different from and even contrary to that of their cultural predecessors. They are no longer images of another way of life but*

rather freaks or types of the same life, serving as an affirmation rather than negation of the established order (Marcuse 1966:62).

408   In a recent poll by the American Film Institute, Grapes of Wrath (1940, directed by John Ford, staring Henry Fonda) was voted the 7th most inspiring movie. Its author John Steinbeck received the 1962 Nobel Prize for Literature.

409   Deleuze (1995:179) emphasised that *Kafka was already standing at the point of transition between the two kinds of society*, a pre-modern and a modern society. This has been *described in The Trial [with] the most ominous judicial expression.*

410   Next to *Modern Times*, Fritz Lang's *Metropolis* (filmed in 1927) also shows the reality of the human conditions in mass manufacturing (www.imdb.com.title/tt0017136/).

411   The BBC comedy series *The Office* started with series one on Monday, 9th July 2001 at 9:30pm. Series two was shown in 2003 with specials also shown in 2003 (www.bbc.co.uk/comdey/theoffice/).

412   According to Chomsky's critique on Skinner (1971:26), *It is, he* [Skinner] *claims, a 'fact that all control is exerted by the environment' (p. 82). Consequently, when we seem to turn control over to a person, we simply shift from one mode of control to another' (p. 97). The only serious task, then, is to design less 'aversive' and more effective controls, and engineering problem.* Chomsky (1971:33) concludes, *in fact, there is nothing in Skinner's approach that is incompatible with a police state in which rigid laws are enforced by people who are themselves subject to them and the threat of dire punishment hangs over all.*

413   Deleuze (1995:182) idea of *new ways of manipulating money* has been described in Galbraith's *A Theory of Price Control* (1952a).

414   Before elaborating further on Orwell's mind control, one needs to keep in mind that these five versions of control (i–v) do not represent closed boxes. They can never be neatly packaged into tidy boxes. Some forms of control overlap. In other cases two different forms exist at the same time while there are also times when elements from different versions of control are combined to make them even more powerful. Despite all this, they assist us in a broad understanding of control at work.

415   Adorno (1944:16) has challenged the one-dimensional belief that progress is always good by noting, *today progress and barbarism are so intertwined as mass culture that only barbaric asceticism against this latter and against the progression of the means may again produce that which is unbarbaric.*

416   While these forms of domestication have largely disappeared in advanced industrialised countries, in those places where capitalism is still in the process of taking hold, forms of worker punishment and domestication are a daily occurrence. Processes illustrated by Engels (1892), E. P. Thompson (1963) and Silver's *Forces of Labor* (2003) are still with us.

417   Already in the year 1883, Lafargue emphasised domesticating effects of what is today termed as *primary* and *secondary* socialisation in 19th century words. He wrote *twelve hours of work a day, that is the ideal of the philanthropists and moralists of the eighteenth century, modern factories have become ideal houses of correction in which the toiling masses are imprisoned, in which they are condemned to compulsory work for twelve or fourteen hours, not the men only but also women and children.* Today, these processes are less visible as corporate mass media seek not to remind us of capitalism's historic mission of domestication (Zengotita 2005).

418 Despite HRM's insistence on training, expressed in almost every HRM textbook, there is also the opposite of training (Monk 1997:12ff.)

419 See Whyte's *Organisational Man* (1961). Primary socialisation could well be described in Marcuse's terms (1966:77) as *the individual must adopt to a world which does not seem to demand the denial of his innermost needs – a world which is not essentially hostile. The organism is thus being preconditioned for the spontaneous acceptance of what is offered. Inasmuch as the greater liberty involves a contraction rather than extension and development of instinctual needs, it works for rather than against the status quo of general repression – one might speak of 'institutionalised de-sublimation. The latter appears to be a vital factor in the making of the authoritarian personality of our time.*

420 The more traditional labour relations perspective tended to focus narrowly on social relations at work is no longer capable of reflecting the true state of the interchanges between work and society. Similarly, a rather one-sided and restrictive HRM-managerial view is equally no longer a truthful reflection on this interchange. For one, both tend to exclude external fractures and secondly, HRM's pathologies silently support secondary socialisation.

421 Cf. Altheide & Johnson (1980:2), Adorno (1944:3) commented on this, *regardless of how much he knows about this subject, and must, if he wishes to pursue a career, displays a professional tunnel vision even narrower than that of the most narrow-minded expert* and he will be fine.

422 In the work domain management seeks to achieve one-dimensionality when *multi-dimensional language is converted into one-dimensional language, in which different and conflicting meanings no longer interpenetrate but are kept apart; the explosive historical dimension of meaning is silenced* (Marcuse 1966:202). But not only management – and with it HRM – has realised the importance of one-dimensional thinking. In politics, too, one-dimensionality is used, especially ever since Margaret Thatcher, once prime minister of Britain, coined the so-called *TINA*-phrase. In politics as in management *TINA*'s meaning is one-dimensional. It portrays: *There Is No Alternative* (TINA) to global managerial and free-market capitalism. In TINA, the numerical large range of different ideas such as neoliberalism, managerialism, privatisation, global competition, free markets, free trade, and above all capitalist globalisation are directed towards one goal, the goal of advanced capitalism. This is the only way which all modern societies can go. See also: a review of Korten's book *The Post Corporate World: Live after Capitalism* (http://www.ratical.org/many_worlds/seeingPCW.pdf).

423 Quoted from Feenberg (2004:68). On the power of technology, Adorno (1944:78) emphasised *the quantification of technical processes, however, its compartmentalisation in the smallest operations, for the most part independent of experience and education, turns the expert status of the new-styled directors to a considerable extent into a mere illusion, behind which is concealed the privilege of being appointed.*

424 The invisible hand of the market is pretended to be a *natural* force. It quietly removes the active hand of socially constructed managerialism. Economic realities such as stagnant or declining wage, worsening of working conditions, rising prices, debts, etc. are presented as natural phenomena, almost like the weather to mask the reality of conscious policies made by managers, corporate shareholders, and capitalists.

425 See: Zengotita (2005). In the words of Orwell (1949:214), *the invention of print, however, made it easier to manipulate public opinion, and the film and the radio carried the process further.*

426 Unlike *participatory* workplace or *industrial* democracy (Albert 2006), the public act of *giving up your vote* is quite different. What is essentially practised in those countries that have been awarded the label democratic countries is *representative* democracy. Jean-Jacques Rousseau (*The Social Contract, 1762*) described the shortcomings of *representative* democracy as practised in England. He wrote *the English people believe they are free, but they are grossly mistaken. They are only so during the election of members of parliament. As soon as these have been elected, the people are immediately consigned to slavery; they are nothing. The way they use their freedom during the brief moments when they possess it means that they thoroughly deserve to lose it (quoted from Canfora 2006:65)*. It appears that not much has changed since the days of Jean-Jacques Rousseau.

427 *In Democracy in Europe – A History of an Ideology,* Canfora (2006:248–252) summed up democracy as: *the term democracy had a short and very marginal life of just three centuries in ancient Greece, between 500BC and 200BC. It then disappeared from the Western world for a very long period, slowly re-emerging much later, until it was consecrated beginning with the French revolution.* As recent as two centuries ago Kant wrote in Perpetual Peace [*Zum Ewigen Frieden, 1795*], that *democracy was the path that led to despotism...in the early 1920s in Germany and elsewhere* [democracy became] *a counterweight to socialism (or to communism), especially when the socialist regimes of Eastern Europe asserted themselves. This was an enormous propaganda gain for Western governments: to be able to appropriate that whole world for themselves. Meanwhile, they were in fact making great strides towards restoring the most uncontrolled free-market economy, and were by now making use of state bodies (some of the illegal!) that would stop at nothing in oppressing communism. It was a gift from God for them to be able to call all this democracy...what has prevailed in the end – or rather as things stand now – is freedom. It is defeating democracy. This freedom is not, of course, for all, but for those who are strongest in competition, be they nations, religions, or individuals.*

428 Habermas (1988) saw the public domain as distinctively different from the economic domain or the world of work. Originally, the public domain wasn't governed by market forces but to be seen as an open theatre for debating and deliberating rather than buying and selling. In late capitalism, this kind of public domain, if it ever fully existed as a practical reality, has been increasingly colonised via corporate media. Late capitalism, in its appearance as mediated democracy, has been fragmented by competing interest groups displaying the manufacturing and manipulation of public opinion (Frazer 1990). *Habermas'* concept of a public domain has never existed inside labour-management relations as instrumental rational imperatives govern discourses.

429 On the fragmentation of work into Taylor's narrow work tasks, Adorno (1944:12) commented, *in the movements which machines demand from their operators, lies already that which is violent, crashing, propulsively unceasing in Fascist mistreatment.*

430 Control mechanisms of these five stages could also be described in cultural terms: a) the power culture with direct control, b) the technology culture where power resides in technique, c) the admin culture where power is established inside rules, d) the enforcement culture where power is enforced via systems, and finally, the person culture where power is administered through internalised structures.

431 See: Kerr, Dunlop, Harbison, & Myers' *Industrialism & Industrial Man* (1960).

432 The role of intellectual labour or management has been described by Adorno (1944:50). He noted, *the ones who are most powerful are those who do the least*

themselves, while shifting as much of the burden as they can onto others, to who they lend their name while pocketing the advantage.

433   See: Galbraith's (1958) *The Affluent Society* and *The New Industrial State* (1969). On affluence and material wealth, Adorno (1944:75) noted, *material success binds individual [Individuum] and society not merely in the comfortable and meanwhile dubious sense, that the rich can escape loneliness, but in a far more radical sense: if the blind, isolated self-interest is driven only far enough, then it passes over, along with the economic one, into social power and reveals itself to be the incarnation of a universally binding principle.*

434   By *service industry* one could understand a society *producing*(!) more than half of its wealth through non-manufacturing activities. In other words and apart from truly servicing jobs such as hairdressing, etc., most workers are engaged in the distribution of goods manufactured elsewhere.

435   Management as master of the modern production assigns numbers to human beings to turn them into Objects of Power. Management controls the numbers – it controls resources and human resources. It gives numbers to humans, to human resources or to *Menschenmaterial* (the German word for human resource) whether on a plastic ID card for human resources or engraved into the arm of Nazi-Germany's *Menschenmaterial* (Bauman 1989).

436   Argumentation can be seen as a reason-giving exercise aimed at supporting a claim that is linked to rationality under a coherent set of agreed-upon rules, procedures, and codes of conducts. The original idea of arguments was aimed at enhancing understanding. It was not a managerially designed competition for winning and loosing an argument. Argumentation was a method of truth-finding, not a method of competition and contest.

437   The management idea of a plurality of different interests inside a corporation is supported by the idea of different cultures inside a corporation. See: Alvesson's *Understanding Organisational Culture* (2002), Alvesson & Willmot's *Studying Management Critically* (2003).

438   *The power and efficiency of this system, the thorough assimilation of mind with fact, of thought with required behaviour, of aspirations with reality, militates against the emergence of a new subject. They also militate against the notion that the replacement of the prevailing control over the productive process by 'control from below' would mean the advent of qualitative change. This notion was valid, and still is valid where the labourers were, and still are, the living denial and indictment of the established society* (Marcuse 1966:256). See also: Orwell (1949), Zuboff (1988), Sewell & Wilkinson (1992); Barker (1993), Lyon (2001), Cairns et al. (2003).

439   A means-ends view of people reduces human resources. It *departs from Kant's dictum never to treat people as a means but rather as ends only* (Cheney & Carroll 1997:596; cf. Sennett 2006).

440   Company culture has been seen as: a) a sense of company identity and a notion of a *'we'*. It implies boundaries between companies. b) It constructs a work culture as cognition or cognitive competence governed by a corporate language and corporate vista. c) A pattern of evaluations consisting of a set of specific corporate values and norms, defining good and bad, setting parameters on what is and what is not to be done. Corporate culture operates as a symbolic system by means of communicative processes (cf. Feldman 1998).

441   Adopted from Alvesson and Deetz (1996:192).

442   The term *Panopticon* is closely associated with the term post-modernism. Post-modernism can be seen as being *epistemological* in character expressed as mod-

ernism or post-modernism or as *epochal* expressed as modernity or post-modernity (Morris 2001:119).

443　On the relative harsh demands of such a career system, Adorno (1944:20) noted, *the iron nerves and calm under fire which are the crucial prerequisites for applicants of highly paid positions, are the picture of the asphyxiated silence, which the employers of the human resources manager later impose politically.*

444　An in a mass-mediated society, human-to-human communication is to a significant extent replaced by a human-media communication. Human-to-human communication is mediated via reporters, TV presenters, and journalists. They take on the role of primary communicators establishing a false reality, the impacts of which have been expressed by Watson (2003:5) as: *it is something else, however, when journalists ignore abuses of the public language by people of influence and power, and reproduce without comments words that are intended to deceive and manipulate. When this happens journalism ceases to be journalism and becomes a kind of propaganda; or a reflection of what Simone Weil called 'the superb indifference that the powerful have for the weak'.*

445　The process of primary socialisation can also include the concept of *cultural capital* or cultural socialisation, viewing access to a certain way of speaking, such as management talk for MBAs, a certain way of managerial behaviour, a certain corporate culture code, and a certain dress or fashion taste as being part of corporate socialisation. Any lack of corporate-culture socialisation leads to a failure of socialisation into higher levels of a hierarchically structured world of management.

446　See: Deleuze (1995:178–182).

447　The attempt to cloak today's pathologies of working regimes as normal has been seen by Adorno (1944:19) as, *…the absolute hegemony of the economy did not mock every attempt at explicating conditions by the psychic life of their victims* [creating conditions that] *have to show that contemporary sickness exists precisely in what is normal.*

448　On managerial time regimes, Adorno (1944:51) noted, *no fulfillment may be attached to labor, which would otherwise lose its functional obscurity in the totality of purpose, no spark of sensibility [Besinnung] may fall in free time, because it might spring into the work-world and set it aflame.*

449　Society has developed a raft of instruments to make the working time regime appear normal. Some have been outlined by Adorno 1944:12), *when time is money, it seems the right thing to do to save time, above all one's own, and one excuses such thriftiness with all due respect for the other. One is straightforward. Every veil which steps between human beings conducting business is felt to be a disturbance of the functioning of the apparatus, in which they are not only objectively incorporated, but to which they belong with pride. That they greet each other with the hellos of tried-and-true indifference instead of doffing their hats, that they send each other interoffice memos devoid of addresses or signatures instead of letters, are the endemic symptoms of the sickness of contact.*

450　See: Morgan (1986:18) and Hyman (1989:37).

451　For example, when governments, work organisation experts and trade unions sought to introduce group work as part of a *Humanisation of Work* project during the 1970s and 1980s, management rejected this. But when changes in the production system (lean production, Just-in-time, Kanban, Japanisation, etc.) demanded the introduction of teams, management was quick to follow suit. This time it was not humanity but work intensification that drove management (Murakami 1999a, 1999b, 2000c).

452 Marcuse (1966:149) has emphasised that *scientific management and scientific division of labour vastly increased the productivity: of the economic, political, and cultural enterprise. Result: '"the higher standard of living. At the same time and on the same ground, this rational enterprise produced a pattern of mind and behaviour which justified and absolved even the most destructive and oppressive features of the enterprise. Scientific-technical rationality and manipulation are welded together into new forms of social control.*

453 See *attac*, anti-capitalism, trade unions, communist parties, some socialist parties, anarchist movements, anti-consumerism, anti-globalisation movements, and Hippie communes such as Christiania in Denmark, Nimbin in Australia, etc.

454 The term *conditioning* reflects two models of behavioural psychology. One is *classical conditioning* invented by Pavlov (1928), the second *instrumental conditioning* that operates with positive and negative reinforcements and punishment (Skinner 1953).

455 See: Bauman (1989); Cheney & Carroll (1997).

456 Albert (2006:93) noted, *there is no such thing as a neutral educational process. Education either functions as an instrument which is used to facilitate the integration of the younger generation into the logic of the present system and bring about conformity to it, or it becomes the practice of freedom – the means by which men and women deal critically and creatively with the reality and discover who to participate in the transformation of their world.*

457 Eisenberg and Goodall's (2001) book, *Organisational Communication: Balancing Creativity and Constraint*, pursues bridging the gap between primary and secondary socialisation by pretending to *help students bridging the gap between what they learn in school and what they experience at work.*

458 Every website of almost any management school or business college testifies to this.

459 It comes in the standard advertisement or marketing package that artificially creates a demand by sending out messages that one needs to oblige to and most importantly, where to go or which products to purchase (the modular MBA, etc.) in order to fulfil a system demand directed towards highly functional training.

460 Quoted from: (Brown & Lauder 2001:58).

461 See Bowles & Gintis (1976, 1981, 2001).

462 See: Mandell's *The Privatisation of Everything (2002)*.

463 See Freire's *Pedagogy of Freedom: ethics, democracy, and civic courage* (1998), *Pedagogy of the Oppressed* (2000), and *Education for Critical Consciousness* (2005).

464 See also: Bowles & Gintis (1981, 2001).

465 *Exchange*-knowledge – symbolised in the sign-value of a degree (MBA) – exchanges labour-power for money by enhancing labour's bargaining position in the labour exchange at the point of the labour process. *Use*-knowledge is functionally related to managerial demands, stretching from reading, writing, mathematics, etc. to highly specified university knowledge such as operations management, marketing, and HRM. These forms of use- and exchange knowledge have almost no meaning in everyday life of human beings but are highly valued by employers.

466 Quoted from John Gardner, former secretary of the US Department of Health, Education & Welfare (see Bowles & Gintis 1976), internet download: http://www.webster.edu/~corbetre/philosophy/education,bg/bg-ch-3.html

467 For the general role of punishment in modern societies, see: Rusche's *Punishment and social structure* (2003).

468   Marcuse (1966:250) wrote on socialisation, *massive socialization begins at home and arrests the development of consciousness and conscience.*

469   On worthiness and trustworthiness, Adorno (1944:38) noted, *Only that which they do not need to know counts as understandable; only what is in truth alienated, the words moulded by commerce, strikes them as trustworthy.*

470   *Marketing, as the marketeers will tell you, is 'rooted in the exchange process'. Increasingly that's where universities are also rooted* (Watson 2003:168).

471   Author is a term that refers to authority and authenticity. Unfortunately, textbook authors hardly ever produce something with an authentic character as their task in managerial socialisation is directed towards the summing up of managerial knowledge rather than producing something original or critical. According to Harding (2003:26), such *textbooks are weighty tonnes, in terms of pounds and ounces. They are some 600 pages long, and...contain a closely-argued text relived by few illustrations or diagrams.* All too often textbooks are not written to enhance critical understanding. They are written to make one accept and acknowledge *facts* that are socially constructed by managerial writers without understanding of the factors that make these facts. *It seems evident to me*, philosopher Gadamer wrote (1976:33), *that acceptance or acknowledgement is the decisive thing for relationships to authority. It lives not from dogmatic power but from dogmatic acceptance.*

472   Quoted from Marcuse (1966:89).

473   Many critical issues *remain concealed in the purely functionalised application of science for the purpose of dominating the world* (Gadamer 1976:124).

474   Increasingly life and communication in society as *in business language is now productivity-driven* (Watson 2003:4; cf. Sennett 2006).

475   The term *ff* is known as *folios,* following pages, *fortissimo* (music), or *fast forward.* Hence the conditioned educational customers of *ff* can adapt to functional knowledge by quickly memorising key terms of managerialism. Their fast-forward conditioning is supported by a raft of books with titles such as *The One-Minute Manager* or *The Quick MBA.*

476   The process originates from Ivan Petrovich Pavlov (1849–1936), Russian physiologist, Nobel Prize winner for medicine (1904) and inventor of classical conditioning. See also Skinner's *Science and Human Behaviour (1953) and* Chomsky, N. (1971). The Case against B. F. Skinner, *The New York Review of Books,* December 30th.

477   The term *fetishism* was coined by the French psychologist *Alfred Binet* (1857–1911) and derives from the European perception of the amulets used in traditional West African religions. Freud saw that *fetish*-objects are linked to the fetishes in which savages believe their Gods to be embodied. Somewhat similarly, Marx' theory of *Commodity Fetishism* also invokes the notion of a magical belief in the power of inanimate objects (Macey 2000:127).

478   Former US-President, Thomas Jefferson (1743–1826), spoke of *inalienable rights.* These are no longer inalienable. Today, they are sold and bought on the market. Jefferson also argued that *human* rights are *natural* rights. Violation of these rights negates the contract which binds a people to their rulers and that therefore there is an inherent *Right to Revolution.*

479   Those who are unwilling or unable to be converted into useful industrial entities bear the full brand of the corporate mass media that forces everyone into a one-dimensional line. They are portrayed as parasites, living off welfare, useless, asocial, anti-social, etc. More descriptions can be downloaded from almost any tabloid newspaper almost anywhere.

480   This is largely the task of *organisational behaviour* (OB). OB has amassed a large volume of managerial writings. The task assigned to OB is that subjects have to be converted into objects of organisational power. Their *human* behaviour has to be replaced with *organisational* behaviour.

481   As Marcuse (1966:36) noted, *the slaves of developed industrial civilization are sublimated slaves, but they are slaves, for slavery is determined neither by obedience nor by hardness of labour but by the status of being a mere instrument, and the reduction of man to the state of a thing. This is the pure form of servitude: to exist as an instrument, as a thing.*

482   During the early 1900s a vigorous debate was launched about the future direction of capitalism splitting its participants into two camps. One group favoured an economic analysis that would see the future development of capitalism leading to one single gigantic corporation, i.e. monopoly, while the other group saw a development directed towards a few large multi-national corporations that have divided their markets into manageable domains, i.e. oligopoly.

483   It appears as a given fact or a brute fact (Searle 1996, 2002) as long as the factors that create the facts remain hidden because this could uncover the fact that these facts are not brute but social facts. They are facts that need human input to become facts and in this case they need the input of an ideologically motivated fact-creator.

484   The 1/3–2/3 conditioning ratio between primary socialisation and secondary socialisation/working life seems to appear as if the dream of any behavioural psychologist has become true. Early and successful conditioning is able to set the parameters and patterns of future behaviours (animals and humans) and values (humans) for the rest of their lives.

485   The push towards managerialism has not only been recognisable in the privatised *education industry* (sic) but also in state run colleges as well as universities. The outcome of these developments has been twofold. Firstly, curricular developments in today's educational institutions have been restructured to the effect that they reflect the demands of managerialism. Secondly, the *academic* subject of *management science* (sic) has levelled itself up to college or university level. All these developments have resulted in sufficiently conditioned human resources once they enter the world of work.

486   Marcuse (1966:38) noted on participation that *neither partial nationalisation nor extended participation of labour in management and profit would by themselves alter this system of domination – as long as labour itself remains a prop and affirmative force.*

487   Adorno (1944:3) noted that *he is no 'professional' [in English in original], ranks in the hierarchy of competitors as a dilettante, regardless of how much he knows about his subject, and must, if he wishes to pursue a career, display a professional tunnel vision even narrower than that of the most narrow-minded expert.*

488   Despite the illusions of an equalising or even *democratic* consumption or mass consumerism, these forms of existence do not indicate an end to hierarchies. As Marcuse (1966:10) pointed out, *if the worker and his boss enjoy the same television program and visit the same resort places, if the typist is as attractively made up as the daughter of her employer, if the Negro owns a Cadillac, if they all read the same newspaper, then this assimilation indicates not the disappearance of classes, but the extent to which the needs and satisfactions that serve the preservation of the Establishment are shared by the underlying population.* These forms have not ended hierarchies. They are signs of system integration of workers through consumption.

489 See: Abrahamson (1996); Levy, Alvesson & Willmot (2003); Linstead et al. (2004:21).

490 Even though the term human is used, the reality of HRM often shows the opposite once the real HRM is exposed (Legge 1995).

491 See: Chandler (1992:11); Boxall & Purcell (2003:28).

492 See: Bauman (1989:24); Marsden & Townley 1996:672).

493 This is very loosely based on Habermas (1997a:274).

494 See Kohlberg (1971, 1981, 1984) for different levels of moral and ethical consciousness; Singer (1985) for a discussion on ethics; and Laffer (2005:273f.) for *The Critical Failure of Workplace Ethics*.

495 The insertion of the invented term suizing(!) indicates two things. Firstly, suicide is a word related to the human condition. It also shows the sometimes highly negative effects that downsizing – mass dismissal of workers and firing – have on humans. Secondly, the term suizing also indicates that companies have all too often followed the managerial fashion of downsizing like a fashion (Abrahamson 1996) without considering its long term consequences as a lack of workers and skills has often had a negative effect on companies during times of economic upswings.

496 While enhancement is one of the preferred terms used by managerialism, Watson (2003:38) emphasised that *enhance is the McDonald's of corporate English.*

497 See: Hyman (1987:41); Langley (1989); Dutton & Ashford (1993); Orlikowski & Yates (1994); Smith et al. (1994); Barker (1999); Emrich et al. (2001)

498 Such thinking operates inside a particular Orwellian logic expressed in 1984 (1949:220), *an [organisational] member is required to have not only the right opinion, but the right instincts. Many of the beliefs and attitudes demanded of him are never plainly stated, and could not be stated without laying bare the contradictions inherent in [HRM].*

499 On the pathologies of modern society, Adorno (1944:12) commented, *in the profit-based economy, the practical social orders [Ordnungen] of life, while claiming to benefit human beings, cause what is human to wither, and the wider they spread, the more they cut off everything which is tender.*

500 In their chapter on *Organisations as Strategic Creations*, Conrad and Poole (1998:8) wrote, *organisations are designed and operated as they are because of the choice their members make. Employees are constantly making choices.* The authors have managed to totally eclipse any historical development of the organisational form of a com-*pany* between its conception as bread sharing among feudal free-*lance* militias to today's asymmetric power relations that follow Taylor's division of labour into management and labour. The military origins as much as the brute facts of a profit oriented corporate world is shrouded behind the veil of a neutral sounding term: *an organisation* in which workers – now called employees – *are constantly making choices!* No word is wasted on the fact that workers find themselves *in things that shape their lives* [and that] *they do so, not by giving, but by accepting the laws of things – not the law of physics but the law of their society* (Marcuse 1966:13). Above all, they have to accept the laws of management and managerialism.

501 See: Legge (1995:97); Billsberry (1996); Parzych (2000); Boxall & Purcell (2003:47); Merrier (2006).

502 See: Bundel (2004:125ff, 146, 148); DeCeri & Kramer (2005:312–313, 468–470).

503 *Semantics* is part of semiotics also including *syntactic* and *pragmatic* communication. *Semantics* addresses how signs relate to their reference, or what signs

(words, etc.) stand for. *Syntactic* study is the study of the relationship among signs. Signs virtually never stand by themselves. They are almost always part of a larger sign system, or group of signs that are organised in a particular way. IR, HRM, PRP, etc. are signs that cannot define themselves. People need to define them. They are socially constructed. Finally, *pragmatic* studies look at how signs make a difference in people's lives, or the practical use and effect of signs. The sign *strike* is received in a different way in the labour domain than it is in the management domain as it has a different effect.

504 Even though post-modernism might call something like managerialism a *narrative* or even a grant narrative, managerialism is much more than a mere story, a tale, or a fictional account. The invention and use of managerialism is closely related to societal relations. Managerialism is not just a narrative or a story to be told (Barry & Elmes 1997), it is the intentional construction of *meaning in the service of power* (Thompson 1990:7) or an ideology.

505 Ideology can be seen as *meaning in the service of power* (Thompson 1990:7). One of the core achievements of managerial ideology is their capability to harmonise. This enables the framing of facts – that are managerially constructed – as reality. Managerial realities do not even have to confirm each other as these ideologies cover social and economic contradictions. They establish a faked harmony between different managerial realities and the methods used to blanket them. In general, ideologies often refer to a system of beliefs, even a system of illusory beliefs, and also to a process of meaning and production of ideas. Ideologies are also related to ideas serving as a weapon for social interests. The core problem of ideology is what is in its *content* as it carries ideas and values. But also the *context* of an ideology is significant. Ideologies impact on meanings by which they are constructed and shared. Fundamentally, *ideologies* are not individually but socially determined because they are created by a group or a class. Inside the world of work, ideologies are prevalent in the social construction of the division of labour, the social idea of management, business and business as associations. They are also – and some might even say predominantly – found in corporate mass media. According to Berger & Luckmann (1967) and Fiske (1990:166) *ideology* has become the category of illusions and *false consciousness*. It is seen as a thought alienated from the real social being of the thinker.

506 This is not to be confused with Kant's idea of a *categorial imperative* developed in *The Groundwork of the Metaphysics of Morals* (Johnson 2004:1). Kant *argued that moral requirements are based on a standard of rationality he dubbed the Categorical Imperative. Immorality therefore involves a violation of the categorial imperative and is thereby irrational. Yet he argued that conformity to the categorial imperative (a non-instrumental principle) and hence to moral requirements themselves, can nevertheless be shown to be essential to rational agency. This argument was based on his striking doctrine that a rational will must be regarded as autonomous, or free... an autonomous will.* Managerial imperatives or system imperatives that are enforced upon the individual do not conform to Kant's idea of *a non-instrumental principle.* They are the exact opposite. When a moral imperative is not based on the *autonomous or free will,* then, according to Kant, it is immoral. Therefore, instrumental or managerial actions or principles cannot be seen as moral in Kant's understanding.

507 Unlike *economic classes* – labour and capital – that are divided based on their relationship in the political economy – one owns the means of production while the other sells the only thing it possesses, i.e. labour power. *Social classes*

can be reduced to show merely social differences. These are to be found in the classical three sociological denominators: a) income, b) education, and c) profession. On this basis, the *working class* or *proletariat* (*Oldspeak*) has been divided into *socially constructed* and not *economically determined classes*. This, of course, serves four purposes. Firstly, it allows the ideological splitting of those who have to sell their labour into two *social* classes, middle class (white collar) and lower class (blue collar). Secondly, the class that actually owns the means of production – the *bourgeoisie* (*Oldspeak*) – has become the *upper class* (*Newspeak*), i.e. *up* = good = a place to aspire to! Thirdly, class divisions move from the real division in society, i.e. the economic division, into the realm of sociology. Real existing economic divisions are now based on socially invented categories and no longer on economic determinants. Lastly, while ideologically cloaking the economic relations in society, it gives the illusion that there are three classes (lower, middle, upper) and not two: labour or proletariat versus capital or bourgeoisie. Consequently, conflict and contradictions in society have been ideologically *overcome* by taking out the dialectics of thesis (labour), anti-thesis (capital), and synthesis (what ought to be) in favour of *what is*, stated as: there are three social classes in society.

508   While the term middle class carries features of a sociological *invented-ness* based on income, education, and occupation, their material existence is based on participation in the labour market that turns the middle class, in socio-economic terms, into a white-collar working class. Above that, the middle class shows strong features of a *petty bourgeois* lifestyle that has, according to Adorno (1944:23), endured *the contradictions between high-flown materials and narrow-minded Spiessbürgerlichkeit [petty bourgeoisie]* but it is also constantly...*threatened by a scarcely less urgent danger: by the economic pressure of the market.*

509   Anti-consumerism has been secured in the margins of society as issues such as Buy-Nothing Days, No-Logo, Clean-Clothes, Anti-Sweat-Shop-movements, Boycott-Days, McLabel, and No-Shopping movements are hardly reported by a mass-media apparatus that depends on advertising income.

510   The difference between *affluence* and *affluenza* can be seen in Galbraith (1958) *The Affluent Society* and Goldthorpe et al. (1969) *The Affluent Worker in the Class Structure* for affluence and in Hamilton & Denniss (2005) work on *Affluenza – When too much is never enough. Gandhi has also summed it up* when he said *the world has enough for everybody's need but never enough of everybody's greed.* The exact opposite has been expressed in *Greed is God.*

511   The adoption of love as an attribute for consumption has been expressed in statements such as *I love chocolate.* A recent newspaper advertisement for a large department store stated, *Father's Day gifts your Dad will love* implying that when purchasing the latest electric shaver model – for the last 50 years this has been a battery powered plastic stick with a moving blade – *your dad will love you.* It is the daily exposure of messages like these that inserts a commercial good into a social relationship *commodifying* and *fetishising* everyday life.

512   We are made to believe that we have to hunt for the newest car even though the changes from the previous model are largely cosmetic while the fundamentals stay the same. We are made to believe that we have to have the latest toothbrush even though the basic item (a plastic stick with a few bristles attached to it) has not changed much during the last 50 years.

513   In *The Critique of Pure Reason* of 1781 (http://www.gutenberg.org/dirs/ etext03/cprrn10.txt), Kant wrote *our age is the age of criticism to which everything must be subjected.*

514 While one of the core ideas of management is the doctrine of *means-ends*, it is used to focus on *means* while pushing the *ends* – what is this all good for, is it ethical (Kohlberg 1981, 1984) – into the background where it can be neglected and made to vanish into thin air.

515 The invention of scientific management by Taylor (1911) and the invention of scientific management studies as an academic field located at universities greatly supported the view that management and the ideology of managerialism are scientific.

516 See Habermas (1988) *Structural Transformation of the Public Sphere* (Cambridge: MIT-Press) and *Civil Society and the Political Public Sphere*, in: Habermas (1997a). *Between Facts and Norms* (Oxford: Polity Press).

517 As Orwell (1949:318) wrote, *countless words such as honour, justice, morality, internationalism, democracy, science and religion have simply ceased to exist.* While in Orwell's novel it is the government's *Ministry of Truth* that makes these words disappear, in today's reality, it is the mass media that create a mediated reality (Zengotita 2005) that structures our image of the world. And it has made many words – almost – disappear, marginalised or has altered their meaning. Imperialism is now called globalisation and deprived of its intentional destructive meaning. Useless people who live off the surplus created by workers were once seen as scavengers, parasites, sponges, or as the ugly face of capitalism, are today turned to the Paris Hiltons of our times and portrayed as someone to be aspired to. At the same time the victims of the system (unemployed, poor, non-process-able people) and those who oppose it (hippies, etc.) are portrayed as parasites.

518 Exactly the same doctrine applies to the market-driven modern textbook that formats the minds of the modern students, adapts them to the conditions of the working regime, and turns them into affirmative characters. The modern textbook avoids any controversies, is easily digestible, and includes nice tables and figures, invented case studies and silly anecdotes, all of which are designed not to upset the textbook market. More than anything, these market products are commercial goods conforming to marketable ideas that do not have to be ideas of truth. Their success is measured on the numbers of editions and volumes sold, not on their truth content. But as all true ideologies they cannot dive too deep into pure fictions. Some – however distorted – link to some sort of reality has to be maintained. The best textbooks are therefore those that can cover the contradictions and pathologies of working regimes by using so-called *practical* and *real life* examples to cover them inside nice and colourful boxes, short summaries, and childish figures. What occurs is the conversion of textbooks from a use-commodity into an exchange commodity. Their ability to be exchanged [book for money] supersedes their usefulness.

519 On this Adorno (1944:34) commented, *no sooner are they granted a certain measure of wealth, than they enthusiastically affirm their fate…*

520 In advanced societies, money is nothing more than the replacement of commodities that have use- and exchange value with the ultimate exchange value medium. Money's great property is that it is almost totally divorced from use-value. It is inedible, one cannot write on it, even as wallpaper it is pretty useless. The unique character of money comes from its exchange property, as it is exchangeable into almost anything. Herein lies the overwhelming fetish of money.

521 When those revolutionary forces temporarily disconnected the reproductive from the productive domain, they were able to communicate revolutionary

ideas to other members of society. This led to two kinds of revolutions: democratic revolutions that sought to end feudalist domination in the reproductive domain and working-class revolutions that sought to end the domination in the productive domain.

522 It was a brief moment in human history when the communicative domain had lost its ideological influence, as the ideological apparatus of the church had not yet been transferred into the ideological apparatus of corporate mass media. Today, this process has been completed. The Sunday indoctrination through the church has been replaced by the daily evening indoctrination through the mass media. The difference between feudalist hegemony and present forms of hegemony is that under feudalism an individual had to attend church while today's individual does not even have to leave the bedroom to receive the corporately mediated worldview. What we have today might even turn out to be more powerful than the power Orwell envisioned his 1984 *Telescreen* would have.

523 Under feudalism the limited amount of goods that were needed had mostly been homemade with use-value as the prime motive. Under early capitalism these goods became commercial commodities serving use-value and exchange-value. With mass consumption, advanced or consumer capitalism, a third level was added. The importance of use-value of goods declined as the market became saturated. However, as so-called *brand names* distance consumers from the price of a good, the exchange-value becomes increasingly secondary. Increasingly, goods are becoming *sign-value* driven. This indicates that consumers purchase goods not because of their use-value or exchange-value but because they are a sign of affluence or *Affluenza*. The idea of *sign-value* covers a range of goods from the faked *Gucci-sign on an equally faked* handbag to the obnoxiously large designer labels *'outside'* of clothing or the 500XLS sign on the back of a car. What is purchased is an imaginary life-style represented by a *sign* and not a commodity for its use- or exchange value. The value of these items lies in the *sign*. Similarly, the sign of *MBA* or *PhD* on a business card – sometimes – exceeds the use- and exchange-value of the *education* (sic) purchased. Lastly, the *sign-value* of a company label on the same card may also exceed the actual working conditions found at these companies.

524 See: Braverman (1974); Edwards (1979); Burawoy (1979, 1985); Hyman (1989) and Jaffee (2001).

525 While previous forms of control (Edwards 1979) have been restricted to work regimes and Barker (1993, 2005) has added a special form of panoptical control to the teamwork organisation of work, increasingly control has moved outside of work. More than ever before, control at work is supplied from the off-work domains of communication and reproduction.

526 Eriksen & Weigard's (2003) *Understanding Habermas – Communicative Action and Deliberate Democracy*; Gastil & Levine's (2006) *The deliberative democracy handbook*; Gilabert's (2005) *The Substantive Dimension of Deliberate Practical Rationality*; Gimmler's (2001) *Deliberative Democracy, the Public Sphere and the Internet*; Kalyvas' (2001) *The Politics of Autonomy and the Challenge of Deliberation*; Lösch's (2005) *Deliberative Politik. Moderne Konzeptionen von Öffentlichkeit, Demokratie und politische Partizipation*; and Oquendo's (2002) *Deliberative Democracy in Habermas and Nino*.

527 Today's discussions on workplace or industrial democracy are largely excluded from modern workplaces. They tend not to feature in textbooks for students of management or business.

528 An index entry of *'democracy'* is absent from almost all standard textbooks on management and HRM. Even a recent *collection* on the world of work or industrial relations (Ackers & Wilkinson 2003) mentions democracy only twice, under *Psychology and IR* and under *Consumer Capitalism*.

529 Even though most members of advanced societies would tick the yes-box when asked *Do you live in a democracy?*, in reality democracy has been successfully removed from two of the three domains (communicative and productive). In the remaining domain (reproductive), democracy has been converted into a system integrative element supported through the communicative domain.

530 To *technify* something is to make it appear technical when in fact it is a socially constructed process. It gives the appearance of being technical when it is not. This process of converting a *social act* into a *technical act* results in *technification*.

531 Even though modern production processes do, in some incidences, demand access to workers' knowledge, this is done in highly structured communicative forums such as team meetings where a managerial appointed sub-supervision – now called team-leader – meets with *his* team. Quality Circles, etc. operate in similar *fashion* as long as they are fashionable (Abrahamson 1996).

532 *Mechanical Solidarity* is social cohesion based upon resemblances and similarities among individuals in a society, and is largely dependent on common rituals and routines. This has been common in prehistoric and pre-agricultural societies. It became less dominant when modernity replaced these earlier forms of societies. *Organic Solidarity* is social cohesion based upon the dependence between individuals in a more advanced society. Though individuals perform different tasks and often have different values and interests, the order and very survival of society depends on their reliance on each other to perform their specific task (Durkheim 1893).

533 On this, Adorno (1944:47) commented, *just as, under the unrestrained primacy of the production process, the wherefore of reason disappears, until it degenerates into the fetishism of itself and of externalised power, so too does it reduce itself down to an instrument and comes to resemble its functionaries* [management T.K.], *whose thought-apparatus only serves the purpose of hindering thought.* In other words, by turning social relations into a fetish – the *fetish-ising* of social relations – humans are not only alienated from themselves and others but are also severely hindered in understanding the true character of social relations.

534 Marx argued that the capitalist economy leads to the *fetishisation* of goods and services, and the devaluing of the worth of a good or service, while instead focusing on its price in the market. In many critical contexts the term is used to describe the tendency of people to identify strongly with products or services they consume, especially those with commercial brand names and obvious status-enhancing appeal, e.g. an expensive car or pricey jewellery.

535 See: Mandell (2002).

536 The managerial ideology of *performance related pay* is, of course, only related to human resources as top management's and CEOs' salaries are divorced from company profits, downturns, share prices, and the economy. For example, Britain's economy and workers wages grew on average by 4 per cent during the 1990s, CEOs' salaries increased by 20% annually.

537 One of the earliest conditioning systems enforced onto newly born humans are time regimes. From our earliest stages onwards, we are conditioned to the clock for eating, sleeping, and toilet times. Today, when workers enter work-

places time-keeping issues are no longer controversial. During early forms of capitalism this was radically different. The conditioning of labour to the clock alone occurred through the use of extremely cruel, brutal, and violent means (Engels 1892; Thompson 1963).

538 While compared to the stage of early capitalism for most of today's workers prison is a less likely occurrence due to refined methods of non-violent system integration (Foucault 1995), the panoptical image of prison control remains a favourite metaphor of today's control systems operative at work.

539 The teaching curriculum at any standard business or management school hardly contains anything *useful* for the private individual because the knowledge gained or the training received are not directed towards *private use* but towards *company use*. When purchasing a garden hose, the new techniques in material process handling or supply chain management are hardly brought to bear. When purchasing a car, the latest techniques in using corporate balance sheets or creative accounting (Enron) are hardly used. Even in marriage, the latest HRM techniques on recruitment and selection are not used and if they were to be applied, the outcome might not be the one anticipated.

540 Bowles & Gintis (1976, 1981, 2001); Reich (1992); Albert (2006).

541 The range of pathologies associated with the present system spans from environmental destruction, global warming, unemployment, underemployment, and insecurity in employment to the gender wage gap, the export of misery to the third world, sweatshops, child labour, bondage slavery, workplace bullying, mobbing, sex slaves, daily industrial accidents, poverty, hunger, starvations on mass levels, etc.

Bibliography

Abrahamson, E. 1996. Management Fashion, *Academy of Management Review*, vol. 21, no. 1.

Ackers, P. & Wilkinson, A. 2003. *Understanding Work and Employment – Industrial Relations in Transition*, Oxford: Oxford University Press.

Ackroyd, S. 2004. Methodology for Management and Organisation Studies – Some Implications of Critical Realism, in: Fleetwood, S. & Ackroyd, S. (eds) *Critical Realist Approach in Organisation and Management Studies*, London: Routledge.

Adams, R. 1993. Understanding, Constructing, and Teaching Industrial Relations, in: Adams, R. & Meltz, N. (eds) *Industrial Relations Theory*, London: Scarecrow Press.

Adams R. 1993a. All Aspects of People at Work: Unity and Division in the Study of Labour and Labour Management, in: Adams, R. & Meltz, N. (eds) *Industrial Relations Theory*, London: Scarecrow Press.

Adorno, T. W. 1944. *Minima Moralia – Reflections From the Damaged Life*, Dennis Redmond (2005) translation: http://www.efn.org/~dredmond/MinimaMoralia.html

Adorno, T. W., Frenkel-Brunswick, E., Levinson, D. J., & Nevitt, R. 1964. *The Authoritarian Personality*, New York: John Wiley.

Adorno, T. 1976. Sociology and Empirical Research, in: Adorno, T. et al. (eds). The Positivist Dispute in German Sociology, London: Heinemann.

Adorno, T. W. & Horkheimer, M. 1944. *The Culture Industry: Enlightenment as Mass Deception*, Transcribed by Andy Blunden 1998; proofed and corrected Feb. 2005, web-download, November 2005.

Agger, B. 1979. *Western Marxism: An Introduction: Classical and Contemporary Sources*, Santa Monica: Goodyear.

Agger, B. 1998. Critical Social Theories: An Introduction, Oxford: Westview Press.

Albert, M. 2006. *Realizing Hope – Life beyond Capitalism*, London: Zed Books.

Altheide, D. & Johnson, J. 1980. *Bureaucratic Propaganda*, Boston: Allyn and Bacon.

Alvesson, M. 1996. *Communication, Power and Organisation*, New York: deGruyter.

Alvesson, M. & Deetz, S. 1996. Critical theory and postmodernism approaches to organisational studies, in: Clegg, S. et al. (eds) *Handbook of Organisation Studies*, Thousand Oaks: Sage.

Alvesson, M. & Deetz, S. 2005. Critical Theory and Postmodernism: approaches to organisational studies, in: Grey, C. & Willmott, H. (eds) *Critical Management Studies – A Reader*, Oxford: Oxford University Press.

Alvesson, M. 2002. *Understanding Organisational Culture*, London: Sage.

Alvesson, M. & Willmot, H. (eds) 2003. *Studying Management Critically*, London: Sage.

Anthony, P. D. 2005. The Ideology of Work, London: Routledge, excerpt reprinted in Grey, C. & Willmott, H. (eds) *Critical Management Studies – A Reader*, Oxford: Oxford University Press.

Austin, J. L. 1962. *How to do things with words*, Oxford: Oxford University Press.

Barbash, J. 1997. Industrial Relations as Problem Solving, in: Barbash, J. & Meltz, N. (eds) *Theorising in Industrial Relations – Approaches & Applications*, Sydney: ACIRRT.

Baritz, L. 1960. The Servants of Power. *A History of the Use of Social Science in American Industry*, Middletown: Wesleyan University Press.

Barker, J. R. 1993. Tightening the Iron Cage: Concertive Control in Self-Managing Teams, *Administrative Science Quarterly*, vol. 38, no. 2.

Barker, J. R. 1999. Communication, Organisation, and Performance, *Administrative Science Quarterly*, vol. 44, no. 3.

Barker, J. 2005. Tightening the Iron Cage: Concertive Control in Self-Managed Teams, in: Grey, C. & Willmott, H. (eds) *Critical Management Studies – A Reader*, Oxford: Oxford University Press.

Barratt, E. 2003. Foucault, HRM and the Ethos of the Critical Management Scholar, *Journal of Management Studies*, vol. 40, no. 5.

Barry, M. 2006. *Company: A Novel*, New York: Doubleday.

Barry, J. et al. 2001. Between the Ivory Tower and the Academic Assembly Line, *Journal of Management Studies*, vol. 38, no. 1.

Barry, D. & Elmes, M. 1997. Strategy Retold, *Academy of Management Review*, vol. 22, no. 2.

Baudrillard, J. 1975. *The Mirror of Production*, St. Louis: Telos Press.

Baudrillard, J. 1998. *The Consumer Society – Myths and Structures*, London: Sage.

Bauman, Z. 1989. *Modernity and Holocaust*, Oxford: Blackwell.

Bell, D. 1960. *The End of Ideology*, Glencoe: Free Press.

Bell, D. 1973. *The Coming of the Post-Industrial Society*, Harmondsworth: Penguin.

Berger, P. & Luckmann, T. 1967. *The Social Construction of Reality*, New York: Garden City.

Biegler, W. P. & Norris, M. 2004. *The New Science of Strategic Execution – How Established Firms become Fast, Sleek Wealth Creators*, London: Praeger.

Billsberry, J. 1996. *The Effective Manager*, London: Sage.

Bing, S. 2006. Book Review on Max Barry's Company: A Novel, *The Guardian Weekly*, vol. 174, no. 15.

Birnbaum, N. 1969. *The Crisis of Industrial Society*, Oxford: Oxford University Press.

Birnbaum, N. 1971. *Toward a Critical Sociology*, Oxford: Oxford University Press.

Blundel, R. 2004. *Effective Organisational Communication*, London: Prentice Hall.

Bolinger, D. 1968. *Aspects of Language*, New York: Harcourt & Brace.

Bolinger, 1980. *Language – The Loaded Weapon*, London: Longman.

Bonß, W. 1984. Critical Theory and Empirical Research: Some Observations, in: Fromm, E. (eds), The Working Class in Weimar Germany, London: Berg.

Bowles, S. & Gintis, H. 1976. *Schooling in Capitalist America: Educational Reform and the Contradictions of Economic Life*, New York: Basic Books.

Bowles, S. & Gintis, H. 1981. Contradictions and Reproduction in Educational Theory, in: Barton, L. (eds) *Schooling, Ideology, and Curriculum*, Sussex: Falmer Press.

Bowles, S. & Gintis, H. 2001. *Schooling in Capitalist America Revisited*, http://www-unix.oit.umass.edu/~bowles

Boxall, P. & Purcell, J. 2003. *Strategy and Human Resource Management*, Basingstoke: Palgrave.

Braverman, H. 1974. *Labor and Monopoly Capital*, New York and London: Monthly Review Press.

Brewis, J. & Linstead, S. 2004. Gender and Management, in: Linstead, et al. (eds), *Management and Organisation – A Critical Text*, London: Palgrave.

Brown, M. & Kelly, R. (eds) 2006. You're History!, London: Continuum.

Brown, P. & Lauder, H. 2001. *Capitalism and Social Progress – The Future of Society in a Global Economy*, London: Palgrave.

Brown, W. 1998. Funders and Research: The Vulnerability of the Subject, in: Whitfield, K. & Strauss, G. 1998 (eds), Researching the World of Work, Ithaca: Cornell University Press.

Bundel, R. 2004. *Effective Organisational Communication*, London: Prentice Hall.

Burawoy, M. 1979. *Manufacturing Consent*, Chicago: Chicago University Press.

Burawoy, M. 1985. *The Politics of Production*, London: Verso.

Burrell, G. 1994. Modernism, postmodernism and organisational analysis 4: the contribution of Jürgen Habermas, *Organization Studies*, vol. 15, no. 1.

Cairns, G. et al. 2003. Organisational Space/Time: From Imperfect Panoptical to Heterotopian Understanding, *ephemera* (ephemeraweb.org), vol. 3, no. 2.

Canfora, L. 2006. *Democracy in Europe – A History of an Ideology*, London: Blackwell.

Caprariis, L. 2000, Fascism for Export? The Rise and Eclipse of the Fasci Italiani all'Estero, *Journal of Contemporary History*, vol. 35, no. 2.

Chalmers, A. F. 1994. *What is this thing called Science?*, 2nd edition, Milton Keynes: Open University Press.

Chandler, A. 1962. *Strategy and Structure*, Cambridge: MIT Press.

Cheney, G. 2004. Bringing ethics in from the margins, *Australian Journal of Communication*, vol. 31, pp. 35–36.

Cheney, G. 2006. Afterword: Casework and Communication About Ethics, in: May, S. (eds), *Case Studies in Organizational Communication*, London: Sage.

Cheney, G. & Carroll, C. 1997. The Person as Object in Discourses in and around organizations, *Communication Research*, vol. 24, no. 6, pp. 593–630.

Chomsky, N. 1967a. The Responsibility of Intellectuals, *The New York Review of Books*, February 23rd.

Chomsky, N. 1967b. On Resistance, *The New York Review of Books*, December 7th (internet download).

Chomsky, N. 1967c. The Responsibility of Intellectuals, *The New York Review of Books*, *February 23rd*. The New York Review of Books, *February 23rd* (internet download).

Chomsky, 1968. Philosophers and Public Philosophy, *Ethics*, vol. 79, no. 1.

Chomsky, N. 1968a. *Language and Mind*, New York: Harcourt Brace.

Chomsky, N. 1971. The Case against B. F. Skinner, *The New York Review of Books*, December 30th (internet download).

Chomsky, N. 1975. *The Logical Structure of Linguistic Theory*, Chicago: Chicago University Press.

Chomsky, N. 1976. *Reflections on Language*, London: Fontana Press.

Chomsky, N. 1994. Democracy and Education, *Mellon Lecture*, Loyola University, Chicago, October 19th, download: www.zmag.org/chomsky/talks/.

Chomsky, N. 1997. Market Democracy in a Neoliberal Order: Doctrines and Realities, *Z Magazine*, November (internet download).

Chomsky, N. 2002. *Understanding Power*, New York: Norton.

Chomsky, N. 2002a. *On the Nature of Language*, Cambridge: Cambridge University Press.

Clampitt, P. 2001. *Communicating for Managerial Effectiveness*, London: Sage.

Clausewitz, C. *1873. On War* (Originally published as 'Vom Kriege' in German by Dümmlers Verlag, Berlin, 1832). London: N. Trübner also by Routledge & Kegan Paul, 1908 & Penguin 1968.

Comte, A. 1853. *Essential Writings on positivism* (original translation by Harriet Martineau, 1853), reprint 1975 by New York: Harper.

Conrad, C. 1992. Corporate Communication and Control, in: Toth, E. & Heath, R. (eds), Rhetorical and Critical Approaches to Public Relations, Hillsdale (NJ): Lawrence Erlbaum Press.

Conrad, C. & Poole, M. 1998. *Strategic Organisational Communication*, London: Harcourt Brace.

Conrad, C. & Haynes, J. 2001. Developments of Key Constructs, in: Jablin, F. & Putnam, L. (eds), *The New Handbook of Organisational Communication – Advances in Theory, Research, and Methods*, London: Sage.

Cooke, B. 2003. The Denial of Slavery in Management Studies, *Journal of Management Studies*, vol. 40, no. 8.

Cornfield, D. & Hodson, R. (eds) 2002. *Words of Work – Building an International Sociology of Work*, London: Kluwer Academic Publishers, ISBN 0–306–46605–8 (hardback), xiii + 378 pages.

Craig, R. T. 1999. Communication Theory as a Field, *Communication Theory*, vol. 9, no. 2.

Dahl, R. A. 1957. The Concept of Power, *Behavioural Science*, vol. 2, pp. 210–215.

DeCeri, H. & Kramer, R. 2005. *Human Resource Management in Australia*, 2nd Edition, Sydney: McGraw-Hill.

Deetz, S. 1992. *Democracy in an Age of Corporate Colonization*, Albany: State University of New York Press.

Deetz, S. 2001. Conceptual Foundations, in: Jablin, F. & Putnam, L. (eds), *The New Handbook of Organisational Communication – Advances in Theory, Research, and Methods*, London: Sage.

Defoe, D. 1719. *Robinson Crusoe*, London: Penguin Classics, 2003.

Deleuze, G. 1995. *Negotiations 1972–1990*, New York: Columbia University Press.

Descartes, R. 1628. Rules for the Direction of our native Intelligence, in Descartes, R. 1988 edition of *Descartes Selected Philosophical Writings*, Cambridge: Cambridge University Press.

Dickens, L. 2000. Feminist Intuition, People Management, vol. 6, no. 14, pp. 48–49.

Disco, C. 1979. Critical Theory as Ideology of the New Class: Rereading Jürgen Habermas, Theory & Society, vol. 8, no. 2.

du Gay, P. 1996. *Consumption and Identity at Work*, London: Sage.

Dunlop, J. 1958. *Industrial Relations Systems*, New York: Holt.

Durkheim, E. 1893. *The Division of Labor in Society*, New York: Free Press, 1933.

Dutton, J. E. & Ashford, S. J. 1993. Selling issues to Top Management, *Academy of Management Review*, vol. 18, no. 3.

Dux, G. 1991. Communicative Reason and Interest: On the Reconstruction of the Normative Order in Societies Structured by Egalitarianism or Domination, in: Honneth, A. & Joas, H. (eds). *Communicative Action – Essays on Jürgen Habermas' The Theory of Communicative Action*, Cambridge: Polity Press.

Eagleton, T. 1994. *Ideology*, London: Longman Press.

Edwards, P. 2003. The Future of Industrial Relations, in: Ackers, P. & Wilkinson, A. (eds), *Understanding Work and Employment – Industrial Relations in Transition*, Oxford: Oxford University Press.

Edwards, P. 2006. *Industrial Relations and Critical Realism: IR's Tacit Contribution, Warwick Papers in Industrial Relations*, no. 80, March 2006 (download).

Edwards, R. 1979. *Contested Terrain*, London: Heinemann.

Einstein, A. 1949. *Philosopher-Scientist*, Cambridge: Cambridge University Press, also: www.marxist.prg/refernce/archive/Einstein.

Eisenberg, E. & Goodall, H. 2001. *Organizational Communication – Balancing Creativity and Constraint*, Bedford: St. Martin Press.

Eldridge, J. 1975. Panaceas and pragmatism in industrial relations, *Industrial Relations Journal*, vol. 6, no. 1.

Engels. F. 1874. *Von der Autorität*, Almanacco Repubblicano per l'anno 1984, reprinted in: Marx-Engels Werke, vol. 18, 5th edition, Berlin: Dietz Press.

Engels, F. 1892. *The Condition of the Working Class in Britain in 1844*, London: Allen & Unwin (reprint 1952).

Emrich, C. G., Holly, H. B., Feldman, J. M. & Garland, H. 2001. Images in words: Presidential rhetoric, charisma, and greatness, *Administrative Science Quarterly*, vol. 46, no. 3.

Eriksen, E. & Weigard, J. 2003. *Understanding Habermas – Communicative Action and Deliberate Democracy*, London: Continuum.

Etzioni, A. 1959. Authority Structure and Organisation Effectiveness, *Administrative Science Quarterly*, vol. 4, no. 1.

Fayol, H. 1949. *General and Industrial Management*, London: Pitman.

Feenberg, A. 1988. The Bias of Technology, in: Pippin, R. et al. (eds) *Marcuse-Critical Theory and The Promise of Utopia*, London: Macmillan Press.

Feenberg, A. 2002. *Transforming Technology – A Critical Theory Revisited*, Oxford: Oxford University Press.

Feenberg, A. 2004. Heidegger and Marcuse – The Catastrophe and Redemption of Technology, in: Abromeit, J. & Cobb, M. (eds), *Herbert Marcuse – A Critical Reader*, London: Routledge.

Feldman, S. 1998. Playing with the Pieces: Deconstruction and the Loss of Moral Culture, *Journal of Management Studies*, vol. 35, no. 1.

Fiedler, F. E. 1996. Research on Leadership Selection and Training: One View of the Future, *Administrative Science Quarterly*, vol. 41, no. 2.

Fiske, J. 1990. *Introduction to Communication Studies*, London: Routledge.

Fleetwood, S. & Ackroyd, S. (eds) 2004. *Critical Realist Approach in Organisation and Management Studies*, London: Routledge.

Flöistad, G. 1970. Social Concepts of Action: Notes on Habermas' Proposal for a Social Theory of Knowledge, *Inquiry*, vol. 13.

Ford, H. II 1946. Human Engineering Necessary for Further Mass Production Progress, *Automotive and Aviation Industries*, XCIV, 2 (15th January 1946).

Forester, J. 1985. Critical Theory and Planning Practice, Forester, J. (eds) *Critical Theory and Public Life*, Cambridge: MIT Press.

Forester, J. 1989. *Planning in the Face of Power*, Berkeley: University of California Press.

Foster, H. 1985. *Postmodern Culture*, London: Pluto Press.

Foucault, M. 1994. *The Order of Things: An Archaeology of the Human Science*, London: Vintage Books.

Foucault, M. 1995. *Discipline and Punish: The Birth of the Prison*, New York: Vintage Books.

Fox, A. 1966: Managerial Ideology and Labour Relations, in *British Journal of Industrial Relations*, vol. 4, no. 3, pp. 366–378.

Fox, A. 1973. Industrial Relations: A Social Critique of Pluralist Ideology, pp. 185–233, in: Child, John (ed.): *Man and Organisation*, London: Unwin Press.

Fox, A. 1974. *Beyond Contract*, London: Faber.

Frazer, N. 1990. Rethinking the Public Sphere: A Contribution to the Critique of Actually Existing Democracy, *Social Text*, no. 25/26, pp. 56–80.

Freire, P. 1998. *Pedagogy of Freedom: ethics, democracy, and civic courage* (translated by Patrick Clarke, foreword by Donaldo Macedo, introduction by Stanley Aronowitz), Lanham: Rowman & Littlefield Publishers.

Freire, P. 2000. *Pedagogy of the Oppressed* (translated by Myra Bergman Ramos, introduction by Donaldo Macedo), New York: Continuum, 2000.

Freire, P. 2005. *Education for Critical Consciousness*, London: Continuum.

Fuller, S. 2003. *Kuhn vs. Popper: The Struggle of the Soul of Science*, Cambridge: Icon Books.

Gadamer, H. G. 1974. *Truth and Method*, Evanston: Northwestern University Press.

Gadamer, H. G. 1976. *Philosophical Hermeneutics*, Berkeley: University of California Press.

Galbraith, J. K. 1952. *American Capitalism, The Concept of Countervailing Power*, Boston: Houghton Mifflin.

Galbraith, J. K. 1952a. *A Theory of Price Control*, Cambridge: Harvard University Press.

Galbraith, J. K. 1958. *The Affluent Society*, Boston: Houghton Mifflin.

Galbraith, J. K. 1969. *The New Industrial State*, Harmondsworth: Penguin.

Gandhi, M. 1925. *Seven Social Sins*, quoted from the weekly journal: *Young India*.

Gastil, J. & Levine, P. (eds) 2006. *The deliberative democracy handbook: strategies for effective civic engagement in the twenty-first century*, Burlington: Ashgate.

Giddens, A. 1979. *Central Problems in Social Theory*, London: Macmillan.

Giddens, A. 1984. *The Constitution of Society*, Berkeley: University of California Press.

Giddens, A. 1992. *Sociology – A Brief but Critical Introduction*, London: Macmillan.

Giles, A. & Murray, G. 1997. Industrial Relations Theory and Critical Political Economy, in: Barbash, J. & Meltz, N. (eds): *Theorising in Industrial Relations – Approaches & Applications*, Sydney: ACIRRT.

Gilabert, P. 2005. The Substantive Dimension of Deliberate Practical Rationality, *Philosophy and Social Criticism*, vol. 31, no. 2.

Gimmler, A. 2001. Deliberative Democracy, the Public Sphere and the Internet, *Philosophy and Social Criticism*, vol. 27, no. 4.

Goldthorpe, J. H., Lockwood, D., Bechhofer, F. & Platt, J. 1969. *The Affluent Worker in the Class Structure*, Cambridge: Cambridge University Press.

Goodrich, C. L. 1920. *The Frontier of Control*, London: Pluto Press

Gorz, A. 1982. *Farewell to the Working Class*, London: South End Press.

Gouldner, A. 1952. The Problem of Succession in Bureaucracy, in: Merton, R. et al. (eds) *Reader in Bureaucracy*, New York: Free Press.

Gouldner, A. W. 1976. *The dialectic of ideology and technology: the origins, grammar, and future of ideology*, New York: Seabury Press.

Grant, D. 2004. Introduction, in: Grant, D. et al. (eds) *The Sage Handbook of Organisational Discourse*, London: Sage.

Grey, C. & Willmott, H. 2005. *Critical Management Studies – A Reader*, Oxford: Oxford University Press.

Gusfield, J. 1980. Introduction, in: Altheide, D. & Johnson, J., *Bureaucratic Propaganda*, Boston: Allyn and Bacon.

Grint, K. 2005. The Sociology of Work, 3rd Edition, London: Polity Press.

Habermas, J. 1968. Knowledge and Human Interests, Boston: Beacon Press, in: McNeill, W. & Feldman, K. (eds) 1998. *Continental Philosophy – An Anthology*, Oxford: Blackwell.

Habermas, J. 1975. Towards a Reconstruction of Historical Materialism, *Theory & Society*, vol. 2, no. 3.

Habermas, J. 1976a. The Analytic Theory of Science and Dialectic, in: Adorno, T. et al. (eds) *The Positivist Dispute in German Sociology*, London: Heinemann.

Habermas, J. 1976b. A Positivistically Bisected Rationalism, in: Adorno, T. et al. (eds) *The Positivist Dispute in German Sociology*, London: Heinemann.

Habermas, J. 1979. *Communication and the Evolution of Society*, Boston: Beacon.

Habermas, J. 1985. *The Philosophical Discourse of Modernity*, Cambridge: Polity Press.

Habermas, J. 1987. *Knowledge and Human Interests*, Cambridge: Polity Press.

Habermas, J. 1988. *Structural Transformation of the Public Sphere,* Cambridge: MIT Press.

Habermas, J. 1997. *The Theory of Communicative Action: Reason and the Rationalisation of Society,* Volume I & II, reprint, Oxford: Polity Press.

Habermas, J. 1997a. *Between Facts and Norms,* Oxford: Polity Press.

Habermas, J. 2001. *On the Pragmatics of Social Interaction – Preliminary Studies in the Theory of Communicative Action.* Cambridge: MIT Press.

Habermas, J. 2006. *Political Communication in Media Society,* Key Note at the 56th Annual Conference of the International Communication Association, Dresden (Germany), June 19th to 23rd, 2006.

Hamel, G 1996. Strategy as Revolution, *Harvard Business Review,* May–June.

Hamilton, C. 2003. *Growth Fetish,* Sydney: Allen & Unwin.

Hamilton, C. & Denniss, R. 2005. *Affluenza – When too much is never enough,* Sydney: Allen & Unwin.

Hamilton, R. 1982. *Who Voted for Hitler?,* Princeton: Princeton University Press.

Handel, M. (eds) 2003. *The Sociology of Organizations – Classic, Contemporary and Critical Readings,* London: Sage.

Harding, N. 2003. *The Social Construction of Management – Texts and Identities,* London: Routledge.

Harford, T. 2006. *The Undercover Economist,* Oxford: Oxford University Press.

Hartley, P. & Bruckmann, C. 2002. *Business Communication,* London: Routledge.

Heath, J. 2003. *Communicative Action and Rational Choice,* Cambridge: MIT Press.

Hegel, G. 1807. Phenomenology of Spirit, in: McNeill, W. & Feldman, K. (eds) 1998. *Continental Philosophy – An Anthology,* Oxford: Blackwell.

Hegel, G. 1821. The Philosophy of Right, in: McNeill, W. & Feldman, K. (eds) 1998. *Continental Philosophy – An Anthology,* Oxford: Blackwell.

Held, D. 1997. *Introduction to Critical Theory – Horkheimer to Habermas,* Cambridge: Polity Press.

Herman, E. S. & Chomsky, N. 1988. *Manufacturing Consent – The Political Economy of the Mass Media,* New York: Pantheon Books.

Herman, E. S. & McChesney, R. W. 1997. *The Global Media – The New Missionaries of Corporate Capitalism,* London: Continuum.

Hirschman, A. 1970. *Exit, Voice, and Loyalty: responses to decline in firms, organizations, and states,* Cambridge: Harvard University Press.

Hobsbawn, E. 1989. *The Age of Empire 1875–1914,* London: Vintage Books.

Hobsbawn, E. 2004. History: a new age of reason – return to asking the big why questions, *Le Monde Diplomatique* (Engl. Edition), December 2004, pp. 1 & 11.

Horkheimer, M. 1937. Traditional and Critical Theory, in: Horkheimer, M. *Critical Theory – Selected Essays,* translated by O'Connell, M. J. et al. (1972), New York: Herder.

Horkheimer, M. 1947. *The Eclipse of Reason,* New York: Oxford University Press.

Howard, M. 2003. *Strategy,* Encyclopaedia Britannica, www.search.eb.com.

Hyman, R. 1979. *Industrial Relations,* London: Macmillan.

Hyman, R. 1987. Strategy or Structure, *Work, Employment & Society,* vol. 1. no. 1.

Hyman, R. 1989. *The Political Economy of Industrial Relations,* London: Macmillan.

Jaffee, D. 2001. *Organization Theory: Tension and Change,* New York: McGraw.

Jay, M. 1974. *The Dialectical Imagination – A history of the Frankfurt School and the Institute of Social Research 1923–1950,* London: Heinemann.

Johnson, R. 2004. *Kant's Moral Philosophy* (first published Mon. Feb 23, 2004; substantive revision Thu. Feb 26, 2004: http://plato.stanford.edu/entries/kant-moral/.

Jones, G. S. 1983. *Languages of class: studies in English working class history, 1832–1982*, Cambridge: Cambridge University Press.

Kalyvas, A. 2001. The Politics of Autonomy and the Challenge of Deliberation: Castoriadis contra Habermas, *Thesis Eleven*, no. 64.

Kant, I. 1781. Critique of Pure Reason, in: McNeill, W. & Feldman, K. (eds) 1998. *Continental Philosophy – An Anthology*, Oxford: Blackwell.

Kant, I. 1788. *Critique of Practical Reason* (translated by Lewis White Beck, 1993) New York: Macmillan.

Kant, I. 1790. *Critique of Judgement* (translated by Werner S. Pluhar, 1987), Indianapolis: Hackett Publishing.

Kaufman, B. 1993. *The Origins & Evolution of the Field of Industrial Relations in the United States*, Ithaca: Cornell University Press.

Kellner, D. 1984. *From 1984 to One-Dimensional Man: Critical Reflections on Orwell and Marcuse, http:///www.gseis.ucla.faculty/kellner/kellner.html, accessed August 2006.*

Kellner, D. 1991. Introduction to the Second Edition, in: Marcuse, H. 1966. *One-Dimensional Man: Studies in the Ideology of Advanced Industrial Societies*, Boston: Beacon Press.

Kellner, D. 2006. Boundaries and Borderlines: Reflections on Jean Baurdillard and Critical Theory, http://www.uta.edu.huma/illuminations/kell2.htm, accessed August 2006.

Kelly, J. 1998. *Rethinking Industrial Relations – Mobilisation, Collectivism and Long Waves*, London: Routledge.

Kerr, C., Dunlop, J., Harbison, F. & Myers, C. 1960. Industrialism & Industrial Man, *International Labour Review*, vol. 135, no. 3–4 (reprinted in 1996).

Knowles, W. 1955. Personnel Management, New York: American Book Co.

Kochan, T. 1980. *Collective Bargaining and Industrial Relations*, Homewood (IL): Richard Irwinn.

Kochan, T., Katz, H. & McKersie, R. 1986. *The Transformation of American Industrial Relations*, New York: Basic Books.

Kochan, T. 2003. *Restoring Workers' Voice: A Call for Action*, distributed via reinet@cru.fr (5th December 2003), Cambridge: MIT Workplace Centre, August 2003.

Kohlberg, L. 1971. From is to ought, in: Mishel, T. (eds) *Cognitive Development and Epistemology*, New York: Academic Press.

Kohlberg, L. 1981 & 1984. *Essays on Moral Development* (vol. 1 & 2), San Francisco: Harper & Row.

Krippendorff, K. 1994. A Recursive Theory of Communication, in: Crowley, D. & Mitchell, D. (eds) *Communication Theory Today*, Cambridge: Polity Press.

Krippendorff, K. 1995. Undoing Power, *Critical Studies in Mass Communication*, vol. 12, no. 2.

Krizan, A. C., Merrier, P. & Jones, C. L. 2005. *Business Communication*, 6th Edition, Mason: Thomson South-Western.

Kroll, M. J., Toombs, L. A. & Wright, P. 2000. Napoleon's tragic march home from Moscow, Lessons in Hubris, *Academy of Management Executive*, vol. 14, no. 1.

Kuhn, T. 1970. *The Structure of the Scientific Revolution*, Chicago: University of Chicago Press.

Lafargue, P. 1883. *The Right to be Lazy*, written in Saint Pelagie Prison, translated by Charles Kerr and first published by Charles Kerr Cooperative, download: www.marxist.org/archive/lafargue/1883/lazy.

Laffer, G. 2005. The Critical Failure of Workplace Ethics, in: Budd, S. & Scoville, J. (eds) *The Ethics of Human Resources and Industrial Relations*, Champaign: Labor and Employment Relations Association.

Langley, A. 1989. In search of rationality: the purpose behind the use of formal analysis in organizations, *Administrative Science Quarterly*, vol. 34, no. 4.

Legge, K. 1995. *Human Resource Management – Rhetoric and Reality*, London: Macmillan.

Legge, K. 2005. *Human Resource Management – Rhetoric and Reality – Anniversary Edition*, London: Macmillan.

Levy, D. L., Alvesson, M. & Willmott, H. 2003. Critical Approaches to Strategic Management, in: Alvesson, M. & Willmott, H. (eds), *Studying Management Critically*, London: Sage.

Linge, D. E. 1976. Editor's Introduction, in: Gadamer, H. G., *Philosophical Hermeneutics*, Berkeley: University of California Press.

Linstead, S., Fullop, L. & Lilley, S. 2004. *Management and Organisation – A Critical Text*, Basingstoke: Palgrave.

Locke, J. 1689a. A Letter Concerning Toleration, translated by William Popple, http://www.constitution.org/jl/tolerati.htm

Locke, J. 1689b. An Essay Concerning Human Understanding, produced by Steve Harris and David Widger, http://www.gutenberg.org/etext/10615

Lockwood, D. 1964. Social Integration and System Integration, in: G. K. Zollschau & W. Hirsch (eds) *Explanations in Social Change*, London: Routledge & Kegan Paul.

Lösch, B. 2005. *Deliberative Politik. Moderne Konzeptionen von Öffentlichkeit, Demokratie und politischer Partizipation*, Münster: Dampfboot-Verlag.

Lukács, G. 1971. Lukács on his Life and Work, *New Left Review*, I/68, July–August.

Lyddon & Smith 1996. Industrial Relations and History – Editorial, *Historical Studies in Industrial Relations*, vol. 1, no. 1.

Lyon, D. 2001. *Surveillance Society: Monitoring Everyday Life*, Buckingham: Open University Press.

Macey, D. 2000. *The Penguin Directory of Critical Theory*, London: Penguin Books.

Mandell, B. 2002, The Privatisation of Everything, *New Politics*, vol. 9, no. 1.

Mander, J. 2001 The Rules of Corporate Behaviour, in: Goldsmith, E. & Mander, J. (eds) *The Case Against the Global Economy – and for a turn towards localisation*, London: Earthscan Press.

Marcuse, H. 1964a. *Soviet Marxism: A Critical Analysis*, Boston: Beacon Press.

Marcuse, H. 1964b. *Industrialization and Capitalism in the Work of Max Weber*, republished in Negations, 1968.

Marcuse, H. 1966. *One-Dimensional Man: Studies in the Ideology of Advanced Industrial Societies*, Boston: Beacon Press.

Marcuse, H. 1968. *Negations – Essays in Critical Theory*, Boston: Beacon Press.

Marcuse, H. 1969. *An Essay on Liberation*, Boston: Beacon Press.

Marglin, S. 1974. What do bosses do? – The origins and functions of hierarchy in capitalist production, *Review of Radical Political Economy*, vol. 6, no. 2.

Marris, R. 1966. *The Economic Theory of 'Managerial' Capitalism*, London: Macmillan.

Marsden, D. 1999, *A Theory of Employment Systems – Micro-Foundations of Societal Diversity*, Oxford: Oxford University Press.

Marsden, R. & Townley, B. 1996. The owl of Minerva: reflections on theory and practice, in: Clegg, S., Hardy, C. & Nord, W. R. (eds) *Handbook of Organisation Studies*, London: Sage.

Marx, K. 1846. Letter to P. V. Annenkov on Pierre-Joseph Proudhon's book on The Philosophy of Poverty, 28th December 1846, printed in: Tucker, R. (eds) 1972. *The Marx-Engels Reader*, 2nd Edition, London: Norton Press.

Marx, K. 1848. *The Communist Manifesto*, www.sozialistische-klassiker.org/ME/ME03.html.

Marx, K. 1890. *Das Kapital – Kritik der politischen Ökonomie (Capital – A Critique of Political Economy)*, Hamburg: 4th edited version by F. Engels, reprinted 1986: Berlin: Dietz-Press.

Maslow, A. H. 1943. A theory of human motivation, *Psychological Review*, vol. 50, no. 4.

Mayo, E. 1945. *The Social Problems of an Industrial Civilisation*, Boston: Harvard University Press.

McCarthy, B. 2000. In the beginning were Beatrice and Sidney: five ages of Industrial Relations, *paper presented at: 50th BUIRA Conference* at Warwick University 7th–9th July 2000.

McGee, M. 1980. The ideograph: A link between rhetoric and ideology, *The Quarterly Journal of Speech*, vol. 66, no. 1: 1–16.

McGregor, D. 1960. *The Human Side of Enterprise*, New York: McGraw-Hill.

Meltz, N. 1997. Theorising in Industrial Relations, in: Barbash, J. & Meltz, N. (eds): Theorising in Industrial Relations – Approaches & Applications, Sydney: ACIRRT.

Mendieta, E. 2002. *The Advances of Transcendental Philosophy – Karl-Otto Apel's Semiotics and Discourse Ethics*, Lanham: Rowan & Littlefield Publishers.

Merrier, P. 2006. *Business Communication*, 6th Edition, Mason: Thomson South-Western.

Metall, 2006. *Wo ist die Hoffnung*, Metall (IGM-Frankfurt), vol. 58, no. 5.

Miles, R. E. & Snow, C. C. 1978. *Organisational Strategy, Structure & Process*, New York: McGraw-Hill.

Miller, K. 2000. Common Ground from the Post-Positive Perspective, in: Corman, S. & Poole, M. (eds) *Perspectives on Organisational Communication*, New York: Guilford Press.

Mills, C. W. 1951. *White Collar: the American middle classes*, Oxford: Oxford University Press.

Mintzberg, H. 1973. *The Nature of Managerial Work*, London: Harper & Row.

Mintzberg, H. 1987a. The strategy concept I: Five Ps for strategy, and Strategy concept II: Another look at why organizations need strategies. *California Management Review*, 30(1): 11–32.

Mintzberg, H. 1987b. Crafting Strategy, *Harvard Business Review*, July–August: 67–81.

Monbiot, G. 2005. Dogs of War – With Pedigree, *The Guardian Weekly*, vol. 172, no. 7, Sydney edition.

Monk, R. 1997. *Just Managing*, Sydney: McGraw-Hill.

Moore, B. 1966. *Social Origins of Dictatorship and Democracy – Lord and Peasant in the Making of the Modern World*, Boston: Beacon Press.

Morgan, G, 1986. *Images of Organisations*, London: Sage.

Morgan, G. 1993. *Imaginization – the Art of Creative Management*, London: Sage.

Morris, M. 2001. *Rethinking the Communicative Turn – Adorno, Habermas, and the Problem of Communicative Freedom*, Albany: State University of New York Press.

Morrow, R. 1994. *Critical Theory and Methodology*, London: Sage.

Mumby, D. 1988. *Communication & Power in Organisations: Discourse, Ideology, and Domination*, Norwood (NJ): Ablex-Press.

Mumby, D. 1997. The Problem of Hegemony: Reading Gramsci for Organisational Communication Studies, *Western Journal of Communication*, vol. 61, no. 4: 343–375.

Mumby, D. 2000. Common Ground from the Critical Perspective, in: Corman, S. & Poole, M. (eds) *Perspectives on Organisational Communication*, New York: Guilford Press.

Mumby, D. 2001. Power and Politics, in: Jablin, F. & Putnam, L. (eds), *The New Handbook of Organisational Communication – Advances in Theory, Research, and Methods*, London: Sage.

Murakami, T. 1999. Post- or Neo-Fordism: Trade Union Policies for Teamwork at General Motors Holden, *Policy, Organisation & Society*, no. 17, summer, pp. 87–104.

Murakami, T. 2000a. Review Essay: New Critical Theory for the New Millennium, *Philosophy & Social Criticism*, vol. 36, no. 6, pp. 109–112.

Murakami, T. 2000b. Think Outside the Square you Live in! Exploring a New IR Theory, in: Gurgess, J. & Strachan, G. (eds), *Research on work, Employment and Industrial Relations 2000*, Newcastle: University of Newcastle (Australia).

Murakami, T. 2000c. Anglo-Saxon Industrial Relations and German Critical Theory, in: BUIRA (eds). *BUIRA 50th Conference*, Coventry: University of Warwick, Industrial Relations Research Unit, Great Britain, Refereed Workshop Papers, paper no. 36.

Nealon, J. & Giroux, S. S. 2003. *The Theory Toolbox – Critical Concepts for Humanities, Arts, and Social Science*, Lanham: Rowan & Littlefield.

Neumann, F. 1944. *Behemoth: The Structure and Practice of National Socialism, 1933–1944*, London: Victor Gollancz.

Offe, C. & Wiesenthal, H. 1980. Two Logics of Collective Action: Theoretical Notes on Social Class and Organisational Form, in: Zeitlin, M. (eds), *Political Power and Social theory – A Research Annual*, vol. 1, Greenwich: JAI Press.

Offe, C. 1984. Ungovernability, in: Habermas, J. (eds). *Observations on the Spiritual Situation of the Age*, Cambridge: Cambridge University Press.

Offe, C. 1985. *Disorganised Capitalism – Contemporary Transformations of Work and Politics*, Oxford: Polity Press.

Offe, C. 1988. Technology and One-Dimensionality: A Version of the Technocracy Thesis? in: Pippin, R. et al. (eds) *Marcuse-Critical Theory and The Promise of Utopia*, London: Macmillan Press.

Ohmae, K. 1983. *The Mind of the Strategist: Business Planning for Competitive Advantage*, New York: Penguin.

Oquendo, A. 2002. Deliberative Democracy in Habermas and Nino, *Oxford Journal of Legal Studies*, vol. 22, no. 2.

Olson, M. 1971. *The Logics of Collective Action*, Cambridge: Harvard University Press.

Orlikowski, W. J. & Yates, O. J. 1994. Genre repertoire: the structuring of communicative practice in organisations, *Administrative Science Quarterly*, vol. 39, no. 4.

Orwell, G. 1946. *Politics and the English Language*, http://orwell.ru.library/essays

Orwell, G. 1949. *Nineteen Eighty-four*, London: Secker & Warburg.

Osborne, R. 2005. *Civilisation – A New History of the Western World*, London: Cape.

Parker, M. 2002. *Against Management – Organisation in the Age of Managerialism*, Cambridge: Polity Press.

Parkin, A. C. 1996. On the Practical Relevance of Habermas' theory of Communicative Action, *Social Theory and Practice*, vol. 22, no. 3.

Parks, B. et al. 1994. A marketer's guide to Clausewitz: lessons for winning market shares, *Business Horizons*, vol. 37, no. 4.

Parzych, P. 2000. *The Basics of Employee Communication*, Cincinnati: South-Western Educational Publication.

Pavlov, I. P. 1928. *Lectures of Conditioned Reflexes*, New York: International Publishing.

Penrose, J., Rasberry, R. & Myers, R. 2004. *Business communication for Managers – An Advanced Approach*, Mason (USA): Thomson South-Western.

Peters, T. & Waterman, R. 1982. *In Search for Excellence*, New York: Harper & Row.

Pfeffer, J. & Fong, C. 2004. The Business School 'Business': Some Lessons from the US Experience, *Journal of Management Studies*, vol. 41, no. 8.

Piven, F. F. & Cloward, R. 1971. *Regulating the Poor: The Function of Public Welfare*, New York: Pantheon Books.

Polanyi, K. 1944. *The Great Transformation – The Political and Economical Origins of our Time*, New York: Farrar & Rinehart.

Poole, S. 2006. *Unspeak*, London: Little Brown.

Popper, K. 1965. *The Logic of Scientific Discovery*, New York: Harper Press.

Popper, K. 1999. *All Life is Problem Solving* (translated by Camiller, P. from 'Alles Leben ist Problemlösung'), London: Routledge.

Porter, M. E. 1980. *Competitive Strategy: Techniques for Analysing Industries and Competitiveness*, New York: The Free Press.

Pringle, D. C. & Kroll, M. J. 1997. Why Trafalgar was won before it was fought: Lessons from resource-based theory, *Academy of Management Executive*, vol. 11, no. 4.

Putman, L. 1995. Bargaining as Organisational Communication, in: McPhee, R. & Tompkins, P. (eds), *Organisational Communication: Traditional Themes and New Directions*, London: Sage.

Putnam, L. & Fairhurst, G. 2004. Discourse Analysis in Organisations – Issues and Concerns, in: Jablin, F. & Putnam, L. (eds), *The New Handbook of Organisational Communication – Advances in Theory, Research, and Methods*, London: Sage.

Radford, G. P. 2005. *On The Philosophy of Communication*, Belmont: Wadsworth.

Ramsay, H. 1977: Cycle of Control: Worker participation in sociological and historical perspective, in: *Sociology*, vol. 11, 1977, pp. 441–506.

Redding, W. C. 1972. *Communication within the organization: an interpretive review of theory and research*, New York: Industrial Communication Council.

Reich, R. 1992. *The Work of Nations – Preparing Ourselves for 21st Century Capitalism*, New York: Vintage Books.

Reich, W. 1946. *The Mass Psychology of Fascism*, New York (1970): Farrar, Straus & Giroux.

Reitz, C. 2000. *Art, Alienation, and the Humanities – A Critical Engagement with Herbert Marcuse*, New York: State University of New York Press.

Rice, J. 2003. The Implications of Complexity Theory for Industrial Relations Theory, in: Holland, P., Teicher, J. & Turberville, S. (eds) *Reflections and New Directions*, Association of Industrial Relations Academics of Australia and New Zealand Conference, 4–7 February 2003, Monash University.

Rusche, G. 2003. *Punishment and social structure* (Georg Rusche and Otto Kirschheimer, with a new introduction by Dario Melossi), New Brunswick: Transaction Publishers.

Rorty, R. 1979. *Philosophy and the Mirror of Nature*, Princeton: Princeton University Press.

Rorty, R. 1982. *Consequences of Pragmatism*, Minneapolis: University of Minneapolis Press.

Rousseau J. J. 1755. *Discourse on the Origins of Inequality, http://oll.libertyfund.org & www.libertarian-alliance.org.uk*.

Rousseau, J. J. 1762. *The Social Contract*, edited by Roger Masters, 1978), New York: St. Martin.

Salaman, G. and & Asch, D. 2003. *Strategy and Capability: Sustaining Organizational Change*, Oxford: Blackwell.

Saunders, S. F. 2004. *Hawkwood: Diabolical Englishman*, Toronto: McClelland & Stewart.

Searle, J. R. 1969. *Speech Acts – An Essay in the Philosophy of Language*, Cambridge: Cambridge University Press.

Searle, J. R. 1979. *Expression and Meaning: Essays in the Theory of Speech Acts*, Cambridge: Cambridge University Press.

Searle, J. R. 1996. *The Construction of Social Reality*, London: Penguin Press.

Searle, J. R. 2002. *Consciousness and Language*, Cambridge: Cambridge University Press.

Selznick, P. 1943. An Approach to a Theory of Bureaucracy, *American Sociological Review*, vol. 8, pp. 51–54.

Sennett, R. 1980. *Authority*, London: Secker & Warburg.

Sennett, R. 2006. *The culture of the new capitalism*, New Haven: Yale University Press.

Sewell, G. & Wilkinson, B. 1992. Someone is watching over me: Surveillance, Discipline and the Just-in-Time Labor Process, *Sociology*, vol. 26, pp. 271–289.

Shalin, D. 1992. Critical Theory and the Pragmatist Challenge, *American Journal of Sociology*, vol. 98, no. 2.

Shannon, C. & Weaver, M. 1949. *The Mathematical Theory of Communication*, Urbanan: University of Illinois Press.

Shenhav, Y. 1999. *Manufacturing Reality – The Engineering Foundations of the Managerial Revolution*, Oxford: Oxford University Press.

Shirer, W. 1950. *The Rise and Fall of the Third Reich – A History of Nazi Germany*, New York: Ballantine Books.

Silver, B. J. 2003. *Forces of Labor: Worker's Movement and Globalisation since 1870*, Cambridge: Cambridge University Press.

Simon, J. J. 2005. Albert Einstein, Radical: A Political Profile, *Monthly Review*, www.monthlyreview.org.

Simon, H. A. 1965. *Administrative Behavior: a Study of Decision-Making Processes in Administrative Organization* (2nd ed.), London: Collier-Macmillan.

Simonds, A. P. 1982. On Being Informed, *Theory and Society*, vol. 11, no. 5.

Singer, P. 1985. *Ethics*, Encyclopaedia Britannica, Chicago, 1985, pp. 627–648 (http://www.utilitarian.net/singer/by/1985—.htm).

Singer, P. W. 2004. The Business of War – Mercenary Motives, *Le Monde Diplomatique*, Manchester: The Guardian Weekly Press.

Skinner, B. F. 1953. *Science and Human Behaviour*, New York: Macmillan.

Smith, A. 1759. *The Theory of the Moral Sentiments*, http://www.adamsmith.org/smith/tms/tms-index.htm.

Smith, A. 1776. *The Wealth of Nations – Books I–III*, London: Penguin Books (reprinted 1986).

Smith, K. G., Smith, K. A., Olian, J. D., Sims, H. P., O'Bannon, D. P. & Scully, J. A. 1994. Top Management Teams Demography and Process: The Role of Social Integration and Communication, *Administrative Science Quarterly*, vol. 39, no. 3.

Spulber, D. F. 2004. *Principles of Management Strategy*, Boston: McGraw-Hill.

Starkey, K. et al. 2004. Rethinking the Business School, *Journal of Management Studies*, vol. 41, no. 8.

Stehr, N. 1994. *Knowledge Society*, London: Sage.

Taylor, F. W. 1911. *The Principle of Scientific Management*, New York: Norton Press (reprinted in Handel, M. (eds) 2003. The Sociology of Organizations – Classic, Contemporary and Critical Readings, London: Sage).

Thompson, E. P. 1963. *The Making of the English Working Class*, London: Victor Gollancz.

Thompson, J. B. 1990. *Ideology and Modern Culture – Critical Social Theory in the Era of Mass Communication*, Oxford: Polity Press.

Thompson, P. 2003. Disconnected Capitalism, *Work, Employment & Society*, vol. 17, no. 2, pp. 359–378.

Thompson, P. 2004. Brands, Boundaries and Bandwagons – Critical Reflections on Critical Management Studies, in: Fleetwood, S. & Ackroyd, S. (eds) *Critical Realist Approach in Organisation and Management Studies*, London: Routledge.

Tompkins, P. K. & Cheney, G. 1985. Communication and Unobstrusive Control, in: McPhee, R. D. & Tompkins, P. K. (eds) *Organisational Communication: Traditional Themes and New Directions*, Beverly Hills: Sage.

Tompkins, P. K. & Wanca-Thibault, M. 2001. Organisational Communication – Prelude and Prospects, in: Jablin, F. & Putnam, L. (eds), *The New Handbook of Organisational Communication – Advances in Theory, Research, and Methods*, London: Sage.

Tzu, Sun 600. *The Art of War – The oldest military treatise in the world*, translated by Giles, L. (1910), London: Luzac & Co.

UN 1948. *Declaration of Human Rights*, adopted and proclaimed by General Assembly resolution 217 A (III) of 10th December 1948, New York: United Nations.

Violanti, M. T. 2006. Should we stop using the letter C?, May, S. (eds), *Case Studies in Organizational Communication*, London: Sage.

Volosinov, V. N. 1929. *Marxism and the Philosophy of Language*, translated by Matejka & Titunik (1973), Cambridge: Harvard University Press.

Walsh, et al. 2006. *The Measurement and Management of Strategic Change – A Guide to Enterprise Performance Management*, Sydney: Pearson Press.

Washburn, J. 2005. *University Inc. – The Corporate Corruption of American Higher Education*, New York: Basic Books.

Watson, D. 2003. *Death Sentence – The Decay of Public Language*, Sydney: Knopf.

Watzlawick, P., Beavin, J. & Jackson, D. 1967. *Pragmatics of Human Communication: A Study of Interactional Patterns, Pathologies, and Paradoxes*, New York: Norton.

Webb, B. & Webb, S. 1894. *The History of Trade Unionism*, London: Longman.

Weber, M. 1922. *Wirtschaft und Gesellschaft*, edited: Marianne Weber (5th edition as Studienausgabe), Tübingen: JCB Mohr.

Weber, M. 1924. *Economy and Society*, Berkeley: University of California Press (reprint in: Handel, M. (eds) 2003. The Sociology of Organizations – Classic, Contemporary and Critical Readings, London: Sage).

Weber, M. 1947. *The Theory of Social and Economic Organization*, Oxford: Oxford University Press.

Weber, M. 1948. Science as a vocation, in: Gerth, H. & Mill, C. W. (eds) *From Max Weber: Essays on Sociology*, London: Routledge.

Weick, K. E. 1995. *Sensemaking in Organisations*, London: Sage.

Wert-Gray, S. Center, C. Brashers, D. & Meyers, R. 1991. Research topics and methodological orientation in organisational communication: a decade in review, *Communication Studies*, vol. 42, pp. 141–154.

Whipp, R. 1998. Qualitative Methods: Technique or Size?", in: Whitfield, K. & Strauss, G. 1998 (eds), *Researching the World of Work*, Ithaca: Cornell University Press.

Whitfield, K. & Strauss, G. 1998 (eds), *Researching the World of Work*, Ithaca: Cornell University Press.

Whittington, R. 1993. *What is strategy – and does it matter?*, 2nd Edition, London: Routledge.

Whittington, R. 2003. The Work of Strategizing and Organizing: for a Practice Perspective, *Strategic Organization*, vol. 1, no. 1.

Whyte, W, H. 1961, *The Organisation Man*, Harmondsworth: Penguin.

Wills, P. 1977. *Learning to Labor – how working class kids get working class jobs*, New York: Columbia University Press.

Wing, C. 1837. *Evils of the Factory System Demonstrated by Parliamentary* Evidence, London: Frank Cass.
Wood, J. 2004. *Communication Theories in Action*, Belmont: Wadsworth.
Zengotita, T. 2005. *Mediated – How the Media shapes your World and the Way you Live in it*. New York: Bloomsbury.
Zizek, S. 1989. *The Sublime Object of Ideology*, London: Verso Press.
Zuboff, S. 1988. *In the Age of Smart Machines*, New York: Basic Books.

Index